JUDGING RIGHTS

JUDGING RIGHTS

Lockean Politics and the Limits of Consent

Kirstie M. McClure

Cornell University Press

Ithaca and London

First published 1996 by Cornell University Press.

Library of Congress Cataloging-in-Publication Data

McClure, Kirstie Morna.
 Judging rights : Lockean politics and the limits of consent / Kirstie M. McClure.
  p.   cm.
 Includes bibliographical references and index.
 ISBN 0-8014-3111-5 (cloth : alk. paper)
 1. Locke, John, 1632–1704—Contributions in political science.
 2. Consensus (Social sciences) 3. Government, Resistance to.
 4. Judgment. 5. Rule of law. I. Title.
 JC153.L87M385 1996
 320′.01–dc20   96-8393

Printed in the United States of America

⊗ The paper in this book meets the minimum requirements
of the American National Standard for Information Sciences—
Permanence of Paper for Printed Library Materials, ANSI Z39.48-1984.

for my grandmother

Frances Trader McClure

Contents

Acknowledgments

The debts that have accumulated around this book defy repayment by mere mention, but mentioned they must be. My thinking about Locke, liberalism, and the history of political thought owes much to Sheldon Wolin, under whose ministrations this research first began. The exemplary friendship of Teresa de Lauretis urged it along, gave it a home, and helped it prosper. The form in which it now appears profited greatly—though perhaps not so much as they might wish—from the generous comments and incisive criticism of Donald Moon, Nancy Hirschmann, Richard Flathman, and William Connolly. One benefits, of course, as much from the spirit of collegiality as from the letter of criticism. On this count, the Johns Hopkins University has proved more than congenial as a place to work the fence-lines between history and theory. The Hopkins history department deserves special mention, both for its general ambience and for the particular virtue of its weekly collocation in "the Seminar." I am grateful as well for ongoing conversations with J. G. A. Pocock, Gabrielle Spiegel, and Dorothy Ross in History, Jonathan Goldberg, Mary Poovey, and John Guillory in English, Jerome Schneewind in Philosophy, Nancy Streuver in the Humanities Center, and Katherine Verdery in Anthropology. Whatever merits this book might have are inseparable from the support and encouragement of these friends and colleagues.

This project has been furthered by a number of institutions as well. Initial research was supported by a National Science Foundation fellowship and a summer grant from the Committee on European Studies at Princeton University. The political science department at Johns Hopkins University has been generous with release time and with support for the graduate students whose labors greatly eased its completion. Next to last, then, but far from least, I want to thank Jennifer Thomas, Jason Frank, Carol Pech, Mark Cushman, and Davide Panagia for their able assistance.

Finally, it has been a pleasure to work with the editors and staff of Cornell University Press. The good will, good humor, and good sense of Roger Haydon, in particular, have been greatly appreciated.

K. M. M.

JUDGING RIGHTS

Introduction

> The magistrate's concernments will always teach him to
> use no more rigor than the temper of the people and the
> necessity of the age shall call for. . . .
>
> But I too forwardly intrude myself into the council cham-
> ber, and like an impertinent traveller, which am concerned
> only with which way the dial points, lose time in searching
> after the springs and wheels that give it motion: It being
> our duty not curiously to examine the counsels but cheer-
> fully to obey the commands of the magistrate in all things
> that God hath left us free.
>
> —John Locke
> *Two Tracts* (1660)

In the three decades between 1660 and the first public appearance
of the *Two Treatises of Government*, John Locke had become an impertinent traveler indeed. Previously secured from interrogation by
a reverence for peace, the springs and wheels of civil power became
subject to increasingly severe scrutiny. Emblematic of this shift is the
recurrent question his *Treatises* addressed to the proper boundaries
of political power, "Who shall be Judge?"—as well as its oft repeated
answer, "The Body of the People." On Locke's account, such popular judgments on the excesses of their governors were relatively
rare: "Such revolutions," the reader is assured, "happen not upon
every little mismanagement in publick affairs. *Great mistakes* in the
ruling part, many wrong and inconvenient Laws, and all the *slips* of
human frailty will be *born by the People,* without mutiny or murmer."
A "design" against their liberties, however, evidenced by a "long

train of Abuses, Prevarications, and Artifices," was another matter.[1] Lurking beneath these assertions, however, is the thornier question of the grounds on which such judgments might be made. What is to distinguish between a great mistake and an abuse? How are civil authorities to avoid, or civil subjects to recognize, the excesses of political power that justify resistance? What are the stakes and implications of such judgments, and what conception of the political do they underwrite? Finally, across the seemingly vast distance traveled between the *Tracts* and the *Treatises,* what intellectual paths and discursive byways serve to mark Locke's metamorphosis from a supporter of order for its own sake to a defender of resistance?

To raise these questions is perhaps to add another impertinence to Locke's own. The issue of the boundaries of civil power, both for Locke and for subsequent articulations of what was to become liberal political theory, is generally thought to be resolved, more or less adequately to be sure, by the notion of consent. It is this notion that is usually advanced as the minimal ground for differentiating between a "legitimate" or "acceptable" polity and its tyrannical or despotic counterpart.[2] But this is too easy an answer for understanding the particular political sensibility articulated in Locke's *Treatises.* One does not, after all, simply consent—one consents to something that one finds either necessary or desirable. Consent, in other words, is a judgment one makes, and a judgment that presupposes certain reasons, evidence, or grounds that count as sufficient to persuade. The point, as I shall suggest, was not lost on Locke, for while the *Treatises* indeed proffer consent as the original basis of government, their political emphasis extends far more broadly into an articulation of

1. *Two Treatises of Government,* ed. Peter Laslett, rev. ed. (1960; reprint, with amendments, Cambridge: Cambridge University Press, 1963), by book and paragraph, 2.225. Hereafter cited as *Two Treatises.*

2. The terms, respectively, are Martin Seliger's in *The Liberal Politics of John Locke* (New York: Frederick Praeger, 1969), pt. 3; and John Dunn's from *The Political Thought of John Locke: An Historical Account of the Argument of the "Two Treatises of Government"* (Cambridge: Cambridge University Press, 1969), esp. chaps. 10 and 13. Some of the difficulties attendant upon this linkage between consent and the legitimacy of a regime are discussed by John Gough, *John Locke's Political Philosophy, Eight Studies,* 2d ed. (Oxford: Clarendon Press, 1973), 52–79; Hannah Pitkin, "Obligation and Consent," pts. 1 and 2, *American Political Science Review* 59, no. 4 (1965): 990–99 and 60, no. 1 (1966): 39–52; and John Dunn, "Consent in the Political Thought of John Locke," in *Life, Liberty, and Property: Essays on Locke's Political Ideas,* ed. Gordon Schochet (Belmont, Calif.: Wadsworth Publishing Co., 1971).

the grounds and circumstances of judgment that constitute sufficient reason for its withdrawal or revocation.[3] Locke's rendering of this issue has a certain casuistic flavor, and in this respect his defense of resistance right centers not only on the question of what it is reasonable to consent to, but the more trenchant problem of how one, in conscience, is to know the limits of one's obligation. In this respect, the political sensibility forwarded by the *Treatises* involves rather more than a theory of government by consent, for it is intimately interwoven with an account of the sort of knowledge requisite to properly political judgment—not simply, as it happens, by "the Body of the People" as a collective subject but, much to the horror of one late-eighteenth-century editor, by any one of its individual members.[4]

Locke, of course, is generally taken to be a liberal, and liberalism is generally viewed as a relatively coherent set of principles centering on the defense of individual rights and liberties, the security of property, and the notion of limited government. So conceived, the liberal tradition in political theory is often seen as a continuing elaboration or development of these principles from the seventeenth century to the present. From this perspective, Locke, Montesquieu, Hume, Smith, Bentham, Kant, Constant, Tocqueville, the Mills, and numerous others—including such otherwise disparate contemporary thinkers as John Rawls, Robert Nozick, and Richard Rorty—can be lumped more or less neatly into the category "liberals." Historically speaking, however, this categorization may obscure more than it reveals, and not only for the seemingly peevish and pedantic reason that the term "liberal" achieved its partisan valence as a marker of political identity and ideological specificity only in the nineteenth

3. See, for example, Locke's use of Hooker in *Two Treatises*, 2.134n: "Sith Men naturally have no full and perfect Power to Command whole Politick Multitudes of Men, therefore utterly without our Consent, we could in such sort be at no Mans Commandment living. And to be commanded we do consent when the Society, whereof we be a part, hath at any time become consented, without revoking the same after by like universal agreement." As it does not in Hooker, however, the revocation of consent becomes in Locke a matter of individual judgment, no more dependent upon universal agreement than is the appropriation of individual property in the state of nature.

4. See, for example, Locke, *Two Treatises*, 2.207–8, and Laslett's note there regarding the Elrington edition of 1798. Locke suggests that though prudence most likely will prevent the right from disturbing established governments, individual citizens "have a right to defend themselves" from unlawful acts on the part of governors, "and to recover by force, what by unlawful force is taken from them" 2.208.

century. Even if we accede to nineteenth-century historiographical
retrojections of liberal partisanship onto the past, a dilemma remains. For despite the persistence of the language of rights and liberties, despite the continuity of concern for safeguarding property,
and despite the tenacious emphasis on the rule of law, theorists conventionally regarded as liberals have differed among themselves in
crucial respects. Most important for the purposes pursued here, they
have diverged substantially in their conceptions of the proper nature, scope, purposes, and objects of political power. Equally important, if far less obvious, is the fact that such differences have tended
to be embedded in differing expectations and presuppositions regarding the character and extent of social knowledge, the terms in
which that knowledge might be framed, and the bearing of such
knowledge on political power, judgment, and action. There is, to put
the point somewhat differently, a significant if generally neglected
connection between various "liberal" theorists' accounts of the character, content, and aims of political life and the manner in which
these things are to be known.

The supposition that politics and knowledge are intimately related, to be sure, is by no means peculiar to liberalism; indeed, in the
most general of terms its Western antecedents can be plausibly
traced back to classical Athens. The relatively recent emergence and
diffusion of empiricism, rationalism, and the scientific method, however, have substantially transformed the character of that relationship. Broadly speaking, in place of the classical quest for the kinds of
knowledge appropriate to a properly political life, moderns have
tended rather to focus theoretical attention on the kinds of politics
commensurate with the state of human knowledge. In this context,
from the seventeenth century to the present, political reflection, no
less than its historical and scientific cousins, has been persistently
implicated in controversies over the fundamental questions of epistemology: What of the world is accessible to human knowledge, and
how are such things to be known?

To say this, however, is not to suggest an epistemologically seamless political modernity. There is a world of difference between the
dominant assumptions structuring the knowledge claims of the
twentieth century and those of the seventeenth, a difference that is
particularly vivid with regard to the presumed nature and regulative
principles of the underlying order of reality to be instantiated by

genuine knowledge. Whether such assumptions be characterized as a
metaphysics, a cosmology, or an episteme, those of the seventeenth
century, like those of the late middle ages, tended predominantly
toward the notion of a steady state. Such terms as harmony, balance,
equilibrium, and convenience typified for the age the character of
order that genuine knowledge sought to reveal.[5] Amidst the flux and
change of material appearances there was generally believed to be a
God-given order of nature, an order governed by principles or laws
of nature that directed the movements of things in a harmony analogous to the visibly regular motions of the heavens themselves. And,
most significantly for my reading of Locke, with respect to human
society in seventeenth-century England that order was preeminently
conceived in moralistic rather than sociological or historical terms.
By the late eighteenth and early nineteenth centuries, with the cata-
clysms of European revolution and the rising lights of secular and
scientific thought, this image of a divinely ordained moral order had
largely receded from the horizon of what counted as genuine knowledge. In its place arose perspectives emphasizing the dynamic characteristics of social change and growth to be typified perhaps most
succinctly by the notion of empirical social processes. With respect to
knowledges of human affairs, particularly in the nascent disciplines
of economics, history, sociology, and psychology, the order that
knowledge aimed to represent was increasingly conceptualized as
one of a worldly facticity unfolding in time. The goal of political and
social inquiry, in this later context, was not simply to chronicle the
facts of a changing world but to discern their patterns, to disclose
their tendencies, and, insofar as it was possible, to foresee or pre-
dict their direction in a way that would permit some measure of
control over their consequences. Whether warranted by historical research, rational inference, or statistical compilations, the object and
content of such knowledges was increasingly conceived to be the
complex yet regular association of facts as they followed from antecedent to consequent, from cause to effect.

5. For very different accounts of this, see Johann Huizinga, *The Waning of the
Middle Ages: A Study in the Forms of Life, Thought, and Art in France and the Netherlands in
the XIVth and XVth Centuries* (London: E. Arnold & Co., 1937); E. A. Burtt, *The Metaphysical Foundations of Modern Science: A Historical and Critical Essay* (New York: Doubleday, 1954); and Michel Foucault, *The Order of Things: An Archeology of the Human Sciences* (New York: Vintage Books, 1973).

Locke's writings, however, preceded the transformation of knowledge that spurred the development of such empirically oriented sciences of society by nearly a century. To be sure, his epistemological investigations in the *Essay concerning Human Understanding* laid much of the foundation upon which such later forms of knowledge would be built, but that work was decidedly skeptical of the possibility of a science of nature, much less a science of the social world.[6] Articulated long before the consolidation of the latter into the now familiar if increasingly frayed disciplinary divides of the social or human sciences, Locke's contributions to the controversies of his day cast human affairs as a realm fraught with "uncertainty and variableness," a domain of flux and contingency in which "nothing remains long in the same state."[7] His political writings, in particular, are devoid of the notions of regular or developing social, economic, or historical processes that occupy so central a place in later thought. But despite his doubts as to the empirical orderliness of the social world or certain knowledge of human affairs, Locke nonetheless subscribed to the principle of harmonious order as the underlying reality to which genuine knowledge must aspire. On his account, however, this order originated not in human artifice but in God's design. Bluntly put, it was a moral order divinely prescribed to beings capable of salvation rather than one of a knowable and patterned facticity of temporal processes.

Following from this, Locke's rendering of the political was in

6. See, for example, Locke's view of natural science in the *Essay concerning Human Understanding*, ed. Peter H. Nidditch (Oxford: Clarendon Press, 1975, by book, chapter, and paragraph, 4.3.29). The following passage from Locke's *Of the Conduct of the Understanding* is typical of his reaction to attempts to understand human society through the methods of mathematical science or chemistry; "Some men have so used their heads to mathematical figures that, giving a preference to the methods of that science, they introduce lines and diagrams into their study of divinity or politic inquiries as if nothing could be known without them; and others, accustomed to retired speculations, run natural philosophy into metaphysical notions and the abstract generalities of logic; and how often may one meet with religion and morality treated of in the terms of the laboratory, and thought to be improved by the methods of chymistry. But he that will take care of the conduct of his understanding, to direct it right to the knowledge of things, must avoid those undue mixtures, and not by a fondness for what he has found useful and necessary in one transfer it to another science, where it serves only to perplex and confound the understanding." John Locke, *Of the Conduct of the Understanding*, ed. Thomas Fowler, 2d ed. (1882; reprint, New York: Lenox Hill 1971), sec. 24, p. 51.

7. Locke, *Two Treatises*, 2.157.

many respects a static one, composed principally of moral and juridical relations between right-bearing individuals and focused centrally on retributive justice. The task and charge of civil law, from this perspective, was primarily to define and secure the right order of relations between such individuals by denominating as "crime" those actions that violated the principles of moral order embodied in God's design by the complementary notions of natural law and natural right. This, in turn, as I shall argue, established within Lockean political theory an essentially moralistic form of political understanding, judgment, and action—a sensibility that pivoted on the prevention and punishment of injury as the privileged means for maintaining moral relations between individuals. Here, however, the question of the source and proper expression of the knowledge necessary to such maintenance took on central significance. Generated in the context of intense political and religious conflict, both confronted with and contributing to the dissolution of older ways of knowing, the Lockean political sensibility stands rooted in the sands of an anxious skepticism.[8] In effect, Locke's response to the remoteness of certainty in human affairs was a theoretical fusion of the problem of knowledge with the question of judgment, and the political meaning and implications of his acquiescence in uncertainty resonate through a series of questions that trail implicitly and explicitly behind.

What was the relationship between the moral order of God's design and the political order of human artifice? What, within this frame, did it mean to make a political judgment? What were its distinguishing features? Its possibilities and limitations? What realms of human activity and experience constituted its proper objects? In what form should it be articulated? Who should be empowered to make such judgments? In what circumstances, by what criteria, and with what authority? Though raised by earlier thinkers in a variety of contexts, these concerns comprise much of the core of Locke's theoretical project—and his defense of political resistance gave them a decisively practical edge. By tracking Locke's engagement with these dilemmas across his various writings, this book undertakes an

---

8. On anxiety as an element of Lockean politics see Sheldon S. Wolin, *Politics and Vision: Continuity and Innovation in Western Political Thought* (Boston: Little, Brown and Company, 1960), 294; and, more recently, Uday Singh Mehta, *The Anxiety of Freedom: Imagination and Individuality in Locke's Political Thought* (Ithaca: Cornell University Press, 1992).

exploration of the problematic of judgment in his work. Its aim is to elucidate the moral meaning and sources of that problematic, to explore its bearing upon and circulation through his principal political writings at some length, and finally, to sketch some of its implications for the question of Locke's relationship to subsequent historical articulations of liberal political theory. In the remainder of these introductory remarks, however, I would like to suggest something of the genesis of the present study and the manner in which it will be pursued, as well as its relationship to a number of previous treatments of Locke's work.

The question of judgment that frames this reading of Locke initially emerged not solely as a curiosity about the seventeenth century, but also as a quandary about the meaning of rights in the contemporary United States. In the Bakke decision of 1976, for instance, the Supreme Court sought a principle to balance the rights of members of more traditionally privileged social groups with the rights of those historically subject to discrimination. In part accepting the practice of reserving a proportion of medical school admissions for women and minorities as a matter of "reverse discrimination" injurious to white men, the Court began to bound the scope of programs designed to remedy the historical exclusion of the former from opportunities to participate in significant arenas of social, political, and economic life. Viewed by progressive and liberal defenders of affirmative action as a conservative "backlash" in favor of privilege, the decision seemed to many an attempt to slow or obstruct the processes of racial and gender integration that such programs took as their goal, and more recent moves to dismantle such programs entirely are open to the same description.

In the contemporary American political idiom, of course, "backlash" is generally taken to signify an essentially reactionary political posture, an attempt to impede or roll back social progress. This usage, however, is a relatively recent accretion. Before the term entered political discourse as a figure for reaction, its literal or denotative meaning had to do with a mechanical dysfunction. The *OED* locates the emergence of its deployment as a political metaphor in the 1950s (and there in relation to desegregation), and as late as 1949 a standard American dictionary held fast to the mechanical meaning, defining "backlash" as a "jarring reaction, or striking back, caused in badly fitting machinery by irregularities of velocity or a reversal in motion," a "play or movement in connecting parts resulting from looseness."[9] If we draw such mechanistic images forward into the figurative use of the word in political discourse, a rather different picture of "backlash" emerges, as well as a number of questions. In the context of the contemporary liberal state, for example, is there a sense in which the language and practice of rights might be seen as analogous to "badly fitting machinery"? Might the increasingly divergent conflicts among liberal, libertarian, conservative, and communitarian perspectives on questions of rights be understood as arising from a political analogue of "irregularities of velocity" or "reversals of motion"? I will not chase these contemporary conundrums here, but as a heuristic device the image of such discordance is at least suggestive. Particularly in light of the widespread modern assumption of the movement of social processes in time, it provides a provocation to rethink the problematic of rights in light of the historicity of its governing notion of order.

By juxtaposing such countervailing rights claims as those addressed by the Bakke decision with earlier usages of the language of rights, a more precisely framed problem emerges, one that points to a paradox in the history of liberal political understanding. In the early modern period, particularly in the hands of thinkers like Locke, the radical edge of the language of rights was honed as a moral claim of individuals, whether singly or in combination, against the excesses of their governors. Ostensibly a language of limitation, its primary political concern was to delineate the proper boundaries of state power over the liberties and properties of its citizens and to discriminate between the due exercise of such power and its arbitrary excess. While the language of rights in this context may not have been the fighting creed of onetime popular imagery, its Janus-like response to both traditional privilege and popular insurgency nonetheless combined a moral defense of resistance with a delimitation of properly political concerns.[10] And yet, by the late twentieth century many aspects of liberal rights-claiming practices not only tend to appeal to state power to redress inequities arising in the domain of social processes, but in so doing tend increasingly to augment its legislative and regulatory authority as well as extend its administrative purview over broad arenas of contemporary social life.

9. *Webster's New Collegiate Dictionary* 2d ed., s.v. "backlash."
10. Wolin, *Politics and Vision* (Boston: Little, Brown and Co., 1960), 294.

Affirmative action programs, in this regard, are but one promontory
of a greater berg, emblematic of more pervasive historical developments in which a panoply of modern knowledges inform not only
governmental interventions in employment, health, education, and
the like, but fiscal and monetary policies as well. The language of
rights, it would seem, as well as the liberal state in whose birth it
assisted, has been in many respects transformed from a guarantor of
personal rights and private life against political interference into a
powerful administrator of social practices armed with an extensive
bureaucratic network devoted to the management of social processes
in time.

   From one perspective, this development could be seen as a consequence of modernization, a result of far-reaching social, demographic, economic, and technological changes over time. It might be
accounted for, in other words, by reference to the size and complexity of modern industrial society, to the dilemmas generated by increasing numbers of individuals engaged in increasingly diverse activities bumping up against one another more often, and in ever
more complex ways. Given this, or so the argument might go, what
else can be done but look to a tolerably just administration of social
life? The interventionist and bureaucratic state, on this view, is perhaps an unfortunate necessity but a necessity nonetheless, and one
through which the language of rights might yet provide a modicum
of security to individuals against both undesirable private practices
and unreasonable excesses of social power and prestige. Such an account may, however, be less than adequate. As I hope to suggest
through this rereading of the Lockean corpus, the potential for such
a strong state authority is deeply embedded in early modern articulations of the language of rights itself. The elaboration of that potential may well be connected to historical changes, but not simply those
of an empirical—social, demographic, economic, or technological—
nature, for it is discernible in the grounds of knowledge and criteria
of judgment underwriting the articulation of state power as early as
the seventeenth century. More specifically, in the context of Locke's
writings, I shall suggest that this potential is intimately bound up
with the manner in which these criteria, as initially formulated
within the moralistic framework of natural law, were both associated
with and transformed by what Michel Foucault described as the epis-

temic shift of the early modern period.[11] What I mean to suggest is the possibility that the apparent historical continuity of what some might style the "liberal tradition" from the seventeenth century to the present may mask an important disjuncture or segmentation in the language of rights. This language, in other words—and more particularly what I shall characterize as the theistic individualism of its central political vocabulary of law, right, liberty, equality, and property—undergoes a substantial shift in political meaning and emphasis as the dominant framework of knowledge in which it is articulated moves from the static and theologically grounded moralism of natural law to more worldly empirical and scientific understandings of the operation of social processes in time.

But why Locke? Locke's work, I suggest, provides a peculiarly fecund site for grappling with the question of the relationship between the language of rights, the power of the state, and the problem of knowledge. To begin with, his various writings are situated at a significant moment in the history of the language of rights. By the seventeenth century, England was becoming in political, economic, and military terms a recognizably modern national state, and Locke's justification of political resistance, as well as his defense of legislative supremacy, can be understood as intimately related to a shift in the political focus of the language of rights from a localistic to a national arena of struggle and contestation. This aspect of Locke's historical location is accompanied, however, by a second of similar importance, for his writings are situated as well on the cusp, as it were, of the modern episteme. On the far side of that temporal division, although the empiricism of his epistemological investigations became pivotal for the later emergence of scientific understandings of society and social processes, his use of the language of rights, the political sensibility he articulated in defense of it, and the epistemological grounds on which these rest were articulated in decidedly moralistic terms and undergirded by a theistic understanding of natural law as a divinely ordained imperative to moral order. On the near side of that division, however, the positive tasks Locke assigned to political power in the production of security, prosperity, and the public good

11. See, in particular, Foucault, *Order of Things,* in which the rise and development of modern social knowledges is traced out of the representations of resemblances, correspondences, and analogies characteristic of previous understandings.

look forward to more emphatically secular and recognizably modern state functions. Further, Locke's various contributions to the political and intellectual culture of the period were both sufficiently broad and sufficiently precise to explore the question of judgment in some detail. Here, his explicit and persistent concern with the question of moral conduct offers an unusually rich resource for investigating the kinds of knowledge and criteria of judgment he considered appropriate to a range of practical dilemmas arising in political and social life. The diversity of these materials, too, ranging as they do across the domains of religion, politics, education, economics, and, most important, epistemology itself, provides an immensely suggestive corpus for considering the stakes and implications of such judgments in a variety of contexts.

Finally, and in combination with the above, Locke's posthumous reputation as a founder of liberalism makes his work both an intellectually fruitful and a politically significant site for opening the question of the historical relationship between the liberal language of rights and the problematic of political judgment. Long considered an exponent of limited government and a defender of rights as moral claims against state power, Locke would seem to be the "liberal" thinker least friendly to the possibility of a strong administrative state. But by considering his positive articulation of state power—by attending closely, that is, to the tasks with which his theoretical construction invests the political—I mean to suggest a rather more complex picture. By exploring the relationship between Locke's moralism, his epistemological investigations, and his deployment of the language of rights, I hope not only to offer a more nuanced theoretical account of the Lockean political sensibility than considerations of philosophical, doctrinal, or ideological coherence have hitherto provided, but also to intimate in rough contours something of the problematic legacy it bequeathed to later liberalisms.

The book is broadly divided into two parts, the first devoted to an account of the theistic resonances internal to Locke's political vocabulary, and the second directed to examining that vocabulary—in action, so to speak—in the context of his more explicitly articulated political theory, as well as in relation to various elements of the broader political discourses and dilemmas of his time. Part I, loosely following recent work on the ordering function of metaphor in scientific understanding, situates Locke's political project within the

dominant cosmological metaphor of the period, the theistic image of
the world as a divinely created "architecture of order."[12] Although
much of this account is consistent with the historical scholarship that
emphasizes the theological foundations of Lockean politics, my aim
is not only to evidence the theistic grounding and moral weight of
Locke's political concerns but more precisely to suggest the semiotic
indebtedness of his political vocabulary to the structural features of
the architectural metaphor.[13] This, in turn, underwrites an attempt
in Part II to rethink and reassess the theoretical character and implications of Locke's account of political judgment and action, particularly as this bears on the meaning of rights in relationship to his
positive conception of political power.

The focus, then, of the two chapters of Part I is on the metaphor
of the "architecture of order" as a structuring device for Locke's
political vocabulary. Metaphor, as Donna Haraway provocatively observes, "is a property of language that gives boundaries to worlds,"
and this was one of the broadest and most widely circulated of such
images in the late medieval and early modern period.[14] A visual representation of the "world picture" itself, the architectural metaphor
for God's created cosmos both provided a hierarchical structure differentiating the human from the non-human world and enabled,
through a wide range of elaborations, diverse accounts of the proper
relationship between the two in God's design. The burden of these
chapters is to articulate the ways in which Locke's specific deployments of the vocabulary of law, right, liberty, equality, and property
are closely bound to and structured by this metaphoric invocation of
the larger design of order embodied in God's creation. Such terms, I
shall argue, can be understood not simply as a priori assumptions or
axioms within a logical system, but as notions at once embedded in

12. For general accounts of the operation of metaphor in the philosophy of science
see Max Black, *Models and Metaphors: Studies in Language and Philosophy* (Ithaca: Cornell University Press, 1962); and Mary Hesse, *Models and Analogies in Science* (South
Bend, Ind.: Notre Dame Press, 1966). For an exploration of the role of competing
metaphors in the paradigmatic redefinition of a specific scientific discipline see Donna
Haraway, *Crystals, Fabrics, and Fields: Metaphors of Organicism in Twentieth-Century Developmental Biology* (New Haven: Yale University Press, 1976).
13. In addition to Dunn, *Political Thought;* see James Tully, *A Discourse on Property:
John Locke and His Adversaries* (Cambridge: Cambridge University Press, 1980); and
John Marshall, *John Locke: Resistance, Religion, and Responsibility* (Cambridge: Cambridge University Press, 1994).
14. Haraway, *Crystals, Fabrics, and Fields,* 10.

and orchestrated by a larger and more encompassing representation
of a created cosmos, a representation most fruitfully understood as
providing not a 'theory' of human nature but a theistically driven
and hierarchically ordered imaginary of the contingency and perils
of the human condition.[15]

The obvious question is why this particular metaphor should be
given analytical privilege. Certainly it was far from the only image
pressed to the service of political discourse in the period. It was,
however, one of the most broadly disseminated and generally accessible cosmological constructs, and as such both informed the casuistic
debates of the time and provided a common frame of reference for
a diverse if conflictual range of apparently more worldly or prag-
matic political concerns. In light of this, and on the strength of recent historical scholarship emphasizing the ethical and theological
moorings of Locke's various writings, the metaphor of God's architecture offers a relatively uncontentious starting point to explore the
moral freighting of his political vocabulary. It provides a broad
heuristic or context of interpretation that has at least a claim to historical plausibility as a schema common to Locke and his contemporaries, including a relatively extensive popular audience. Further, because Locke himself persistently deploys the metaphor throughout
his life, it cannot be seen as a presentist imposition on his work, nor
does it force him at the outset into a particular political or theoretical
"tradition" that is itself subject to interpretive objections with respect
to questions of a canon, on the one hand, or issues of his meaning to
his audience on the other.[16] Because the metaphor is now obsolete,

15. E. M. W. Tillyard, *The Elizabethan World Picture* (New York: Macmillan, 1944),
took this hierarchical imaginary as both constituitive and regulative of English political culture in the period, focusing in particular on the relationship it implied between
the upper echelons of the social order and innate superiority as a central motif in
Elizabethan literature. More recently, and in terms more congenial to the account
offered here of Locke's various appropriations of the image, Jonathan Dollimore has
argued that literary deployments of that hierarchy frequently emphasized not only
the dissociation of social rank from natural superiority or inferiority, but the moral
leveling of individual agents, regardless of worldly station and status, through the
character of their deeds. See Jonathan Dollimore, *Radical Tragedy: Religion, Ideology,
and Power in the Drama of Shakespeare and His Contemporaries* (Chicago: University of
Chicago Press, 1984).

16. Such present-oriented framing devices are characteristic of both Leo Strauss's
account of Locke in *Natural Right and History* (Chicago: University of Chicago Press,
1953); and C. B. Macpherson, *The Political Theory of Possessive Individualism: Hobbes to
Locke* (Oxford: Oxford University Press, 1962). With regard to the question of "tradition," I do not mean to suggest that Locke cannot be read as participating in any one

an account of its operation in his work may also open a theoretical space for considering the historicity of Locke's political thought in ways that are inaccessible to more narrowly contextualist, eventmental, or ideological reconstructions of his meaning or intentions.[17]

What I refer to throughout the book as Locke's political vocabulary, of course, preceded by quite some time the development of an identifiably liberal political discourse, however generously one may be inclined to view anachronistic usages. The juridical terminology of law, right, liberty, and property, in particular, had long been characteristic of the English political idiom, and although equality was perhaps a more recent accretion, it had been well integrated into common usage by the seventeenth century. To be sure, this vocabulary has proved persistent through the development of later, self-professedly liberal accounts of political understanding, and it continues to play a significant role in structuring political perception, struggle, and controversy. With the admirable exceptions of John Dunn, James Tully, and John Marshall, however, in most scholarly interpretations of Locke's work the image of a divinely created world that framed his use of the terms and structured their mutual relations is seldom granted much import.[18] By reconstructing this architecture and suggesting some of the ways in which the insistent but

---

of a number of traditions. Such readings can be quite illuminating, as is the case with Julian H. Franklin, *John Locke and the Theory of Sovereignty: Mixed Monarchy and the Right of Resistance in the Political Thought of the English Revolution* (Cambridge: Cambridge University Press, 1978); as well as the reading of Locke in the context of natural law theories in Tully, *Discourse on Property.* Nonetheless, I take it as important that what are now regarded as Locke's explicitly political works, that is, the *Two Treatises* and his various letters on toleration, are polemical tracts addressed to a broad public. The *Treatises,* in particular, are notoriously ecumenical in the mélange of perspectives they draw upon. While their placement in the context of a particular tradition may bring to light important aspects of their meaning, there is little reason to privilege such contextualizations as securing or settling their meaning in any final sense.

17. Here I am thinking primarily of Laslett's reading of Locke in the context of the Exclusion Crisis in the introduction to his edition of Locke, *Two Treatises;* the account of that text as an expression of radical Whig ideology in Richard Ashcraft, *Revolutionary Politics and Locke's "Two Treatises of Government"* (Princeton: Princeton University Press, 1986); and the rendering of Locke's ideological indebtedness to the Calvinist idea of the "calling" in Dunn, *Political Thought.*

18. Even Dunn, however, curiously neglects the possibility that this imagery may be importantly constitutive of Locke's meanings. While he duly notes the presence of the image in Locke's work, he nonetheless turns rather quickly to identify more narrowly defined social carriers of its meaning, eventually locating the key to Locke's theory in the notion of Calvinist social values and the idea of the "calling." See Dunn, *Political Thought,* esp. chap. 9.

complex moralism of its language of justification undergirds the core political categories of Locke's theoretical enterprise, I hope to establish a basis for seeing that project in a new light. While this treatment will necessarily intersect with previous scholarly analyses, it differs in both conception and intention from most of this literature. In particular, it attempts to pursue a loose agnosticism with regard to the interpretive divide between present-minded accounts of Locke's relevance and more historically precise contextual reconstructions of his meanings in his own time. In evoking the metaphor of macrocosmic architecture as a context for interpreting his work, I hope at the outset to relieve his political vocabulary of its familiarity by insisting on the broad historicity of its meaning. Of those scholars concerned with the situatedness of Locke's writings in the discursive context and argumentative strategies of their own time and place, I ask a measure of generosity, or at least tolerance, toward an approach less governed by the documentary, eventmental, and inferential commitments of the historian's craft. Of the more philosophically inclined—and most particularly of those who might press for the continuing relevance or applicability of that vocabulary—I ask that its internal interconnections and connotative range be questioned at the outset, rather than immediately defined and examined for conceptual consistency.

Quick definitions, and the inconsistencies they seem to reveal across Locke's work, are one of the principal sources for the widely disparate theoretical accounts of Locke's politics, as can be seen most clearly from interpretations of the term "property" and its political meaning in Locke's writings. It is, for instance, a common observation that the usage of the term is inconsistent in the *Treatises*, referring at different times broadly to such things as liberty and life or narrowly to material goods and personal possessions. This inconsistency, for one well-known interpreter, reflects a "confusion" in Locke's definition of property that "might be ascribed to the confusion in his mind between the remnant of traditional values and the new bourgeois values."[19] Over the years this contention itself has generated a maelstrom of debate over, as some would have it, the political and theoretical implications of this "inconsistency," or as others insist, over the underlying logic of Locke's argument, its co-

---

19. Macpherson, *Political Theory*, 220.

herence in its historical context, and the consequent inaccuracy of
such broad allegations of conceptual confusion. The present work is
an attempt to recast the terms of this debate, but more importantly it
is an attempt to do so in a manner that sustains some claim to historical purchase and, at the same time, clears a path for subsequent
inquiries into the question of Locke's relationship to later articulations of liberal political theory.

This, to be sure, presents no small interpretive dilemma. There
are, however, good reasons for thinking that the question of Locke's
"inconsistency" that has agitated so many may be poorly posed. One
of the more curious of these reasons, and for some perhaps one of
the more compelling in historical terms, is the fact that Locke apparently prided himself on the cogency of his treatment of property.
"Property," he suggested in a letter to Richard King, "I have no
where found more clearly explained than in a book intitled 'Two
Treatises of Government.'"[20] Hubristic though it may seem, the comment comes from a writer who, when he did find his own treatment
of important topics confused, was known both to acknowledge this
to his intimates and to correct himself in print in subsequent edi-
tions. His constant reworking of the chapter "Of Power" in the *Essay*
is only the most obvious example of this. Given the fact that Locke
read and revised the text of the *Treatises* for three different printings
prior to his letter to King, one cannot help but think he believed
what he said. For those unpersuaded by the subject-centeredness of
such biographical accounts, it could also be pointed out that the
Treatises' seemingly unselfconscious oscillation between the broad
and narrow meanings of "property" was not at all peculiar to Locke,
but common to the usage of the period. The semantic field of the
term, which we shall explore more fully later on, is captured perhaps more robustly by the notion of "propriety," a morally loaded
term connoting that which was properly "one's own," particularly as
this was established by law. Interestingly, in his revisions for the
third edition of the *Treatises*, Locke frequently substituted "property"

20. John Locke, "A Letter to the Rev. Richard King," in *The Works of John Locke in
Ten Volumes*, 12th ed. (London: 1823), 10: 307. I do not here mean to imply that
Locke's conceptual difficulties existed only where he recognized them. The point is
simply that after numerous revisions of the *Treatises* he remained sufficiently per-
suaded of the cogency of the account to single it out as a particularly well-formulated
treatment of the subject.

for his original use of "propriety," a change that Laslett accounts difficult to understand "unless the language had changed between 1680 and 1700."[21] Indeed, it had been changing for some time, but in relation to historical dynamics more deeply sedimented than the high political crises of those two decades. It was, however, not simply the language that was changing but its referential range as well. From the sixteenth century onward, England's expanding commercial economy, with its extensive monetarization of property relations and market exchanges, had radically unsettled the traditional framing of "propriety" as both a moral and a legal category. Not yet narrowed to the more assertively modern sense of "property" as material possessions, however, Locke's use of the term was relatively lucid—if not without its tensions and ambiguities—not only within the theistic framework of God's design but within the ethico-juridical conventions of the common law, itself widely regarded as the distinctively English manifestation of that frame.

On these grounds, and in view of various recent reconstructions of Locke's coherence, it may well be that the confusions attending his treatment of property, as well as a series of other political questions that follow from this, are more likely ours than his. The problem, in other words, may well be that the intervening three centuries have generated sufficient changes in the meanings of and relationships between many of his central terms that, despite the apparent continuity of the vocabulary, we no longer speak the same language.[22] But if this is the case, if the problem of reading Locke entails a translation between two historically divergent political idioms, little is to be gained in dissolving the distance by retrospectively displacing contemporary constellations of meaning onto his usages. The problem of interpretation here, however, is not merely one of avoiding anachronism, as if it were possible, Ranke-like, to provide settled positive demarcations of such slices of time. Events and regimes may have their beginnings and ends, but political vocabularies are more protean creatures and their metamorphoses in time may well defy the impulse to enclose them in a distant past. Parsing historical pe-

---

21. See Laslett's note, Locke, *Two Treatises*, at 1.73.

22. A similar point is raised by Christopher Hill in his discussion of the shifts in meaning to which the terms "reason" and "reasonableness" were subject through the seventeenth century. See Christopher Hill, *Change and Continuity in Seventeenth-Century England* (Cambridge: Harvard University Press, 1975), 102–23.

riods in one way rather than another is not merely a matter of setting the record straight, but a matter of articulating, here and now, a relation between past and present. As a consequence, if our contemporary controversies over the meanings of law, right, liberty, equality, and property run the risk of anachronism as guides to the sense of their seventeenth-century antecedents, this suggests not simply questions of conceptual clarity or historical accuracy. Insofar as such researches orient contemporary meanings in time, they raise questions of political significance as well.

This raises a second point. However mistaken it may be to impose modern meanings on seventeenth-century usages, the project of interrogating the historicity of Locke's political vocabulary in relation to that of later liberalism is neither ill conceived nor theoretically illegitimate. But to date, the most persuasive historical arguments for the rough coherence of his theory have limited themselves principally to refuting the allegation of confusion by recovering what they take to be his meanings in their original context. John Dunn's *The Political Thought of John Locke: An Historical Account of the Argument of the "Two Treatises of Government,"* James Tully's *A Discourse on Property: John Locke and His Adversaries,* Richard Ashcraft's *Revolutionary Politics and Locke's "Two Treatises of Government,"* and John Marshall's *John Locke: Resistance, Religion, and Responsibility* are meticulous, careful, and highly compelling reconstructions of the historical Locke. To be sure, they differ on particular points of interpretation, but these differences pertain to what will count as the historical record of Locke's meaning and intentions in his time and place. Self-consciously limited to the project of resurrecting the "real" Locke, they proffer a Locke substantially purged of the questions, confusions, imperatives, and dilemmas of liberal politics in the late twentieth century.[23]

23. In Dunn's and Tully's contributions, and more emphatically so for the present study, "coherence" is not to be understood as "consistency." The latter, as a logical standard, depends upon agreement as to the meaning of terms, a condition not only complicated by Locke's historical distance from twentieth-century usages but, in his own time, a condition hardly to be expected of the unsettled discursive terrain of seventeenth-century English politics. "Coherence," however, is a far looser criterion that addresses not the logical consistency of a theorist's use of terms but the sense in which a theoretical exposition "hangs together." What hangs together and what does not, as well as who it hangs together for, are important questions that necessarily direct attention to variations in usage available at the time. For Dunn and Tully this

From the standpoint and concerns of contemporary political theory, however, these works, while in many respects persuasive in their
historical arguments and provocative in their points of difference,
are overmodest. What is gained by their efforts is a rich sense of the
situatedness of Locke's writings in their historical milieu and of the
complexity of their relationship to his own political commitments
and involvements. Ashcraft's account of the connections between
Locke's conspiratorial activities and the *Treatises'* articulation of radical Whig ideology reinvests that work with a militancy often underplayed by postwar scholarly and textbook accounts that figure him as
a paragon of liberal common sense. Equally salutary reminders of
Locke's distance from modern liberalism are provided by Dunn's reconstruction of his theological commitments and moral concerns, by
Tully's analyses of the bearing of those concerns on Locke's natural-
law arguments regarding property, and by Marshall's impressive historical account of their changes and continuities across the trajectory
of his moral and social thought more generally. These four books
stand as much needed correctives to the excessively secular repre-

---

issue is framed largely by concerns for historical accuracy. Both works are informed
by the methodological imperatives advanced by Dunn himself in "The Identity of the
History of Ideas," *Philosophy* 43, no. 164 (April 1968): 85–194; and by Quentin Skinner, "Meaning and Understanding in the History of Ideas," *History and Theory* 8, no. 1
(1969): 3–53. Although the contexts they establish are different, both works attempt
to reconstruct Locke's meaning and intentions by indicating how he inserted himself
into the frameworks of argumentation available in the period. But this is perhaps to
restrict his meaning too narrowly. It is not unusual to be understood as meaning more
than one intends, and the effort to insulate historical writing from this possibility
greatly constricts the sense in which such texts can be said to have a properly "historical" meaning. The attribution of intentions beyond what a theorist actually states is
always a matter of inference and interpretation, and this in turn is indeed dependent
upon a particular context of interpretation. In historical study, however, there is no
such creature as an uninterpreted context: that is, there is no stable field of meaning
"out there" with respect to which particular historical texts can be held accountable. A
historical context, in other words, is itself a constructed range of more or less conventionally accepted referents within which certain sorts of meanings can be understood
as possible. In effect, the meaning of a historical text can be as broad or narrow as the
context within which it is placed. No context, however, is simply given, for it—no less
than the meanings that are derived from it—is a construction of the interpreter. The
exclusion of the present from such contextualizations is quite impossible. Tully's most
recent book, *An Approach to Political Philosophy: Locke in Contexts* (Cambridge: Cambridge University Press, 1993), is a superb example of how supple the notion of context can become when reflexively oriented toward issues and theoretical perspectives
arising in the interpreter's present.

sentations typical of most twentieth-century commentary. But what is lost is a theoretical understanding, a political sense if you will, of why anyone here and now should consider this important. However this problem might be addressed with respect to thinkers more distant from the Anglo-American liberal tradition, Locke's posthumous election as a founder of that tradition and the significance of his reputation and writings for the reflexive self-understanding of subsequent theorists and actors both within and without it cannot be so easily relegated to a distant if in some sense recoverable past. A reading of Locke's writings, in short, need not crudely presume that he provides solutions to our contemporary problems to suggest that his nominally historical meanings may percolate well beyond his own time. Indeed, our own efforts to discern those meanings are necessarily implicated in that percolation, precisely because they articulate a relation between his past and our present—and this is no less the case for those who figure that relation under the signs of rupture and distance than it is for those who write it as continuity.

In addition to the fact that Locke remains, as it were, "alive" in this sense, it is also the case that the ostensibly Lockean political vocabulary of law, right, liberty, equality, and property remains at the heart of contemporary political discussion. That vocabulary itself has been solidified, regularized, and institutionalized over the past three hundred years in ways that extend its historical horizon from the English constitutional crises of the seventeenth-century to the political struggles and controversies of the present. Clearly, dominant forms of twentieth-century political argumentation do not use this language to understand the same world that Locke did. The works of Dunn, Tully, and Marshall, in particular, provide sufficient testimony to remind us of this, should such a reminder be necessary. Neither Calvinist "callings" nor early modern controversies within the conceptual framework of natural law remain particularly compelling or relevant for twentieth-century political understandings— and even the religious right maintains political silence on the question of the soul's salvation, however noisily they may press for the right to life. But in view of such differences the political and theoretical question becomes one of considering the relationship between the apparent continuity of the central terms of Locke's political vocabulary and the profound changes in political meaning and normative grounding suggested by more temporally delimited historical interpretations. That his articulation of the mutual relations between political power, ethical propriety, and material property might be even loosely coherent given his theological, moral, and epistemological commitments should, in other words, open rather than close the question of his relationship to subsequent political theory and practice.

It is my hope in this book to provide such an opening. My aim, then, is not to argue that Locke's work provides answers to contemporary political questions—a strategy contextualists I think rightly disdain—but rather to suggest that his answers to his questions can illuminate something of the genealogy of our own. Here I think the broad context offered by the metaphor of God's architecture is a productive starting point. Intellectual productions, no less than the tasks of ordinary life, rely heavily upon what Michael Polanyi termed "tacit knowledge," general structuring assumptions that lend a taken-for-grantedness, more or less coherent, to the experienced world. For Locke, just as for most of his contemporaries, the broad image of that architecture provided one such structure. A vivid picture of human existence within a larger cosmos, the order it suggested was expressed not in terms of a mundane facticity but in terms of God's agency in the fabrication of a world whose things and creatures were hierarchically arrayed along a vertical axis by divine design. My purpose in Part I is to articulate the broad contours and multiple levels of that imagery as they can be glimpsed in Locke's writings. Cast as an ethnography of the cultural imaginary of God's architecture, Chapter 1 describes the structure of the world figured by that metaphor and elucidates the meaning and stakes of the problem of judgment within it. Chapter 2 then explores its echoes, its resonances and correspondences, in Locke's articulation of the vocabulary of law, right, liberty, equality, and property.[24]

I have previously noted the interpretive and exegetical functions of the metaphor in discerning something of the historical valences of this vocabulary. To begin to draw out its specifically political character, however, both in the context of Locke's particular usages and with respect to its legacy for subsequent expressions of liberal theory, we require something more. While the metaphor, in other words, might provide the most general categories through which

24. Others have touched upon elements of this subject in relation to Locke's religious beliefs, most notably Dunn and Marshall in the works cited at note 13. Here, however, it will be treated more on the order of a cultural hegemon.

Locke's views of the political and social world were framed, it does not tell us much more than that. It suggests little of the challenges embraced by his contributions to the political literature of late-seventeenth-century England, and it certainly does not suggest how the political point of these contributions might have been opened to differential rearticulation in later, less theistically inflected times. To address these issues, a view of the conflicts of the period is necessary, as well as a more general characterization of Locke's theoretical project within them. This is the task of Part II, which shifts to a more historically situated attempt to locate the connections between that project and the language and practice of rights in the period. I consider Locke's articulation of the language of rights in the context not only of the disarray that had characterized English political discourse since midcentury, but of the political tasks it embraced over the tumultuous decade that culminated in the 'Glorious Revolution.' To this end, the introduction to Part II takes up the question of the relationship between the metaphor of God's architecture and the more familiar problems and perspectives of Locke's immediate political context. The political and theoretical character of his project in that context is explored in greater detail in Chapters 3 through 5, while Chapters 6 and 7 turn to a series of more general considerations raised by Locke's positive construction of political power. As the interpretation of Lockean politics developed across these chapters presumes familiarity with the details of the "architecture" presented in Part I, a rehearsal here of the broader perspective pursued in Part II would be prone either to tedium or to excessive reduction. Readers desirous of more extensive preliminaries will find partial satisfaction in the remarks introducing Part II, but at this point, rather than summarize at the beginning what is achieved only at the end, let me dispense with further explanation and invite you to an exploration of God's architecture.

Part I

AN ARCHITECTURE
OF ORDER

1

An Architecture of Order:
Metaphor, Morality, and the
Problem of Judgment

> So, if the world itself be but an house, if the earth, which
> *hangeth upon nothing,* be the foundation, and the glorious
> spheres of heaven the roof. . . , if this be the habitation of
> an infinite Intelligence, the Temple of God; then we must
> acknowledge the world was built by him, and, conse-
> quently, *that he which built all things is God.*
>
> —*John Pearson*

The image of the world as an edifice designed and built by an infinitely knowing maker was a commonplace in seventeenth-century understandings of the cosmos.[1] Through this architecture of creation the ordered hierarchies of Christian Scripture, medieval Scholasticism, and "heathen philosophy" alike resonated, echoing their diverse choruses of subordinate relations of rank and degree. In an earlier age this order was preeminently understood to be one of analogy from greatest to least, of similitude and correspondence within and between each link in the "great chain of being."[2] Macro-

1. John Pearson, *Exposition of the Creed* (1659), ed. Robert Sinker (Cambridge: Cambridge University Press, 1899).

2. See Arthur O. Lovejoy, *The Great Chain of Being: A Study in the History of an Idea* (Cambridge: Harvard University Press, 1965) for the classic history of this concept. Francis Oakley, *Omnipotence, Covenant, and Order: An Excursion in the History of Ideas from Abelard to Leibniz* (Ithaca: Cornell University Press, 1984) suggests an alternative order, equally hierarchical but grounded in God's will and promise of a covenant rather than subsisting in the nature of things. See also Edward P. Mahoney, "Metaphysical Foundations of the Hierarchy of Being according to Some Late-Medieval and Renaissance Philosophers," in *Philosophies of Existence: Ancient and Medieval,* ed. Parviz Morewedge (New York: Fordham University Press, 1982), 165–257.

cosm and microcosm were parallel images of detail and design: as God had differentiated the world of created beings by degrees of perfection, so had he ordered the ranks of human society into hierarchical relations of station and status. In the intellectual world of Stuart England, however, this vision of God's order confronted another, one for which the structured edifice of creation was equally hierarchical but within which the notion of essential correspondences between macrocosm and microcosm was conspicuously absent if not, indeed, resolutely denied. One such denial, characteristic of the opposition faced by the older vision, was trenchantly put by John Spencer, who castigated the notion of a "very rigid and strict analogy and conformity between the Macrocosm and the Microcosm, the World and Man," calling it a "conceit as dear to some Ancient and Modern Writers as their very eyes."[3] Among the numerous tracts of the age in which this refiguration of the world's architecture found voice was John Locke's *Two Treatises of Government.* Refusing the idea of a divinely ordained social hierarchy, Locke asserted there to be "nothing more evident, than that Creatures of the same species and rank promiscuously born to all the same advantages of Nature, and the use of all the same faculties, should also be equal one amongst another without Subordination or Subjection."[4] This God-given natural equality of human agents and their "*perfect Freedom . . .* within the bounds of the Law of Nature" stand, of course, at the center of the *Treatises*' political world.[5]

3. John Spencer, *A Discourse concerning Prodigies: Wherein the Vanity of Presages by Them Is Reprehended and Their True and Proper Ends Asserted and Vindicated,* 2d ed., corrected and enlarged (London: J. Field for Will Groves, 1665), 70.

4. John Locke, *Two Treatises of Government,* ed. Peter Laslett, rev. ed. (1960; reprint, with amendments, Cambridge: Cambridge University Press, 1963), by book and paragraph, 2.4. See also 1.67 for a similar construction. Hereafter cited as *Two Treatises.*

5. Ibid. Wolfgang von Leyden has claimed that "the law of nature as it occurs in Locke's philosophy is not the same as one of Galileo's or Newton's so-called laws of nature: it is not concerned with physical phenomena, their motion or regularity." See Wolfgang von Leyden, "John Locke and Natural Law," in *Life, Liberty and Property: Essays on Locke's Political Ideas,* ed. Gordon J. Schochet (Belmont, Calif.: Wadsworth Publishing Co., 1971), 12. This is perhaps an oversimplification. It is true that Locke took the human species as his primary theoretical focus and hence in most of his works is principally concerned with the "law" appropriate to human agents rather than that governing physical phenomena. Although the former of these is marked by its voluntary and the latter by its necessary character, both derive from the same source, that is, God's intended design of the cosmos as a whole.

As the structure of a house may be unaffected by redesigning the plan of a single floor, the architecture of Locke's larger cosmos remained hierarchical. Despite his leveling of the social microcosm, the rest of the structure stood firm. The floors and bearing walls of God's edifice, as it were, which distinguished the human place from the greater and lesser aspects of God's creation, held fast—as Locke's own phraseology suggests. To the human species, as to "all the several degrees and ranks of Creatures," the creator had granted faculties appropriate to the condition and circumstances in which he made them—just as to bodies, substances, and matter that same "Wise Architect" had imparted "the original Rules and Communication of Motion."[6] This architecture of created nature, as the work of a perfect and infinitely knowing being, was a design of "order, harmony, and beauty"[7] within which humanity's space was but a small part—though a part no less subject to God's design of harmony and order than the rest. Rearrange their rooms as they might, human agents resided in a mansion not of their own making, and the structural boundaries of that dwelling remained the divinely ordained limits of both their nature and their competence.

It is out of this architecture of order that Locke's conception of politics emerged. His vision of political society thus locates the dynamics of social existence within a divine scaffolding that defined not simply human nature, but the nature of the cosmos as a whole and the place the human species was meant to occupy within it. Despite the sustained attention that his political writings have received in the last forty years, the relationship between his well-known participation in the leveling of the social microcosm and his retention of the hierarchical image of the larger cosmos has never been examined as a question of political significance.[8] His declarations of hu-

6. The phrases are drawn from John Locke, *Essay concerning Human Understanding*, ed. Peter H. Nidditch (Oxford: Clarendon Press, 1975), by book, chaper, and paragraph, 2.9.12 and 4.3.29, respectively. Hereafter cited as *Essay*.

7. Ibid., 4.10.10.

8. Philosophers and historians of philosophy, particularly those interested in questions of epistemology, have noted Locke's retention of the macrocosmic structure. See, for instance, Michael R. Ayers, "Mechanism, Superaddition, and the Proof of God's Existence in Locke's *Essay*," *Philosophical Review* 90, no. 2 (1981): 210–51; and Michael R. Ayres, "Locke versus Aristotle on Natural Kinds," *Journal of Philosophy* 78, no. 5 (1981): 247–72. Among social and political theorists, however, the significance of the question has been suggested in Louis Dumont, "Religion, Politics, and Society in the Individualistic Universe," *Proceedings of the Royal Anthropological Institute for*

man freedom and equality tend to be read as a priori assumptions, as givens that open out onto such now familiar questions as the relationship between freedom and authority or between the individual and the community, or alternatively, onto questions about the place of his political writings amidst the multiple political languages of his period. I will suggest, however, that what are commonly taken as significant elements of Locke's political vocabulary—law, right, liberty, equality, and property—as well as his broader theological, metaphysical, and epistemological concerns, are powerfully framed, related, and set in motion by the structuring metaphor of God's hierarchical design. In the chapter following we will consider the bearing of this ordered structure upon that political vocabulary itself. But for the moment, before venturing into the politics of the peculiar space allotted humankind by its divine architect, we might pause to survey the Lockean vision of the larger whole by drawing out the links and points of connection between his various enunciations of that structure. Suspending modern tendencies to disbelief in such things, let us note some of the details of its divine construction, walking its halls and exploring its recesses in an effort to glean the character of the human place within it.

I   The Structure of Creation

The vastness and perfection of God's created cosmos are recurrent themes in Locke's writings, as present in his last supervised edition of the *Essay concerning Human Understanding* as in the early *Essays on the Law of Nature*. The opening of the latter work succinctly characterizes the extent of God's creation as well as his sovereignty over it:

> Some divine being presides over the world—for it is by His order that the heaven revolves in unbroken rotation, the earth stands fast and the stars shine, and it is He who has set bounds even to the wild sea and prescribed to every kind of plants the manner and periods of germination and growth; it is in obedience to His will that all living things have

1970: 33–41; and, more generally, in the introductory materials to Louis Dumont, *Homo Hierarchicus: The Caste System and Its Implications*, rev. ed. (Chicago: University of Chicago Press, 1980). I am indebted to Natalie Davis for directing me to Dumont's work.

their own laws of birth and life; and there is nothing so unstable, so uncertain in this whole constitution of things as not to admit of valid and fixed laws of operation appropriate to its nature.[9]

The entire world was thus ordered and governed by laws in accordance with God's eternal will and purpose. Indeed, it was the sensible perception of this order and measured regularity within the physical world that provided Locke, like so many of his Christian predecessors and contemporaries, with his principal arguments for the existence of such an all-powerful maker. After careful consideration and contemplation of "the beauty of the objects to be observed, their order, array, and motion, [the mind] thence proceeds to an inquiry into their origin, to find out what was the cause, and who the maker of such an excellent work, for . . . this could not have come together casually and by chance into so regular and in every respect so perfect and ingeniously prepared a structure."[10] This alone, or so Locke wrote, should suffice to persuade us of the existence of a "powerful and wise creator of all these things, who has made and built this whole universe and us mortals who are not the lowest part of it."[11]

Locke often likened this universe to a magnificent and timeless machine in which the parts are each subject to their own particular principles of operation, yet participate and interact in a larger harmony and accord intended by God's design. The laws governing this design, however, are "Secrets of Nature"; things within this order are not, as they appear, "independent of other Things," but are linked to them with hidden connections and influences of God's making.[12] It is these unknown relations that invisibly produce the "sensible Qualities" and motions through which human agents come to perceive the things of the world.[13] Put differently, although the order and regularity of created nature can be readily observed, the

9. John Locke, *Essays on the Law of Nature*, ed. Wolfgang von Leyden (Oxford: Clarendon Press, 1954), First Essay, 109. Hereafter cited as *ELN*. Von Leyden dates the composition of these essays roughly between 1660 and 1664, with earlier drafts of six of them written sometime between 1654 and 1663. See his introduction, 7–13.
10. Ibid., Fourth Essay, 153. See also Ibid., Second Essay, 133; and Locke, *Essay*, 1.4.9.
11. *ELN*, Fourth Essay, 153.
12. *Essay*, 4.6.11.
13. Ibid.

deeper relations between its parts—the causes and principles of their mutual relations—though real, are inaccessible to the prying curiosity of human eyes. As Locke puts it, "how much the Being and Operation of particular Substances in this our Globe, depend on Causes utterly beyond our view, is impossible for us to determine. We see and perceive some of the Motions and grosser Operations of Things here about us; but whence the Streams come that keep all these curious Machines in motion and repair, how conveyed and how modified, is beyond our notice and apprehension."[14] While this asserts human agents' inability to truly know the extent or regulative principles of the universe they inhabit, there appears to be little doubt of the unity and interdependence of its elements in God's grand design: "The great Parts and Wheels . . . of this stupendious Structure of the Universe, may, for ought we know, have such a connexion and dependence in their Influences and Operations one upon another, that, perhaps, Things in this our Mansion, would put on quite another face, and cease to be what they are, if some one of the Stars, or great Bodies incomprehensibly remote from us, should cease to be, or move as it does. This is certain, Things, however absolute and entire they seem in themselves, are but Retainers to other parts of Nature, for that which they are most taken notice of by us."[15]

Locke thus represented the order of nature as a seamless web of connection, harmony, and interdependence among all created things. At the same time, though, it remained a decidedly hierarchical order as well. Constituted by a vast chain of divinely determined ranks and degrees, it spanned in range and complexity from the simplest inert matter to the most perfect mind, the creator himself. Though Locke, unlike the "judicious Hooker" who haunts much of Locke's work, never offered a sustained explication of this hierarchy,

14. Ibid. This is the case not only with regard to substances, but with regard to sentient creatures, and in this context there are moral considerations as well: see Locke's curious discussion of changelings and monsters at 4.4.13–17. It is on the basis of the limits of this capacity that he argues against the possibility of an explanatory or demonstrably true science of physical nature (4.3.24–29). Able to know only what we can observe and denied access to the essences of substances, we can demonstrate the regularities of nature but never penetrate to their causes. As we shall see later, because humans share the principal property of the law that governs them, i.e., reason, and because no intelligent being can be supposed to be ruled by a law that cannot be known, Locke argues for the possibility of a demonstrative science of morality.

15. Ibid., 4.6.11. See also 4.3.24, 28, 29.

his texts nonetheless consistently intimate characteristics that differentiate among several of its "ranks and degrees." Thus it is *"Perception . . .* which *puts the distinction betwixt the animal Kingdom, and the
inferior parts of Nature,"*[16] while the capacity for "Abstracting" into
"general Ideas" establishes a "perfect distinction betwixt Man and
Brutes."[17] Further, and for Locke hypothetically, the ability to retain
in memory and even simultaneously envision "all their past knowledge," among other more perfect expressions of God-given faculties
found in humans, marks "Angels" and the "superior ranks of
Spirits" apart from the human species.[18] Again, for each of these
ranks and aspects of creation Locke supposed God to have ordained
certain faculties and laws of operation appropriate to its place and
purpose in the larger design. Considering the discernible order in
the physical world and the fitness of living creatures' faculties for
their conditions and habitats, the notion that humankind alone was
without such a law and faculties commensurate with their position
appeared quite absurd.[19] As the acme of terrestrial beings, partaking
in some measure of God's own intellectual nature, the human species occupied a unique place in the architecture of creation. Possessed of the faculties of abstraction and understanding as well as
perception, capable of speech and invention, reason and choice, humanity must be subject to a law appropriate to such an elevated condition. An all-wise and powerful creator could make nothing without
a purpose, as it would be "contrary to such great wisdom to work
with no fixed aim."[20]

Reflection upon their own faculties, Locke suggested, should convince human agents that they too are ordained to fulfill a purpose in
God's design. No individual could believe, "since he perceives that
he has an agile, capable mind, versatile and ready for anything, furnished with reason and knowledge, and a body besides which is

16. Ibid., 2.9.11.
17. Ibid., 2.11.10.
18. Ibid., 2.10.9. On Locke's account, of course, our middling place in God's architecture renders any ideas we may have of the capacities of creatures or spirits above
us but "extravagant conjecture," although he seems quite willing to engage in such
conjecture when it serves the purposes of his argument. Ibid., 2.23.13.
19. On the general proportionality of faculties to condition, see ibid., 2.9.12, 13;
with specific reference to the human species, see especially 2.23.12; and Locke, *ELN*,
First Essay, 117 and Seventh Essay, 199.
20. Locke, *ELN*, Fourth Essay, 157.

quick and easy to be moved hither and thither by virtue of the soul's authority, that all this equipment for action is bestowed on him by a most wise creator in order that he may do nothing, and that he is fitted with all these faculties in order that he may thereby be more splendidly idle and sluggish." In short, "God intends man to do something." Just what this entails is to be inferred both from "the end in view for all things" and from "man's own constitution and the faculties with which he is equipped." Taken together, these considerations should suffice to show that, "since man is neither made without design nor endowed to no purpose with these faculties which both can and must be employed, his function appears to be that which nature has prepared him to perform. That is to say, when he in himself finds sense experience and reason, he feels himself disposed and ready to contemplate God's works and that wisdom and power of His which they display, and thereupon to assign and render praise, honour, and glory most worthy of so great and so beneficent a creator." Further, and again urged by their senses and reason, Locke's human agents find themselves driven "to procure and preserve a life in society with other men" not only by "life's experience and pressing needs," but also by a "certain propensity of nature."[21] Locke thus represented God's will for members of the human species in terms of a dual purpose: that they both honor and reflect his own glory and that they pursue a life in society with their fellows. In effect, this duality of function in God's design parallels precisely the duality of their created nature as both intellectual and corporeal beings, as well as the twofold foundation of their knowledge, reason and sense experience.[22]

21. All quotations in this paragraph are from ibid. Locke continues: "Further, he feels himself not only to be impelled by life's experience and pressing needs to procure and preserve a life in society with other men, but also to be urged to enter into society by a certain propensity of nature, and to be prepared for the maintenance of society by the gift of speech and through the intercourse of language, in fact as much as he is obliged to preserve himself" (ibid., 157–59). The *Two Treatises* follow a similar course: "God having made Man such a Creature, that, in his own Judgement, it was not good for him to be alone, put him under strong Obligations of Necessity, Convenience, and Inclination to drive him into *Society*, as well as fitted him with Understanding and Language to continue and enjoy it" (Locke, *Two Treatises*, 2.77).

22. For another account of the character and some of the implications of the politics of this dualism in the liberal tradition, see Eldon J. Eisenach, *The Two Worlds of Liberalism: Religion and Politics in Hobbes, Locke, and Mill* (Chicago: University of Chicago Press, 1981).

In conformity with these purposes and consistent with the excellence of their created nature, Locke construes God's law for human creatures as both similar to and different from the laws governing the other aspects of creation. On the one hand, as an integral element of the divine design, the whole of which pointed to God's power and glory, its similarity lay in its prescription of a parallel order and harmony for human relations. Variously identified as "the Law of Nature," "Reason," the "Law of Reason," and "the Voice of God,"[23] God's rule willed the peace and preservation of the species as a whole. Duly understood and followed, the order prescribed by this rule for human agents was one of "Peace, Good Will, Mutual Assistance, and Preservation" in human society.[24] Its difference, on the other hand, from the laws of operation ordained for the lower orders of creation, is rooted in the uniqueness of the human species even among corporeal beings. Of all earthly creatures, human agents alone were created capable not only of reason, which they shared in a limited sense with the higher animals, but of memory, abstraction, consciousness, and, most importantly, accountability.[25] The law appropriate to such a created condition thus aimed at *"the direction of a free and intelligent Agent* to his proper Interest"; it provided "a rule and pattern of living"; it was, in short, a moral law, consistent with the rational nature of the species, which its individual members must voluntarily choose to follow in the course of their actions.[26]

Locke thus inscribed the human place in God's architecture of the cosmos as a privileged one. Situated at the pinnacle of the earthly hierarchy, the species' purpose is both to reflect and to express the power and wisdom of its maker. But despite the recurrent insistence on God's perfection and the rootedness of the whole construct in the existence of such a deity, this universe is, in an important sense, human-centered. Though God intends the order and beauty of natural creation "for no other end than His own glory,"[27] human agents alone are spiritually and intellectually capable of recognizing and

23. Locke, *Two Treatises*, 2.7, 2.6, 1.101, 1.86.
24. Ibid., 2.19.
25. Locke, *Essay*, 2.11.11; 2.28.25, 26; 1.11.10; 2.27.9, 10; 1.27.13, 17.
26. The three phrases are from Locke, *Two Treatises*, 2.57; John Locke, *Two Tracts on Government*, ed. Philip Abrams (Cambridge: Cambridge University Press, 1967), hereafter *Tracts*, Latin Tract, 222; and Locke, *ELN*, First Essay, 113.
27. Locke, *ELN*, Fourth Essay, 157.

rendering the requisite "praise, honour, and glory" due its maker. The whole of the earth itself is thus "given to Men for the Support and Comfort of their being," as are all the "inferior Creatures" provided for their "use" and "comfortable preservation."[28] As God's "Workmanship," human agents are "sent into the world by his order and about his business," and by the same divine hand that world is furnished "with things fit for Food and Rayment and other Necessaries of Life, Subservient to his design, that Man should live for some time upon the Face of the Earth, and not that so curious and wonderful a piece of Workmanship by its own Negligence, or want of Necessaries, should perish."[29] So framed, human creatures roamed their earthly mansion at will, free to use whatever they found at hand for the "convenience" and comfort of corporeal life. This was a world designedly hospitable to human comfort, curiosity, and capacity for invention. Its orderly constitution not only provided the materials necessary to the bodily well-being of its human tenants but, given due consideration, raised their thoughts to the contemplation of their maker and the moral laws he had ordained for their mutual relations.

The "work" or function of the human species within this design was consequently driven by two great concerns: that its members provide for their terrestrial life and sustenance and that they perform their moral duties.[30] Put somewhat differently, on Locke's rendition of the human position in the architecture of order, the earthly pursuits of the species were subject to two distinctly different sorts of descriptions, each denominated by reference to its purpose. Typically, he referred to these activities as those aiming at the "Conveniences of Life," on the one hand, and the "Vertues" or "Duty" on the other, with each sort distinguished on the basis of the end it served.[31]

28. Locke, *Two Treatises*, 2.26, 1.87.

29. Ibid., 2.6, 1.86. For an extended treatment of this workmanship model and its role in Locke's political theory, see James Tully, *A Discourse on Property : John Locke and His Adversaries* (Cambridge: Cambridge University Press, 1980).

30. Locke describes these duties as being of three sorts: "To God, to their neighbor, and themselves" (Locke, *ELN*, Fourth Essay, 159), and begins an elaboration of this in the Seventh Essay. As we shall see, these duties are quite different both in what they demand and in how they are known, and these differences become quite important for the character and legacy of Lockean politics.

31. For considerations of convenience, see Locke, *Essay*, 1.1.5, 2.23.12, 4.11.8, 4.12.10; and Locke, *Two Treatises*, 2.26, 32, 34. For the issue of virtue or duty, see Locke, *Essay*, 1.1.5, 2.23.12. This framing of the problem in terms of final causes is a

Actions, then, "the great business of Mankind" in earthly life, were useful or "convenient" insofar as they conduced to the maintenance or improvement of bodily life, but they were "moral" or virtuous as they conformed to God's rule for the species, the law of nature.[32] Where the first sort of description was appropriate to activities aiming at the comfort and preservation of terrestrial existence, the second spoke to the mutual relations of human individuals as moral creatures capable of eternal rewards.[33]

I will return later to these differing descriptions of human activities as I begin to explore Locke's political vocabulary. At this point, however, my concern is to suggest the manner in which their Lockean meanings are at once embedded in and structured by the image of a hierarchical order of created nature within which the human species occupies a distinct place. The character of this structure, this "architecture of creation," has been shown to be one of order and harmony, of balanced regularity, of connection and interdependence in the rule-governed operations of its parts. For human creatures, no less than for the rest of creation, Locke presumed there to be "fixed laws of operation" appropriate to their status as "free intelligent agents." These laws, like all God's laws, were defined by his purposes and expressive of his will, but the uniqueness of the human place within this architecture required that the rules prescribed to human agents differ in kind from all the rest. In a word, they invested human action with a moral rather than simply physical or instinctual dynamic. As a result, the order and harmony at which they aimed—the "peace and preservation of all mankind" during their earthly sojourn—could be realized only to the extent that human individuals freely recognized and adopted these laws as guides to action. At the same time, however, the sphere of actions to which this moral law referred pertained most importantly to the mutual relations of human agents with their fellows, and as such was strictly distinguished from their relationships to the inferior aspects of cre-

---

characteristic Lockean construction, and one of the points on which he is critical of Descartes. See Lord Peter King, *The Life of John Locke, with Extracts from His Correspondence, Journals, and Common-Place Books,* 2 vols. (London: H. Colburn and R. Bentley, 1830), esp. 2:133–39.

32. Locke, *Essay,* 2.22.10, 1.3.8, 2.28.5.

33. Typically, on Locke's view, the latter set of concerns were the most difficult to bear in mind. Compare, for example, his discussions of the relationship between knowledge, faith, and the fate of one's soul in the *Essay,* 2.21.60 and 4.3.6.

ation. That latter sphere of activity had as its primary referent the material well-being and physical comfort of the species and centered upon each individual's due use of the subordinate things and creatures of God's cosmos for the benefit of life. Moral relations, though, had another end in God's design and ultimately spoke to a different and higher purpose than mere earthly life. Created as equals within God's hierarchy, human beings were not "made for one anothers uses,"[34] and the order prescribed for their mutual relations for Locke was emphatically one of "Vertue," not "convenience." This construction of human agents' peculiar place within the divine architecture thus implied differentiated connections between the condition of individuals and the various other aspects of God's creation. To be sure, they all served one "Sovereign Master" who had commanded a moral law to guide and regulate their conduct, but they served him in different ways depending upon the activities they undertook and the relations in which they engaged.[35]

The central importance of this law in Locke's representation of the human condition raised two crucial and intimately related questions: the specific content of the law of nature, and the manner in which human agents might come to know it. If God willed for them to order their actions by the criterion of virtue, it was essential that they be capable of knowing just what was demanded of them. Though expressed more or less prominently in his various works, these questions both guided and plagued Locke's intellectual efforts throughout his life. No small amount of attention has been paid to these problems by later commentators, and conflicting claims abound as to whether he ever succeeded in addressing them to his own, or anyone else's, satisfaction. Whether or not Locke did, in fact, give an adequate account of them by any standards, or whether even his attempts to do so lend a strain of inconsistency to his thought as a whole, his texts persistently suggest the ultimate stakes of moral

34. Locke, *Two Treatises*, 2.6.
35. Despite his interest in the nascent sciences and his close association with Newton, Boyle, Sydenham, and other luminaries of the period's scientific community, this question of God's law for human actions persisted as a continuing problematic in Locke's writings and formed the primary impetus for the *Essays on the Law of Nature* and the *Essay concerning Human Understanding*. It appears as a recurrent theme as well in his more explicitly political writings, his inquiries into religion and the grounds of toleration, and as we shall see later, even provided an implicit framework for his economic investigations.

knowledge and obligation for creatures capable of salvation.[36] Rather than assessing the adequacy or consistency of Locke's numerous attempts to come to terms with the problem of knowing what was specifically required of human agents by the law of nature, it might be worth considering why it was important to explore the question in the first place. What was the character, function, and meaning of the law of nature in the created condition of the human species? How does this law inform Locke's representation of various human activities within the architecture of order? What is entailed by his phrasing the question of natural law as a question of epistemology? And, finally, what bearing do such considerations have on Locke's construction of the political?

II Virtue and Convenience: The Moral Law as Human Boundary

On Locke's account of God's creation, the law of nature, as the expression of his will, was the sole determinant of worldly order and

36. The difficulty of settling the issue apparently neither deterred him from attempting the task, whatever its results, nor diminished his investment in its importance. The extensive literature on this controversy includes the following important contributions: Richard Aaron, *John Locke*, 3d ed. (Oxford: Clarendon Press, 1971); Richard Howard Cox, *Locke on War and Peace* (Oxford: Clarendon Press, 1960); John Dunn, *The Political Thought of John Locke: An Historical Account of the Argument of the "Two Treatises of Government"* (Cambridge: Cambridge University Press, 1969); Sterling Lamprecht, *The Moral and Political Philosophy of John Locke* (New York: Columbia University Press, 1918); Raymond Polin, *La politique morale de John Locke* (Paris: Presses universitaires de France, 1960); Leo Strauss, *Natural Right and History* (Chicago: University of Chicago Press, 1953); Elliot W. Urdang and Francis Oakley, "Locke, Natural Law, and God," *Natural Law Forum* 11 (1966): 92–109; John W. Yolton, *Locke and the Compass of Human Understanding: A Selective Commentary on the "Essay"* (Cambridge: Cambridge University Press, 1970); James Tully, *A Discourse on Property: John Locke and His Adversaries* (Cambridge: Cambridge University Press, 1980); Neal Wood, *The Politics of Locke's Philosophy: A Social Study of "An Essay concerning Human Understanding"* (Berkeley: University of California Press, 1983); John Colman, *John Locke's Moral Philosophy* (Edinburgh: Edinburgh University Press, 1983); W. M. Spellman, *John Locke and the Problem of Depravity* (Oxford: Clarendon Press, 1988); and David Wooton, "John Locke: Socinian or Natural Law Theorist?," in *Religion, Secularization, and Political Thought: Thomas Hobbes to J. S. Mill*, ed. James E. Crimmins (London: Routledge, 1989), 39–67. For my present purposes, however, the issue is not whether Locke resolved the question or whether the various ways in which he addressed it throughout his life are consistent. Rather, I am concerned here with the stakes of the problem (of knowing the law of nature) itself, that is, with why it might have invited theoretical attention as a question worthy of address for issues surrounding the operation of political authority.

harmony. Without following the "fixed principles of operation" ascribed to them by God's design, the things of this world would be
devoid of order or connection. This was no less the case for the
human species than it was for the rest of his architecture. Amid the
noisy and buzzing plentitude of appearance and experience there
existed a fundamental order of nature that governed the myriad
movements of all created things in a harmony not unlike that of the
heavens themselves. For human agents, as we have seen, the peculiar
characteristic of this law was its moral and voluntary character, but
its end was the same order and harmony prescribed to the other
elements of creation. The function, then, of the law of nature was
the right ordering of human actions with respect to God and their
fellows, both immediately for the peace and preservation of the species in terrestrial existence and ultimately for the possibility of salvation in the life to come. According to this rule, as Locke observed in
a different context, "all men alike are friends of one another and are
bound together by common interests," and its fundamental precept
"forbids us to offend or injure without cause" any of our fellows.[37]
By reason of this "Law common to them all," God has constituted
human beings as a "great and natural Community" and his rules
provide "the tye, which is to secure them from injury and violence."[38]

To acknowledge the law of nature as a rule of conduct was to
order one's actions in accordance with "Vertue." For Locke, the
"true and only measure of Vertue" was to make one's actions "conformable to God's will, or to the rule prescribed by God," and this
meant doing that which "is in its own nature right and good."[39] In
substance, the fundamental charge of this rule was the elimination
of force and violence from human affairs, and its precepts directed
human agents to pursue peaceful and just relations among themselves. Further, because they expressed the will, power, and wisdom
of a perfect maker and because they aimed at the same end of order
and harmony, the various precepts of this law were of necessity perfectly consistent with one another. Locke alluded to this internal harmony of the law of nature and the order it prescribed time and time

37. Locke, *ELN*, Fifth Essay, 163. The qualification "without cause" becomes a
pivot of political significance in the *Two Treatises*, where it is linked to executive right.
See Locke, *Two Treatises*, 2.6, where the single exception to the prohibition of injury
("unless it be to do justice to an offender") is stated.

38. Locke, *Two Treatises*, 2.128, 8.

39. Locke, *Essay*, 1.3.18.

again, though perhaps most succinctly and explicitly in the early *Essays on the Law of Nature*, where we find the confident assertion that "virtuous actions themselves do not clash nor do they engage men in conflict: they kindle and cherish one another."[40] In short, because the "duties of life are not at variance with one another," truly virtuous actions never required that one moral good be balanced against or sacrificed for another.[41] In accordance with the perfection of his nature and with his role as creator, these rules of morality received their obligatory force from their status as the will of God: "He has a Right to do it, we are his Creatures: He has Goodness and Wisdom to direct our Actions to that which is best: and he has Power to enforce it by Rewards and Punishments, of infinite weight and duration, in another Life."[42] On the basis of this vision, Locke presents God's law for the human species as "the only true touchstone of *moral Rectitude*" or righteousness.[43] As such it embodies an objective, universal, and eternal moral code to which every human agent was obliged—and on the basis of which their deeds in this life would be judged in God's final accounting.[44] Although the particular actions conformable to this law might in some cases vary with times and circumstances, its binding force was "perpetual and universal."[45] To do one's duty in this life was to merit one's reward in the next,

40. Locke, *ELN*, Eighth Essay, 213.
41. Ibid.
42. Locke, *Essay*, 2.28.8. For Locke's most developed discussion of the distinction between knowledge of moral precepts and knowledge of their obligatory force, see *The Reasonableness of Christianity*, in *The Works of John Locke in Ten Volumes* (1823; reprint, Scientia Verlag Aalen, 1963), 7:135–47. For the controversy over the voluntaristic vs. the rationalistic basis of Locke's ethics see, for instance, Raghuveer Singh, "John Locke and the Theory of Natural Law," *Political Studies* 9, no. 2 (1961): 105–18; Strauss, *Natural Right and History;* Leo Strauss, "Locke's Doctrine of Natural Law," *American Political Science Review* 52, no. 2 (1958): 490–501; Wolfgang von Leyden's introduction to Locke, *ELN;* Philip Abrams' introduction to Locke, *Tracts;* and G. A. J. Rogers, "Locke, Law, and the Laws of Nature" in *John Locke: Theory of Knowledge*, ed. Vere Chappell (New York: Garland Publishers, 1992), 502–18.
43. Locke, *Essay*, 2.28.8. See also 1.3.6, as well as Locke, *Reasonableness of Christianity*, esp. 111–12.
44. On the objective character of the obligation here, see Locke, *ELN*, especially the Seventh and Eighth Essays, as well as Locke, *Reasonableness of Christianity*, particularly the early part of the essay on the Law of Works. For his reiteration of the connection between this obligation and salvation, see Locke, *ELN*, First Essay, 119, and Fourth Essay, 183, 185–89. Some of Locke's strongest statements on the certainty of God's final judgment appear in the *Essay*. See especially Locke, *Essay*, 1.3.6; 2.21.60, 70; 2.27.22; 2.28.8; 4.3.6; 4.4.14.
45. Locke, *ELN*, Seventh Essay, esp. 191–93.

and when the day of judgment arrived each would receive retribution according to the character of the life they had lived.

This construction opened up two different problems, both of which culminated in the question of how human agents could come to know what was required of them by the law of nature. On the one hand, it suggested the possibility of a demonstrative science of morality, the aim of which would be to derive "from self-evident Propositions, by necessary Consequences" the principal duties to which human agents were subject by God's rule of virtue.[46] This metaphysical project, though repeatedly urged upon him by many of his contemporaries, Locke never attempted. On the other hand, the construction raised more practical questions about the moral status and potential of human social practices and activities, and about the relationship between the created condition of the species and human beings' condition in particular social orders. It was these problems, and in particular the dilemma of practical judgment they suggested, that captured Locke's attention. He briefly stated the issue in one of his journal entries in the following terms: "Virtue, as in its obligation it is the will of God, discovered by natural reason, and thus has the force of law; so in the matter of it, it is nothing else but doing of good, either to oneself or others; and the contrary hereunto, vice, is nothing else but doing of harm. . . . But since men in society are in a far different estate than when considered single and alone, the instances and measures of virtue and vice are very different under these two considerations."[47] Because human agents in society are creatures of culture, for whom the esteem and reputation accorded them by others are important considerations, actions may "become vices amongst men in society, which without that would be innocent."[48] Life among others holds the possibility of being both more

---

46. Locke, *Essay*, 4.3.18. It is here that questions of Christian doctrine also loom large as problems for Locke's moral and religious formulations, especially questions regarding faith and grace. Here, as elsewhere, I sidestep the issue by focusing attention on the issue of practical morality. For the best available historical interpretation of the more complex set of issues I neglect here, see John Marshall, *John Locke: Resistance, Religion, and Responsibility.* (Cambridge: Cambridge University Press, 1994).

47. King, *Life*, 2:94. King gives the source for this as Locke's Commonplace Book of 1661, but according to Abrams there is no such document and the entry occurs in a journal dated 1681. See the introduction to Philip Abrams, ed., *John Locke: Two Tracts on Government* (Cambridge: Cambridge University Press, 1967), 9. It is, however, not important for the present point whether this account of virtue represents an early or a late interest on Locke's part.

48. King, *Life*, 2:95.

complicated and more morally demanding than it is for individuals considered singly in the created condition of the species.

Locke's recognition that human actions are ordered in society by a variety of rules including but not limited to the law of nature occurs repeatedly throughout his works. At the same time, though, his discussions of the issue emerge against the continuing background assumption that there exists an objective, timeless, and universal structure of moral duties appropriate to the human species within God's architecture. Aside from these natural duties, however, he notes two additional sorts of imperatives by which human agents in particular societies in fact order their actions toward God and their fellows. These, respectively, are the "civil law," which arises from the will and power of the magistrate, and the "Law of Opinion or Reputation," which is generated by the private or "tacit" consent of human agents in particular societies and cultures.[49] While both sorts of rules are adopted by particular individuals in various actual societies to order their activities in the world, on Locke's view such actions accord with God's design only to the extent that the rule that guides them itself conforms to the requirements of natural law. Thus actions considered worthy of praise or blame in any given society can be truly virtuous only insofar as they are consistent with that higher law.[50] Similarly, the laws of civil society "are only so far right, as they are founded on the Law of Nature, by which they are to be regulated and interpreted."[51] As we find, however, in the *Essays on the Law of Nature*, this ideal harmony between the rules God had set for the human species and those they set themselves was far from common. Indeed, historically and experientially the imperatives arising in society often seemed just as likely to turn human actions against the dictates of their maker: "There is almost no vice, no infringement of natural law, no moral wrong, which anyone who consults the history of the world and observes the affairs of men will not readily perceive to have been not only privately committed somewhere on earth but also approved by public authority and custom. Nor has there been

---

49. *Essay*, 2.28.9, 10–12. See also Locke, *Tracts*, Latin Tract (trans.), 221–25 which includes the "law of scandal" and "private law" in addition to "divine" and "civil law" in a four-fold typology. These, too, we should note, are hierarchically ordered. I have discussed the political weight of the latter typology in an interpretation of the politics of Lockean toleration. Kirstie M. McClure, "Difference, Diversity, and the Limits of Toleration," *Political Theory* 18, no. 3 (1990): 361–91.

50. Locke, *Essay*, 2.28.10.

51. Locke, *Two Treatises*, 2.12.

anything so shameful in its nature that it has not been either sanctified somewhere by religion, or put in the place of virtue and abundantly rewarded with praise."[52] The potential disparity intimated here between what God demanded of one's actions in the world and what one's polity or culture might require or permit was a moral question of no small significance. For Christian believers in particular, the capacity to recognize such a disjuncture involved the highest of stakes, for what was ultimately at risk was salvation.[53]

Such cognizance of one's moral duties, however, was a difficult task. And Scriptural revelation, the mainstay of faith for centuries, had since the Reformation itself become a source not only of controversial interpretation but of violent conflict as well. For Locke, both England's recent experience and the history of religious wars on the Continent were sad testimony to the terrestrial corruption of Scriptural injunctions.[54] That God commanded order and virtue as rules for human life was perhaps as certain as anything could be, but the specific actions necessitated by this divine injunction were not easily seen, nor was the uncertainty attending the relationship between the various rules one might follow to this end a source of comfort. Individuals were born and educated in a social condition regulated by civil and cultural norms of human constitution, yet in God's final accounting worldly actions were to be judged by their conformity with rules appropriate to their created nature. With salvation thus potentially precarious, it was incumbent upon human agents to judge rightly what their maker required of them. However they comported themselves in their earthly existence, however they conformed to the laws or social norms of their culture, indeed whatever

52. Locke, *ELN*, Fifth Essay, 167.

53. For more extended discussions of the religious aspects of Locke's work see, for instance, Samuel Gring Hefelbower, *The Relation of John Locke to English Deism* (Chicago: University of Chicago Press, 1918); Herbert McLachlan, *The Religious Opinions of Milton, Locke, and Newton* (Manchester: Manchester University Press, 1941); or, more recently, Spellman, *Locke and Depravity*, and Marshall, *Locke: Resistance, Religion, and Responsibility*. The centrality of Locke's religious commitments to his political theory is also stressed by Dunn, *Political Thought*, esp. chaps. 16 through 19.

54. Locke, *Tracts*, English Tract, 160–62, and Latin Tract (trans.), 211. Locke's point here is the same one that he urges in all of his letters on toleration, as well as in *Reasonableness of Christianity*. It is not, for him, that Scriptural precepts are inaccessible; they are distorted by interpreters motivated by worldly ambitions for power to their own purposes and designs, rather than used as a source of moral knowledge. Thus, for Locke, as the interests of power change, so too do interpretations.

their fate or station in terrestrial terms, they all stood as equals before God's final judgment. This, Locke assumed, was a given of creation, a fundamental reality inherent in the human position within the architecture of order. So understood, the dilemma confronting every human agent was one not of metaphysical speculation but of existential risk and practical judgment, for the problem was how to discern the requirements of God's moral rule and, if necessary, distinguish them from the conventional understandings operative in any given society.[55]

III   God's Architecture and Human Action

In subsequent chapters I will address these dilemmas in greater detail and consider their bearing on Locke's political writings at some length. At this point, however, let us draw back somewhat and begin to collect the various strands of meaning orchestrated and structured through Locke's persistent invocation of the architecture of order. Having glimpsed the broad contours of his representation of that cosmic hierarchy, what can we say of his perspective on its human tenants and the place allotted them by their maker? Here, my concern is not to reconstruct Locke's "theory of human nature," but rather to limn the basic features of his representation of the human condition, for what the architectural metaphor suggests is less a particularized focus upon the human species as such than an emphasis upon that species' characteristic relatedness to a larger world created, structured, and ordered by divine design. What sorts of things emerge as aspects of the human condition so understood? What are the characteristic features of the human situation within

55. To be sure, as Locke explains at length in *Reasonableness of Christianity*, for Christian believers the law of faith had supplanted the law of works, but this was true only for Christians and was given them as an act of grace. Given the universal character of God's rule for the human species, the objective character of the rule of virtue governs all alike—pre-Christian as well as non-Christian. It may well be that increasing European awareness of the diverse and often conflicting systems of moral precepts, an awareness that Locke shared, motivates a good part of his emphasis on faith as the primary condition for salvation. Parenthetically, Locke was an avid and persistent collector of the travel literature of his day, and such works comprised a significant proportion of his extensive library. See the introduction to John Harrison and Peter Laslett, eds., *The Library of John Locke*, Oxford Bibliographical Society Publications, n.s., 13 (Oxford: Oxford University Press, 1965).

that design? What kind of a world is this and, given such a world, how and what is the human species meant to be within it?

The essentially theistic character of this Lockean cosmos seems beyond dispute. It appears, however, far less an artifact of sectarian Christian dogma or doctrine than a generalized reflection of Christian faith, albeit one colored by a certain residual scholastic tint. God stands as the sublime architect of a hierarchically structured world in which all things and creatures are subject to principles of operation appropriate to their designed purpose and function within the whole. Because the human species is stationed at the apex of the earthly hierarchy, its unique function is to witness, reflect, and express the perfection of the creator. As observers and beneficiaries of the order and regularity of nonhuman nature, human beings are compelled to recognize the power and wisdom capable of executing so grand a design. As intellectual creatures they are created capable of knowing and acting upon the principles of operation appropriate to their elevated status. By ordering their affairs according to the rule of virtue, they can ensure that human relations fulfill God's intentions for "peace, good will, and mutual assistance" within the species, and thereby reflect his perfection and enact their own unique status as creatures designed for salvation.

First, then, we might note the centrality, indeed the indispensability, of natural law to the order and coherence of the Lockean cosmos as a whole. As we have seen, that created world is one of inherent God-given order, of regularity, interdependence, harmony, and symmetry. Within such a world human agents, no less than the tides, the planets, and the rest of the created cosmos, are subject to a law of motion that prescribes their manner of being in the world. At the same time, however, we should note the privilege of the human species with respect to that law, a privilege guaranteed by its peculiar placement within the scaffolding of the architecture. Distinct from the rest of terrestrial nature, the law to which human beings are uniquely subject is a moral law appropriate to their singular status as rational creatures. In part separable from the natural world, which stands perfect and orderly in its God-given physical determinacy, the human perfection and order enjoined by natural law is possible only insofar as that law is adopted by existential human agents as a rule to guide their actions. It arises, in other words, not from the physical necessities of earthly life but from the choice of human actors to do that which is good and to avoid that which is injurious to their fellows. Although the moral law, like the laws of physical nature, embodies God's will for the creation, its end of peace and harmony for human relations can only be realized to the extent that human agents freely judge, will, and act in accordance with its commands. Again, by so acting, human agents simultaneously fulfill God's intentions for social peace and harmony and realize their own potential perfection as creatures designedly capable of eternal life.

Locke's inscription of the human place in God's architecture of order thus projects a powerful if largely implicit vision of human potentiality that intertwines the promise of Christian salvation with the worldly hope of social peace and harmony in temporal existence. But this is not all. At the same time, the structured hierarchy of this created cosmos situates these possibilities within a world of things and creatures donated by God to the human species for their "use," "convenience," and "comfortable preservation." Inherent in the "nature" of human creatures—that is, in their created condition and designed place in the structured hierarchy of God's architecture— are the necessary capacities and material resources to live both a moral life deserving of salvation and a physical existence of peace, comfort, and abundance. This, needless to say, was no small claim. Of course, that such possibilities inhered in the created condition of the species was no guarantee that they would ever come to pass. It might be the life that God intended, but Locke's texts evidence persistent and worrisome attention to the fact that it was hardly the life lived in society. Both ancient and modern histories as well as the reports of contemporary travelers provided a wealth of examples to the contrary.

But the metaphor of God's architecture provided Locke with more than simply a moral ideal by which to measure or judge existing societies. It also located that ideal within a structure of divine creation that he credited as an existential given. By virtue of the very givenness of that structure and the designedly contingent nature of human action within it, the fulfillment of God's intentions remained an ever-present possibility. This is not to attribute to Locke some sort of millenarian impulse. Rather, it is to suggest that his particular articulation of the imagery of the world's architecture allowed him to problematize the disparity between God's intentions and human experience not as a theological question of fallen souls or the corruption of human nature, but as a question of human action and understanding. Rejecting the idea that the moral corruption of human agents in actually existing societies is somehow necessitated or entailed by original sin, Locke located the disparity between the divine design and human experience in society around the question of the human capacity to discern God's moral rule.[56] In so doing, he rendered both virtue and corruption dependent not upon some presumed quality or flaw of the human soul, but upon human agents' existential ability to discover, understand, and act upon the principles of natural law appropriate to their position in God's architecture. Thus, strictly speaking, the human species in the aggregate is neither good nor evil, but its particular members are designedly capable of both.

We shall delve into some of the more politically significant implications of this construction later, but for present purposes my point is to suggest that the special character Locke attributes to the human station in the created hierarchy leads him to constitute the human condition in terms that emphasize potentiality, capacity, and contingency.[57] In light of this, we might mark a second important characteristic of Locke's perspective on God's architecture, namely the centrality of *action* in his representation of the species. Recall his description of the attributes that render human agents subject to the moral law: "an agile, capable mind, versatile and ready for anything" and "a body . . . which is quick and easy to be moved hither and thither."[58] Such endowments of the species are crisply and explicitly summarized as so much "equipment for action," and again, in the *Essay*, we find action characterized as "the great business of Mankind, and the whole matter about which all Laws are conversant."[59] Conceived within the architecture of creation, action thus assumes the status of a cosmological or ontological fact. In the broadest sense,

56. For his discussion of original sin, see Locke, *Reasonableness of Christianity*, esp. 4–9. While Locke insisted that virtue could be learned, his emphasis on education was hardly optimistic. For a discussion of this aspect of Locke's view of moral pedagogy in relation to Broad-Church and Latitudinarian concerns see W. M. Spellman, "Locke and the Latitudinarian Perspective on Original Sin," in *John Locke: Theory of Knowledge*, ed. Vere Chappell (New York: Garland Publishers, 1992), 519–32.

57. For a similar perspective, see Hans Aarsleff, "The State of Nature and the Nature of Man, in Locke," in *John Locke: Problems and Perspectives*, ed. John W. Yolton (Cambridge: Cambridge University Press, 1969), 99–136.

58. Locke, *ELN*, Fourth Essay, 157.

59. Locke, *Essay*, 2.22.10.

of course, activity is an attribute of all sentient creatures. But human agents' subjection to the moral law and their elevated status as moral beings distinguishes their actions from those of the subordinate ranks of nature's creatures. Though similarly driven by the bodily needs of temporal existence, human agency is directed by quite different faculties, faculties appropriate both to the unique sorts of creatures that human beings designedly are and to the peculiar nature of the law they are under. Whereas "inferior Animals," for example, are determined "by their Sense, and Instinct," human agents are "directed" by their "Senses and Reason."[60] Instinct functions as a "principle of operation" divinely implanted in animals to lend a physical and immediate determinacy to the order and coherence of their actions in the natural world. But because, on Locke's account, the human "principle of operation" lacks such determinacy, the domain of action as a whole is potentially a matter of morality insofar as individuals' chosen actions are consistent or inconsistent with the requirements of moral law.[61]

It is here, in the cosmological status of human action in God's architecture, that Locke situates the fundamental problematic of human life and identifies the sources of tension and ambiguity that generate its essential dynamic. This view of action lies at the root of his assertion in the *Essay* that "our Business" is to understand those things "which concern our Conduct" and to discover "those Measures, whereby a rational Creature put into that State, which Man is in, in this World, may, and ought to govern his Opinions, and Actions depending thereon."[62] To glimpse not only the complexity but also the political implications of this project, we would do well to appreciate its embeddedness in a cosmological context presumptively confronted as an ontological given, a world preconstituted, structured, and ordered by divine design. Within this structure, however, actions are inherently diverse. Fleeting and transient instants, every human action is by its nature "perishing the moment it begins."[63] But because human agents are creatures capable of eternal life and subject to a moral law, intelligent agents whose actions are

60. Locke, *Two Treatises*, 1.86.
61. The example of cannibalism here is the most obvious; see Locke, *Two Treatises*, 2.57.
62. Locke, *Essay*, 1.1.6.
63. Ibid., 2.27.2.

freely chosen, they are accountable to their maker for the use they make of their freedom. Although distinguishable in terms of such varied attributes as "Causes, Means, Objects, Ends, Instruments, Time, Place, and other circumstances,"[64] actions remain the identifiable, if separate and discrete, deeds of particular agents whose moral worth will be the object of God's judgment on that day of days when he shall reward or punish each according to their merit.

From this conception of distinctly human action we might infer a series of more specific characteristics implied by Locke's imagery of the human situation. Perhaps most obviously, and seemingly most consistent with previous treatments of his corpus, is the individualism such a perspective implies. The meaning of this individualism is not, however, generated through structured oppositions to such concepts as society, collectivism, or communitarianism, as a long lineage of modern commentators would have it. Rather, it is an artifact of creation, at once a theological imperative and an existential fact, simultaneously prior to and operative within actual human life. On this account, only human individuals think, will, and judge their actions, and each individual is accountable to God for the moral worth of the temporal life that is constituted by such decisions over time. Further, and implicit in this linkage of action and moral accountability, Locke's representation of the human condition is importantly centered upon the problem of judgment. Here, the characterization of human agents in terms of their created potential for moral action finds both a dimmer and a darker side in their corollary potential for mistaken, or worse, corrupt judgment. Because human actions are freely chosen and because each action is the product of individual decision, any attempt to understand the disparity between the moral life God intends for human agents and the lives they actually experience and express in society is necessarily resolved into the question of the nature, source, and proper criteria of moral judgment. This, arguably, is precisely the project undertaken in the early *Essays on the Law of Nature* and, in a more expansive context, in the *Essay concerning Human Understanding*. To engage the complexity of the question of judgment across Locke's various formulations, however, it is important to consider its indebtedness to this vision of the world's architecture of order, for that imagery suggests that Lockean individuals inhabit a world that is morally marked in crucial respects.

64. Ibid., 2.22.10.

The nonhuman world of material things and creatures and the so-cial world of their own species are not simply an undifferentiated background against which individuals each struggle to achieve their separate purposes. Rather, these contexts of action are pre-constituted by divine design as different levels of a hierarchically structured reality. This structure both contains human agents in a fabric of God's purposes and confronts them with the dual tasks of sustaining their temporal existence and treating their created equals in a manner consistent with their potential as creatures deserving of salvation.

There are two additional aspects of this image of the human situation that bear further elaboration. First, the human position within and relationship to the hierarchy, like the structure itself, is a given of creation. The divine source of this givenness, however, stipulates two distinct criteria of judgment for particular human actions, each defined by reference to the purpose of the action and to the status of its appropriate object in the created hierarchy. Toward one's equals in the order of nature the first rule of action is "virtue," while to the inferior ranks of things and creatures "convenience" is the proper guide. Here we find a division in Locke's ontology of human action and judgment. As biological creatures intent upon preservation or comfort, human agents assume an instrumental stance toward all aspects of nature subordinate to their elevated status in God's design. As rational beings capable of salvation, however, they possess the capacity to consider the intrinsic worth or moral status of particular actions with God's rule of virtue as a guide. Thus construed, Locke's observation that we are not authorized "to destroy one another, as if we were made for one anothers uses, as the inferior ranks of Creatures are for ours"[65] appears not simply as a proto-Kantian moral imperative, but as a topographical marker of the situatedness of human action and judgment within the world's architecture. "Human nature," from this point of view, is not so much something individuals possess as something they enact—something they perform insofar as they adopt the appropriate rules of action in the proper context.

Second, and following from this, although the structure of creation defines how God intends human agents to act, the existential fact of their freedom carries with it a potential for transgression as well. At once contingent and governed, individuals do in fact act.

65. Locke, *Two Treatises*, 2.6.

But with each deed they participate in a fabric of God's making and thereby constitute themselves as particular kinds of beings within a preestablished framework of divinely determined meaning. While the order and coherence of properly human life is expressed by conformity to the rule of virtue, animal existence too has its own predetermined meaning and coherence, constituted by its own peculiar principle of operation. Animal life aims only at survival, and Locke presents its characteristic rule as force and violence. To act on this rule is to succumb to the finitude, the confinement to temporal existence characteristic of beasts, regardless of the agent's biological nature. As the *Treatises'* characterization of criminal action suggests, by violating the law of nature "the Offender declares himself to live by another Rule than that of *reason* and common Equity."[66] In failing to act in accordance with the rule of virtue the transgressor of natural law thus enacts the objective nature of a beast: he "becomes degenerate, and declares himself to quit the Principles of Human Nature, and to be a noxious Creature."[67] Such creatures, however they may have the appearance of human individuals, "are not under the ties of the Common Law of Reason"—they follow "no other Rule, but that of Force and Violence, and so may be treated as Beasts of Prey."[68]

Taken together, these characteristics of the human condition operate in Locke's texts as a set of metatheoretical givens, generated through the metaphor of God's architecture as a cultural imaginary. The subjection to moral law, the centrality of action and individual accountability, the distinction between virtue and convenience, the notion of a morally marked world, the idea of properly *human* nature as something performed in deeds rather than inherent in the species: such things never appear as explicit premises in what we might now consider Locke's recognizably political arguments. Nonetheless, they persistently structure significant aspects of his more explicitly articulated political theory. Indeed the premises and concepts often taken as fundamental to that theory—what I characterized earlier as Locke's political vocabulary—are in important ways not simply informed, but defined, structured, and set in motion by the implicit cosmology of the architecture of order.

66. Ibid., 2.8.
67. Ibid., 2.10. See also Dunn, *Political Thought,* 107–9.
68. Locke, *Two Treatises,* 2.16. See also 2.172, 181, 182.

2

Echoes of the Architecture:
Laws of Virtue,
Rights of Convenience

> But the greatest error of all the rest is the mistaking or
> misplacing of the last or furtherest end of knowledge.
> [Knowledge is] . . . a rich storehouse for the glory of the
> Creator and the relief of man's estate.
>
> —Francis Bacon
> *The Advancement of Learning*

Unlike many of the philosophers, jurists, and Scholastics who
preceded him, Locke never articulated his perceptions of the
world's architecture into an explicit cosmological vision. From pass-
ing references and occasional remarks, the hierarchy of God's creation appears as something presumed to be the case, rather than
something requiring definition or defense.[1] It is, in effect, an unex-

1. This hierarchy, of course, had been an explicit staple of earlier thought. In its
formal structure, Locke's allusions to such a hierarchy follow Hooker's eloquent elab-
oration, *The Laws of Ecclesiastical Polity*, in *The Works of That Learned Divine Mr. Richard
Hooker*, ed. John Keble, 2d ed., 3 vols. (Oxford: Oxford University Press, 1841), bk. 1.
For an account of Tudor and early Stuart understanding of the concept, see E. M. W.
Tillyard, *The Elizabethan World Picture* (New York: Macmillan, 1944); and, more generally, Arthur O. Lovejoy, *The Great Chain of Being: A Study in the History of an Idea*
(Cambridge: Harvard University Press, 1965). Locke's reluctance to spell this out explicitly is what one might expect from his epistemological explorations—specifically
from his suggestion that the knowledge necessary for distinguishing with certainty
between cosmological ranks, involving as it does the question of divinely determined
essences, is beyond the powers of human intellect. In this respect, Locke (as well as his
equally skeptical contemporary, Hobbes) occupies a curious historical place between
thinkers and epochs far more confident in their claims to knowledge. The theological
systems of the religious tradition from Augustine, through Aquinas, to Hooker, and

amined structure, evidenced here and there by a curious distinction or an odd turn of phrase, but never set forth in so many words. However fascinating the further reaches of that cosmos to minds of a more imaginative or grandly speculative bent, Locke's intellectual energies typically flowed in rather less sublime channels. Nonetheless, even his self-confessedly more mundane and worldly interests bear the traces of this imagery of the human place and function in God's architecture of order. That the species was God's workmanship, that he had prescribed a uniquely moral law to order human actions, that individuals were created capable of knowing and acting upon that law, and that their salvation hung upon their fidelity to it— these aspects of Locke's theistic cosmology resonate throughout his writings on politics, economics, education, religion, and epistemology.

And yet, though Locke may have described himself in the *Essay* as an under-laborer, his project of "removing rubbish" in the way of moral knowledge is somewhat less than modest, for it attempts to persuade his readers of the moral and practical irrelevance of more sublimely speculative or abstract philosophical endeavors.[2] Not only do the far corners and hidden causes of the created world escape our capacities, they have little bearing upon our proper concerns. But this, as Locke represents the larger scheme of things, cannot detract from the practical importance and moral status of what may yet be known. "Men have Reason," he suggests, "to be well satisfied with what God hath thought fit for them, since he has given them . . . Whatsoever is necessary for the Conveniences of Life, and Infor-

---

the immediately preceding Baconian science, were more certain that their perceptions mirrored the world as it really was. By the late eighteenth century, despite the insistent voice of Humean skepticism in England, Linneaus again asserted epistemological confidence with the claim that in constructing his categories of botanical classification he was "standing in the eye of God." For treatments of the question in Locke's more immediate context, see Henry G. Van Leeuwen, *The Problem of Certainty in English Thought, 1630–1690* (The Hague: Martinus Nijhoff, 1963); and Barbara Shapiro, *Probability and Certainty in Seventeenth-Century England: A Study of the Relationships between Natural Science, Religion, History, Law, and Literature* (Princeton: Princeton University Press, 1983), esp. chap. 2.

2. See, for instance, John W. Yolton, *Locke and the Compass of Human Understanding: A Selective Commentary on the "Essay"* (Cambridge: Cambridge University Press, 1970); John W. Yolton, "The Science of Nature," in *John Locke: Problems and Perspectives,* ed. John W. Yolton (Cambridge: Cambridge University Press, 1969), 183–93; and Neal Wood, *The Politics of Locke's Philosophy: A Social Study of "An Essay concerning Human Understanding"* (Berkeley: University of California Press, 1983).

mation of Vertue; and has put within the reach of their Discovery
the comfortable Provision for this Life and the Way that leads to a
better."[3] Whatever the limits of the human capacity to grasp the vastness of the created world, individuals are apparently well equipped
to discern both what is necessary to their preservation in this life and
what conduces to their fitness for the next.

In this stylized division of human knowledge, Locke both affirms
and elaborates on the human position and function in God's architecture of creation. As we have seen, to describe an action in terms
of "virtue" or "convenience" is both to indicate the end at which it
aims and to invest it with particular referents and relations within
the architecture of created nature. Thus virtuous actions take the
moral law for their rule and express the agent's moral potential,
whereas acts of convenience are instrumental to the maintenance or
improvement of terrestrial existence. The former pertain to a
sphere of moral relations between human agents as created equals in
the order of nature; the latter involve the use of things that have an
inferior status within that hierarchy. To command the mind to the
pursuit of virtue and convenience is thus to channel the intellect in
two directions. On the one hand, the "Information of Vertue" points
to the study of moral law, duty, and obligation; on the other, pursuit
of "the Conveniences of Life" suggests investigations of the potential
utility of physical nature for the species' comfort and preservation.[4]
This distinction between virtue and convenience, between what
might be called moral and material ends, is thus central not only to
Locke's image of the hierarchy of order and his conception of human action, but to the knowledge requisite for such action as well.
And since these human creatures are preeminently cast as creatures
of action, the precise meaning, character, and implications of such a
distinction are part and parcel of the moral status and potential ascribed to Lockean humanity.

    3. John Locke, *Essay concerning Human Understanding*, ed. Peter H. Nidditch (Ox-
ford: Clarendon Press, 1975), by book, chapter, and paragraph, 1.1.5. Hereafter cited
as *Essay*.
    4. For an interesting interpretation of these aspects of the *Essay*, see Wood, *Politics
of Locke's Philosophy;* and the earlier essay, Neal Wood, "The Baconian Character of
Locke's *Essay*," *Studies in the History and Philosophy of Science* 6, no. 1 (1975): 43–84. For
a perspective concerned principally with the problem of morality in the *Essay*, see
John Colman, *John Locke's Moral Philosophy* (Edinburgh: Edinburgh University Press,
1983).

The capacity of the species to know and follow God's moral law is, of course, a recurrent theme not only of Locke's explorations of morality and epistemology but of his political writings as well. The connections, however, between the concepts of virtue and convenience and his more generally recognized political vocabulary are not at all obvious. While the intervening centuries have witnessed the institutionalization of Locke's more explicit political terminology in common language as well as constitutional theory and practice, the imagery of measured hierarchies characteristic of his theistic cosmology has fared poorly by comparison. Early modern intellectuals might seriously debate whether the hand of God was necessary to wind the mechanism of a clocklike cosmos, but there was little doubt of either its existence or his part in its creation. Accordingly, my task here is to bridge these centuries for our decidedly more secular understanding by suggesting the relationship between the imagery of Locke's theistic cosmology and what are commonly taken to be the core concepts of his political theory. To this end, before turning to Locke's more obviously political concerns, let us begin by attending closely to the central terms of his political vocabulary as they resonate with his account of the created or natural condition of the human species. As a preliminary to this I will first clarify the significance and ontological status of the state of nature in the *Second Treatise,* as this epitomizes Locke's imagery of the created condition. We will next explore his conceptualizations of natural law and natural right, particularly in light of their filiations within the larger structure of the architecture of order; then we will consider in similar fashion his notions of liberty, equality, and property. With this view of Locke's political vocabulary as a basis, we will be prepared to turn in Part II to his account of the "original" of political power and its function in his account of political society.

I   The State of Nature

For Locke, no less than for his contemporary Hobbes or his eighteenth-century critics Hume and Rousseau, the determination of what was "natural" to the human species was a necessary preliminary to political theorizing. Thus the *Second Treatise* opens by claiming that "to understand Political Power right, and derive it from its Orig-

inal, we must consider what State all men are naturally in."[5] Yet
Locke's rendering of this nature, infused as it was with the presumption of divine agency in the world's creation, confronts the modern
reader with an interpretive dilemma. What, given this assumption, *is*
"the State all men are naturally in"? For Hobbes, Hume, and Rousseau, the natural condition of humankind principally referred to its
worldly characteristics or behavior as observed or inferred by human
agents; Locke's account of natural humanity had as its central reference the created condition of the species. Where they, in other
words, emphasized what they found to be the actual or descriptive
characteristics of the species—its physical passions, worldly desires,
and material interests—he began with an image of humanity as it
was divinely constructed within and in relation to a larger created
cosmos. Even the *Second Treatise,* in conception and execution one of
the more secular of Locke's works, opens with a depiction of human
agents as "all the Workmanship of one Omnipotent, and infinitely
wise Maker; all the Servants of one Sovereign Master, sent into the
World by his order and about his business." All "furnished with like
Faculties," members of the human species were created as common
participants in "one Community of Nature."[6]

The worldly egalitarianism of this construct, what I referred to
earlier as the leveling of the human microcosm, may well have been
of relatively recent origin. But the intellectual context and cultural
imagery in which it emerged, the creationist foundation and the hierarchical structure of Locke's larger cosmology, was in many respects closer to worldviews typical of the late Middle Ages than to
the more pointedly naturalistic perspective of the eighteenth-century
Enlightenment. Nonetheless, and particularly with respect to his political writings, Locke's conceptual indebtedness to the earlier period
tends to pale before his temporal and thematic proximity to the
later. All too often, though, our historical interpretations of past
thinkers center on their prodigious insights into a world only beginning to emerge, rather than on their, from this perspective, anachronistic, naive, or unreflective retention of older categories of
thought. And yet, the theistic freighting and ontological status of

5. John Locke, *Two Treatises of Government,* ed. Peter Laslett, rev. ed. (1960; reprint, with amendments, Cambridge: Cambridge University Press, 1963), by book and
paragraph, 2.4. Hereafter cited as *Two Treatises.*
6. Ibid., 2.6.

Locke's state of nature betrays just such a continuity, for his participation in the rupture of natural hierarchies in the social microcosm
was accompanied by a persistent if subtle reiteration of the larger
architecture of the macrocosm as a whole.

For Locke, that which is natural owes its presence in the world to
God's design. Its existence, its place and function in the whole, and
its manner or principle of operation are ordained by divine intention. With respect to the human species, as we have seen, this structured creationism appears in his portrayal of natural humanity at
the earthly apex of God's architecture. As free, active, intelligent
agents, subject to the rule of virtue, human beings are both uniquely
capable of morality in the terrestrial order and uniquely accountable
for the conformity of their actions to that rule. What Hume damned
as metaphysics and falsehood, what Bentham ridiculed as "nonsense
upon stilts," appears in Locke's texts as an unquestionable fact of
creation: natural law exists as a universal and eternal God-given
standard of good and evil that human agents neglect at the peril of
their souls. In light of this, to consider Locke's state of nature, to
explore the character and dynamics of the political world he derives
from it, we would do well to consider the reality thus attributed to
the moral imperatives of natural law. As signifiers of God's intentions, the rules of virtue mark the boundary between the potential
divinity of the human species and the earthly finitude of animal existence. On Locke's account, the moral law has a *real* existence in the
order of things, an existence as given and as certain as that of God
himself. And equally real is the promise of salvation for those who
conform their actions to its rule. Indeed, and again echoing the hierarchical structure of God's architecture, this potential immortality
was the "great and inestimable advantage" of human agents "above
other material Beings."[7]

Certain, too, in this context was the inevitability of God's judgment. Despite its apparent removal from such concerns, the *Second
Treatise* circulates an emphatic warning to those who would, perhaps
even rightly, take justice into their own hands. "He that *appeals to
Heaven*," Locke observes, "must be sure he has Right on his side; and
a Right too that is worth the Trouble and Cost of the Appeal, as he
will answer at a Tribunal, that cannot be deceived, and will be sure

7. Locke, *Essay*, 4.4.15.

to retribute to every one according to the Mischiefs he hath created to his Fellow-Subjects; that is, any part of Mankind."[8] The weight and significance of these theistic elements in the *Treatises'* portrayal of the state of nature tend to be underplayed or unappreciated by most twentieth-century political commentary. Even John Dunn, otherwise acutely attuned to the persuasiveness and power of theological concerns in Locke's work, is a case in point. Acknowledging the state of nature as "that state in which men are set by God," he yet intimates his own commitment to secular modernity by casting such a concept generally as "that classically feeble expository cliché of the natural-law thinkers," and Locke's natural state in particular as "simply an axiom of theology."[9] It is, he argues, neither anthropological nor historical. In his attempt to refute those who would overly sociologize Locke's state of nature, however, Dunn errs in the opposite direction, suggesting that it "has literally no transitive empirical content whatsoever." "For empirical specification," he continues, "in Locke's conception, was in itself contamination by history and the analytical function of the concept lay precisely in its ahistoricity."[10] By presuming that what is empirical or historical exhausts the range of things actually existing, this characterization signals its own participation in the modern disenchantment of the world, denying the status of reality to anything not observed, recorded, or inferred in material experience by human agents. But for anyone convinced of the soul's immortality, of the existence of angels and spirits, indeed of the real existence of God himself, such a constriction of existence would deny reality to a considerable part, and for the human species

8. Locke, *Two Treatises* 2.176. See also 2.21, 241.

9. John Dunn, *Political Thought of John Locke: An Historical Account of the Argument of the "Two Treatises of Government"* (Cambridge: Cambridge University Press, 1969), 97, 100, 103.

10. Ibid., 103. This might be called the theist face of Locke's realism or, alternatively, the realist face of Locke's theism. In any case, it is not far removed from the question of the consistency between Locke's empiricist theory of knowledge and his embrace of atomism, taken up by David E. Soles, "Locke's Empiricism and the Postulation of Unobservables," *Journal of the History of Philosophy* 23, no. 3 (1985): 339–69. Although his suggestion that Locke viewed the inability of seventeenth-century science "to discover the atomic real essences of objects" as a "contingent limitation to be overcome"(368) is questionable at best, his larger point is perspicuous. Both with regard to "insensible" corpuscular objects and with regard to the hierarchical ordering of things and creatures by various degrees of perfection, Soles argues, Locke's "rule of anology" provides a strong probabilistic warrant for inferences from sensation and experience to the existence of unobservables.

a fundamental part, of the created world. True, on Locke's view human understanding of such things is rooted in faith and probability, but this is hardly a mark against their existence.[11]

Although he recognizes the theological basis and normative status of the state of nature in Locke's work, Dunn's acquiescence in a more assertively modern empiricist or materialist understanding of what is real leads him to cast that condition as equivalent to the prelapsarian state of Christian theology, separated from social history by a "profound chasm." This, in turn, leads him to characterize Locke's account of "social development" in the natural state as intimately bound up with the Fall. Dunn suggests, for example, that "the sin of Adam . . . is responsible for the persistent insecurity and uncertainty which arise from the treatment which men meet at the hands of other sinful human beings."[12] On Locke's rendition, however, the state of nature and the social condition may belong not so much to distinct temporalities as to different planes of being. On the one hand, taken as terrestrial existence, the social or political state neither abolishes nor supersedes the objective moral order ordained as fitting for human life. "The Obligations of the Law of Nature," Locke observes, "cease not in Society but only in many Cases are drawn closer, and have by Humane Laws known Penalties annexed to them, to inforce their observation."[13] In political society legislators no less than common citizens remain subject to the imperatives of virtue: "The *Rules* that they make for other Mens Actions, must as well as their own and other Mens Actions, be conformable to the Law of Nature, *i.e.* to the Will of God, of which that is a Declaration."[14] In this context the creation of political society may well imply a metamorphosis of the experiential world of human agents, but it cannot abolish the objective and eternal reality of moral obligation, nor can it obviate the accountability of each individual to God's final judgment.

At the same time, though, Locke does employ the concept of the state of nature as both existentially prior to and normative for particular polities. This usage, however, should not be confused with a prelapsarian state of innocence irrevocably lost to human agents, for

11. See, for example, Locke, *Essay*, 1.4.16; 4.10, esp. 9-19.
12. Dunn, *Political Thought*, 103, 115.
13. Locke, *Two Treatises*, 2.135.
14. Ibid.

the fall from purity suggested by the biblical account of Adam and Eve's transgression in Eden sits uneasily with the more eclectic range of religious sentiments that percolate through Locke's various writings.[15] To the extent that the Scriptural story is relevant to the *Treatises'* representation of natural humanity, it is perhaps best interpreted in relation to Locke's suggestion elsewhere that by their disobedience Adam and Eve and all their descendants became mortal: "As Adam was turned out of paradise so all his posterity were born out of it, out of the reach of the tree of life; all like their father Adam in a state of mortality void of the tranquility and bliss of paradise."[16] The loss of Eden, on this account, did not entail a final loss of moral capacity, but rather implied a transformation of the human condition, a change marked by the assumption of all of the difficulties of ordinary human life. "Paradise," Locke continued, "was a place of bliss as well as immortality; without drudgery and without sorrow. But when man was turned out he was exposed to all the toil, anxieties and frailties of this mortal life."[17] It is, however, quite unnecessary to equate this account of the origin of human frailty and mortality with inherent sinfulness. The human species for Locke was not morally tainted by original sin; Adam's descendants were not born in a state of guilt nor were they doomed "to a state of necessary sinning and provoking God in every action that they do."[18]

These observations reinforce what I suggested earlier: that on Locke's perspective the disjuncture between the peaceful and virtuous life God intends for man and the corruption evidenced by

15. W. M. Spellman, *John Locke and the Problem of Depravity* (Oxford: Clarendon Press, 1988), tends to support Dunn's view. But see John Marshall, "John Locke's Religious, Educational, and Moral Thought," *Historical Journal* 33, no. 4 (1990): 993–1001, for a pertinent critical review of this and other recent literature on the question. Locke's eclecticism with regard to both method and doctrine, as well as his general distance from constructions of inherent sinfulness current in his period, is emphasized in: Arthur Wainwright's introduction to John Locke, *A Paraphrase and Notes on the Epistles of St. Paul to the Galatians, Corinthians, Romans, Ephesians. To Which is Prefixed an Essay for the Understanding of St. Paul's Epistles by Consulting St. Paul Himself*, ed. Arthur Wainwright (Oxford: Oxford University Press, 1987); and John Marshall, *John Locke: Resistance, Religion, and Responsibility* (Cambridge: Cambridge University Press, 1994). Wainwright's edition of Locke, *Paraphrase and Notes*, is one of the works reviewed in Marshall, "Locke's Religious, Educational, and Moral Thought."

16. John Locke, *The Reasonableness of Christianity*, in *The Works of John Locke in Ten Volumes* (1823; reprint, Scientia Verlag Aalen, 1963), 7:7.

17. Ibid. Compare Locke, *Two Treatises*, 1.44–45, 2.32.

18. Locke, *Reasonableness of Christianity*, 6.

much of human history points not to a fatal flaw in the human soul, but rather to the difficulties confronting the capacity of human agents to discern accurately what God requires of them. Both the early essays on natural law and the later *Reasonableness of Christianity*, as well as the *Treatises* and the *Essay concerning Human Understanding*, consistently identify these obstacles with the operation of contrary imperatives promulgated by earthly powers: with civil law, religious authority, tradition, and custom. As it initially appears in the *Second Treatise*, of course, the state of nature contains none of these impediments to moral judgment. It is, I would suggest, an attempt to represent the natural state of the species in a manner consistent with the broad imagery of their created condition in God's architecture. In other words, the state of nature evokes a condition in which neither social convention, temporal authority, nor inherited belief confounds the human capacity to discover the moral law. In this sense it might be read as intimating a peculiarly human and mortal sort of innocence, a postlapsarian moment in which human agents might yet enact the moral potential of their created nature.

So understood, the state of nature opens Locke's account of the "original" of political power with a vision of the human condition as it was intended by God to be in his architecture of order, a state of "peace, good will, and mutual assistance." Yet, secured though it may be in the firmament of divine purposes, this natural state seethes with political meaning and nuance from the outset. It provides the terrain, as it were, upon which Locke marshals much of the vocabulary that is later to become the common tender of liberal political discourse: law, right, liberty, equality, and property. However familiar these concepts may have subsequently become, in Locke's hands they remained embedded in a theistic world view. Let us turn then to the first two terms of this vocabulary and explore in more detail their points of contact with the architecture of order, for if the state of nature is the terrain in which Lockean political power finds its roots, natural law and natural right establish its parameters and delineate its moral topography within the larger design of God's cosmos. As we shall see, while law and right formally define the objective moral boundaries that mark this terrain as properly human, it is liberty, equality, and the possession of property that describe the created character of its inhabitants in relation both to each other and to that larger whole.

II Human Action and Moral Meaning: The Complementarity of Law and Right

If the "state all Men are naturally in" evokes the created condition of the human species, and if natural law is the rule of virtue set by God for its elevated position in the hierarchies of his creation, then natural law and natural right can be seen as demarcating the structural boundaries of properly human activities in that state. As we have seen, the place and function of human agents in God's architecture is constituted by the superiority of their intellectual faculties over the rest of created nature and, concomitant with this, by the uniquely moral quality of the law appropriate to such a created condition. It should come as no surprise, then, to find in Locke's presentation of the relationship between law and right a politicized resonance of this image of the world's divinely created hierarchy. The first explicit statement of this relation occurs in his early explorations of the law of nature, where he distinguishes between "natural law" and "natural right" by suggesting that "right is grounded in the fact that we have the free use of a thing, whereas law is what enjoins or forbids the doing of a thing."[19] In this formulation, both law and right pertain specifically to human activities: to act lawfully is to perform or forbear such actions as the law requires, while to act within one's rights is to operate in a domain where one may freely determine one's actions, independently of such external rules or standards. The realm of right so conceived is a realm of freedom, but it can only be understood as such in relation to the law that, by framing its boundaries, makes it possible. Bluntly put, the exercise of rights is a uniquely human activity made possible only by the existence of law. As the point appears in the *Second Treatise*, "The end of Law is not to abolish or restrain but to preserve and enlarge Freedom: for in all the states of created beings capable of Laws where there is no Law there is no Freedom."[20] It is, in other words, only the

19. John Locke, *Essays on the Law of Nature*, ed. Wolfgang von Leyden (Oxford: Clarendon Press, 1954), First Essay, 111. Hereafter cited as *ELN*.

20. Locke, *Two Treatises*, 2.57. For a similar point and more extended discussion, see James Tully, *A Discourse on Property: John Locke and His Adversaries* (Cambridge: Cambridge University Press, 1980), esp. 43–48, 127–30. For the topic more broadly treated, see Richard Tuck, *Natural Rights Theories: Their Origin and Development* (Cambridge: Cambridge University Press, 1979).

knowledge of what is required or prohibited by law that establishes the scope of right or liberty.

Locke's account of the relationship between law and right has been variously construed by modern interpreters. Both Dunn and James Tully, for example, recognizing the embeddedness of Locke's understanding of human action in a system of divine purposes, see his notion of rights as an expression of human agents' duty or obligation to preserve themselves and others.[21] Leo Strauss, on the other hand, and Richard Cox in a somewhat different context, both stress the cognitive inaccessibility of natural law and moral obligations in all of Locke's writings save the *Treatises*. On this basis both of the latter scholars view Locke as effectively discounting such requirements and asserting rather the primacy of rights over the performance of duties as prescribed by the law of nature.[22] These several perspectives are rooted in a recognition of the apparent centrality and thematic importance of natural law for Locke's political theory, but they differ substantially in the weight they accord to his admission of the difficulty of knowing that law, particularly in their respective treatments of the extent to which that difficulty might subvert his seeming reliance upon natural law as a moral basis for political society.

In their attempts to come to terms with Locke's political writings, however, none of these well-known readings attends closely to his presupposition of a hierarchy in created nature.[23] In neglecting the salience of this imagery for Locke's notions of law and right, they neglect as well the implication of a parallel order that such an assumption confers upon the moral character of actions within that structure, and this is particularly the case with regard to his representation of the state of nature. As we have seen, Locke differenti-

21. Tully, *Discourse on Property*, 43–50, 62–64, 101–4; Dunn, *Political Thought*, chaps. 8 and 9.

22. See Leo Strauss, *Natural Right and History* (Chicago: University of Chicago Press, 1953), esp. 248; Richard Howard Cox, *Locke on War and Peace* (Oxford: Clarendon Press, 1960). As noted by Laslett in his edition of Locke, *Two Treatises*, p. 313, a variation on this point was voiced by Elrington in his annotation of the fourth edition of the *Treatises* (1798), with particular reference to Locke's construction of executive right in the state of nature.

23. Dunn, *Political Thought*, chaps. 8 and 9, is once again an exception in his attempt to present this, but he stops short of exploring the depths and implications of his own insight as he then shifts to a discussion of Locke's "conjectural sociology" (see esp. 87–91, 96–113).

ated between the moral status associated with various types of human activities both in terms of the end they served and with respect to the created rank of their objects or referents. If we recall in this context his insistent distinction between virtue and convenience, the language he uses to differentiate between natural law and natural right suggests a striking parallelism in the differential moral status accorded to actions based on law and those grounded in right. To act as required by law, on this account, is to act in accordance with "virtue." It is to fulfill one's obligations as a rational creature by conforming to God's prescription of moral order, for natural law is the system of moral imperatives which human agents must respect not only to ensure social peace but, in so doing, to enact their moral character. But to follow the parallel further, if natural right is "grounded on the fact that we have the free use of a thing," the exercise of rights becomes associated with the realm of "convenience" and use, not "virtue." To describe any particular action as a matter of "right" so conceived is to suggest its embeddedness in the preservation of mortal or earthly existence. But it is at the same time to characterize such an action as one appropriately directed, in the first instance, to the ranks of things and creatures subordinate to the human species' elevated position in the hierarchy of created nature. Thus, from this perspective, the exercise of natural rights properly refers to the activity of using things and creatures for the preservation, maintenance, or improvement of terrestrial existence.[24]

This characterization of right, however, does not imply the emancipation of human agents from their natural duties. Rather, it desig-

24. There is, to be sure, a loose sense in which specific actions exercising such rights also fulfill a duty to God. As his "property" each of us is "bound to preserve ourselves." Thus we have a "right" to choose freely from the creatures and things of lower nature what we require for our comfort and preservation, but we are not free to starve ourselves, for that right subtends the duty of preservation. Hence the rather curious remark that "there can be some degree of righteousness" in such activities as "eating, drinking, and sleeping." John Locke, *Two Tracts on Government,* ed. Philip Abrams (Cambridge: Cambridge University Press, 1967), Latin Tract, 213. In a very different context, Locke seems to conceive his "executive right" of punishment as involved with the "use" of criminals (Locke, *Two Treatises,* 2.8). In this sense, the violators of natural law are rendered "thinglike" not only with respect to God's final judgment, but with respect to that of their fellows as well. Thus in destroying a criminal who has become a "noxious beast," Locke's natural agent can be seen as, in some sense, preserving terrestrial existence. For a discussion of this "executive right," see also Dunn, *Political Thought,* 107–11.

nates a sphere of freedom or liberty in which specific actions and their referents are morally indifferent, matters of choice rather than obligations stipulated by the precepts of natural law. Here, the natural right or freedom to use the resources of nature is a fact of creation no less than natural law itself: to claim a right is to refer to "the fact that we have the free use of a thing"; it is to assert that such an action is one permitted by or indifferent to natural law. Within the situation structured by the metaphor of God's architecture, in other words, both natural law and natural right express God's will for the human species, specifically, by establishing the objective moral parameters of properly human action in the created condition of the species. Natural law marks a domain in which human agents are morally obliged to act as the rule of virtue prescribes. There, by following God's will in determining their actions toward their fellows, they act in accordance with the divine element of their nature, with their reason and their created potential for moral action in this world and salvation in the next. The domain of right, on the other hand, is constituted by relation as a sphere of liberty in which particular human agents are free to follow their own individual preferences and judgments of worldly satisfaction. There they may direct their actions as they each see fit or "convenient" for the preservation and comfort of their own mortal existence, without further regard to the moral law and without fear of God's ultimate judgment.

Perhaps the most important aspect of the conceptual relationship suggested here between natural law and natural right lies in its exclusion of any possible tension or conflict between the two. Because the domain of right is by definition free of obligations imposed by natural law, no act properly a matter of natural right can violate the moral rule. It is, in other words, a formal characteristic of a natural right that it is necessarily consistent with natural duty. This simple analytic truth has important implications for understanding the moral status of rights in the *Treatises'* presentation of the natural condition of the species, for in that state the law of nature operates as the sole defining feature of moral order. In stipulating the actions required or prohibited by God's will as consistent with his purposes, it mandates that relations between members of the human species be peaceful and free of violence. If natural law thus proscribes all injurious acts, and natural right is a domain of choice left free by law, no proper exercise of a natural right can be injurious. Similarly, since the exercise of rights is by definition consistent with natural law and the observance of natural law is the necessary and sufficient condition for peace and order in human society, the sphere of actions designated by right contains no possibility of internal moral conflict. In short, formally speaking, by divine design it is impossible for the rightful actions of any one natural agent to conflict with or infringe upon those of any other. Further, for any individual agent, since all possible actions duly grounded in natural right are consistent with natural duty, the choice between particular actions in any given context can never, properly speaking, present a moral dilemma. To restate the matter in terms of the distinction between virtue and convenience, to the extent that they conform to the objective domain of natural right as defined by law, individual judgments of personal convenience cannot entail human injury. By the same token, for any particular agent any number of rightful actions may be convenient for a given end or purpose, but so long as such options are permitted by the rule of virtue, the choice between them is morally indifferent. Finally, as we shall explore more fully later, it should also be noted that because this complementarity of law and right follows from the assumption that the domain of the former constitutes that of the latter, should knowledge of natural law become problematic so too would legitimate claims of rightful convenience.

At various points in both the *Two Treatises* and his earlier *Essays on the Law of Nature,* as well as in the *Essay concerning Human Understanding,* Locke emphasizes that it is a matter of utmost importance that these very different domains of action and criteria of judgment not be confused. Each text repeatedly insists that individuals' determinations of moral virtue or obligation be strictly distinguished from judgments of personal convenience and worldly advantage. In the *Essays on the Law of Nature,* for example, those who contend that morality is rooted in the "instinct" of self-preservation and the pursuit of "safety" and "welfare" are taken to task for committing precisely this error. Were moral obligations founded upon individual preferences of what was "useful" to preservation, "virtue would seem not so much man's duty as his convenience, nor will anything be good except what is useful to him; and the observance of this law would be not so much our duty and obligation, to which we are bound by nature, as a privilege and an advantage to which we are led by expediency."[25] Similarly, in a passage from the *Treatises* unmistakably saturated with the imagery of the architectural metaphor, Locke notes with abhorrence the extreme case of such confusion in the example of cannibalism. This, he observes, is evidence of how a man's "busie mind" can "carry him to a Brutality below the level of Beasts, when he quits his reason, which places him almost equal to Angels."[26] In acting contrary to the species' created capacity to apprehend rationally God's rule that we are not "made for one another's uses" as the lower animals are for ours, the cannibal becomes more savage than beasts, whose violent appetites remain a product of instinct rather than a perversion of reason and freedom.

We find a more complicated example of the same sort of operation in the *Essay concerning Human Understanding*, where Locke discusses a community of robbers. Unlike the cannibal who simply, if perversely, abandons the moral rule, "Confederacies of the greatest Villains" may yet keep "Faith and Rules of Justice one amongst another." But such conformity to morality is illusory, for in such company God's moral precepts are adopted as "Rules of Convenience" rather than as expressions of virtue in recognition of moral duty. In that context, Locke suggests, "it is impossible to conceive, that he embraces Justice . . . who acts fairly with his fellow High-way-men, and at the same time plunders, or kills the next honest Man he meets with. Justice and Truth are the common ties of Society; and therefore even, Outlaws and Robbers, who break with all the World besides, must keep Faith and Rules of Equity amongst themselves, or else they cannot hold together."[27] In taking convenience as their

---

25. *ELN*, Sixth Essay, 181. In a more explicitly political context, compare Locke's quarrel with Proast over the legitimacy versus the utility of force in the hands of the civil magistrate: "Granting force, as you say, . . . useful to the salvation of men's souls; yet it does not follow that it is lawful for the magistrate to use it; because . . . the magistrate has no commission or authority to do so. . . . For though it be a good argument; it is not useful, therefore not fit to be used; yet this will not be good logic, it is useful, therefore any one has a right to use it. For if its usefulness makes it lawful, it makes it lawful in any hands that can so apply it; and so private men can use it." John Locke, *Second Letter concerning Toleration*, in *The Works of John Locke in Ten Volumes* (1823; reprint, Scientia Verlag Aalen, 1963), 6:80. That which is useful, in short, like all judgments for which convenience is a guide, is always constrained by a consideration of what law allows.

26. Locke, *Two Treatises*, 2.58.

27. Locke, *Essay*, 1.3.2.

guide, such criminals presume a freedom which in Locke's view they objectively lack as rational creatures capable of moral judgment and obligation. Observing justice among themselves as a matter of mutual advantage rather than as a duty prescribed by the rule of virtue, they render instrumental and relative the acts and practices which, by the latter criterion, designedly possess an intrinsic moral status. However peaceful or harmonious the internal relations of such communities might be, the violence of their members' actions toward others transgresses the objective boundaries of natural order and contradicts their created potential for moral action.

In Locke's representation of the created order, then, the virtue prescribed by natural law and the conveniences permitted by natural right structure the ontological boundaries of properly human activities. In formal terms, the domains of action to which they refer are separated in three essential respects. First, they are distinguished in terms of their purposes. As conformity to God's law, "virtue" describes the intrinsic goodness of acts as these confirm the moral capacity of human agents and their created potential for eternal life. "Natural right" and "convenience," on the other hand, denominate actions that are instrumental to the preservation and comfort of mortal or bodily existence. Second, they are distinguished with reference to their respective objects. Virtue is the appropriate guide prescribing peace and order for interactions with other human beings, while convenience is a rule for actions utilizing the things and creatures of subordinate nature. Finally, and implicit in both the former respects, they are differentiated in terms of the character and criteria of judgment appropriate to their respective domains of action. In contrast to the realm of law and virtue, where one's duty is to follow God's moral rule proscribing the injury of others, the sphere of right or convenience is one in which individuals are free to act as they find most conducive to their own particular preservation and comfort. In effect, while the former is posited as an objective, universal, and eternal standard of good or evil acts, the latter, by contrast, is constituted as a domain of instrumental activity, indifferent to the rule of morality, in which individuals are free to pursue their own purposes and preferences as they see fit. To determine an action on the grounds of convenience is thus to weigh its worldly consequences in accordance with one's individual preferences; to do so on the basis of law, on the other hand, is to recognize an objective moral duty independent of one's preferences or this-worldly considerations of private advantage.

This construction of the formal complementarity between law and right is a given within Locke's imagery of God's architecture. Given, too, as we have seen, is the human species' created capacity to discern the distinctions this complementarity presumes between the proper ends, objects, and criteria of judgment for activities so defined and so situated. God having "put within reach of their Discovery the comfortable Provision for this life and the Way that leads to a better," human agents are designedly capable of orienting themselves within this morally marked world in a manner consistent with their maker's intentions. By respecting the hierarchical separation of humankind from the subordinate ranks of nature, by treating their created equals in conformity with the natural law of virtue and duly orienting their judgments of convenience to the rightful use of things and creatures necessary to their preservation, individuals in the state of nature might express the highest potential of their nature. So long, in other words, as individual agents conform their actions to the distinct object boundaries and criteria of judgment ordained by God's design, they will realize his intention that the natural condition of the species be one of "peace, good will, and mutual assistance." Such a happy condition, of course, corresponds to Locke's initial presentation of the state of nature in the *Second Treatise*, and is suggested in references to that state in other works as well—indeed, it is the manner in which this peaceful condition becomes corrupt that necessitates the creation of political society. Before we move to an examination of that process, however, let us round out our picture of the natural state as implied in the architectural metaphor by considering Locke's description of its original inhabitants.

III   Natural Humanity: A World of Free and Equal Possessors

In Locke's rendering of the world's architecture, considerations of law and right, virtue and convenience, function not only as divinely ordained demarcations of possible human actions but also as criteria of judgment for existential human agents. On Locke's account these agents are constituted as specific sorts of beings within that structure, that is, as beings whose characteristic features have been molded by the same divine hand that formed the architecture they inhabit. We might take the *Second Treatise*'s initial characterization of the state of nature as Locke's most concise description of these features. Human agents, he suggests, exist by nature in "*a State of perfect Freedom,*" a state in which they may "order their Actions, and dispose of their Possessions, and Persons as they think fit, within the bounds of the Law of Nature, without asking leave, or depending upon the Will of any other Man." This condition is one of equality as well, "wherein all the Power and Jurisdiction is reciprocal, no one having any more than another."[28] Here we find the "natural," that is, God-given characteristics of human agents to reside in their freedom, their equality and, more subtly, in their common status as possessors.

This freedom and equality, of course, can be read as the major premises underpinning the central argument of Locke's political theory, just as the mention of possessions can be read as reference to a natural proprietary capacity that foreshadows his treatment of property right in the fifth chapter of the *Second Treatise*. But the meaning and function of these terms in his political writing can also be read as more complicated than that of a priori assumptions in a logical argument. As we have seen, Locke's theistic perspective locates the human condition within a hierarchy of created nature and presumes each individual member of the species to be destined, as it were, for the bench of God's final judgment, presenting a life composed of discrete actions to be considered for its conformity to the moral law. Locke's representation of the freedom and equality of human agents in the natural state thus follows from and points to a more expansive understanding of the human condition than the logic of his explicit political "argument" in the *Treatises* might suggest. Because these free, equal, and possessing agents confront a world that is morally marked by an objective and hierarchical structure of law and right, the meaning of their freedom and equality, as well as their status as possessors, is both richer and more fraught than the characterization of these attributes as "premises" can adequately capture. Each of these attributes, in other words, is invested with nuance by its inscription within the imagery of the architecture of order and, conse-

28. Locke, *Two Treatises*, 2.4.

quently, by its relationship to the divine intentions that perfected that design. If human agents are distinguished from the lower orders of creation by their subjection to moral law and their potential for salvation, their characterization as free and equal possessors operates as a description of beings designedly fit for such an elevated place and function in God's hierarchy. Although, within the cultural imagery of the architectural metaphor, the complex interconnections implied by this description may well have been perceived as all of a piece, for the purposes of exposition we will here consider each in turn, drawing out the connections between them where appropriate. Again, as was the case in the preceding treatment of law and right, my intent is to suggest the relationships between these terms, to elucidate their embeddedness in the hierarchy of creation, and thereby to suggest something of their distance from what is commonly taken to be their sense.

Liberty

Locke's indebtedness to the structured hierarchies of God's creation and the moral topography of law and right is perhaps most evident in his treatment of natural liberty. Clear too, however, is his emphasis on independence, on the existentially real and divinely ordained individuation of action, judgment, and accountability inherent in this structure. Consider, for example, the initial formulation of liberty in the *Second Treatise* as the "perfect freedom" of human agents to "order their Actions" and "dispose of their Possessions, and Persons" as they think best, "within the bounds of the Law of Nature," independently of "the Will of any other Man."[29] As we have seen, the structured complementarity of natural law and natural right in God's design not only establishes the latter as a realm of freedom, but simultaneously centers it on the use of things serviceable for terrestrial preservation and renders its scope dependent upon the boundaries or limits defined by law. In the created or natural condition of the species the moral law's prohibition of injury establishes the boundary of properly human liberty as a liberty defined and delimited by the rule of virtue. The "State of *Liberty*," Locke cautions, "is *not a State of Licence*." "Man," he notes, may have "uncontroleable Liberty" with respect to "his Person or Possessions,"

29. Ibid.

but this nonetheless excludes a "Liberty to destroy himself, or so much as any Creature in his Possession, but where some nobler use, than its bare Preservation calls for it."[30] Governed by the universal and objective obligations of natural law, properly human liberty is thus circumscribed by a variety of moral imperatives. Most importantly, with respect to relations between members of the species, that law "teaches all Mankind, who will but consult it, that being all equal and independent, no one ought to harm another in his Life, Health, Liberty, or Possessions."[31]

To put the point briefly, the liberty attributed to human agents in the natural state pertains to their discretionary power over what is properly theirs as individuals: their persons, their actions, and their possessions. The "perfection" of this liberty, however, refers not to its scope or extent, for it is always bounded by the existence of law. Rather, its perfection lies, on the one hand, in its consistency with the moral imperatives of natural law and, on the other, in the fact that its exercise is the business of the individual agent, independent of the will of any other person. To be free, on this view, is to order one's actions in accordance with the designed structure of law and right that marks the boundary between human and animal existence. Only by respecting this boundary, as we have seen, does the agent express a properly human character. What this might mean in practical terms is explicitly framed by the distinction and hierarchical separation between human agents' mutual interactions and their activities with respect to the rest of the created world. Following this distinction, Lockean liberty simultaneously encompasses a conception of freedom as protection or insulation from the interference of others and one, as well, that evokes a notion of self-mastery, within the bounds set by law, over those things necessary to sustain life. With respect to one's equals in the hierarchy, it is to be free "from restraint and violence from others which cannot be, where there is no Law."[32] Liberty lies in the protection afforded by the moral law's prohibition of injury, but further, it is to be free of the will of others, to order what is one's own "without asking leave, or depending on the Will of any other Man."[33] This broad construction of protection, in turn, provides the bridge to Locke's positive conception of liberty

30. Ibid., 2.6.
31. Ibid., 2.6.
32. Ibid., 2.57.
33. Ibid., 2.4.

as self-mastery. Locke specifies the content of this second sense of human freedom as an individual's right "to dispose and order, as he lists, his Person, Actions, Possessions, and his whole Property, within the Allowance of those Laws under which he is; and therein not to be subject to the arbitrary Will of another, but freely follow his own."[34] Here Locke again mirrors the distinction between law and right, virtue and convenience, in the morally marked architecture of God's creation. The dual sense of liberty reflects, on the highest level, the conformity of human action to the natural law prohibition of force or injury in relations between human agents. On a second and subordinate level it refers to the free use of things, as each judges convenient, within the realm of right defined by law.

Freedom in the latter sense, as we shall discuss more fully when we turn to property, can only be understood as a product of the species' created capacity to discover the moral law. The "liberty of an individual," as Locke suggests in a comment on children, "is *grounded* on his having *Reason,* which is able to instruct him in that Law he is to govern himself by, and make him know how far he is left to the freedom of his own will."[35] Again, in terms of the language of virtue and convenience, this is to say that private judgments of convenience in the free use of what is one's own are congruent with properly human liberty only insofar as they follow from an apprehension of law. The stakes are high here. In yet another evocation of the natural hierarchy, Locke suggests the potential danger implicit in human actions unbounded by such a recognition of law: "To turn [a minor] loose to an unrestrain'd Liberty, before he has Reason to guide him, is not the allowing him the privilege of his Nature, to be free; but to thrust him out amongst Brutes, and abandon him to a state as wretched, and as much beneath that of a Man, as theirs."[36] So conceived, Lockean liberty assures terrestrial autonomy to each member of the species. At the same time, it encloses human agents within the parameters of their own judgment and establishes personal accountability for the moral character of their actions in the world. Granted the free use of subordinate nature within the objective boundaries of the law of nature, Locke's natural agents are constituted as moral islands, self-sufficient in their natural liberty or right to provide for themselves the necessities of life. Further,

34. Ibid., 2.57.
35. Ibid., 2.63.
36. Ibid.

they are self-determining in their judgments of the bounds of this liberty. Their insulation from their fellows lies not simply in their freedom from the violence of others, but in their individual right to determine their own actions and their right to use the lower ranks of things and creatures independently of the will or permission of any-one else.

In effect, framed within the hierarchical imagery of the architec-ture of order, Locke's account of liberty in the *Treatises'* natural state articulates a similarly hierarchical bifurcation of human freedom. Pertaining at the highest level to relations between members of the human species, it suggests independence of both the violence and the will of others, while its positive expression is channeled into self-mastery in the use of subordinate nature. In this respect Locke's account of natural liberty thus points in two directions simul-taneously, each of which is conceptually imbricated with the remain-ing two terms of his central political vocabulary. On the one hand, since the perfection of natural freedom consists in its being bounded by law, the independence characteristic of human agents in that state points to natural law and its function as a moral guide to the actions and mutual relations of the species as created equals. The second connotation of freedom, on the other hand—that is, freedom in the use of things and the mastery of what is one's own—directs attention to Locke's conception of rights, particularly as this is manifested in his treatment of property.

Equality

The prominence of natural liberty in the *First Treatise*'s polemic against the divine authority of Filmer's patriarchs is obvious. Less commonly emphasized, though, is the fact that this liberty is itself persistently welded to representations of the fundamental equality of members of the human species. It is, Locke suggests, "very evi-dent" that all who share "in the same common Nature, Faculties and Powers, are in Nature equal, and ought to partake in the same com-mon Rights and Privileges, till the manifest appointment of God, who is Lord over all, Blessed for ever, can be produced to show any particular Persons Supremacy, or a Mans own consent Subjects him to a Superior."[37] The opening paragraphs of the *Second Treatise* reit-

37. Ibid., 1.67. See also 1.25–27.

erate the certainty of this conviction, observing that there is "nothing more evident, than that Creatures of the same species and rank promiscuously born to all the same advantages of Nature, and the use of all the same faculties, should be equal one amongst another without Subordination or Subjection."[38] Indeed, it is in this context that Locke, in an unusual invocation of authorities, marshals "the Judicious Hooker" to his cause. For the latter, Locke notes, it is the "relation of equality between ourselves and them, that are as our selves" that grounds the "several Rules and Canons, natural reason hath drawn for direction of Life."[39] As this deployment of the great Anglican divine might suggest, Locke's account of human equality, like his larger cosmology, remains essentially Christian in derivation. As Dunn has argued, it reflects the "creaturely equality of all men in virtue of their shared species membership," an equality that originates in "their shared position in a normative order, the order of creation."[40] In this evident truth, both human liberty and moral obligation find their roots.

From Locke's perspective this equality is not, as we later moderns might say, a "fundamental value"—it is a fact of creation. And, as we have seen, that creaturely equality entails far more than a narrowly conceived ethical or moral equality. It further implies a series of parallel or designedly equivalent relations between each individual member of the species and the other elements in the hierarchy of God's architecture. Clearly, all are equally obliged by the law of nature to observe the prohibition of harm. But further, all are equally entitled to possess the things of this world that conduce to their comfort and subsistence, to use the inferior ranks of nature for their individual "convenience" and comfortable preservation. God, Locke suggests, set "Mankind above all other kinds of Creatures, in this habitable Earth of ours," and gave "to Man, the whole species of Man, as the chief Inhabitant, who is the Image of his Maker, the Dominion over the other Creatures."[41] Being situated, as it were, on the same plane of the created hierarchy, all humanity is equally subject to the objective structure of the moral law and equally master of the lower orders of creation. As members of the same species com-

38. Ibid., 2.4.
39. Ibid., 2.5.
40. Dunn, *Political Thought*, 99, 106–7. See also 112, 121.
41. Locke, *Two Treatises*, 1.40.

monly constituted by their maker as moral agents, human beings are not only equally obligated to observe the rule of virtue but equally invested with the liberty or right to use the nonhuman world of things and creatures as they each deem fit for their individual comfort and preservation.

Natural liberty and equality are thus integral to and definitive of the place allotted humankind within the architecture of order. Natural liberty is rooted in the created equality of human agents, and that equality is defined by their equal possession of natural liberty bounded by law. The relationship between the two terms, however, is not simply circular, for they are mutually and reciprocally implied by Locke's representation of divine intentions for the human species as a whole, both in terms of their potential for salvation and in terms of their relatedness to the terrestrial world in this life. Liberty and equality characterize human agents in a manner at once consonant with and constitutive of their unique status as moral beings, as independent participants in a natural community ordered by law. Abstract as it may appear to the more secular and empirical modern mind, Locke's account of liberty and equality describes the real and necessary characteristics of the species within the morally marked world of God's creation. Taken together, of course, his liberty and equality constitute a denial of "natural," understood as divinely ordained, political inequality in the form of patriarchal power. At the same time, though, they presume that the species is subject to divine authority, and they oblige its members to observe the divinely structured boundary between law and right, and in this respect they also refuse the inequality naturalized by de facto acquiescence in the right of the strongest.

In explicit terms, Locke presents this natural equality of the created condition as one "wherein all the Power and Jurisdiction is reciprocal, no one having more than another."[42] The use of the term "jurisdiction" is crucial, for the equality evoked here is not one of physical capacity or bodily power. It is not, as it was for Hobbes and later moderns, reducible to the plane of material existence. Indeed, the equality to which Locke refers is consistent with a variety of worldly inequalities that originate in the consent or recognition of others. "*Age* or *Virtue* may give Men a just Precendency: Excellency

42. Ibid., 2.6.

of Parts and Merit may place others above the Common Level: *Birth* may subject some, and *Alliance* or *Benefits* others, to pay an Observance to those to whom Nature, Gratitude, or other Respects may have made it due."[43] Distinct from the inequalities generated within such circumstantial, contingent, or "instituted" relations, the equality in which Locke locates all human agents by nature is one of "Jurisdiction or Dominion one over another." Specifically, it embodies the "equal Right that every Man hath, to his Natural Freedom," which Locke characterizes as their natural right to "order their Actions, and dispose of their Possessions, and Persons as they think fit, within the bounds of the Law of Nature, without asking leave or depending upon the Will of any other Man."[44] Once again, Lockean equality in the natural state is intimately associated with his conception of liberty. It suggests the equality of free and active beings, of self-constituting and self-determining moral agents within a framework of divine purposes. It is an egalitarianism of rights and obligations understood as the peculiar descriptive characteristics of human activities distinct from all the lower orders of terrestrial creation.

Locke's representation of human equality, however, is not only a matter of subjection to the moral law, for this in turn entails an equality of active powers. In part this active component inheres in individuals' "dominion" over subordinate nature. But his account of the natural condition—and this is of no small political consequence—renders human agents equal, as well, in their shared status as executioners of the moral law. Law, on Locke's view, was dependent upon active enforcement, and the law of nature was, in this respect, no different from "all other Laws that concern Men in this World." As with them, it would "be in vain, if there were no body that . . . had a *Power to Execute* [it]."[45] Thus in the natural state the execution of natural law is "put into every Man's hands, whereby every one has a right to punish the transgressors of that Law." And, as Locke continues, "if any one in the State of Nature may punish another, for any evil he has done, every one may do so. For in that

43. Ibid., 2.54.
44. Ibid. For contrast, see the extensive discussion of "instituted relations" in Locke, *Essay*, 2.18.3.
45. Locke, *Two Treatises*, 2.7. Compare 2.219 and the discussion there of implications for political society when civil laws lack an executor. We shall explore this issue at length in Part II.

State of Perfect Equality, where naturally there is no superiority or
jurisdiction of one, over another, what any may do in Prosecution of
that Law, every one must needs have a Right to do."[46] In embedding
this "strange doctrine" of executive right in natural equality, Locke
further elaborates the created condition of the species in a manner
that effectively reinforces the individuation of its members as separate and autonomous moral agents. We have seen already that this
individualism stands simultaneously as an existential fact and as a
theological imperative: only individuals consider, will, and judge
their actions, and all are equally accountable for the moral worth of
a life so determined. Consonant with this, Locke's construction of
human equality invests individual agency not only with the Hobbesian right and power to provide for one's own bodily needs and determine one's own individual actions, but with the reciprocal jurisdiction to judge and punish the actions of others for their deviations
from the moral law. In this, Locke counters both the divine authori-
tarianism of Filmer and the naturalistic chaos of the Hobbesian state
of war with an alternative vision. Authority and juridical power, on
the account offered by the *Treatises,* is neither centralized within nor
banished from the natural state, but distributed and dispersed, one
might even say democratized, as a defining characteristic of human
beings per se as moral agents.[47]

    In their mutual subjection to natural law and their shared execu-

---

46. Ibid., 2.7.
47. It might be objected that my use of the term "democratized" to describe the
egalitarian distribution of executive right is off the mark. Within the constraints of
Locke's natural condition, because the law that governs it is of God's making, the only
power to be distributed is that of its enforcement. It is possessed by one (Filmer's
patriarch, for example), by the few, or by the many, and insofar as these principles of
distribution classically distinguish between monarchy, aristocracy, and democracy, I
see no reason why its generalized distribution cannot be called democratic. Further,
on Locke's account the exercise of this right is not restricted to the injured party.
Because executive right is common to all, the injured party may be assisted by "any
other Person who finds it just," ibid., 2.10. This is not, perhaps, a collective process in
the sense of generating a common public or sovereign will—interestingly, save for the
fable of initial foundings, little in Locke's work is collective in that sense—but nothing
precludes it from being collaborative. So long as no one is excluded in principle from
the exercise of such power, describing it as democratically distributed seems to me
quite appropriate, and the more particularly so since that distribution is replicated in
Locke's account of resistance right. Unlike various continental views that granted resistance right to a specified few (parliamentarians or nobles, for instance), his is general across the population as a whole.

tive power to give it force, human agents in the state of nature are
assured to be free, equal, and independent, and at the same time are
presented as members of a natural community defined and ordered
by law. Though the dual themes of freedom and equality are both
evident and often noted, the meaning of the "independence" these
entail bears further specification. In effect, the characteristic equality
of Locke's natural agents and their rightful freedom within the
boundaries of law insulates them from one another and places them,
each separate and self-determining, within the morally marked grid
of God's created order.[48] Possessed of common yet individuated dominion over the lower ranks of God's creation, solely responsible for
the manner in which they conduct their individual lives, Lockean
humanity is thus particularized into independent moral persons,
each confronted with the necessity of containing their actions within
the objective structure of natural law and natural right. Each individual is sole author of a life and each is accountable for the conformity of the actions that comprise that life over time to the imperatives of natural law. Each, in other words, both judges and is judged
by the rule of virtue that defines the excellence of the human species
in God's design. No earthly authority intercedes between these Lockean individuals and their maker, save for the capacity for judgment
and punishment attributed universally to all members of the species.
They are each thus uniquely and individually responsible for their
actions, both immediately to their fellows and, ultimately, to God's
final judgment.[49]

Like liberty, then, Locke's natural equality is conceived in terms of
the species' characteristically doubled relatedness to both law and
right as the objective moral boundaries of its members' activities in
the natural state. It refers, on the one hand, to their subjection to
natural law as a guide to human virtue, and, on the other, to their
shared dominion over nonhuman nature and their common jurisdiction over one another. Where the first of these defines humankind,
as if from the perspective of God, as "one Community, . . . one
Society distinct from all other Creatures,"[50] the latter two begin to

48. They remain, however, dependent upon God, as Tully discusses in greater detail in *Discourse on Property*, chap. 2, esp. 36.

49. See, for example, Locke, *Two Treatises*, 2.20–21, 176; compare the discussion of
the person in Locke, *Essay*, 2.27.26.

50. Locke, *Two Treatises*, 2.128.

suggest something of their mutual relatedness from the standpoint of terrestrial experience and bodily needs. While the creaturely equality of the state of nature individuates the members of the human species as moral agents, however, it does not construe them as solitary beings. Typically, Locke attributes what he presents as the species' natural sociability to divine design: "God having made Man such a Creature, that, in his own Judgement, it was not good for him to be alone, put him under strong Obligations of Necessity, Convenience, and Inclination to drive him into *Society,* as well as fitted him with Understanding and Language to continue and enjoy it."[51] Again enlisting Hooker, Locke both evokes the elevated status of the human species in God's architecture and suggests a material basis for their terrestrial association. The laws of nature, he notes, drawing on the *Ecclesiastical Polity,* are binding on humankind even if *"they have never any settled fellowship, never any Solemn Agreement amongst themselves what to do or not to do."* But such solitude is neither natural nor fitting for the sorts of creatures human beings are meant to be in the divine plan. As Locke's citation of Hooker continues, *"we are not by our selves sufficient to furnish our selves with a competent store of things, needful for such a Life, as our Nature doth desire, a Life, fit for the Dignity of Man; therefore to supply those Defects and Imperfections which are in us, as living singly and solely by our selves, we are naturally induced to seek Communion and Fellowship with others."*[52] For Locke's free and equal individuals, no less than for Hooker, a significant basis for human sociability was the necessity of providing for the conveniences of life by assuring a "competent store of things." Here, we turn to the remaining characteristic of human agents in the state of nature, their status as "natural" possessors of property.

Property

If, as I have suggested, the domain of right refers in the first instance to the human use of subordinate nature for bodily preservation and comfort, the idea of "property" for Locke would seem to stand as the epitome of right. In this he follows a common usage of the period that identified property as "the highest right a Man can

51. Ibid., 2.77.
52. Ibid., 2.15.

have to a thing."[53] Indeed, as it is characterized in the *First Treatise*, "the utmost Property Man is capable of" is "to have a right to destroy any thing by using it."[54] The consistency of this formulation with Locke's understanding of "convenience" is most clearly suggested in the *First Treatise* as well. Property, we find there, not only originates in "the Right a Man has to use any of the Inferior Creatures, for the Subsistence and Comfort of his Life," it exists for the "sole Advantage of the Proprietor, so that he may even destroy the thing, that he has Property in by his use of it, where need requires."[55] As a matter of right, intended by God for the sole advantage of its possessor, the use of property is thus an activity appropriately judged on the grounds of individual or private convenience.

So conceived, Lockean property would appear to embody precisely the sort of purely individual or private instrumentality attributed to it by many modern commentators. At the same time, however, Locke's usage of the term "property" is more extensive than the outward possession and use of objects. Both the scope and the diverse types of property right evidenced in his work have been repeatedly scrutinized for some decades now. Indeed, since C. B. Macpherson's highly original study, the controversy over the political meaning of Lockean property may well be said to dominate contemporary interpretations of his political theory.[56] Still, despite this sus-

53. Elisha Coles, *An English Dictionary* (1676; reprint, Menston: Scolar Press, 1971), s.v. "Property." See also John Kersey, *Dictionarium anglo-britannicum* (London: J. Wilde, 1708), s.v. "Property." As Tully has noted, Jean Barbeyrac remarked upon Locke's broad use of the term: "Mr Locke means by the word 'property' not only the right which one has to his goods and possessions, but even with respect to his actions, liberty, his life, his body; and, in a word, all sorts of right." See Jean Barbeyrac, "A Historical and Critical Account of the Science of Morality," the introduction to Samuel Pufendorf, *Of the Law of Nature and Nations*, ed. Jean Barbeyrac, trans. Basil Kennett (London: J. Walthoe, R. Wilken [etc.], 1729), p. 4. For discussion see James Tully, *An Approach to Political Philosophy: Locke in Contexts* (Cambridge: Cambridge University Press, 1993), 109–17.

54. Locke, *Two Treatises*, 1.39.

55. Ibid., 1.92.

56. C. B. Macpherson's initial contribution was his "Locke on Capitalist Appropriation," *Western Political Quarterly* 4, no. 4 (1951): 550–66. For discussions of this debate see Tully, *Approach to Political Philosophy*, chaps. 2, 3, and 4: "After the Macpherson Thesis," "The Framework of Natural Rights in Locke's Analysis of Property," and "Differences in the Interpretation of Locke on Property." Prior analyses of Locke on property include Paschal Larkin, *Property in the Eighteenth Century, with Special Reference to England and Locke* (Dublin: Cork University Press, 1930); Willmoore Kendall, *John Locke and the Doctrine of Majority Rule* (Urbana; University of Illinois Press, 1941); J. D.

tained attention, too few have paused to consider Locke's conception of property in terms of either its human meaning or its moral status as these underlie its explicit and obviously central role in his constitution of political society. I will take up the question of the relationship Locke articulated between property and political power in the next chapter; for now, following from the relationship suggested above between natural law and natural right, on the one hand, and liberty and equality, on the other, I will first explore the prior and more fundamental connection Locke establishes between property and the human condition. In this context I will direct attention to two specific aspects of his treatment of property. First, I will exam-

Mabbott, *The State and the Citizen* (London: Hutchinson's University Library, 1947); John Gough, *John Locke's Political Philosophy, Eight Studies* (Oxford: Clarendon Press, 1950). Shortly after Macpherson's original article, Strauss published his *Natural Right and History,* a work that concurred in fundamental respects with Macpherson's linkage of Locke to unlimited capitalist appropriation, though from a significantly different interpretive standpoint. Subsequent treatments of the question of property in Locke's work are voluminous, but among the more important contributions are the following: Melvin Cherno, "Locke on Property: A Reappraisal," *Ethics* 68, no. 1 (1957): 51–55; C. H. Monson, "Locke and His Interpreters," *Political Studies* 6, no. 2 (1958): 120–33, which treats parts of the debate; Raymond Polin, *La politique morale de John Locke* (Paris: Presses universitaires de France, 1960); Jacob Viner, "'Possessive Individualism' as Original Sin," *Canadian Journal of Economics and Political Science* 29, no. 4 (1963): 548–59; Macpherson's reply, "Scholars and Spectres: A Rejoinder to Viner," *Canadian Journal of Economics and Political Science* 29, no. 4 (1963): 559–62; Peter Laslett, "Market Society and Political Theory," *Historical Journal* 7, no. 11 (1964): 150–54; Alan Ryan, "Locke and the Dictatorship of the Bourgeoisie," *Political Studies* 13, no. 2 (1965): 219–30; J. P. Day, "Locke on Property," *Philosophical Quarterly* 16, no. 64 (1966): 207–20; Martin Seliger, *The Liberal Politics of John Locke* (New York: Frederick Praeger, 1969), chaps. 5 and 6; Dunn, *Political Thought;* Edward J. Hundert, "The Making of *homo faber:* John Locke between Ideology and History," *Journal of the History of Ideas* 32, no. 1 (1972): 3–22; Karl Olivecrona, "Appropriation in the State of Nature: Locke on the Origin of Property," *Journal of the History of Ideas* 35, no. 2 (1974): 211–30; Karl Olivecrona, "Locke's Theory of Appropriation," *Philosophical Quarterly* 24, no. 96 (1974): 220–34; Robert Nozick, *Anarchy, State, and Utopia* (Oxford: Basil Blackwell, 1974); Hillel Steiner, "The Natural Right to the Means of Production," *Philosophical Quarterly* 27, no. 1 (1977): 41–49; Gordon Schochet, *Patriarchalism in Political Thought: The Authoritarian Family and Political Speculation and Attitudes, Especially in Seventeenth-Century England* (Oxford: Basil Blackwell, 1975); Thomas Scanlon, "Nozick on Rights, Liberty, and Property," *Philosophy and Public Affairs* 6, no. 1 (1976): 3–25; Edward J. Hundert, "Market Society and Meaning in Locke's Political Philosophy," *Journal of the History of Philosophy* 15, no. 1 (1977): 33–44; Tully, *Discourse on Property;* Wood, *Politics of Locke's Philosophy;* Neal Wood, *John Locke and the Theory of Agrarian Capitalism* (Berkeley, Calif.: University of California Press, 1984); Alan Ryan, *Property* (Minneapolis: University of Minnesota Press, 1987); and Jeremy Waldron, *The Right to Private Property* (Oxford: Clarendon Press, 1988).

ine a variety of forms in which property appears in his rendition of
the created condition of the human species, and the connections
these embody with the larger architecture of order. With this as a
point of departure, I will then consider what it might have meant for
him to characterize property as a "right" appropriate to the human
species by nature.

The centrality and pervasiveness of property in the *Treatises* is as
unquestionable as its characterization as a right of nature. Like liberty and equality, however, Lockean property resonates with the
echoes of the architectural metaphor, and though the hierarchy it
embodies is subtle, it is nonetheless important. In its most elevated
sense, on the highest tier of the architecture, property typifies God's
relation to his creation.[57] As the "Maker of Heaven and Earth," God
himself appears as the "sole Lord and Proprietor of the whole
World."[58] It is this proprietary relationship between creator and creation that underlies the fundamental precept of natural law, the prohibition of injury between human agents: being all God's "Workmanship . . . they are his Property, whose Workmanship they are,
made to last during his, not one anothers Pleasure."[59] Similarly, it is
the presumption of God's property in the creation that defines, qual-
ifies, and circumscribes Locke's representation of the human species'
natural property in the subordinate ranks of things and creatures:
"For however, in respect to one another, Men may be allowed to
have propriety in their distinct Portions of the Creatures; yet in respect of God . . . , Mans Propriety in the Creatures is nothing but
that *Liberty to use them,* which God has permitted."[60] On Locke's account, this extended sense of God's proprietorship of the created
world is the source of both natural law and natural right for the
human species.[61] In the hands of an all-wise and all-powerful maker,
in other words, property and sovereignty are inseparable. As God's
property, individuals are denied the use of their fellows, just as they
are granted the use of the things and creatures below their elevated
position in the hierarchy of creation. God's jurisdiction with respect

57. For a more extensive discussion of this see Tully, *Discourse on Property*, esp. 35–
42.
58. Locke, *Two Treatises*, 1.39.
59. Ibid., 2.6.
60. Ibid., 1.39.
61. See Tully, *Approach to Political Philosophy*, chaps. 2 and 3.

to them is thus perfect and absolute; it is the epitome of dominion understood as the rightful power to order their mutual relations and their interactions with nonhuman nature. As Locke put the point in the *Essay*, God "has a Right" to give us laws. "We are his Creatures: He has Goodness and Wisdom to direct our Actions to that which is best: and he has Power to enforce it by Rewards and Punishments, of infinite weight and duration, in another Life."[62]

The intimate connection suggested here between property right and sovereign power is, of course, precisely what Locke denies Filmer's patriarchs in terrestrial existence. At the same time, though, we might note that even this totality of divine power was conditioned by and expressed through law. God may be omnipotent and omniscient, but even his actions are ordered by the law of nature: "The Freedom of the Almighty hinders not his being determined by what is best."[63] As supreme legislator, he orders the world by perfect reason; his will is by definition nonarbitrary, and the moral laws he sets to human actions are presumed integral to the design and proper functioning of the whole of his creation. In this respect even the divine proprietorship of the world that Locke presents as the extreme and perfect instance of property right is bounded by a conception of purpose and order that excludes arbitrary action. The physical laws given to nonhuman nature assure the harmony and integrated function of the whole, while the moral law set to human agency is "*the direction of a free and intelligent agent* to his proper Interest," prescribing "no farther than is for the general Good of those under that Law."[64] In this sense, though human creatures are both God's "property" and his subjects, their divine governance appears solely in terms of laws, with these determined by the criterion of the good of the species as a whole.

With this brief glimpse of the measure of God's property in his creation, we are prepared to discern just how short of such power and jurisdiction Locke's account of human property right falls. Most

---

62. Locke, *Essay*, 2.28.8.

63. Ibid., 2.21.49. See also Locke, *Two Treatises*, 2.195.

64. Locke, *Two Treatises*, 2.57. On this reading, refusal to conform to the moral law does not leave human beings undetermined by any law. Rather, it leaves them subject in this life only to the laws governing the biological or physiological processes of animal life. Like any other beasts, they eat, sleep, grow, decline, and die, their bodies eventually returning to organic matter. Of course, on Locke's account such a refusal is enacted at the risk of one's soul.

important, on the plane of terrestrial existence—a "state of medi-
ocrity" substantially removed from the perfection of divine power
and knowledge—he severs the relationship between possession and
sovereignty. In Locke's view of the created condition of the species
this separation follows necessarily from God's proprietorship. Construed in the first instance as his creatures, human agents are equally
subject to the law of nature, all subordinate to the rule of virtue as
the perfect expression of his will. No one of them is endowed by
nature with the sovereign right to prescribe rules for the actions of
their fellows. In the created condition of the species such dominion
would be not only a usurpation of God's right, but unnecessary as
well, since the precepts of natural law are presumed both accessible
to all and sufficient to ensure peace and order in human relations.

Locke's denial of natural superiority in the human microcosm is,
to be sure, accompanied by a powerful assertion of the species' natural dominion over the lower ranks of creatures. And yet, as we have
noted, the "property" he grants his natural agents is both broader
and more complex than the simple possession and use of material
things. Indeed, the semantic field of Lockean "property" extends to
all that which, in the seventeenth century, could properly be called
one's own, encompassing one's person, actions, life, limbs, labor,
health, and liberty, as well as outward possessions or material goods.
It is, however, not simply the diversity of Locke's conception of
property right that challenges twentieth-century understanding, but
the fact that the right, or liberty of action, embodied by such diverse
forms itself admitted of varying degrees.[65] In this regard, it is important to note that for Locke the property right natural to the human
species pertains more specifically to the liberty of action that its use

---

65. This is not to suggest that rights in the twentieth century are not diverse. Philosophers, for example, may speak of subjects bearing "bundles of rights" as a way of
differentiating between various ways of distributing diverse sorts of rights to a variety
of social subjects. The diversity of rights on Locke's account, however, not only privileges distinctions between higher and lower degrees as the proper principle of sort-
ing, but assumes that such degrees are built into the ontological structure of the world
by God. Tully, whose analyses of the complexity of Lockean property is not altogether
foreign to the considerations presented here, nonetheless suggests that Locke's "definition of property does not specify what degree of control one has over the object
except that it cannot be taken without consent, and this is true of any right." Tully,
Approach to Political Philosophy, 121. While this is generally accurate with regard to
Locke's explicit *definitions* of property, in the discussion that follows I hope to indicate
that his descriptive phraseology persistently gestures toward just such degrees.

entails than to the particular objects or things of which it is predicated.[66] While the "utmost Property" a person might have in a thing was the rightful power to destroy it through use or consumption, lesser forms of property right entailed more restricted understandings of proper use. In the *Second Treatise*, for example, while Locke notes that "every Man has a *Property* in his own *Person*," he yet asserts that "no Body has an absolute Arbitrary Power over himself . . . to destroy his own Life."[67] Similarly, though the human species is granted a property in the subordinate ranks of nature, even this does not invest any particular human agent with a liberty "to destroy . . . so much as any Creature in his Possession, but where some nobler use, than its bare Preservation calls for it."[68]

As these examples suggest, and as noted earlier with respect to Locke's supposition of the complementarity of natural law and natural right, the liberty of action embodied in this understanding of right is defined or circumscribed by law. In most of his treatment of the property right appropriate to human agents in the state of nature, Locke continues to articulate this harmonious relationship between law and right in constructions that consistently imply the boundedness of property right by considerations of proper use. And what is "proper" in this context is itself consistently structured by reference to the law of nature. In this sense, the diverse forms of Lockean property—the property one has in one's person, actions, life, limbs, health, possessions, and so forth—are linked by their common relation to his understanding of right as an individual liberty of use for the preservation and maintenance of earthly life. They suggest, in other words, an extended sense to the use of those "things" over which, within the boundaries of action defined by nat-

66. As Tully suggests, "proper" refers to the extent of the agent's "moral power" over what is his or her own. In its basic outline, my reading is very similar to Tully's, but from my perspective the phrase "liberty of use" covers both of his distinctions, between "liberty of use" and "exclusive" rights and between "objective" and "subjective" rights. See Tully, *Discourse on Property*, esp. chaps. 3 and 5.

67. Locke, *Two Treatises;* 2.27, 2.135. See also 2.23.

68. Ibid., 2.6. Today, advocates of animal rights would deny that human consumption constitues a nobler use of a creature than its preservation. If nothing else, this may suggest that the modern leveling of the architecture of creation has dissolved not only the higher divisions of the old worldview, but the lower as well. For Locke such claims would have made no sense, since rights were only possessed by intelligent beings capable of moral law. For examples of God's donation of property in subordinate nature, see ibid., 1.86, 92; 2.26.

ural law, the individual has sole mastery or control "without asking leave, or depending upon the Will of any other Man."[69] The ever-present qualification of this liberty, however, is "within the bounds of the law of nature." Lockean property is indeed the epitome of right, but the domain of liberty suggested by such right cannot be understood without reference to the rule which, by determining its boundaries, both defines it as morally permitted and marks it as properly human. In this context, the scope of human liberty in the use of property is variously structured by its relationship to the precepts of natural law that command the preservation of both one's self and others and that prohibit the injury of one's fellows.

One way of unpacking this construction of property right is to consider it initially from the perspective of God's proprietorship. For Locke, the world is its maker's property and "nothing was made by God for man to spoil or destroy."[70] From this standpoint, given the finitude of human life, the liberty of use granted human agents in the things of this world is but a temporary propriety in things over which only God has genuine dominion. On the plane of terrestrial existence in the natural state, however, the extent of human liberty in the use of various forms of property is hierarchically structured in conformity with the distinction between the human species and the lower ranks of created nature. The most exclusive property attributed to human agents in Locke's natural state is the "*Property*" one has "in his own *Person*"; this "no Body has any Right to but himself."[71] Created "free, equal, and independent" in the order of nature, all human agents are possessed of this self-propriety. The property right in one's person is thoroughly individuated, yet its meaning in Locke's rendering of the human condition is simultaneously bound up with the manner in which the use of this "possession" is structured by law. Indeed, as he characterizes it in the *Essay*, the term "person" itself is a "Forensick Term appropriating Actions and their Merit; and so belongs only to intelligent Agents capable of a Law, and Happiness and Misery." It is, he continues, through the extension of this "self" in consciousness "beyond present Existence to what is past" that the person "becomes concerned and accountable, owns and imputes to it *self* past Actions."[72]

69. Ibid., 2.4.
70. Ibid., 2.31.
71. Ibid., 2.27.
72. Locke, *Essay*, 2.27.26.

In effect, like liberty and equality, the property one has naturally in one's person points in two directions, to two levels of articulation in the architecture of order. It suggests, on the level of purely terrestrial existence, the existential liberty of use one has in one's own body: the liberty to begin, continue, or abstain from any particular action, for example, to move, eat, sleep, drink, or not as one wills.[73] At the same time, however, and in relation to what Locke presents as higher concerns, it suggests as well the relationship between any such action (as the concrete and purely personal expression of this existential liberty) and law—specifically the moral law that defines the boundaries of the liberty proper to creatures capable of salvation. To own one's self, in other words, is to "own" one's actions, to be self-determining. To have such a property in one's own person is to be responsible, to be accountable as an individual moral agent for the conformity of those actions to the law. With respect to this property in one's person, as noted above, Locke locates the boundary of right, the scope of proper use in the first instance, in the prohibition of suicide.[74] Our lives and our bodies, on this account, however private, are not ours in any absolute sense. We do not make them, but have them, as it were, on loan from our maker.[75] They are ours to use, not to destroy arbitrarily. Although existentially speaking, as free agents our power over them is complete (that is, we each do with them as we will), cosmologically understood as moral agents in an ordered architecture of divine purposes, to be fully human is to conform our will to the law of nature. Since that law is the voice of God, to do otherwise is to violate his intentions, to perform through our actions a nature far short of our created potential.

Actions, of course, are not only self-regarding. Human agents in Locke's natural condition are under "strong Obligations of Necessity, Convenience, and Inclination" to associate with their created equals in the architecture, just as they are "directed" by their "Senses and Reason . . . to the use of those things, which were serviceable for [their] Subsistence, and given [them] as a means of [their] *Preserva-*

---

73. Ibid., 2.21, esp. 8–12, 21–23. This chapter of the *Essay* is a discussion "Of Power." In it Locke's argument about liberty begins with what I have here referred to as existential or terrestrial liberty, then step-by-step recalls the necessary boundedness of this liberty of voluntary action by the precepts of morality.

74. Locke, *Two Treatises*, 2.135, 23.

75. See the discussion of the person in Tully, *Discourse on Property*, 104–11. This, too, is Locke's ground for denying parents a property in their children, as he argues in the *Two Treatises*, 1.52–54.

tion.[76] His natural agents are thus portrayed as constantly acting with regard both to their fellows and to the subordinate ranks of things and creatures in the hierarchy of creation. As natural proprietors of their actions, though, they are created individually accountable for the conformity of these actions to the law of nature. The natural right or liberty of use entailed by their individual self-propriety is, in this context, bounded not only by the prohibition of suicide, but by the moral imperatives that define their proper relationship to other human agents, on the one hand, and to nonhuman nature, on the other. To take their relations to their fellows first, as created equals, each equally possessed of their self-propriety, they are denied property in each other. Property in general being for the sole advantage of the proprietor, the property of individuals in their respective persons is for their own personal use and convenience to order as they each see fit. In cosmological terms, as we have seen, this follows from the assumption that they are God's property, "made to last during his, not one anothers Pleasure."[77] As they are each granted the use of their own person, so are they denied the use of any other's. To attempt such use would be to violate all of the characteristics set to the species by its maker; it would constitute the denial of the liberty, equality, and independence of the other as these find their concentrated expression in the right all have equally in their self-propriety. To injure another person, on this account, is to infringe not only upon the natural right, liberty, and property they have in their person, but in so doing to invade God's property as well. In this sense the exclusive property right or liberty of use each has in their person and actions is both confirmed and delimited by the moral law's complementary proscription of personal harm.

Though the property Locke's natural agents have in their persons is the most exclusive or private form of property he offers, the most extensive property right they have is the "right to destroy any thing by using it."[78] Such use, while emphatically denied with respect to their persons, is itself definitive of the utmost property they may have in the lower orders of creation. Denied the liberty of self-destruction, they are invested with the right, indeed are subject to the duty, to sustain their lives and persons through the use of subordi-

76. Locke, *Two Treatises*, 2.77, 1.86.
77. Ibid., 2.6.
78. Ibid., 1.39.

nate nature. Like all terrestrial creatures, Locke notes, the human agent is made with a "strong desire of Preserving his Life." This, "having been Planted in him, as a Principle of Action by God himself, Reason, *which was the Voice of God in him,* could not but teach him and assure him, that pursuing that natural Inclination he had to preserve his Being, he followed the Will of his Maker, and therefore had a right to make use of those Creatures, which by his Reason or Senses he could discover would be serviceable thereunto. And thus Man's *Property* in the Creatures, was founded upon the right he had, to make use of those things, that were necessary or useful to his Being."[79] Such use of subordinate nature, however, conforms to God's intentions for the human species only insofar as it conforms to the law that defines it as properly human: "The same Law of Nature," Locke asserts, that gives us "Property, does also *bound* that *Property,* too."[80] As noted previously in a different context, on Locke's view of God's design the human pursuit of subsistence differs in kind from that of the lower orders of creation. Determined by natural instincts rather than by a reasoned apprehension of the law, animals need not, indeed cannot, be understood to be concerned with the "propriety" or moral status of their inclinations to fulfill their subsistence needs. A predator cannot justly be said to have a property in its prey, any more than a plant could be said to have a property in the nutrients it draws from the soil. As free intelligent agents uniquely subject to the moral law, only human agents are capable of property right, a law-bound liberty of action in the use of things necessary to sustain their lives, for only they are created existentially free to choose or discover what is serviceable to that end. The emphatically moral character of the law appropriate to the activities of such self-determining agents thus renders them uniquely capable of property. At the same time, the objective structure of God's intentions for the species, the designed complementarity of law and right, imposes upon each individual the obligation to discern the boundary between what is and what is not permitted them in the use of earthly things.

On Locke's account of the created condition of the species, the individualistic or private character of its members' property in the

79. Ibid., 1.86.
80. Ibid., 2.31.

inferior ranks of nature follows necessarily from the property they each have in their persons. As Locke puts it in *Two Treatises*, though the natural produce of the earth "and [the] Beasts it feeds belong to Mankind in common, as they are produced by the spontaneous hand of Nature; and no body has originally a private Dominion, exclusive of the rest of Mankind, in any of them, as they are thus in their natural state: yet being given for the use of Men, there must of necessity be a means *to appropriate* them some way or other before they can be of any use, or at all beneficial to any particular Man." Locke locates this means of appropriating nature's bounty in the exclusive property each has in their person and actions: the "Labour of his Body, and the Work of his Hands," he suggests, are equally the property of each individual agent. Thus "whatsoever then he removes out of the State that Nature hath provided, and left it in, he hath mixed his *Labour* with, and joyned to it something that is his own, and thereby makes it his *Property.*"[81] This labor, "being the unquestionable Property of the Labourer, no Man but he can have a right to what that is once joyned to." In this Locke finds the distinction between the property of any given individual and that granted by God as common to the species as a whole. A person's labor "added something" to things thus particularized "more than Nature . . . had done; and so they became his private right."[82] It is, in other words, only the person's labor that renders God's donation to the species useful in fact, and thus it is only action that, in Locke's terminology, "begins a property" or "fixes" particular properties in things.[83]

To establish such a private right in a thing by labor, then, is to create an individual title to it, to claim a personal liberty of use in it. It is to mark something as one's own, exclusive of and secure from the will or interference of others. But because property so established arises from human action—"the great business of Mankind, and the whole matter about which all Laws are conversant"[84]—one's

81. Ibid., 2.26.
82. Ibid., 2.27, 28.
83. See, for example, ibid., 2.28, 30. This, for Locke, is consistent with both reason (1.86) and Scripture (1.42, 2.32). For related discussions of the character and implications of this formulation, see Yolton, *Locke and the Compass of Human Understanding*, 187–93; Dunn, *Political Thought*, esp. 67 n. 4; and Tully, *Discourse on Property*, 116–30, 174–76.
84. Locke, *Essay*, 2.22.10.

power over it, though private, remains subject to the moral imperatives of the law of nature. As action, in other words, extends the
exclusive property one has in one's person into the things of subordinate nature by appropriating them for use, so does it extend the
accountability of the person, both into the act of appropriation and,
subsequently, to the manner in which property so established is
used. It is with respect to this "making one's own" of subordinate
nature that Locke attaches the limiting conditions of properly human property in the natural condition of the species. On the one
hand, appropriation itself is bounded by the provision that such action establishes rightful title only "where there is enough, and as
good left in common for others." Given the abundance of God's
original donation, though, the simple appropriation of one's needs
seemed to Locke sufficient to ensure the conformity of action to this
proviso: "The measure of Property, Nature has well set, by the Extent of Mens *Labour, and the Conveniency of Life:* No Mans Labour
could subdue, or appropriate all: nor could his Enjoyment consume
more than a small part; so that it was impossible for any Man, this
way, to intrench upon the right of another, or acquire, to himself, a
Property, to the Prejudice of his Neighbor, who would still have
room, for as good, and as large a Possession (after the other had
taken out his) as before it was appropriated."[85] Legitimate appropriation is bounded directly by the natural law's proscription of injury to
one's fellows, though Locke confesses such injury to be impossible in
the created condition.

As the need to use the provisions of nature for one's preservation
and comfort creates a title to particular portions of nature's plenty,
so does the proper use of such property sustain it. Individual need,
in this sense, not only begins but conditions the use of such property
as one may establish in the act of appropriation: "As much as any
one can make use of to any advantage of Life before it spoils, so
much may he by his labour fix a Property in. Whatever is beyond
this, is more than his share, and belongs to others." This spoilage
limitation circumscribes the use individuals are entitled to make not
only of the "spontaneous Products of Nature" but of the possession
of land as well. In the first case, if such provisions "perished, in

---

85. Locke, *Two Treatises*, 2.27, 36. See also 2.31, 37. Locke even suggests that, were
it not for the invention of money, this measure would still be appropriate and possible
(2.36). This point will be explored in detail in Part II.

[someone's] Possession, without their due use . . . he offended against the common Law of Nature." For such an excess the agent "was liable to be punished." By wasting nature's goods "he invaded his Neighbor's share, for he had no Right, farther than his Use called for any of them, and they might serve to afford him Conveniences of Life." With respect to land, the same criterion applied. Whatever a natural agent "tilled and reaped, laid up and made use of, before it spoiled, that was his peculiar Right; whatsoever he enclosed, and could feed, and make use of, the Cattle and Product was also his. But if either the Grass of his Inclosure rotted on the Ground, or the Fruit of his planting perished without gathering, and laying up, this part of the Earth, notwithstanding his Inclosure, was still to be looked on as Waste, and might be the Possession of any other."[86] Here, just as with the property attributed to one's person, human property in the things and creatures of subordinate nature, however private, cannot be seen as absolute. Once again, although in existential terms individuals' physical power over them is complete— that is, as free agents they do with them as they will—cosmologically their status as moral agents obligates them to conform their judgments of material convenience, their actions in the appropriation and use of their particular property, to the rule of virtue, natural law. And once again, to exceed these bounds is to transform properly human liberty into license and thereby violate the highest potential of the species.

In terms of external goods, that which is legitimately established and properly sustained as one's own, within the allowance of natural law, is rightfully used by the criterion of its possessor's personal "convenience." But it is natural law, and not simply the individual's terrestrial judgment of such convenience, that confirms such property as a natural right. To put the point somewhat differently, while human agents are existentially free to judge any appropriation or use of the things of this world convenient to their personal preservation or comfort, for this to be properly human liberty, for it to enact their moral nature, it must conform to the objective structure of law and right ordained by God's design. Lockean property, in this sense, is indeed for the "sole advantage of the proprietor," but what is advantageous here is not simply that which individual agents do in fact

86. Ibid., 2.31, 37, 38.

judge convenient. Rather, Locke suggests the necessary moral boundedness of such judgments by the objective imperatives of natural law, as these circumscribe properly human liberty and express God's intentions for the preservation both of the species as a whole and of each of its members.

Recognizing these various qualifications of the use Locke accounts as permitted in one's person and possessions, we might ask what it meant for him to characterize property as a "right" appropriate to human agents by nature? To begin with, the extent of the term's referents—one's person, actions, life, health, limbs, and external goods—focuses its field of meaning clearly on the things of this life. It endows individuals with the liberty to preserve and sustain their own lives as they each find convenient to that end. Indeed, in Locke's hands, property right appears as a concentrated expression of human liberty: in terrestrial terms one's property is the condensation of what is one's own, that which is insulated from the interference of others, and that over which one thus has complete mastery. At the same time, however, Lockean property remains a fundamentally moral category as well. As a unique and distinctively human capacity in God's architecture of order, the possession and use of property is an activity that, to be properly human, must conform to the law of nature. On this account, in short, one is not simply master of one's own, but accountable for its proper use as this is bounded by law.

On Locke's representation of the human condition, property and accountability, right and law, liberty and obligation, all function as differing but parallel descriptions of God's intentions for the human species, distinct from all the lower ranks of terrestrial creation. Property may include everything that pertains to terrestrial life, but how one conducts one's self in such worldly activities has important consequences, for that conduct is subject to sanction both in this life and in the life to come. The place and meaning of property in the created condition of the species thus remains intimately and inseparably connected with the moral law. Law, in this context, is the defining feature of natural community. It unites human agents as equal moral persons by a common rule of mutual obligation and duty to preserve both themselves and others. Right, liberty, equality, and property, on the other hand, individuate the members of this community as particular moral agents, as owners of their persons, actions, and possessions, and render them each mutually and reciprocally accountable for the proper use of what is theirs.

It has been my intention in this chapter to elaborate the nature and extent of the relationship between the structured hierarchies of Locke's theistic cosmology and his portrayal of the natural state of the human species. My point has not been to suggest that he was obsessed with salvation, much less to imply that religion per se should be seen as a dominant theme in his work. Rather, by tracking some of the semiotic linkages of the central terms of his political vocabulary within the measured byways of the architectural metaphor of God's creation, I hope to have shown that that cultural imagery, replete with its faith in the Christian promise of salvation, structured his thought in ways inaccessible to interpretive perspectives that exclude such considerations out of hand. Most important, I have suggested that from a Lockean perspective such things as God, the human soul, natural law and its complement natural right, and indeed salvation itself, were neither myths nor mere social constructions in the face of the unknown, but aspects of real existence that human agents neglected only at the risk of their future state.

This retention of the hierarchical structure of earlier cosmologies infuses the *Treatises'* account of the natural condition of the human species with a certain subtlety, one generally unacknowledged by most modern treatments of Locke's thought. In particular, it casts what I have called his political vocabulary—his usage of natural law, natural right, liberty, equality, and the possession of property—as a constellation of terms, the interconections and mutual resonances of which are generated through the framework of divine intentions for the species. Each of these terms carries with it the echoes of the architecture from which it emerged, and each is importantly related to each of the others in a manner that structurally defines the human condition in relation to the rest of that larger cosmos. Natural law and natural right, differentiated hierarchically in the first instance by the created rank of their referents, define the objective moral boundaries of properly human action in that state. So conceived, they circumscribe human agents' terrestrial activities in a manner that distinguishes them from the lower orders of creation. To act within these boundaries is to express the highest potential of their created nature—their capacity for moral action and their fitness for the promise of salvation. Natural liberty, equality, and property, on the other hand, characterize human agents themselves as creatures designedly fit to inhabit this morally marked world, as independent agents individually responsible for the conformity of their actions to the objective domains of law and right divinely established as appropriate to their condition.

Recalling the characteristics of the human situation suggested in our initial consideration of the architecture of order, we may isolate several noteworthy features of the state of nature so understood, each of which bears significantly upon the political sensibility articulated in Locke's various writings. First, although it is an image of the world as God created it, the concrete manifestation of the peace and harmony he intends is fundamentally dependent upon human judgment. Although the architecture inhabited by the human species is morally marked, the contingent nature of human action within it centers the problem of realizing God's intentions on the capacity of individuals to judge rightly what is required of them. It requires, in other words, that human agents duly discern the boundaries of law and right in particular contexts and that they regulate their actions accordingly. Second, we might note the meaning and character of the notion of order that emerges from this understanding. As embodied by the complementarity of law and right, virtue and convenience, the order appropriate to the created condition of the human species is a fundamentally moral order. The harmony and accord at which it aims refer, in the first instance, to the elimination of injury and violence between members of the human species as free, equal, and independent moral agents. It presumes that however diversely human beings might pursue their earthly preservation and comfort, however different their individual preferences and evaluations of the conveniencies of subordinate nature might be, so long as their actions toward their own species conform to the moral law, the order that God intends can be realized in practice.

It posits, to put the point somewhat differently, the existence of an order that refers wholly to the conformity of human actions to the law of nature, independent of whatever consistency or regularity may or may not obtain across human practices in the rightful pursuit of worldly comfort and convenience. It is, on this account, a matter of indifference to the moral rule that any number of individuals agree or disagree in common practice with respect to anything that a single individual might do by right. Such practices, however regular or consistent they might be in the behavior of any given group, differ in kind from the moral order prescribed to human actions by God's rule of virtue. What I am suggesting here is that any empirically observable social practice is, within this perspective on the human condition, nothing more than a generalized, one might even say habitual, repetition of particular acts. So conceived, its relationship to the moral order ordained by God for human society is a matter of the conformity of its constituent acts to the law of nature, and more particularly to the prohibition of injury. It is, for example, in Lockean terms indifferent to the order proper to human society that the members of any given community be vegetarians, fish-eaters, or proponents of any other culturally specific preference of subsistence goods. Should such culinary practice ever include cannibalism, however, the practice may be regular and systematic, but hardly orderly in the moral sense emphasized by Locke's rendering of God's design.

Third, we might note the substantive division of human knowledge implicit in Locke's distinction between individuals' judgments of law or virtue and their judgments of right or convenience. This division, as Locke presents it, refers to differences not only in the objects or referents of such judgments, but in the criteria of judgment appropriate to each realm. Moral knowledge and knowledge of the potential utility of the things and creatures of subordinate nature, in other words, differ on Locke's account not simply in their referents but in the operations of the human intellect appropriate to their exercise. Linked to the prospect of salvation, moral knowledge requires recognition of the intrinsic moral status of particular actions and the consistent alignment of individual preferences and worldly purposes to the moral requirements of the law of nature stipulated by the prohibition of injury. Knowledge of the conveniences of nature, by contrast, entails an instrumentalist or consequentialist orientation of human thought, one which takes its bearings from worldly considerations and private estimations of preference, expediency, or advantage. But again, for God's intentions of terrestrial harmony to be realized in practice, such judgments of private convenience in the rightful use of one's own, one's liberty or property, must accord with an apprehension of what the law allows.

Finally, and following from this, the ordained complementarity of law and right entails a very specific connection between knowledge of the moral law and the free determination of convenience appropriate to the realm of right. When Locke asserts, "Where there is no law, there is no freedom," he is specifying the character of the relationship between moral knowledge and properly human liberty, between God's rule of virtue and individuals' rightful judgments of their private convenience. The cosmological fact of human freedom, as we have seen, is intrinsic to human agents' unique status as rational creatures capable of law, but on Locke's account such freedom presupposes that the individual is "capable to know that Law, that so he might keep his Actions within the Bounds of it."[87] Knowledge of the moral law, in other words, is what delineates the scope and content of natural right. Thus the complementarity of natural law and natural right in the created condition of the human species makes moral knowledge requisite to the expression of properly human liberty, to the exercise of natural rights, and to the free pursuit of private convenience that these entail. Once again, the possibility of social peace and moral order that this complementarity promises is dependent upon human agents' due determination of and active conformity to the boundary of law and right ordained by divine design.

All this, admittedly, takes us far afield from what are generally taken to be Locke's political concerns. Why, one may well ask, should we attend to the apparently idealized morality of his cosmology when the concrete problem he addresses is that human agents are "no strict Observers of Equity and Justice"?[88] As his examples of cannibalism and criminality suggest, despite the designed complementarity of law and right, virtue and convenience, in practice Locke's free and equal possessors are quite capable of subverting this design. The political issue is not joined by simply suggesting that such subversion is itself consistent with the species' freedom and the duality of its created nature. Corrupt or immoral action, in this context, while confining the agent to the temporality of organic nature, nevertheless situates the problem of politics squarely in the earthly

87. Ibid., 2.59. On Locke's account, with respect to both natural and civil law, this capacity is to be presumed by their having reached a "State of Maturity." In the same place he continues, "When he has acquired that state, he is presumed to know how far that Law is to be his Guide, and how far he may make use of his *Freedom*, and so comes to have it; till then, some Body else must guide him, who is presumed to know how far the Law allows a Liberty."

88. Ibid., 2.123.

world of birth and death, growth and decay. So what, to put the question directly, might Locke's retention of the hierarchy of the macrocosm and faith in God's promise of immortality have to do with those decidedly more mortal and practical political concerns?

This question demands more than evidence, however persuasive, that Locke's apparent moralism exceeded simple lip service to either traditional or contemporary sectarian conceptions of Christian duty. It requires that the connections be drawn concretely between the ideal morality implicit in his adherence to the hierarchical imagery of God's architecture and his more explicitly articulated political theory. At the same time, our travels through that architecture suggest that the political problematic Locke addresses, insofar as it is expressed in human action, pivots crucially upon the question of judgment. More specifically, it suggests an exploration of his political writings with an eye both to the kind of knowledge and criteria of judgment they construct as appropriate to the political realm, and to the character of the conception of political power such constructions inform. These connections, as I hope to show more fully in Part II, appear in Locke's construction of the state of nature and his narrative account of the creation of political society. I have already suggested that the *Treatises'* presentation of that original state is an evocation of the created condition of the human species within a hierarchically structured and morally marked world of divine design. Taken baldly, this perspective is by no means new.[89] But where others have noted this in the context of defending the authenticity of Locke's ethical positions, I find in it the foundation and skeletal structure upon which he crafted a political understanding commensurate with a concern for the grounds of moral knowledge and the principles of human action.

Locke's conception of the human condition, in other words, with its focus upon the problems of judgment and action and its emphasis upon each individual's accountability both to God and to their fellows for the deeds of their mortal life, links his ethical, political, and epistemological investigations. From this perspective, the *Treatises'* account of the "original" of civil government can be read as an exploration of the sources of tension and ambiguity consequent upon

89. See Dunn, *Political Thought,* esp. chaps. 8 and 9; Raymond Polin, "Locke's Conception of Freedom," in *John Locke: Problems and Perspectives,* ed. John W. Yolton (Cambridge: Cambridge University Press, 1969), 1–18.

human activities in the natural state that eventually confound the human capacity to discern properly the designed boundary between natural law and natural right. Here, Locke's hierarchical cosmology looms large as a key to the conception of politics proffered by the *Treatises,* for his acceptance of the architecture of order both evidences the stakes involved in his account of political society and, by virtue of this, establishes certain constraints upon the kind of political order he can envision. But this is to get ahead of ourselves. To make good these claims, let us turn to his political writings.

Part II

A POLITICS OF JUDGMENT

Introduction

> . . . to know that which before us lies in daily life, that is
> the prime Wisdom.
>
> —John Milton

Although the broad metaphor of God's architecture had long accompanied English understandings of the world, by the seventeenth century the philosophical discipline, intricate distinctions, and
multiple relations of similitude and correspondence that had characterized earlier accounts of that structure had lost both their rigor
and their clarity. Nonetheless, allusion to its broad contours continued if not to dominate at least to channel subtly the attention and
discourse of those who would write about the world.[1] Fortified here

---

1. The metaphor is, of course, a matter of direct concern to Hooker, whose construction of the architecture in Book I of his *Ecclesiastical Polity* stands as one of the
most eloquent and explicit of its English articulations. See Richard Hooker, *The Laws
of Ecclesiastical Polity*, in *The Works of That Learned Divine Mr. Richard Hooker*, ed. John
Keble, 2d ed., 3 vols. (Oxford: Oxford University Press, 1841), bk. 1. Its echoes are
also to be found in far less likely places. Harrington, hardly a devotee of such speculative systems, nonetheless carries its resonances, as suggested by the following example
from his *Aphorisms Political*, in *The Political Works of James Harrington*, ed. J. G. A.
Pocock (Cambridge: Cambridge University Press, 1977), 773: "LXXXV: To make
principles or fundamentals belongeth not unto men, unto nations, nor unto human
laws. To build upon such principles or fundamentals as are apparently laid by God in
the inevitable necessity or law of nature is that which truly appertaineth unto men,
unto nations, and unto human laws. To make any other fundamental, and then build
on them, is to build castles in the air." Compare this with Locke on the same issue:
"Municipal Laws of Countries . . . are only so far right as they are founded on the
Law of Nature, by which they are to be regulated and interpreted." John Locke, *Two
Treatises of Government*, ed. Peter Laslett, rev. ed. (1960; reprint, with amendments,
Cambridge: Cambridge University Press, 1963), by book and paragraph, 2.12. Here-
after cited as *Two Treatises*. Locke and Harrington may perhaps have differed in the
particular contents they would have attributed to the law of nature, but its hierarchi-

105

by reference to customary practice, enriched or challenged there by travelers' accounts of the larger world, complicated, deepened, or indeed questioned elsewhere by emerging scientific perspectives as well as Reformation theology, the image and broad categories of that hierarchical cosmos nonetheless persisted in providing the scaffolding upon which much of both common understanding and scholarship arranged their perceptions of the world.[2] Intellectual debate in this context, however, particularly over questions of politics and religion, tended to focus less upon the validity or appropriateness of the architecture's categories than upon judgments of their boundaries in the world of experience. Accepting the notion of individual moral accountability, and agreeing that there were such framing elements in God's design as, for instance, virtue and convenience, arguments centered upon how these categories were to be distinguished and where their limits were to be drawn in practice. The ongoing controversy over the question of religious imposition is a prime example. The contributors to the debate all agreed that there existed *adiaphora,* things or actions "indifferent" to God's laws, but they contested what was to be included in the category and why as a ground for conflicting positions on the power of the civil magistrate to determine the ceremonies of worship.[3]

---

cal relation and regulative function with respect to civil law and its charge to legislators are common to both.

2. Indeed, the growing looseness of the metaphor as a cosmological understanding in the seventeenth century both allowed for and was pressured by the epistemic transformation that reorganized empirical knowledge and redefined its place in human understanding over the next century. For a recent description of this see Michel Foucault, *The Order of Things: An Archeology of the Human Sciences* (New York: Vintage Books, 1973). While Foucault focuses specifically on the invention of the "human sciences," earlier writers had glimpsed something not unlike the shift he identifies in other areas. See, for example, E. A. Burtt, *The Metaphysical Foundations of Modern Science: A Historical and Critical Essay* (New York: Doubleday, 1954). For a similar thesis in relation to religion and poetry, Basil Willey, *The Seventeenth-Century Background: Studies in the Thought of the Age in Relation to Poetry and Religion* (Garden City, N. Y.: Doubleday, 1953). For a fascinating and ambitious contribution to understanding these shifts in seventeenth-century knowledges in England, see Barbara Shapiro, *Probability and Certainty in Seventeenth-Century England: A Study of the Relationships between Natural Science, Religion, History, Law, and Literature* (Princeton: Princeton University Press, 1983).

3. For an account of Locke's relation to this controversy, see Philip Abrams's introductory essay to John Locke, *Two Tracts on Government,* ed. Philip Abrams (Cambridge: Cambridge University Press, 1967). Abrams's edition also contains an appendix that provides a fine bibliography of the major primary source materials through

As the seventeenth century wore on, the grip of earlier, more speculative Scholastic disputes on English intellectuals loosened in the face of emphatically worldly concerns. For a nation whose citizens were increasingly politicized over the relationship between their religious beliefs and their commitments in this world, one of the issues that pressed insistently to the fore was that of the moral meaning of action and experience in common life and, more particularly still, in political practice. By midcentury revolution and regicide, as well as the persistent question of religious liberty, provided ample grist for the mills of controversy and polemic. More subtly but no less surely, such long-term factors as agricultural improvement, the development of national and international markets, the extension of a money economy, and the uneven emergence of wage labor pressed hard against customary understandings of property rights and political power as well as such traditional elements of Christian morality as the duty of charity and the prohibition of usury. Yet the taken-for-grantedness of God's design, the persistence of belief in his promise of salvation, and the certainty of his final judgment often operated to center such disputes both implicitly and explicitly, depending on the matter at hand, on the issue of what was commanded, what permitted, and what prohibited by God's rule. At issue, too, at the root of such discussion, was the larger question of how such things might be known.

Further, for most seventeenth-century thinkers this welter of change and controversy could not be neatly separated into such distinct domains as religion, politics, economy, and society. For the many who retained even its loose imagery, the metaphor of God's

---

which this controversy found voice. A contemporary analogy might be helpful in clarifying the claim that the validity of such categories could be faithfully upheld even as the question of their placement in the world became more hotly debated. American participants in current controversies over welfare reform or health care, for instance, appear to concur that the social world is a world of causes and effects, but in the context of particular issues—like drug addiction, poverty, welfare dependency, urban violence, and the like—they are by no means agreed as to which social phenomena properly belong in which category. Not unlike the categories that flowed from the image of God's agency and design in seventeenth-century England, the categories of cause and effect continue to structure political debate. The power of theistic imagery in the earlier period is in this respect similar to the power of the notions of cause and effect today. Both are presumed to structure the reality of the world, and the problem of determining their boundaries in the quotidian world of appearance and experience is the very stuff of political contestation.

architecture permitted no such organization of knowledge apart from questions of morality and salvation. True, earlier in the century Bacon had argued for the liberation of natural philosophy from the hold of theological systems, but the fruit of his labor was a long time ripening. And if it was hard in the seventeenth century to carve out an autonomous realm of physical nature from the body of faith, it was more difficult still to do so in discussions of human society. But however compelling the metaphor of God's architecture in its emphasis on the moral stakes of human action, it was nonetheless permissive in the range and variety of conceptual constructs in light of which such morality might be defined and interpreted. It was an image whose organizing assumptions retained much of their hold, but whose boundary disputes over the placement of its categories in the world of experience came to be more and more tendentious. Here, particularly with respect to questions of morality and conduct, the problem of the possible source, nature, purpose, and extent of moral knowledge roiled below the surface of controversy. At the same time, while the architectural metaphor may have functioned as one of the broadest frameworks organizing perceptions of the world in seventeenth-century England, it was certainly not the only one. With respect to the political realm in particular there was another, more recent and indigenous notion, less indebted to Scholastic artifice and articulated specifically as a retrospective account of centuries of English political practice: the idea of the Ancient Constitution.[4] Put forth as a rendering of political life as historically lived rather than as a cosmological image of God's design, it centered upon common usage, precedent, and tradition, on customary practice rather than theologically rooted metaphysical abstractions. Drawn from the practical and conceptual resources of the common law, assumed to be consistent with God's rule rather than defended as such, this notion included among its core categories the same juridical terms that had long provided a focus for English political contestation and debate: law, right, liberty, juridical equality, and property.

4. See J. G. A. Pocock's classic study, *The Ancient Constitution and the Feudal Law: A Study of English Historical Thought in the Seventeenth Century*, 2d ed. (Cambridge: Cambridge University Press, 1987). For an interesting perspective on the antecedents of this view in medieval thought, see Walter Ullmann, *Principles of Government and Politics in the Middle Ages* (London: Metheun, 1961); and Walter Ullman, *History of Political Thought in the Middle Ages* (Hammondsworth: Penguin, 1965).

In terms of the immediate political conflicts of late Tudor and Stuart England, the moralism of the theistic metaphor and the prudential language of precedent and custom were by no means mutually exclusive; both could claim a purchase on English political understanding and allegiance. Indeed, in the face of the extreme Scripturalism of late-sixteenth-century Puritans, Richard Hooker's *Ecclesiastical Polity* can be seen as a masterful fusion of the two perspectives.[5] But the great Anglican intellectual synthesis of the claims of custom and the concern for salvation soon wore thin. As the tensions of the seventeenth century developed and sharpened, the fabric of that compromise was subject to increasing strain. In moral and religious terms it was rent by the assertive resurgence of sectarian Scripturalism, as well as by monarchical gestures toward Catholicism and the emergence of various strands of absolutist theory. The claims of custom and tradition, on the other hand, became increasingly ambiguous and controversial as both local communities and the nascent English state confronted not only the immediate challenge of dissenting sects, but the unfolding consequences of deeply rooted social and economic change.[6] By midcentury innumerable controversies over the scope, nature, and meaning of political power suc-

5. See F. J. Shirley, *Richard Hooker and Contemporary Political Ideas* (London: Society for Promoting Christian Knowledge, 1949).

6. For a general account of the period in Europe, see Theodore K. Rabb, *The Struggle for Stability in Early Modern Europe* (Oxford: Oxford University Press, 1975); for England in particular, see J. H. Plumb, *The Growth of Political Stability in England, 1660–1730* (London: Macmillan, 1967). Other more specific areas of interest and change are suggested in such works as P. G. M. Dickson, *The Financial Revolution in England: A Study in the Development of Public Credit, 1688–1756* (London: Macmillan, 1967); Christopher Hill, *Puritanism and Revolution: Studies in Interpretation of the English Revolution of the Seventeenth Century* (London: Secker and Warburg, 1958); Christopher Hill, *Society and Puritanism in Pre-Revolutionary England* (New York: Schocken Books, 1964); J. P. Kenyon, *The Stuart Constitution, 1603–1688: Documents and Commentary* (Cambridge: Cambridge University Press, 1966); William M. Lamont, *Godly Rule: Politics and Religion, 1603–60* (London: Macmillan, 1969); Michael Walzer, *Revolution of the Saints: A Study in the Origins of Radical Politics* (Cambridge: Harvard University Press, 1965); and J. R. Weston, *Monarchy and Revolution: The English State in the 1680s* (London: Blanford Press, 1972). The difficulties for a nation whose political understanding was largely formed by the common law are put trenchantly by Sir Charles Ogilvie, *The King's Government and the Common Law, 1471–1641* (Oxford: Basil Blackwell, 1958). By the close of that period, he argues, "the country had outgrown its ancient 'Constitution,' which had come to result in an inescapable series of deadlocks." (160). This outcome, for Ogilvie, was rooted in fundamental economic and social changes, particularly the emergence of new forms of property and new kinds of economic activities.

cessively converged on the problem of justifying political action, especially as this touched upon the power of Parliament, the prerogative of the monarch, and the duty of obedience. Whether articulated in terms of the Ancient Constitution or framed in the language of God's design, controversies between crown and parliament, between Puritan, Presbyter, and Anglican, and between merchant, lord, and freeholder all tended increasingly to betray the incapacity of existing constructs to coherently differentiate friend from foe or consistently legitimate particular courses of action rather than others. Royalist and revolutionary, mob and magistrate alike condensed, stretched, assimilated, and combined such languages to their own purposes, revealing the disruption of all in the face of new political tasks and alignments.[7]

From the perspective of the twentieth century, the situation might be characterized as a legitimation crisis, as the failure of existing ideological constructs to lend coherence to political experience and action.[8] Seventeenth-century adherents of these views, however, would have found such a description profoundly disturbing. Scripture was not simply belief or ideology but God's truth, just as the Ancient Constitution was an account of English liberties in historical fact. That such truths and facts could be marshaled to different purposes by conflicting parties indicated to contemporaries not the inco-

7. For two interesting examples of the disarray of political idioms earlier in the century, see Keith Wrightson, "Two Concepts of Order: Justices, Constables, and Jurymen in Seventeenth-Century England," and John Walter, "Grain Riots and Popular Attitudes to the Law: Malden and the Crisis of 1629," both in *An Ungovernable People: The English and Their Law in the Seventeenth and Eighteenth Centuries,* ed. John Brewer and John Styles (London: Hutchison and Co., 1980), 21–46 and 47–84. For the problem in the context of political ideology at midcentury, see Quentin Skinner, "History and Ideology in the English Revolution," *Historical Journal* 8, no. 2 (1965): 151–78; and Quentin Skinner, "The Ideological Context of Hobbes's Political Thought," *Historical Journal* 9, no. 3 (1966): 286–317. An insightful and challenging account of political rhetoric, publishing, and pamphleteering from the civil wars to the Restoration is provided by Elizabeth Skerpan, *The Rhetoric of Politics in the English Revolution, 1642–1660* (Columbia: University of Missouri Press, 1992). It is hardly surprising in such a context to find both Hobbes and Locke, among others, railing at the "abuse of language" and seeking, in their various ways, more settled patterns of linguistic usage.

8. See J. G. A. Pocock, *The Machiavellian Moment: Florentine Political Thought and the Atlantic Republican Tradition* (Princeton: Princeton University Press, 1975), esp. chaps. 9, 10, and 12, as well as Skinner's two articles cited in the previous note. A similar characterization of the confusion of political languages in the period can be found in Pocock's contextualization of James Harrington in his introduction to *The Political Works of James Harrington* (Cambridge: Cambridge University Press, 1977).

herence of their favored construct, but the insidious character and evil design of the opposition. Whether the accusation was framed as the subversion of traditional liberties, of civil authority, or indeed of God's design itself, the charge was the same: the distortion of truth for particular advantage. In recognition of this, the problem of political justification in the period would perhaps be better described as a crisis less of ideology narrowly conceived than of political understanding in the broadest sense.

As we descend from the heights of God's architecture to Locke's particular interventions in political argument in the period, we might best begin by attending closely to his own description of his enterprise. The preface to the reader of the *Treatises*, for instance, proffers the hope that they will be "*sufficient to establish the Throne of our Great Restorer, our present King William; to make good his Title, in the Consent of the People, which being the only one of all lawful Governments, he has more fully and clearly than any Prince in* Christendom: *And to justify to the World, the People of* England, *whose love of their Just and Natural Rights, with the Resolution to preserve them, saved the Nation, when it was on the very Brink of Slavery and Ruine.*"[9] Locke's condensation of available political languages here is worthy of note. William is accounted the "Restorer," presumably not simply of order but of traditional liberties and the English Constitution as well. The *Treatises* will establish his "Title" in the "Consent of the People," calling simultaneously on the idiom of popular sovereignty and the language of property to make clear his right to the throne. But further, the text will "justify to the World" the English people, who, on the grounds of their "Just and Natural Rights . . . saved the Nation" from "Slavery and Ruine." Here, I think, in addition to the obvious juridical resonances, the theological connotation of "justification" is intimated as well, along with its foundation in God's moral law. Locke's own prefatory account of his project thus draws upon a wide range of available associations to suggest the simultaneous creation of a new king and restoration of an old order, by the consent of a "People" whose acts in so doing are to be accounted justified—free from guilt or penalty of sin because within the bounds of righteousness.[10]

9. Locke, *Two Treatises,* preface, p. 171.
10. For an account of the languages circulating at the time of the *Treatises'* publication see Mark Goldie, "The Revolution of 1689 and the Structure of Political Argument," *Bulletin of Research in the Humanities* 83, no. 4 (Winter 1980): 473–564, as well

There is, however, good reason to see this project of justification as directed to a more determinate audience than "the World." The full text of the *Two Treatises of Government* was published only in English during Locke's lifetime, and his subsequent personal revisions saw print only in his native tongue.[11] The seemingly banal observation that his aim was to justify the English people to themselves may hence be more significant than it first appears. That the text could, for instance, serve the purposes of such justification to its author's satisfaction as well in 1689 as in the context of its original composition suggests that the political question he hoped to answer for his English audience was of greater moment than the particular circumstances of either the Exclusion Crisis or the Glorious Revolution. He seeks, after all, to justify not a particular *event*, but the deeds of a "*People*," and to do so in their own eyes he must address them in terms they could understand, terms adequate to but not delimited by the circumstances of the moment. This, in turn, suggests the possibility of a broader theoretical account of Locke's political project in the *Treatises* than many contextualist reconstructions of his thought typically encompass, but one that is nonetheless more locally nuanced than philosophical readings typically permit. In casuistic terms, to "justify" the actions of a "People" in late Stuart England was to offer its constituent members an account of how and why their deeds were consistent with the care of their souls. At the point of the *Treatises*' publication, it was to offer a characterization of the political realm that could reconcile England's recent political history with the moral imperatives of God's law.[12] In so doing, particularly given the equivocal character of extant political languages, Locke advanced a mode of political understanding capable of comprehending the contemporary diversity of antiabsolutist modes of argument under the broader construct of reasoned judgment and natural law. To

---

as the works by Skinner and Pocock cited above. With regard specifically to the problem presented by the *Treatises*' simultaneous imbrication within multiple "traditions" of political discourse and the context of its publication, I think no one has framed the dilemma so perspicuously as Gordon Schochet, "Radical Politics and Ashcraft's Treatise on Locke," *Journal of the History of Ideas* 50, no. 3 (1989): 491–510, esp. 508–10.

11. See Laslett's edition of Locke, *Two Treatises*, Appendix A, Checklist of Printings 1689–1960. One French edition (of the *Second Treatise* alone), a translation of the first English edition, was published in Amsterdam in 1691.

12. Indeed, that it found publication only in 1689 might suggest that, once resistance commenced, circumstances became adequate to its purposes.

put the point somewhat differently, Locke's political theory can be seen as offering an exemplar of political judgment. Consistent with his concern for individual moral conduct and accountability, it recalls his admonitions elsewhere that judgment and action must be carefully considered not only with regard to their worldly consequences, but with respect for the conscientious care of one's soul as well.

Locke's opening remarks in *Of the Conduct of the Understanding* might help clarify the point:

> The last resort a man has recourse to in the conduct of himself is his understanding; . . . [he] determines himself to this or that voluntary action upon some precedent knowledge, or appearance of knowledge, in the understanding. No man ever sets himself about any thing but upon some view or other which serves him for a reason for what he does: and whatsoever faculties he employs, the understanding, with such light as it has, well or ill informed, constantly leads; and by that light, true or false, all his operative powers are directed.[13]

The issue, as Locke argued in the *Essay*, was not whether the will was free or not, but rather the manner in which the will itself was subject to the understanding. To be "subject to" something, of course, is to be ruled by it, and the political resonances of Locke's language here are striking. He continues:

> The will itself, how absolute and uncontrollable soever it may be thought, never fails in its obedience to the dictates of the understanding. Temples have their sacred images, and we see what influence they have always had over a great part of mankind. But in truth the ideas and images in men's minds are the invisible powers that constantly govern them; and to these they all universally pay a ready submission. It is therefore of the highest concernment that great care should be taken of the understanding, to conduct it right in the search of knowledge and in the judgments it makes.[14]

13. John Locke, *Of the Conduct of the Understanding*, ed. Thomas Fowler, 2d ed., (1882; reprint, New York: Lenox Hill, 1971), sec. 1, p. 3.
14. Ibid. Compare Locke, *Essay*, 2.21, esp. 5–21, 51–62. Interestingly, this discussion begins with the question of power and culminates in a discussion of wrong judgment.

Indeed, it is this concern for the "images in men's minds" that underlies Locke's criticism in the *Treatises* of "the Pulpit" for having "publickly owned" Filmer's defense of patriarchal power and "made it the Currant Divinity of the Times." As "Teachers," the clergy "have so dangerously misled others" that Locke excuses his own attack on a long-dead adversary to show them "of what Authority this their Patriarch is, whom they have so blindly followed." This business of political understanding is of signal importance. "There cannot," he asserts, "be done a greater mischief to Prince and People, than the Propagating wrong notions concerning government."[15]

Still, it is far from sufficient simply to dismantle the intellectual edifice of patriarchalism. The critic concerned with the perceptions of a wide and heterogeneous public must offer something else in its place to inform political understanding and judgment. As Locke puts the issue in the opening of the *Second Treatise,* having dispensed with Filmer's system:

> He that will not give just occasion, to think that all Government in the World is the product only of Force and Violence, and that Men live together by no other Rules but that of Beasts, where the strongest carries it, and so lay a Foundation for perpetual Disorder and Mischief, Tumult, Sedition, and Rebellion, . . . must of necessity find out another rise of Government, another Original of Political Power, and another way of designing and knowing the Persons that have it, then what Sir *Robert F.* hath taught us.[16]

Locke announces his intent to provide this both by the title of the second essay, "Concerning the True Original, Extent, and End Of

15. These phrases are all from Locke, *Two Treatises,* preface.
16. Ibid., 2.1. Consider, too, the similar contention at 1.106: "The great Question which in all Ages has disturbed Mankind, and brought on them the greatest part of those Mischiefs which have ruined Cities, depopulated Countries, and disordered the Peace of the World, has been, Not whether there be Power in the World, nor whence it came, but who should have it. The settling of this point being of no smaller moment than the security of Princes, and the peace and Welfare of their Estates and Kingdoms, a Reformer of Politicks, one would think, should lay this sure and be very clear in it. For if this remains disputable, all the rest will be to very little purpose; and the skill used in dressing up Power with all the Splendor and Temptation Absoluteness can add to it, will serve only to give a greater edge to Man's Natural Ambition, which of it self is but too keen. What can this do but set Men on the more Eagerly to scramble, and so lay a sure and lasting Foundation of endless Contention and Disorder, instead of that Peace and Tranquility, which is the business of Government, and the end of Humane Society."

Civil Government," and by the opening phrase of its first substantive chapter, "To understand Political Power right."[17]

No inconsiderable amount of ink has been devoted to the question of the intentions informing the *Treatises,* and the lapse of time between the context of their composition and that of their publication adds further complexity to the problem. Without denying the significance of the sequence of events and circumstances surrounding the strange career of Locke's text, I think it possible to characterize a range of its effective meanings in broadly theoretical terms—in terms, that is, that exceed without suppressing the eventmental particularities of the period stretching from the Exclusion controversy to the revolution of 1688–89. Taken from the standpoint of our present as discrete historical phenomena, the Exclusion controversy, the subsequent conspiracies, and the Glorious Revolution indeed offer different casts of characters, different constellations of political forces and arguments, as well as different fates for many of those willing to countenance resistance to Stuart rule. Locke's varying intentions and involvements in these events quite legitimately make their connection to the *Treatises* a matter of historical concern. From the standpoint of political theory, however, there is a sense in which each of these moments involved their contemporaries in the same *sort* of problem that had divided significant segments of the English political nation numerous times before, indeed the same sort of problem that had incited the composition of Filmer's *Patriarchia* some fifty years earlier.

No less than the civil wars of 1642–49 and no less than the Parliamentary trial and execution of Charles I, the Exclusion Crisis of 1679–81 and the clandestine plottings of insurrection and assassination in 1682–83 provoked an acute question of conscientious judgment—a question generalized to the public as a whole by the revolutionary events of 1688–89. For those confronted with rival claims to rightful authority, with conflicting demands on their allegiance, the question was as simple as its answer was vexed: To whom was the duty of obedience owed? For such as might answer a call to arms, in whose defense should those arms be taken up? For those who acknowledged uneasiness over the relationship between their political commitments in this world and their fate in the next—and we have no

17. Title page of the *Second Treatise,* and 2.4, respectively.

reason to think their numbers insubstantial—these were matters of great moment, but they nonetheless presupposed an answer to a prior question. The moral question in this context was not simply which rival power had the better claim or title to obedience, nor was it only a question of whether armed resistance could be justified in the abstract, for such constructions imagine choosers unencumbered by previous commitments of loyalty and obedience. For those situated in the complex networks of obligations and allegiances, oaths and promises that constituted the bonds of English political sociability, however—and especially for the more scrupulous consciences among them—the moral question was whether one could be at liberty to conceive the situation as a matter of choice in the first place. And to this question, at both ends of the decade of the 1680s, the *Treatises* responded resolutely in the affirmative.

That affirmation, however, found its first occasion for public enunciation only in 1689, amidst the growing profusion of printed tracts debating the constitutional, philosophical, and moral grounds of obligation, particularly as these pertained to "the propriety, or impropriety, of transferring allegiance from James II to William III."[18] The modern bibliographer of this literature observes that Locke's *Treatises* are more abstract than all but one of these works, but like the genre as a whole his account of obligation joins the controversy sparked by an act of the Convention Parliament, in April of that year, requiring that oaths of allegiance to William III be sworn by all public officeholders, both local and national, civil and ecclesiastical. The observation is suggestive, not least of all because those affected had previously sworn oaths of allegiance to James II as their "lawful and rightful King." From the standpoint of the twentieth century, this may seem to many an unduly narrow occasion through which to locate any significant portion of the *Treatises'* meaning, but the moral stakes of that controversy suggest otherwise. Oaths taken to obey and defend James imposed obligations on the conscience, obligations which, if still binding, made the act of embracing William a sin. In effect, before one could swear allegiance to William, one had to be freed of those prior obligations of loyalty. Obeyed de facto William could be, but not, in the style of the period, "owned" as a "lawful and rightful King."[19] Unless, of course, one could be con-

18. Goldie, "Revolution of 1689," 476.
19. See J. P. Kenyon, *Revolution Principles: The Politics of Party, 1689–1720* (Cambridge: Cambridge University Press, 1977), chap. 3.

vinced, to an extent that would satisfy the qualms of conscience, that James II had so forfeited his claims to obedience as to leave one free to engage William as king by right.

Evidence from Locke's private papers and correspondence, indicating his attention to the issue both before and after the publication of the *Treatises,* might amplify the point. On 10 June 1689—slightly more than two months before that work was licensed for printing— Locke received a letter from his Quaker friend Benjamin Furly, who recounted two quite different conversations on the question, one with "a scrupulous Cambridge Schollar," the other with "one of our folk." The first, who "thought nothing 'Could discharge him of the oath of Allegiance that he had take to Ja:2 and his successors,'" Furly "had pleasant sport with . . . on R. Filmer's maggot." This the scholar soon abandoned, though he nonetheless insisted on retaining Filmer's conclusion. The second, beset by "the like scruple," Furly thought he had convinced otherwise, but not so: "He gravely told me I had more experience of these things than he, and had said much that he could not answer. But that I had not satisfied his reason." Summing up the two encounters, Furly's tone suggests consternation: "I see not," he confided, "that university learneing, nor inspiration, does make all that pretend to it wise, nor give them Common Sense."[20]

The "reason" that had to be satisfied in this context, however, was not the philosophical faculty of the eighteenth-century Enlightenment. That later reason was a bolder creature, given to more solidly secular abstractions, well insulated from the final judgments of a Protestant God and well removed from a care for the fate of one's soul. The reason of Furly's second interlocutor was woven of a different cloth, referenced to the more finite and particularized, indeed, individuated capacity that Locke called "the understanding." Pertinent to the individual judgment of a particular case, "interested" in one's moral standing in the eye of God, what this reason required was not simply a general account of the consensual basis of government. These existed already in abundance. It demanded something more specific: an account of the conditions under which

20. The letter appears in John Locke, *The Correspondence of John Locke,* ed. E. S. De Beer (Cambridge: Cambridge University Press, 1978), 3: 639. For Locke's own articulation of the significance of oaths see James Farr and Clayton Roberts, "John Locke on the Glorious Revolution: A Rediscovered Document," *Historical Journal* 28, no. 2 (1985): 385–98. For an account of the parliamentary debates over the dilemma, see Henry Horwitz, *Parliament, Policy, and Politics in the Reign of William III* (Manchester: Manchester University Press, 1977), chaps. 1 and 2.

one's consent to established magistracy might be voided—an account, that is, of the conditions under which previous avowals of obedience and allegiance to a monarch might be so "discharged" of their moral force as to free the conscience of obligation. The failure to satisfy these requirements carried consequences of great weight, for what was at stake was one's character as a moral agent, both in the eyes of one's fellows and in the judgment of a not always forgiving God.

Some months after receiving Furly's letter, probably between late autumn of 1689 and February 1690, Locke gestured forcefully to these consequences in papers sent to Edward Clarke. William's right to the throne, he observed, found its source in "the miscarriages of the former reigns," and only a "publique condemnation and abhorrence" of those misdeeds could "justifie" William's title and the public "maintenence of him" in that position. For those who would acknowledge no malfeasance on the part of the Stuart monarchy, "our complaints were mutiny and our redemption rebellion and we ought to return as fast we can to our old obedience."[21] In short, if obedience were James's due, to do otherwise than render it was to commit the sin of rebellion. In practical terms, to be sure, a nation extensively divided on this question was a nation on the brink of civil war. But morally speaking those divisions could not be parsed simply by appeal to preexistent social groupings, as if guided by modern pollsters skilled in the divining of behaviors habitual to those possessed of certain worldly interests or opinions. Such interests in Locke's theistic frame were matters of convenience, matters of choice only insofar as they were consistent with the law of virtue. As a consequence, in moral terms the question of allegiance had to do with what the rule of virtue required or permitted, for only this could "justifie" to the scrupulous conscience what, in the absence of such justification, might otherwise be taken as a mortal sin.[22]

Much has been duly made of the radical character of the *Treatises'* use of natural law in its account of the beginnings and dissolutions of government. Much, too, has been said of Locke's practical capacities not only to accede to but to praise England's ancient liberties and constitutional arrangements.[23] And yet, if the dilemma of conscience

21. Farr and Roberts, "Locke on the Glorious Revolution," 396–97.

22. Locke addresses those of scrupulous conscience at the close of the preface to the *Treatises*, p. 173.

23. See Lois Schwoerer, "Locke, Lockean Ideas, and the Glorious Revolution," *Journal of the History of Ideas* 51, no. 4 (1990): 531–48; Martyn P. Thompson, "Signifi-

just noted can be supposed to hover off-stage from the *Treatises'* explicit arguments, this strange admixture of what we might now call radicalism and conservatism may not be so strange after all. Natural-law reasonings in this context might supply in explicit terms what ancient constitutionalist and historical contract arguments took as a matter of course—that is, the consistency of England's constitutional frame with God's design. In other words, it may be, as John Dunn has argued, that the "political doctrine" of the *Treatises* "was merely the dignifying of the legal order of the English polity," but perhaps this was because Locke sought not so much to recast commonly held opinions as to invest them—one might even say radically—with a moral rather than historical grounding.[24] This, in turn, might be sufficient to suggest the circumstances under which citizens could be understood to be discharged of the moral obligation of obedience to an established magistrate. To be at liberty in this regard, however, might open any number of possible courses of action, including the restoration, renewal, or renovation of the previous constitutional frame.[25] Locke's radical principles, in short, are by no means antithetical to the conservation of well-established legal and constitutional practices, nor do they necessarily signify a refusal of the historical idiom so widely circulated in his period. Indeed, as I shall suggest in the chapters to follow, they complement that idiom even as they presuppose those practices.

From this perspective—here recalling both Furly's lamentation about common sense in the question of obligation and Locke's recognition of potential slippage between redemption and rebellion in

---

cant Silences in Locke's *Two Treatises of Government:* Constitutional History, Contract, and Law," *Historical Journal* 31, no. 2 (1988): 275–94.

24. John Dunn, "The Politics of Locke in England and America," in *John Locke: Problems and Perspectives,* ed. John W. Yolton (Cambridge: Cambridge University Press, 1969), 56. But see also Martyn P. Thompson, "The Reception of Locke's *Two Treatises of Government,* 1690–1705," *Political Studies* 24, no. 2 (1976): 184–91; Charles D. Tarlton, "'The Rulers Now on Earth': Locke's *Two Treatises* and the Revolution of 1688," *Historical Journal* 28, no. 2 (1985): 279–98; and Richard Ashcraft, *Revolutionary Politics and Locke's "Two Treatises of Government"* (Princeton: Princeton University Press, 1986).

25. Without entering into the debate over which social groups Locke may have intended to address, the interpretation offered here suggests something of his strategy of argumentation nonetheless. An account of James II's forfeiture of obedience that could satisfy the consciences of those who, in his terminology, had given their "explicit consent" by sworn oaths of allegiance would necessarily be sufficient to satisfy those whose consent was merely "tacit." Similarly, to "justify" the extremity of action represented by armed resistance in such a case was necessarily to countenance lesser remedies as well.

public perceptions—we might read the *Treatises'* combined enunciation of a range of political languages as following Locke's own rec-
ommendation in his short essay "Of Study." There, in closing, he
reconsiders his earlier exclusion of history as a "useless part" of education. "On the other side," he says,

> I recommend it to one who hath well settled in his mind the principles
> of morality, and knows how to make a judgement of the actions of men,
> as one of the most useful studies he can apply himself to. There he shall
> see a picture of the world and the nature of mankind, and so learn to
> think of men as they are. There he shall see the rise of opinions and
> find from what slight and sometimes shameful occasions some of them
> have taken their rise, which yet afterwards have had great authority . . .
> and passed for sacred in the world, and borne all before them.[26]

A similar and more pointedly political emphasis on moral knowledge
as the necessary basis of both judgment and historical understanding
appears in *Some Thoughts concerning Education,* where Locke suggests
in order of significance the matters of study necessary for a "Gentleman" to be "serviceable to his Country." First, he must have "Knowledge of Vertue" based on the Bible, as well as a "System of Ethicks."
Thus grounded in morality, he is to be taught "the natural Rights of
Men, and the Original and Foundation of Society, and the Duties
resulting from thence." This latter study, Locke insists, "a Gentleman should not barely touch at, but constantly dwell upon and never
be done with." Finally, he should "study Our Law" and "the English
Constitution and Government, in the ancient Books of the Common
Law" as well as contemporary writers. With that in hand, he should
"read our History, and with it join in every King's Reign the Laws
then made." This, Locke suggests, "will give an insight into the reason for our Statutes, and show the true ground upon which they
came to be made, and what weight they ought to have."[27]

Framed in the terms of this curriculum, the *Treatises* can be understood as a contribution to the second tier of a political education.[28]

26. John Locke, "Of Study," in *The Educational Writings of John Locke,* ed. James
Axtell (Cambridge: Cambridge University Press, 1968), 422.

27. Ibid., 109–325. The passages quoted are from paragraphs 186 and 187.

28. For a similar observation, but addressed more specifically to Locke's amalgam
of constitutionalist, contract, and natural-law discourses, see Martyn P. Thompson,
"Significant Silences."

As such, with the notable exception of the repeated invocation of the moral prohibition of harm, they tend to presume rather than present the relevant "Knowledge of Vertue." Generally speaking, they also abjure more particular legal and historical considerations, except where these provide an instance or example of the more immediate dilemma of political judgment that Locke is concerned to resolve. In the *Treatises*, it is not simply reason, but more specifically, reasoned judgment in the individuated sense suggested by Furly's second interlocutor, that becomes the core of the mode of political understanding that underlies both the theoretical "original" of political power and the grounds for political action on the worldly terrain of the historically existent English state. In the former, as we shall see, in combination with natural law such judgment has foundational status for the emergence of civil law and power. In the latter, it appears as the corrective, rather than the corrosive, of custom—as the faculty through which the traditional criteria of justice and common equity are marshaled to accommodate the demands of a changing world. In both cases, the broad criteria of virtue and convenience that we have explored in Locke's cosmological frame continue to structure his political vocabulary of law, right, liberty, equality, and property, as well as his account of reasoned judgment in the political realm more generally. In both cases those criteria can be understood not only to subtend the privilege Locke accorded to the consensual basis of government, but to suggest the limits of that consent as well.

3

Crime and Punishment:
Natural Politics and the
Epistemology of Right

> Let every soul be subject to the higher powers. For there is
> no power but of God: the powers that be are ordained of
> God. Whosoever therefore resisteth the powers resisteth
> the ordinance of God. And they that resisteth shall receive
> to themselves damnation.
>
> —Romans 13: 1–2

To a modern reader the political language of the *Two Treatises* carries an almost intuitive air of familiarity. Government by consent, equality, rights, liberty, property, the rule of law—these notions have, over the past three hundred years, become the legal tender of liberal political discourse and practice. The notion of rights in particular is so pervasive that it could well be said to constitute the core of liberal political understanding. Given the complex internal connections between these concepts and their embeddedness in Locke's theistic cosmology, however, it is difficult to view his political writings as simply a defense of rights narrowly conceived. And constitutionalist though Locke may well have been, his theoretical concerns appear far broader than any legal or constitutional interpretation of his work might suggest.[1] To say this is to deny neither the

1. Compare, for example, Sterling Lamprecht, *The Moral and Political Philosophy of John Locke* (New York: Columbia University Press, 1918); John Gough, *John Locke's Political Philosophy, Eight Studies*, 2d ed. (Oxford: Clarendon Press, 1973); and the more critical views of Martin Seliger, *The Liberal Politics of John Locke* (New York: Frederick Praeger, 1969); or Willmoore Kendall, *John Locke and the Doctrine of Majority Rule* (Urbana: University of Illinois Press, 1941).

significance of rights nor the importance of institutions and consent in Locke's thinking. Rather, it is to insist that such themes are but parts of a more comprehensive theoretical project, the focus of which, bluntly stated in the *Second Treatise,* was "to understand Political Power right."[2]

To "understand" such power in a nation rocked by controversies as varied in scope and content as those of seventeenth-century England was a tall order. Yet the persistent framing of fundamental political questions around the powers of magistracy and the duty of obedience served if not to clarify at least to simplify the focus of the task. In this context, it is curious that the political bearing of Locke's theism and of his faith in the promise of redemption has so little engaged the attention of recent scholars. Indeed, most modern interpreters of Locke's political theory tend to write as though he took up his pen in a situation every bit as secular as our own.[3] As we have seen, however, the central terms of his political vocabulary are semiotically indebted to a theistic framework that lends moral resonance to even the more worldly of his writings. That this is the case should hardly be surprising, for the world of practical politics was no less fraught with theistic drama than the languages in which they were articulated. Not only were the religious controversies of the Civil War and the rule of the Saints still within living memory, but questions of policy regarding religious nonconformity and dissent had not abated since the Restoration. Similarly, it might bear remembering that the Parliamentary catalogue of grievances against James II opened by taking aim at his "endeavor to subvert and extirpate the Protestant Religion, and the Lawes and Liberties of this Kingdome."[4]

2. John Locke, *Two Treatises of Government,* ed. Peter Laslett, rev. ed. (1960; reprint, with amendments, Cambridge: Cambridge University Press, 1963), by book and paragraph, 2.4. Hereafter cited as *Two Treatises.*

3. John Dunn and James Tully, again, are notable exceptions, but more recent work by Gordon Schochet and John Marshall suggests this tendency may be on the wane. In addition to Marshall, "John Locke's Religious, Educational, and Moral Thought," *Historical Journal* 33, no. 4 (1990): 993–1001; see Schochet, "Toleration, Revolution, and Judgment in the Development of Locke's Political Thought," *Political Science* 40, no. 1 (1988): 84–96.

4. "An Acte for Declareing the Rights and Liberties of the Subject and Setleing the Succession of the Crowne," 1688, *Statutes of the Realm,* 1 W. & M. 2, c. 2. Widely available in modernized variants, the document is printed as Appendix I to Lois Schwoerer's excellent study, *The Declaration of Rights, 1689* (Baltimore: Johns Hopkins University Press, 1981).

For Locke, as for many of his contemporaries, worldly actions remained inextricably bound up with the question of one's final fate, and one's greatest duty remained the care of one's soul. That Locke excluded worldly power from most matters of religious doctrine in his various essays on toleration did not mean that action in the political world had no moral connotations, nor did it mean that moral actions had no theological significance.

Locke's account of the relationship between politics and moral duty bore little resemblance, however, either to the vocal Scripturalism of the contemporary pulpit or to the admonitions of the Apostles. One might well imagine him confronting the threat of damnation for resisters with a subtle reading of yet another Pauline injunction: "Render therefore to all their dues: Tribute to whom tribute *is due;* custom to whom custom; fear to whom fear; honour to whom honour." The political problem, he might note (in his insistently juridical way), lay not in the rendering, but in the determining—of what was due, to whom, under what circumstances, and with what sanctions for not so rendering.[5] Even the *Second Treatise* invokes the moral culpability of the wrong rendering epitomized by political rebellion, but its emphasis upon the equality of all before the law of

---

5. Rom. 13.7 AV. To imagine this is not entirely to depart from Locke's texts, for a similar possibility is suggested by his *A Paraphrase and Notes on the Epistles of St. Paul to the Galatians, Corinthians, Romans, Ephesians. To Which Is Prefixed an Essay for the Understanding of St. Paul's Epistles by Consulting St. Paul Himself*, in *Works* (1823, reprint Scientia Verlag Aarlen: 1963), 8: 247–345. In place, for instance, of the "damnation" promised resisters by the King James translation, Locke's paraphrase suggests that those who resist "will be punished by those powers that they resist" (p. 368). Locke's note 1b on Rom. 13. 1–7, especially on the matters of "higher powers" and rendering what is due, refuses Christianity any special privilege with regard to judgments of what is fit to be rendered, but leaves open to citizens the possibility of so judging in particular times and places: "Whether we take 'powers,' here, in the abstract, for political authority or in the concrete, for the persons *de facto* exercising political power and jurisdiction, the sense will be the same, viz. That Christians, by virtue of being Christians, are not any way exempt from obedience to the civil magistrates, nor ought by any means to resist them, though by what is said, ver. 3, it seems that St. Paul meant here *magistrates having and exercising a lawful power. But whether the magistrates in being were or were not such, and consequently were or were not to be obeyed, that Christianity gave them no peculiar power to examine. They had the common right of others, their fellow-citizens, but had no distinct privilege as Christians. And, therefore, we see, ver. 7, where he enjoins the paying of tribute and custom, &c, it is in these words: 'Render to all their dues, tribute to whom tribute is due, honour to whom honour,' &c. But who it was, to whom any of these, or any other dues, of right belonged, he decides not, for that he leaves them to be determined by the laws and constitutions of their country*" (my emphasis, pp. 367–68).

virtue generates a definition of rebellion in terms quite different from simple resistance to the powers that be. Indeed, the whole point of the closing chapter's labored exposition on the dissolution of government was to show that rebellion properly understood was forceful opposition not simply to official persons, but to the authority of the laws and the constitution itself.[6] "This I am sure," Locke insists, "whoever, either Ruler or Subject, by force goes about to invade the Rights of either Prince or People, and lays the foundation for *overturning* the Constitution and Frame of *any Just Government,* is guilty of the greatest Crime . . . a Man is capable of. . . . And he who does it, is justly to be esteemed the common Enemy and Pest of Mankind; and is to be treated accordingly."[7] The "appeal to Heaven" that such action represents is no small matter. Anyone who undertakes it "must be sure he has Right on his side; and a Right too that is worth the Trouble and Cost of the Appeal, as he will answer at a Tribunal, that cannot be deceived, and will be sure to retribute to every one according to the Mischiefs he hath created to his Fellow-Subjects; that is, any part of Mankind."[8] But what was lawful authority? How was "the Constitution and Frame of a Just Government" to be discerned? In the face of such high stakes, how might one "be sure he has Right on his side?"

It is these sorts of questions that Locke's *Second Treatise* addresses, I would suggest, and it addresses them in significant part by drawing upon the English juridical idiom of crime and punishment to analogize the removal of an erring king to just retribution against a common criminal. In thus justifying the actions of the English people, however, the *Treatises* offer more than a rhetorical salve to the uneasy conscience, for the historical mode of understanding, characterized by reference to the facts of English history, was incapable of grounding such judgments. However the historical record might chronicle the tendencies of oppressed peoples "to ease themselves of a burden that sits heavy upon them,"[9] history alone could never invest such action with moral rectitude. If, as J. H. Hexter argues, the fundamental political controversy of the time lay in the opposition between "liberty and the rule of law on the one hand and lawless

6. Locke, *Two Treatises,* 2.226. See also the continuation of this point in 2.227.
7. Ibid., 2.230. See also 2.11, 181, 182.
8. Ibid., 2.176.
9. Ibid., 2.224.

rule, and despotism or tyranny on the other,"[10] this conventional polarity finds Lockean expression in the parallel distinction between lawful action and criminality. Through this distinction, the *Second Treatise* provided an exemplar of political judgment and understanding, independent of Scripture, that was both consistent with common notions of right and answerable to the moral imperatives of a higher law. Bridging the abstract moralism of natural law and the customary claims of the practice of rights, this understanding relied neither upon the complex systems of continental natural-law theorists nor upon the contestable terrain of the Ancient Constitution, however frequently or clearly it deployed elements of each. Rather, it took its roots in the ubiquity of the culture of law itself, and more particularly in the distinctive moral status conventionally attached to judgments of law and right, particularly in the context of crime and punishment.[11]

In condensing this broadly popular understanding on the dual question of the limits of obedience and the origin, extent, and purpose of political power, the political realm of the *Second Treatise* is figured as both a juridical and a moral category. To this end, it begins with a representation of natural politics in the created condition of the species, in a world within which the complementarity of law and right ordained by God's design is realized in practice. This, as we have seen, is dependent upon knowledge of the moral law, but Locke can be understood as approaching this dilemma less from the heights of a philosophical tradition than from a perspective of practical problems of judgment and action broadly familiar to his contemporary English audience. In so doing, he articulates what I shall

10. J. H. Hexter, *Reappraisals in History: New Visions of History and Society in Early Modern Europe*, 2d ed. (Chicago: University of Chicago Press, 1979), 216.

11. For a discussion of the cultural interface between local juridical practice and the legal profession in the period, see Alan Macfarlane and Sarah Harrison, *The Justice and the Mare's Ale: Law and Disorder in Seventeenth-Century England* (New York: Cambridge University Press, 1981), esp. 197. Similarly, by the time of the Stuarts, popular understanding of the common law saw its most significant political function as the protection of the subject from arbitrary rule, as W. J. Jones argues in his *Politics and the Bench: The Judges and the Origins of the English Civil War* (London: Allen and Unwin, 1971). For a brief general overview of the point, see James Sharpe, "The People and the Law," in *Popular Culture in Seventeenth-Century England*, ed. Barry Reay (New York: St. Martin's Press, 1985), 244–70. I borrow the the concept of the phrase culture of law from Howard Nenner, *By Colour of Law: Legal Culture and Constitutional Politics in England, 1660–1689* (Chicago: University of Chicago Press, 1977).

call an epistemology of right, an account of moral knowing that takes sensation, experience, and reflection as sufficient to discern the fundamental imperatives of natural law and suggests the possibility of moral certainty in the recognition and just punishment of crime and injury. Locke's initial rendition of the state of nature, in other words, provides a vision of the conditions and criteria of judgment appropriate to the exercise of political power in the morally marked world of God's design.

I   Political Power and the Problem of Convenience

Although the juridical character of Lockean politics is hardly disputed, little attention has been directed to the centrality of crime and punishment for Locke's various representations of political power. From the earliest tracts on the civil magistrate, through the letters on toleration, the *Treatises,* and the *Essay on Human Understanding,* to *The Reasonableness of Christianity,* that power is principally identified with the operation of retributive justice—with the use of worldly force to punish the breach of law. "We may take it as settled," Locke suggests in the *Tracts* of 1660, "that that institution may be called 'magistrate' which can, of its own right, impose laws on subjects and sanction them, whether it be an assembly—as some desire—or a monarch."[12] Here, as in the *Second Treatise,* attention is drawn to the independence of political power as such from the particular institutional forms through which it may be exercised.[13] The fundamental character of this power lies in its right to impose laws and sanction them, a right characterized later as a "public right" which can in no way be diminished or "prejudiced" by the "ill will of an individual inferior."[14] This juridical conception of civil power finds its most refined expression in the *Second Treatise,* where Locke

12. John Locke, *Two Tracts on Government,* ed. Philip Abrams (Cambridge: Cambridge University Press, 1967), Latin Tract (trans.), 213. Hereafter cited as *Tracts.*

13. Compare, Locke, *Two Treatises,* 2.132, and esp. 2.133, where Locke asserts, "By *Commonwealth,* I must be understood all along to mean not a Democracy, or any Form of Government, but *any Independent Community.*"

14. Locke, *Tracts,* Latin Tract (trans.), 237. Locke here excludes both private grudges and the promptings of individual conscience from resistance. Abrams argues, I think persuasively, that this claim is continuous in Locke's later arguments for toleration, though I take the *Two Treatises* to present a more complex case. See Abrams' introductory essay to Locke, *Tracts,* 98–107.

both elaborates upon its content and gives greater specificity to its proper ends. Political power, as he defines it there, is *"a Right* of making Laws with Penalties of Death, and consequently all less Penalties, for the Regulating and Preserving of Property, and of employing the force of the Community, in the Execution of such Laws, and in the defence of the Commonwealth from Foreign Injury, and all this only for the Publick Good."[15]

The unique characteristic of political power lies in the right of its bearers to determine the lawfulness of actions and to punish transgressions with death. It is this, in conjunction with its peculiar end (the public good) and its distinct charge (to regulate and preserve property as well as defend against and punish injury), that distinguishes the political relation between magistrate and citizen from the variety of other power relations that Locke recognized as operative in society.[16] The *Treatises* represent this power, however, not only as a matter of institutional competence, but as a natural attribute of the human species. *"Political Power,"* Locke observes, "is that Power . . . which every Man has *in the State of Nature* . . . to use such means for the preserving of his own Property, as he thinks good, and Nature allows him; and to punish the Breach of the Law of Nature in others so, as . . . may most conduce to the preservation of himself, and the rest of Mankind."[17] The essential character of political power is thus both intimately related to property and identical in purpose whether wielded by individuals in the state of nature or by governments in civil society. That some, or even most, individuals relinquish their rights to exercise such a power changes neither its nature nor its proper aim. As Locke puts it, "The end and measure of this Power, when in every Man's hands in the State of Nature, being the preservation of all his Society, that is all Mankind in general, it can have no other end or measure, when in the hands of the Magistrate, but to preserve the Members of that Society in their Lives, Liberties, and

---

15. Locke, *Two Treatises*, 2.3. Abrams, in Locke, *Tracts*, 103, comments on Locke's conspicuous neglect of the ends of political power in the *Tracts*.

16. Other power relations for Locke include those specific to "a *Father* over his Children, a *Master* over his Servant, a *Husband* over his Wife, and a *Lord* over his Slave." Locke, *Two Treatises*, 2.2. For elaborations of paternal/parental power, see esp. 2.52, 58, 59, 63–66; of master/servant relations, 2.85; of conjugal power, 2.80–82; and of slavery, chap. 4 entire.

17. Ibid., 2.171. See also 2.87, where these are referred to as "Rights and Privileges" which human agents "hath by Nature."

Possessions."[18] In sum, political power appears here as a particular
sort of right with respect to two quite specific referents and activities.
On the one hand, it is exercised in the preservation of property, in
the broad sense of life, liberty, and worldly goods. On the other, it is
expressed in the punishment, with death if necessary, of any who
violate the law.[19]

In terms of earlier theories of natural law, as Otto von Gierke
suggested long ago, the naturalness of this power was not original to
Locke.[20] In this context, however, the assertion of the strangeness of
executive right might best be seen as directed to a public untutored

18. Ibid. See also Locke's discussion of "civil interests" in *A Letter concerning Tolera-*
tion, ed. James Tully (Indianapolis, Ind.: Hackett Publishing Co., 1983), 28, 47–48.
The issue is also discussed in James Tully, *An Approach to Political Philosophy; Locke in*
Contexts (Cambridge: Cambridge University Press, 1993), 18–20.

19. Hence Locke, *Two Treatises*, 2.3, formally defines political power as "*a Right* of
making Laws with Penalties of Death, and consequently all less Penalties, for the Regulating and Preserving of Property, and of employing the force of the Community, in
the Execution of such Laws, and in the defence of the Common-wealth from Foreign
Injury, and all this only for the Publick Good." There are, as we shall see, significant
differences between this power understood as a natural attribute of individuals and as
an "instituted relation" between governors and governed in civil society. The latter
devolves from "some act, whereby any one comes by a Moral Right, Power, or Obligation to do something. . . . All this sort [of relation] depending upon Men's Wills, or
Agreement in Society, I call *Instituted*, or *Voluntary*; and may be distinguished from the
natural in that they are most, if not all of them, some way or other alterable, and
separable from the Persons, to whom they have sometimes belonged, though neither
of the Substances, so related, be destroy'd." John Locke, *Essay concerning Human Un-*
derstanding, ed. Peter H. Nidditch (Oxford: Clarendon Press, 1975), by book, chapter,
and paragraph, 2.28.3. Hereafter cited as *Essay*. Here, consistent with Locke's presentation in the *Treatises*, the political relation between magistrate and citizens is independent of particular rulers or formal institutions. The latter, as he suggests in the *Trea-*
tises, are historically alterable by human action on the grounds of experience (see, for
instance, Locke, *Two Treatises*, 2.107). In the *Treatises* the differences between natural
and instituted political power are fairly easily summarized. Most obviously, in the
natural state, although equally invested with the power of punishment, individual
possessors of political power do not make law but "reason to" or "discover" it. Further, natural individuals have rights only over such property as is properly their own,
and cannot in any way regulate, determine, or otherwise set rules for the manner in
which others choose to use or dispose of what is theirs. Such differences are important, and they raise significant questions for what it means for Locke to have attempted to translate the political power attributed to individuals in the state of nature
into civil power in a social condition. Elements of this conundrum will be dealt with in
a later chapter; for now we will limit our discussion to what it might have meant for
Locke to refer to this power as a right, particularly one proper to human agents by
nature.

20. Otto von Gierke, *Natural Law and the Theory of Society, 1500–1800*, trans. Ernest
Barker (Boston: Beacon Press, 1960), chap. 2, sec. 1, no. 16, esp. 98–100 and nn.

in the multiple and complex intellectual traditions of natural law, but quite familiar with such a power as the signal characteristic of political rule.[21] What was bizarre about it, as Locke readily acknowledged, was not what it was, but how problematic its egalitarian distribution could become where each was judge in their own case.[22] In admitting the validity of this objection, however, Locke turns its point to a different purpose, inviting his readers to consider its more telling challenge to the claims of absolutist theory, where the ruler, equally subject to the frailties of human judgment, "has the Liberty to be Judge in his own Case, and may do to all his Subjects whatever he pleases, without the least liberty to any one to question or controle those who Execute his Pleasure."[23] In this formulation the question of royal accountability is raised in no uncertain terms, but the notion that the actions of magistrates were themselves subject to a

21. For a recent discussion of such traditions see Deborah Baumgold, "Pacifying Politics: Resistance, Violence, and Accountability in Seventeenth-Century Contract Theory," *Political Theory* 21, no. 1 (1993): 6–27. By untutored here I mean not ignorant but unschooled. The political literature of the period from the Exclusion Crisis onward abounded in references to and discussions of such authorities, and one could hardly say that the reading public or political nation was unfamiliar with a variety of such positions. My point here is not that Locke's audience was unaware of what we now style as "traditions of discourse," or that they had no cognizance of the writers and texts that served as authorities within them. Rather, I am suggesting that in Locke's work the problem of judging between conflicting authorities—or, as was often the case, the same authorities marshaled to conflicting purposes—is displaced. Without denying that the *Treatises* can be read as participating in one or more of those traditions, I take them nonetheless as an attempt to stabilize the juridical idiom common to these various perspectives by drawing upon a different sort of familiarity, that is, the familiarity and experience of indigenous practices of law and right in and around the common law.

22. Locke, *Two Treatises*, 2.13. Indeed, in the seventeenth century it was the self-appointed assumption and periodic exercise of this power by English mobs, particularly in anti-improvement disturbances and food riots, that incited state repression and punishment for treason. Where such mobs restricted their activities within the bounds of traditional understandings of political right, acting simply to "remind" governors of their traditional duties, state action tended more to attempt to redress their grievances. See Buchanan Sharp, "Popular Protest in Seventeenth-Century England," in *Popular Culture in Seventeenth-Century England,* ed. Barry Reay (New York: St. Martin's Press, 1985), 271–308. I should note here that Tully, too, suggests that Locke's executive right plausibly describes elements of English historical practice, but he believes it to approximate the accusatory system generally displaced by the legal revolution of the twelfth century, but still persistent in some aspects of seventeenth-century common law practice. See Tully, *An Approach to Political Philosophy,* 21–23, 28, 35. This is a question that well deserves further investigation.

23. Locke, *Two Treatises*, 2.13.

higher law was hardly news to Locke's audience. Customary law itself found its ultimate validation not solely in its immemorial status,
but in the weight this lent the presumption that it was a manifestation of the Law of God.[24] Similarly, English judges themselves could
be considered bound to administer the law in conformity with principles of morality, justice, and common equity.[25] In emphasizing the
naturalness of this power of punishment, Locke thus reinforces a
common view of the boundedness of political power by the imperatives of moral order. If, however, one rejects the notion of passive
obedience, if one wishes to render the magistrate subject to worldly
sanctions, the crucial political question then becomes how to distinguish between the just and unjust exercise of such power. Locke is
quite explicit about this in the *Second Treatise*, notably in the suggestion that it is precisely the "inconveniences" of the "irregular and
uncertain exercise of the Power every Man has of punishing the
transgressions of others" that motivate the creation of political soci-

24. See, for instance, the assertion of a "serjeant at the Law of England" cited in Sir
Charles Ogilvie, *The King's Government and Common Law, 1471–1641* (Oxford: Basil
Blackwell, 1958), 119. Hooker's argument that the law of nature is evidenced in the
consent of men by customary practice is also relevant, as is Locke's contention in the
Essay that while such customs cannot demonstrate the conformity of a practice with
natural law, they yet can be evidence of their consistency with it. See esp. Locke, *Essay*,
2.28.11, and the notation Locke adds there in the fourth edition.

25. As the issue was put by the Common Lawyer and Judge John Cook in a Letter
to the Lord Deputy of Ireland in August 1655: "If the Honest man have not speedie
Justice, it is the judge's fault, he must Answer it at the Great day of Judgement,
however he may Pleade Custom in these Inferior Judicatures, and his old Plea (that
he would help him as a Private man, but cannot do it as a Judge) will be ridiculous at
the Last Day. For a Judge ought to have a conscience as any Private man, and he
ought to rectify Erroneous Consciences in a Court of Equity." Ogilvie, *King's Government*, 121. This dilemma was voiced in the context of a debate over the role of conscience in judicial decisions. If common law were a reliable guide to God's moral law,
it would be sufficient to determine the justice of cases without the intervention of the
judge's conscience. If its reliability were less than certain, then the operation of conscience might be essential to the rendering of just decisions. While Ogilvie's book casts
such controversies as questions of institutional jurisdiction between Courts of Law and
Courts of Equity, in common practice public understandings of legal judgment were
both muddier and more flexible than rival lawyerly constructions of the issue. See, for
example, Keith Wrightson, "Two Concepts of Order: Justices, Constables, and Jurymen in Seventeenth-Century England," in *An Ungovernable People: The English and
Their Law in the Seventeenth and Eighteenth Centuries*, ed. John Brewer and John Styles
(London: Hutchison and Co., 1980), 21–46. Wrightson argues that the looseness of
local practice and understanding over the century diminished in the face of more
routinized or rule-governed, and to this extent less "equitable," understandings that
accompanied the increasing centralization of state power.

eties in the first place.[26] But to understand the significance of this problem for Locke's political theory and, in particular, to grasp its bearing on his construction of political judgment in general, it will be helpful to return briefly to the architecture of order.

In my account of that architecture I argued that "natural right" denoted a liberty of action, bounded by and complementary to natural law, proper to human agents within the morally marked world of God's design. One of the essential features of Locke's description of natural humanity was the egalitarian distribution of both natural property rights and jurisdiction to judge and punish transgressions of the moral law. So conceived, the power of punishment functioned as the guarantor of moral order and accountability in the created condition: by enforcing the rule of virtue, it was the worldly mechanism that sustained Locke's individuation of the species into separate and autonomous moral agents. This interpretation raises a number of thorny questions for Locke's inclusion of political power as a natural right proper to the species in the original condition. Given the complementarity of law and right, virtue and convenience in that state, is it possible that the power of life and death entailed a judgment of "convenience?" If so, in what sense? Similarly, having noted Locke's parallel bifurcation of human knowledge into virtue and convenience, to what extent might this characterization of political right embody a particular understanding of specifically political knowledge and judgment? Finally, in light of the explicit connection between the exercise of such power and the preservation of property, what, if anything, might this linkage of punishment and convenience have to do with the structured moralism and theological underpinnings of Locke's initial representation of the human condition?

A crucial clue to these connections appears in the chapter on property in the *Second Treatise*. There, Locke's closing remarks on the meaning of property in the state of nature reiterate his earlier characterization of that state as one free of mutually destructive conflict and controversy. The peace of that condition is attributed specifically to the principles regulating the appropriation of property in the original condition:

> It is very easie to conceive without any difficulty, *how Labour could at first begin a title of Property* in the common things of Nature, and how the

26. Locke, *Two Treatises*, 2.127.

spending it upon our uses bounded it. So that there could then be no
reason of quarelling about Title, nor any doubt about the largeness of
Possession it gave. Right and conveniency went together; for as a Man
had a Right to all he could imploy his Labour upon, so he had no temptation to labour for more than he could make use of. This left no room
for Controversie about the Title, nor for Incroachment on the Right of
others; what Portion a Man carved to himself, was easily seen; and it
was useless as well as dishonest to carve himself too much, or to take
more than he needed.[27]

As a summary restatement of the chapter's elaborate narrative of the
origin of property, the passage seems unexceptional. Yet to the modern reader there is something both curious and obscure in the characterization of the natural state as one in which "Right and conveniency went together." That sense of curiosity might well become a
suspicion of contradiction when one recalls that by Locke's own account it is the "inconveniences" attending the exercise of natural
rights, especially the executive right of punishment, that necessitate
the creation of civil government.[28]

To note this, however, is not simply to raise again the question of
the ambiguous status of Locke's state of nature,[29] but to point to yet
another context in which that ambiguity appears—one to which our
ordinary understanding of modern English usage provides no immediate access. It is to identify a previously neglected plane of
meaning on which Locke articulated the character and tasks of the
political realm. This, it might be objected, is a large claim to hang
upon so small a phrase. Such an objection, however, seems hasty in
light of Locke's conceptual linkage of right and convenience in denominating a particular class of activities within God's architecture
of creation. In that context, as we have seen, the terms were con-

27. Ibid., 2.51.
28. Ibid., 2.13, 90, 127.
29. This is a staple of Locke scholarship. See, for instance, John Dunn, *The Political
Thought of John Locke: An Historical Account of the Argument of the "Two Treatises of Government"* (Cambridge: Cambridge University Press, 1969), 96–119; C. B. Macpherson,
The Political Theory of Possessive Individualism; Hobbes to Locke (Oxford: Oxford University Press, 1962), 238–47; Richard Ashcraft, "Locke's State of Nature: Historical Fact
or Moral Fiction," *American Political Science Review* 68, no. 3 (1968): 898–914; Hans
Aarsleff, "The State of Nature and the Nature of Man in Locke," in *John Locke: Problems and Perspectives,* ed. John W. Yolton (Cambridge: Cambridge University Press,
1969), 91–136.

nected in describing actions instrumental to the preservation or comfort of bodily life, particularly in the use of worldly things. An additional clue, as we have noted previously, appears in the sixth of his *Essays on the Laws of Nature*. There, in denying the "instinct" of self-preservation as a proper ground for moral obligation, Locke associates "convenience" with an individual's judgment of "what is useful to him" in terms of "private advantage" or "expediency."[30] So understood, "convenience" is linked to a form of judgment based upon a private consideration of worldly consequences and is contrasted with "duty," which pertains to actions commanded and prohibited by a formal and hierarchical structure of law.

These examples simply restate and reinforce what we have already discerned about Locke's usage of "convenience": that it is identified with the realm of right, with the due use of what is properly one's own, for the preservation of mortal life. "Conveniency," though, in the lexicon of the period, had more expansive meanings as well. Broadly speaking, it suggested the orderly operation or constitution of the elements of a system. Common to both these connotations was the idea of ordering the parts of a whole in a manner appropriate to its purpose or function. Thus as an aesthetic term in architecture "conveniency" suggested the balanced or harmonious disposition of a building's constituent structures. Similarly, in the case of an individual life, "conveniency" might imply not simply immediate utility or advantage, but the harmonious integration of one's activities into a life historically lived. In Locke's political writings the term not only is resonant with these meanings but is structured as well by its constant association with the idea of duty or virtue, understood as the conformity of particular actions with the requirements of law.[31] An analogous and more extensively elaborated vision of the relationship between virtue, duty, convenience, and law appears in Locke's early essays on the civil magistrate, where the terms are embedded in a discussion of the rightful power of rulers—a discussion that not only reiterates their conceptual relationship but situates that relationship in an explicitly and overtly political context. There again, "convenience" is linked to a form of judgment based on consequences and is contrasted with law as a criterion for determining the propriety of actions:

30. John Locke, *Essays on the Law of Nature*, ed. Wolfgang von Leyden (Oxford: Clarendon Press, 1954), Sixth Essay, 181. Hereafter cited as *ELN*.
31. Ibid., 181–83.

> Everyone in those things that fall under his choice ought well to balance
> the conveniencies and inconveniencies on both sides, and to be poised
> on that side on which the weightier consequences shall hang. . . . And
> thus the magistrate is to consider the consequences of those things
> which God hath left free before he determine them by his public de-
> crees, and the subject to consider the consequences of those things
> which the magistrate hath left free before he determine them by his
> private resolution; and would all men thus limit their motions within
> their own sphere they would not be so turbulent and troublesome.[32]

The pivotal phrase here is "in those things that fall under his
choice," for in both the English and Latin tracts this sphere of activities is defined and delimited by reference to a formally hierarchical
structure of law. Thus actions *properly* determined on the grounds of
convenience can only be those that are left free by the rule of law.
Strictly speaking, in other words, the criterion of convenience is appropriate only to a realm of action in which one is free of any obligation imposed by law. Once again, a judgment of convenience
presupposes an understanding of one's obligations, entailing a
knowledge of what the law requires and what it leaves free.

As is clear here, however, Locke distinguishes between various
levels of freedom and law, differentiating stepwise the liberties and
responsibilities proper to rulers and subjects in relation to various
tiers of law. In the Latin tract, these distinctions are put succinctly:
"All the things that are indifferent so far as a higher law is concerned are the object and matter of a lower, and the authority of the
individual prevails in all matters that are not wholly prescribed by
superior law."[33] In the *Treatises'* state of nature, of course, there is no
law but the law of nature, the "rules of virtue" that God has prescribed "betwixt man and man," and consequently "the authority of
the individual prevails" over all actions left free by natural law. In
that context, however, the ascription of social peace to the convergence of "right and conveniency," is a substantive claim: it points to
a condition in which the divinely ordained complementarity of law
and right, virtue and convenience, obtains in practice. Specifically, it
invokes a situation in which actions grounded upon individual determinations of convenience concur with or conform to the objective

32. Locke, *Two Tracts*, English Tract, 156.
33. Ibid., Latin Tract (trans.), 227.

structure of law and right that demarcates properly human activities in the architecture of created nature. It points, in other words, to a situation in which human agents realize God's design of social peace and harmony by correctly discerning and acting in accordance with the ordained boundary between law and right, virtue and convenience.

To be sure, this peaceful condition is superseded by one quite different, one sufficiently beset by controversy to require the establishment of civil government. But if, as I have argued, the due exercise of natural rights for Locke was dependent upon knowledge of natural law, this allusion to the convergence of right and conveniency is significant, for it imagines that the exercise of rights with respect to both property and the power of punishment at one point conformed to the law of nature. If Locke's account of the state of nature is a story of its corruption, it would seem important to grasp precisely what it is that gets corrupted as well as the specific processes by which this occurs. This, in turn, suggests a number of questions, especially in light of the characteristics of the species' natural condition noted in Part I. What is it, for instance, in Locke's presentation of the original state of nature that ensures the convergence of right and conveniency? Given his use of the past tense—convenience and the lawful exercise of rights "went together"—what was it that sundered the original complementarity of law and right? Finally, what bearing might this have on Locke's account of the relationship between property and political power? With these questions in mind, let us turn to a closer examination of the *Treatises'* original presentation of the state of nature, particularly as this suggests the relationship between judgments of right and knowledge of the moral law.

II   Political Understanding: Power and Judgment in the Natural Community

The *Treatises'* account of the "true Original, Extent, and End of Civil Government" embeds the exercise of political power firmly in a framework of divine purposes, but Locke's observation there that "God hath certainly appointed Government to restrain the partiality and violence of men"[34] raises an issue presented more fully in his

34. Locke, *Two Treatises*, 2.13.

third letter on toleration. Political power, he notes in the latter work, is ordained by God, but particular governments are instituted by individuals in a "corrupt state of nature." Finding themselves in such a state, they are "authorized and required by reason, the law of nature, to avoid the inconveniences of that state, and to that purpose put the power of governing them into some one or more men's hands, in such forms, and under such agreements as they should think fit."[35] What the narrative of the *Second Treatise* describes is how this power, whether in the state of nature or in civil society, is bounded in its proper exercise by the moral imperatives of natural law. Through this narrative, Locke's justification of the English people is grounded by evoking a common understanding of political judgment as appropriate to both the natural state and the civil condition. In this, the *Treatises* can be read as suggesting that the grounds and criteria of judgment necessary to discern and legitimately resist the exercise of unlawful power in a civil polity are in some sense equivalent or analogous to those appropriate to the recognition and punishment of criminality in the state of nature. Hence the task of recreating political order becomes significantly parallel to the initial creation of the legitimate polity in a corrupt state of nature.

This notion of a corrupt state of nature, of course, is an issue addressed by a number of modern interpreters of Locke's work. Leo Strauss, for example, finds in it Locke's subversion of traditional conceptions of moral duty. On that reading it is but a vehicle for resuscitating a sanitized version of Hobbes's political world in a form more palatable to the English public. C. B. Macpherson, too, speaks of Locke's systematic dismantling of the moral obligations of natural law as a strategic move, but on that account Locke's purpose is to constitute a political realm justified by the security it provides "possessive individuals" of the rising bourgeoisie in their quest for the unlimited acquisition of property. On both accounts, the peaceful state of nature represents little more than a shallow or devious use of traditional ethical views in the service of quite different ends. What these otherwise disparate interpretations neglect, however, is the depth and complexity of the relationship between Locke's politi-

35. John Locke, *Third Letter on Toleration,* in *The Works of John Locke in Ten Volumes* (1823; reprint, Scientia Verlag Aalen, 1963), 6:225.

cal and moral concerns. Intent upon demonstrating and criticizing the connections between his conception of politics and his defense of property, they effectively sidestep his theistic representation of the moral status of property or political power as appropriate to distinct sorts of activities proper to creatures capable of salvation and subject to a divine imperative of social peace. In focusing on the temporal mechanics, so to speak, of his account of property and political power, they effectively flatten his hierarchical conception of a morally marked world to a single, and singularly secular, plane. Having elaborated the indebtedness of Locke's account of the human condition to a structured architecture of divine design, we are now in a position to offer an alternative view. In particular, the perspective thus far attained suggests the necessity of reexamining Locke's state of nature both in its peaceful formulation and with an eye to the source and dynamic of its corruption, especially as this bears on his account of the relationship between property and political power. This, in turn, may cast new light not only upon the *Treatises'* account of the transition from the state of nature to civil society, but more generally upon the grounds and criteria of judgment they advance as appropriate to the exercise of political power in either condition.

With this in mind, let us return to Locke's allusion to the convergence of right and conveniency in the state of nature. Consider again the passage as a whole:

> It is very easie to conceive without any difficulty, *how Labour could at first begin a title of Property* in the common things of Nature, and how the spending it upon our uses bounded it. So that there could then be no reason of quarrelling about Title, nor any doubt about the largeness of Possession it gave. Right and conveniency went together; for as a Man had a Right to all he could imploy his Labour upon, so he had no temptation to labour for more than he could make use of. This left no room for Controversie about the Title, nor for Incroachment on the Right of others; what Portion a Man carved to himself, was easily seen; and it was useless as well as dishonest to carve himself too much, or take more than he needed.[36]

What is perhaps most striking here is the uncharacteristic tone of confident assurance and certainty that it projects onto human action and judgment in the natural state. There is no suggestion of moral

36. Locke, *Two Treatises*, 2.51.

pravity, no hint of equivocation, no intimation of ambiguity. There is "no reason for quarrelling," "nor any doubt" as to the extent of possession, "no temptation" to accumulate beyond what is necessary for one's own use, "no room for Controversie . . . nor for Incroachment on the Right of others." Human action in this context carries a presumption of obviousness, an explicit transparency: the justice of what one does is "easily seen." Human judgment is invested with a clarity and immediacy with respect to property that lends support to Locke's characterization of the natural condition as one of "Peace, Good Will, Mutual Assistance, and Preservation."[37] If, as I have suggested, Locke grounded the possibility of social peace on the designed complementarity of law and right, this suggestion of the convergence of right and conveniency marks the state of nature as a condition in which the human species actively expressed God's intentions in practice. It evokes, as I suggested earlier, a postlapsarian world in which the species, already subject to earthly finitude and the necessity of labor, evidenced a very human and mortal sort of innocence. Although distanced from the state of purity and perfect obedience that characterized Eden before the Fall, it yet reflects the integrity of Locke's "free intelligent agents" as creatures capable of ordering their affairs in accordance with the moral requirements of God's design.

On this reading, the issues of the content of natural law and the manner in which individuals come to know it become pivotal for engaging the political meanings set in motion by Locke's rendering of the state of nature, for he repeatedly insisted that human agents were created capable of regulating their behavior in conformity with this law as a God-given standard of right and wrong. Unlike Hobbes, for whom effective morality was necessarily conventional and hence no part of the natural condition, Locke represented that state as governed by a law of nature, discoverable to human reason, which "obliges every one" and "willeth the Peace and *Preservation*" of the species as a whole.[38] Indeed, as we have seen, in the morally marked

37. Ibid., 2.19.
38. Ibid., 2.6, 7. See also 2.12: "It is certain there is such a Law, and that too, as intelligible and plain to a rational Creature, and Studier of that Law, as the positive Laws of Common-wealths, nay possibly plainer; As much as Reason is easier to be understood than the Phansies and intricate Contrivances of Men, following contrary and hidden interests put into Words."

world of God's design, knowledge of this law is a necessary element of the appropriate exercise of rights. If, therefore, at some point right and conveniency went together, then this convergence itself attributes to the species, at least once, cognizance of the law that defined the bounds of their natural liberty.

The *Second Treatise,* I would suggest—despite the seemingly abstract or fictive character of its state of nature—approaches this problem of moral knowledge from the perspective of practical problems of judgment and action familiar to Locke's contemporary audience. Theirs was a world of visceral experience, one in which the administration of justice in the recognition and punishment of criminality was a broadly participatory social practice centered in the local community. In the seventeenth century the formal responsibility for prosecuting criminals devolved principally upon the local public itself, resting initially with the victim or the victim's kin and subsequently upon the grand jury or the coroner's jury, although by the eighteenth century this responsibility had gradually shifted to the magistracy. Particularly in felony cases, the participation of the local community in criminal prosecutions was regarded as a significant constitutional principle, supported by the idea that only they had the personal knowledge necessary to the rendering of justice.[39] In practice, however, local knowledge and experience played an even more important role. Strict adherence to the letter of the law could itself prove a source of social conflict in local communities, particularly where formally prescribed penalties were popularly perceived to be excessive. These difficulties were ameliorated locally by widespread practices of extralegal mediation and arbitration, often based on appeals to ideals of neighborhood and social harmony, that attempted to resolve disputes short of formal prosecution and punishment.[40]

39. These observations are drawn from H. H. Baker, "Criminal Courts and Procedure at Common Law, 1550–1800," in *Crime in England, 1550–1800*, ed. J. S. Cockburn (Princeton: Princeton University Press, 1977), 15–48. A direct connection between Locke and practices of informal arbitration is laid out by Henry Horwitz and James Oldham, "John Locke, Lord Mansfield, and Arbitration in the Eighteenth Century," *Historical Journal* 36, no. 1 (1993): 137–59. As a member of the Board of Trade, Locke was commissioned to devise a mode of informal arbitration for disputes between merchants, and drafted a bill to this end that was presented to the board in November 1696.

40. This discussion is based on M. J. Ingram, "Communities and Courts: Law and Disorder in Early-Seventeenth-Century Wiltshire," in *Crime in England, 1550–1800*, ed. J. S. Cockburn (Princeton: Princeton University Press, 1977), 110–34. For further

Even popular disturbances of the period, as Buchanan Sharp has
suggested, can be understood in terms of the characteristic lawmind-
edness of English popular culture.[41] In grain riots, for example, the
themes of local knowledge and direct experience, informal practices
of adjudication, and common understandings of the moral basis of
law and right can be seen as converging in the moral claims advanced by mob action. Rioters evidenced an ambivalent or equivocal
relationship to formal law, often urging magisterial action against
grain merchants or "improvers" for disrupting traditional rights. Indeed, such popular protests "often took the form either of attempts
to enforce the law or appeals to the authorities for aid."[42] Typically,
such agitations were directly concerned with the problem of subsistence and the experience of dearth, particularly as these were related to the price of grain, wages, unemployment, or common rights,
and they generally represented "an attempt to preserve some traditional notion of a just price or community-based standard of a moral
economy."[43]

The mode of political understanding and judgment presented in
the *Second Treatise* resonates with these participatory and experiential
aspects of the popular view of justice and the administration of
rights. In this regard, particularly in the linkage of property and
subsistence needs with the definition of crime and the exercise of the
executive right of punishment, Locke's state of nature proffers an
exemplar of moral knowledge and political practice quite consistent
with popular understandings. His original presentation of property
right and political power in this context can thus be read less as a
theory of natural law than an epistemology of natural right: a model
of political judgment that evokes ordinary sensation and experience
of need and shows how reflection on this could be sufficient to establish the complementarity of law and right in practice, at least in the
original condition of the species. This qualification is significant, as
we shall see in the chapter to follow, but for the moment let us trace

---

accounts of eighteenth-century developments, see Douglas Hay et al., eds., *Albion's
Fatal Tree: Crime and Society in Eighteenth-Century England* (New York: Pantheon, 1975).
　　41. Sharp, "Popular Protest."
　　42. Ibid., 303.
　　43. Ibid., 273–75. For the persistence of this notion, see E. P. Thompson, "The
Moral Economy of the English Crowd in the Eighteenth Century," *Past and Present* 50
(1971): 76–136.

this epistemology of right as it appears in Locke's initial characterization of the peaceful state of nature. Perhaps the best way to proceed is to undertake a speculative reconstruction of the processes by which his free and equal possessors in their created condition might come to understand what is required of them by the moral law. In so doing we should be able to discern the conditions under which and criteria by which judgments of law and right in that state might be taken to ensure the conformity of human action to God's design. Here, then, I will be concerned to show how Locke's natural moral agents might be expected to discover the primary imperatives of natural law and to exercise their natural rights over property and the punishment of crime in accordance with those rules.

III   An Epistemology of Right

We have seen that Locke's notion of moral agents in the state of nature is closely bound to his conception of the person. As articulated in the *Essay*, this originates with a "self," "that conscious thinking thing . . . which is sensible, or conscious of Pleasure and Pain, capable of Happiness or Misery, and so concern'd for it *self*, as far as that consciousness extends."[44] Such elemental self-awareness is shared with lower animals, but unlike the latter, human agents are also endowed with reason, which extends this consciousness in time.[45] Where animals act on instinct and are not responsible for their actions, human consciousness is that of sensible beings capable of both choosing and remembering particular courses of action.[46] Thus when Locke refers to human freedom in the *Second Treatise* as being *"grounded on* . . . having *Reason,"*[47] this suggests not only that human agents are capable of reasoning to the requirements of the law of nature, but that their subsequent actions are intentional choices, not instinctual responses. It is on this basis that they can be said to "own" their actions and thereby be held responsible for them.[48] Thus for Locke "person" is "a Forensick Term appropriating Actions and their Merit; and so belongs only to intelligent Agents capable of a

44. Locke, *Essay*, 2.27.17.
45. Ibid., 2.27.10–11, 13–17.
46. Ibid., 2.27.25–26.
47. Locke, *Two Treatises*, 2.63.
48. Locke, *Essay*, 2.27.17.

Law, and Happiness and Misery."[49] Because individuals as persons
choose their actions, which may or may not be consistent with the
law they are under, they are accountable and thus may be punished
for transgressions.

Because for Locke there are no such things as innate ideas, individuals in the state of nature could only reason to, and thus be
bound by, moral principles through sensation and reflection. Not
only simple recognition of common objects, but even knowledge of
God and the law of nature must be so rooted. "All those sublime
Thoughts," Locke observes, "which towre above the Clouds, and
reach as high as Heaven it self, take their Rise and Footing here: In
all that great Extent wherein the mind wanders, in those remote
Speculations, it may seem to be elevated with, it stirs not one jot
beyond those *Ideas,* which *Sense* or *Reflection,* have offered for its
Contemplation."[50] In the state of nature human agents share with
animals "a strong desire of Self-preservation," and are directed by
their "Senses and Reason" as animals are by their "Sense and Instinct . . . to the use of those things, which were serviceable for . . .
Subsistence, and given [them] as a means of [their] preservation."[51]
Here, moved by the sensations of hunger, thirst, and temperature,
Locke's natural agents may be imagined as selecting from nature's
bounty those things that will best satisfy their needs. At the same
time, Locke represents these natural agents as capable of recognizing their fellows as equals, "there being nothing more evident, than
that Creatures of the same species and rank promiscuously born to
all the same advantages of Nature, and the use of the same faculties,
should also be equal one amongst another without Subordination or
Subjection."[52] Once individuals understand nature as the source of

49. Ibid.
50. Ibid., 2.1.24.
51. Locke, *Two Treatises,* 1.86; see also 2.25. Compare Locke, *Essay,* 4.11.6, and
4.11.8 where, with respect to the things of nature, Locke notes that "*the testimony of our
Senses . . . is not only as great as our frame can attain to, but as our Condition needs.* For
our Faculties being suited not to the full extent of Being, nor to a perfect, clear,
comprehensive Knowledge of things free from all doubt and scruple; but to the preservation of us, in whom they are; and accomodated to the use of Life."
52. Locke, *Two Treatises,* 2.4. See also Locke, *Essay,* 4.12.3, where equality and excess appear as intuitive recognitions independent of abstract maxims. All knowledge
for Locke begins with such recognitions in the experience and sensation of particulars.

their own preservation and their fellows as their equals, reason and reflection must assure them of others' equal right to self-preservation. From these observations, Locke concludes, just as every one "is *bound to preserve himself* . . . so by the like reason when his own Preservation comes not in competition, ought he, as much as he can, *to preserve the rest of Mankind,* and may not unless it be to do Justice on an Offender, take away, or impair the life, or what tends to the Preservation of the Life, Liberty, Health, Limb or Goods of another."[53]

Locke has so far shown that human agents in the original state are capable of reasoning to the two fundamental tenets of the law of nature: self-preservation and preservation of their kind. Still, the propositions that such reasoning yields to their understandings require further stipulation. As he notes in the *Essay,* even the statement *"Men must repent of their Sins"* is inadequate as a moral principle, however true it may be as an abstract rule, "for the word . . . *Sins,* being put, as it usually is, to signifie in general ill Actions, that will draw on punishment upon the Doers; What great Principle of Morality can that be, to tell us we should be sorry, and cease to do that, which will bring mischief upon us, without knowing what those particular Actions are, that will do so?"[54] The *Treatises* provide the requisite connections between the abstract imperatives of the law of nature and the particular actions required or enjoined by that rule in the discussion of property. Echoing traditional understandings of the inviolability of subsistence needs, Locke presents the natural right to nature's goods as both grounded in and limited by the practical principles of labor and use. Though all human agents have a right to their preservation and to the conveniences of life provided by nature for their subsistence, "there must of necessity be a means *to appropriate* them in some way or other before they can be of use, or at all beneficial to any particular Man."[55] Food, clothing, shelter, and other things necessary to individual subsistence and preservation must be actively produced by their own labor.

Here, Locke locates the foundation of property right in the same notion he identifies with moral agency, the person. In the same move,

---

53. Locke, *Two Treatises,* 2.6. The qualification here, "unless it be to do Justice on an Offender," is important, as we shall see below.
54. Locke, *Essay,* 1.3.19.
55. Locke, *Two Treatises,* 2.26.

however, he elaborates the first two criteria for distinguishing between
those actions that conform to the law of nature and those that do not:

> Though the Earth, and all inferior Creatures be common to all Men, yet
> every Man has a *Property* in his own *Person*. This no Body has any Right
> to but himself. The *Labour* of his Body, and the *Work* of his Hands, we
> may say, are properly his. Whatsoever then he removes out of the State
> that Nature hath provided . . . he hath mixed his *Labour* with, and
> joyned to it something that is his own, and thereby makes it his *Property*.
> It being by him removed from the common state Nature placed it in,
> hath by this *labour* something annexed to it, that excludes the common
> right of other Men. For this *Labour* being the unquestionable Property
> of the Labourer, no Man but he can have a right to what that is once
> joyned to, at least where there is enough, and as good left in common
> for others.[56]

With this formulation, personal labor is stipulated as the practical
principle by which individuals in the state of nature can know the
actions required by the imperative of self-preservation and thereby
also know what is properly theirs. Just as one's life itself is a rightful
property, so are those things one labors upon to provide for one's
subsistence. As that same right excludes others from taking one's
life, since all are equal, so are they excluded from the property one
has labored upon to maintain it: "Though the Water running in the
Fountain be every ones, yet who can doubt, but that in the Pitcher is
his only who drew it out?"[57] Here, the sort of knowledge Locke suggests as appropriate to natural property right is quite literally hands-
on. Through labor one knows with the certainty of personal experience the extent of what is justly one's own.

Annexed to this principle of labor is a second practical principle
by which Locke's natural agents may conform their actions to the
natural law that requires the preservation of the species. Though
labor defines the property that can be appropriated for one's own
preservation and convenience, this conduces to the preservation of
all only "where there is enough and as good for others." In this the
right of individuals to appropriate as much as they need is predicated on the assumption that sufficient materials exist for each to do
so without depriving others of their equal right to nature's goods.

56. Ibid., 2.27.
57. Ibid., 2.29.

Were this not to be the case, appropriation even of one's needs could invade the rights of others.[58] Again the criterion provided evokes common sensation and experience, for local recognition of dearth or abundance in the things necessary to maintain life is an experiential judgment, and one likely to be familiar to Locke's seventeenth-century audience. To the objection that these criteria of just appropriation would allow anyone to "ingross as much as he will," Locke replies in the negative: "The same Law of Nature, that does by this means give us Property, does also *bound* that *Property* too."[59] Property rights in the goods of nature are rooted in their usefulness for self-preservation, but this defines their limits as well: "As much as any one can make use of to any advantage of life before it spoils; so much he may by his labour fix a Property in. Whatever is beyond this, is more than his share, and belongs to others."[60] The spoilage principle thus operates as the third practical criterion whereby individuals in the natural state may know the just bounds of their property. The bounty of nature exists for the preservation of all, not for any particular individual to waste or destroy uselessly.[61] To do so, indeed, would be both irrational and unjust. Though each must labor to provide their own subsistence, where the excess product of this labor spoils, they have wasted both their own energies and the product itself, as well as invaded the common right of others. Once again, Locke evokes an experiential understanding of one's needs as the basis for just appropriation, and once again the recognition of property in excess of right is figured as viscerally known.

Thus in the original condition need and labor provide both practical principles of appropriation and experiential grounds for an individual's positive title to property. Similarly, the provisos prohibiting

<hr />

58. See also ibid., 2.34, 36 (in land "as good and as large"), and 37. For the question of the moral problem of marketing surplus in a monetarized economy, see Locke, "Venditio," in John Dunn, "Justice and the Interpretation of Locke's Political Theory," *Political Studies* 16, no. 1 (1968): 84–87. We shall have occasion to consider the "Venditio" more closely in Chapter 7.

59. Locke, *Two Treatises*, 2.31.

60. Ibid.

61. Waste or spoilage in this context was not, as it might appear, an offense against some idea like modern efficiency. Sir Frederick Pollock and Frederic William Maitland, for example, found legal actions for "waste" in English law as early as the thirteenth century. See *The History of English Law before the Time of Edward I*, 2d ed., 2 vols. (1899–1923; reprint with revisions, Cambridge: Cambridge University Press, 1968), 2:9.

spoilage and requiring that enough and as good be left for others establish, in an equally immediate and cognizable fashion, the just bounds of one's appropriation. Significantly, however, these practical guides to what an individual might justly possess also function as sensible and experiential criteria by which unjust appropriation can be readily known. The offenses of those who stole the fruits of another's labor, who allowed their own product to spoil, or who failed to leave sufficient for others needs were, as Locke might say, easily seen. And, as his elaboration of the point in the *Two Treatises* suggests, the same criteria of just appropriation applied to both the collection of nature's "spontaneous Products" and the enclosure of land.[62] In both cases what one might justly possess was limited to that required for use. To exceed this was to injure the common right of others, and excesses under these conditions were patently obvious. The evidence of the senses alone would establish the fact of violation sufficiently to convince both the transgressor and others that such actions were contrary to the law of nature.

Equally clear, it would seem, might be the measures of punishment proportionate to the crime, though Locke defers discussion of "the particulars of the Law of Nature, or its *measures of punishment*."[63] If, for example, the meat of a deer has been allowed to spoil, might not the responsible party, by common understandings of justice and equity, be expected to repay the community a like amount? Or, perhaps, since such spoilage would injure no particular person, no worldly punishment would follow. Restitution, however, might more clearly apply to the cultivation of land, for if the product of one person's enclosure were to spoil they might be deprived of that portion that produced the excess. This, Locke observes, "notwithstanding his Inclosure, was still to be looked on as Waste, and might be the Possession of any other."[64] Recognition of crimes against particular persons and the rule of punishment appropriate to them might be no less evident to the senses. Where the practical principles of labor and use and the proviso "enough and as good" provide sufficient guidance for each to know what is properly their own, "he that had

62. *Treatises*, 2.37–38.
63. Ibid., 2.12.
64. Ibid., 2.38. The example of spoiled meat is Locke's. To allow any of the "spontaneous Products of Nature" to perish in one's possession "without their due use" was to violate the law of nature and leave one "liable to be punished." Ibid., 2.37.

as good left for his Improvement, as was already taken up, needed not complain, ought not to meddle with what was already improved by another's Labour: If he did, 'tis plain he desired the benefit of another's Pains, which he had no right to."[65] If someone, for instance, stole the provisions another had gathered for a week's subsistence, what could be more evident or reasonable than that the offense be made good by restoring to the injured party the like amount? No other measure would be necessary, for the goods of the natural state have simply an "intrinsick value" which "depends only on their usefulness to the Life of Man."[66] At the same time, the injured party would know that this was all they were entitled to by way of reparation. To demand more would be to do an obvious injury to the offender, for which they in turn could be held accountable.

Recalling the theistic grounding of Locke's individualism, these formulations underwrite the effective moral separation or insulation of human agents in their natural state. The epistemology of right grounds the possibility of harmonious natural property relations by guaranteeing to each individual knowledge of what is properly their own, and on this basis they are each free to act within the allowance of the law of nature without the interference, consent, or control of any other person. Their individual determinations of convenience and the character of the life they constitute by their actions is thus a matter of individual responsibility as it is by definition a product of their individual judgment. All these things taken together orchestrate the "convenience" or harmony of the whole. Significantly, however, the convergence of right and conveniency in this context need not imply the optimistic assumption that all members of the species faithfully contain their actions within the divinely structured boundary between natural law and natural right. While the species may have been created capable of correctly discerning the requirements of this boundary in particular instances, the existential fact of human freedom implies the potential for transgression. This, indeed, is what underlies the unique characteristic of political power as a natural right to do lawful harm to offenders. The root of this power, on Locke's account, lay in the nature of law itself, for even the law of nature "would, as all other Laws that concern Men in this World, be

65. Ibid., 2.34.
66. Ibid., 2.37. This natural value is contrasted to monetary value. See also ibid., 2.46, 50, 182, 184.

in vain, if there were no body that . . . had a *Power to Execute* that Law."[67] And, as we have seen, the egalitarian distribution of this power is a fundamental part of Locke's construction of human equality in the natural state.

This inclusion of executive right as an aspect of natural equality introduces a new and portentous twist into what I have described as the divinely ordained complementarity of natural law and natural right. The structural imperative of the morally marked world of God's architecture, as we have considered it so far, is to differentiate between virtuous or moral actions toward one's own species and instrumental or convenient actions directed to the world of things and inferior creatures. The inclusion of the power of punishment in the realm of right can, in this context, only be sustained by the presumption that violators of the natural law rendered themselves "thinglike" by their transgression. It is only by this mechanism that, despite the use of force in punishment, the designed complementarity between law and right can remain in place. And, consistent with the assumption that all rights are circumscribed by law, Locke is quick to note that executive right itself is not to be understood as an "Absolute or Arbitrary Power, to use a Criminal . . . according to the passionate heats, or boundless extravagancy of . . . Will" but must only be such as will "retribute him, so far as calm reason and conscience dictates, what is proportionate to his Transgression."[68] Leaving aside the specifics of proportionality,[69] what does the presence of such a power of

67. Ibid., 2.7.
68. Ibid., 2.8.
69. This, to be sure, is to leave a great deal aside, and it will doubtless not satisfy the myriad objections that could be raised at this point simply to say that I follow Locke, *Two Treatises*, 2.12, in so doing. On one reading this avoidance might seem a typical Lockean abstraction, far removed from the sort of concrete specificity we might like such formulations to embrace. Nonetheless, it is consistent with my suggestion above that Locke's discussion parallels local practices of informal arbitration, where the specific penalties were not matters of statute but judgments settled by mutually agreed upon arbitrator(s). This, indeed, was their point—to make the administration of justice both more accessible to the parties and more responsive to the particulars of the dispute. Interestingly, Horwitz and Oldham's research suggests that, although the original act (*Statutes of the Realm*, 9 Will. 3, c. 15)—framed to sidestep legal delays, expense, and maneuvering by appeal—mandated contempt orders upon those who broke their prior agreement to conform to the arbitrator's judgment, by the latter third of the eighteenth century the practice had resulted in a proliferation of procedural rules for arbitration as well as the professionalization of arbiters. By 1805, they note, over half of the arbitrators were legal professionals. In short, "re-

lawful harm imply for Locke's assertion that, at some point in the natural state, right and conveniency went together? Most important, it suggests that the complementarity of law and right in practice does not entail the utopian assumption that all can be relied upon to conform their actions to God's design. Similarly, it would seem to preclude the supposition that solitary individuals simply provide for their subsistence needs, avoiding violation of the natural law by avoiding contact with others. Rather, it implies that the convergence of right and conveniency includes actions undertaken by executive right. It suggests, in other words, that however some individuals may violate the law of nature, the actions of others in meting out their punishment conform to the moral law.[70]

It is important to attend closely to the *Treatises'* presentation of this issue. Grant the supposition that the epistemology of right, with its experiential grounds of need-based judgments, sufficiently secured property so as to leave "no reason of quarrelling," no "doubt about the largeness of Possession," and "no room for Controversie about the Title" or "Incroachment on the Right of others."[71] It is not, I would suggest, so difficult to discern the basis for Locke's assertion that in sufficiently heinous cases the criminal might be "destroyed as

---

liance upon the court's powers of enforcement was having the unintended result of 'legalizing' court-related arbitration, with all that this development could entail in the way of additional delay and greater expense." Horwitz and Oldham, "John Locke and Arbitration," 158–59.

70. It seems a strange notion of social peace that includes any form of violence. Indeed, from the vantage point of modern pacifism, it may well appear a contradiction in terms. The more explicit modern focus on the simple observable facticity of events, absent all the trappings of a morally marked world of God's design, leads us to think of peace as the absence of overt violence and violence as the negation of peace. Locke's relegation of criminals to subhuman status, from this perspective, appears as little more than a sleight of hand to salvage an otherwise tenuous argument. But the more recent position, rooted as it is in an empirical rather than a moral-theistic understanding of social order, itself reflects the vast distance between Locke's imagery and such contemporary cultural frames. The order Locke expects in human action is judged by its relationship to moral law, not by the mere facticity of actions but in their conformity to the rule of virtue. As criminal violence (force without right) disorders this moral fabric, so punishment of an offender (force with right) returns human affairs to a moral equilibrium. Thus Locke could simultaneously affirm an identity between criminal violence and bestiality, assert the justice of punishment, and find social peace in the sequenced balance of these. A more extensive discussion of punishment is offered in John Locke, *Second Letter concerning Toleration*, in vol. 6 of *The Works of John Locke in Ten Volumes* (1823; reprint, Scientia Verlag Aalen, 1963).

71. Locke, *Two Treatises*, 2.51.

. . . one of those wild Savage Beasts with whom Men can have no Society nor Security."[72] If rightful actions in accordance with law are so easily known, and if, as I have argued, human nature for Locke is something enacted in deeds rather than simply possessed by all, the relegation of criminals to the ranks of beasts is wholly unsurprising, for it is structurally mandated by their act of transgression. In effect, by violating the law they demote themselves from the ranks of humanity to the level of the lesser creatures of God's creation. At the same time, though, such violations are presented as infrequent in the original state. Indeed, on the terms set forth by Locke's political imagery, if the boundaries of rightful convenience are so easily seen, it is difficult to imagine how it could be otherwise. Even after the institution of government, the *Treatises* proffer a social context quite similar to the peaceful state of nature. "In the beginning of things," Locke conjectures, "the equality of a simple poor way of liveing confineing their desires within the narrow bounds of each mans smal propertie made few controversies and so no need of many laws to decide them: And there wanted not of Justice where there were but few Trespasses, and few Offenders."[73] Locke's third letter on toleration evokes a situation similar to that of the *Treatises'* original state of nature, imagining the possibility of a society for whose members "the rivers and woods afforded the spontaneous provisions of life" and who "with no private possessions of land had no enlarged desires after riches or power." Such a community, Locke suggests, could exist "without any municipal laws, judges, or any person with superiority established amongst them." Rather, they could "settle all their private differences, if any arose, by the extemporary determinations of their neighbors, or of arbitors chosen by the parties."[74]

In his deployment of such examples, Locke again can be read as echoing traditional English images of localism, neighborliness, and social harmony, as well as extralegal practices of local arbitration.[75]

---

72. Ibid., 2.11. Locke's deployment of the language of crime and punishment and his relegation of criminals to the ranks of beasts take on a sharper political edge later in the *Second Treatise.* Compare, for instance, the description at 2.172 of the "despot" who, by "revolting from his own kind to that of Beasts by making Force which is theirs, to be his rule of right, . . . renders himself liable to be destroied . . . as any other wild beast, or noxious brute with whom Mankind can have neither Society nor Security."

73. Ibid., 2.107.

74. Locke, *Third Letter on Toleration,* 225.

75. This claim draws on the perspectives provided by recent studies of seventeenth-

These images, as contemporary scholars of English popular culture have argued, manifested broadly popular understandings not of how law actually operated or how such judgments of private controversies were in fact made, but rather of the ways in which laws and judgments should or could operate if such power were secure in the hands of magistrates, judges, constables, juries, and citizens of good character. At times, perhaps, in some locales and in some cases, these practices of political judgment may have tolerably approached the ideal. More often, though, particularly as the century wore on, the administration of English justice was widely seen as becoming more and more problematic, indeed, in the language of the period, more and more corrupt.[76]

Locke's political works identify the dynamic of corruption not with property per se, but with "enlarged desires after riches or power." At one point, the *Treatises* specifically associate it with the multiplication of laws, and link this in turn not to the existence of possessions but to the emergence of "Covetousness and Ambition." By way of contrast, Locke evocatively compares that corrupting dynamic to the peace of an imagined past, to the "great confidence" given "Men one of another" by the "Innocence and Sincerity" of a "poor but vertuous Age."[77] That "Golden Age . . . had more Virtue, and consequently better Governours, as well as less vicious Subjects" than later epochs in which "vain Ambition, and *amor sceleratus habendi,* evil Concupiscence, had corrupted Mens minds into a Mistake of true Power and Honour."[78] As these formulations suggest, the theoretical prob-

---

century law, particularly the following: James A. Sharpe, "Enforcing the Law in the Seventeenth-Century English Village," in *Crime and the Law: The Social History of Crime in Western Europe since 1500,* ed. V. A. C. Gatrell, Bruce Lenman, and Geoffrey Parker (London: Europa Publications, 1980), 97–119, esp. 106–7, 109–10; T. C. Curtis, "Quarter Sessions Appearances and Their Background: A Seventeenth-Century Regional Study," and Ingram, "Communities and Courts," both in *Crime in England, 1550–1800,* ed. J. S. Cockburn (Princeton: Princeton University Press, 1977), 135–54 and 110–34; and Wrightson, "Two Concepts of Order."

76. A pertinent comparison here is between Locke's account of the various occasions for the "dissolution of government" in the *Treatises,* 2 chap. 19, and the accusations of royal corruption of English justice in the Declaration of Rights, particularly those treating the corruption of juries, the judicial usurpation of parliamentary jurisdiction by King's Courts, excessive fines, illegal and cruel punishments, promises of fines and forfeitures prior to the conviction of those accused, and other excesses of royal power. See "An Acte for Declareing the Rights and Liberties of the Subject and Setleing the Succession of the Crowne," 1688, *Statutes of the Realm,* 1 W. & M. 2, c. 2.

77. Locke, *Two Treatises,* 2.107.

78. This, and the remainder of the passage, is paraphrased from Locke, *Two Treatises,* 2.111.

lem to be addressed is not one of a direct or mechanical relationship between property and political power. Social harmony and the violence of corrupt individuals are potential characteristics of both the natural and the civil condition. The corruption of innocence, in other words, can occur in either state, and Locke identifies its dynamic in both contexts with the same phenomena: the emergence of ambition, covetousness, viciousness, luxury, and "enlarged desires after riches or power." At the same time, though, the difficultly is cast in explicit terms as the corruption "of Mens minds into a Mistake of true Power and Honour"—the corruption, in other words, of judgment and understanding. In the chapter to follow I will suggest the source of this corruption and explore its implications for Locke's account of political power in civil society. Before we turn to this, however, it might useful to collect the various strands of the argument thus far.

The *Treatises* represent natural humanity as free and equal possessors in a framework of divine intentions for the peace and preservation of the species as a whole. The egalitarian distribution of rightful power over both property and the punishment of offenders against the moral law individuates the species into separate moral agents and renders them each accountable to their fellows for their proper observance of the designed boundaries between law and right in the appropriation of nature's goods for their subsistence. The natural limits of the appropriation of one's own, the proper extent over which one is free to exercise one's private judgments of convenience, are set by an epistemology of right that ties appropriation to an experiential understanding and judgment of need and use, while the executive right of punishment operates as the guarantor of moral order in the administration of natural justice. In these respects, the *Treatises* advance an image of what might well be called natural politics, an image that presents political power as a natural characteristic of the species democratically distributed to its membership as a whole. In the natural state where the epistemology of right yields knowledge of the moral law, this power is properly exercised by each and all on the basis of their individual judgment. Where this knowledge is effectively available, judgments so grounded necessarily conform to the moral meanings of God's architecture as this is expressed by the designed complementarity of law and right, virtue and convenience. Locke's presentation of natural politics thus stresses the boundedness of properly political power by the imperatives of natural law, even as it gives central significance to the operation of retributive justice.

Finally, and however strange its egalitarian distribution might appear to Locke's contemporaries, this model of political judgment and understanding in significant ways recirculated popular notions of the proper scope, purpose, nature, and boundaries of political power. Particularly in its articulation of the relationship between law and right in matters of property, subsistence needs, criminality, and punishment, it evokes familiar contemporary notions of local knowledge, sociability, and the administration of justice. In so doing, the *Treatises* proffer an exemplary understanding of political power that both invests it with a moral grounding and suggests the moral boundaries of its proper exercise in practice. We shall soon see that, just as this notion of political power remains indebted to conventional understandings, so too does Locke's account of its corruption. But because what is corrupted is human judgment itself, Locke's description of the source and process of that corruption is significant for understanding the relationship between power and right in his presentation of civil society, particularly as this implies a model of judgment for the grounds of legitimate resistance.

4

Money Matters:
Inconveniences and the
Disordering of Natural Judgment

Wide wasting pest! that rages unconfin'd,
And crowds with crimes the records of mankind;
For gold his sword the hireling ruffian draws,
For gold the hireling judge distorts the laws,
Wealth heap'd on wealth, nor truth nor safety buys,
The dangers gather as the treasures rise.
—Samuel Johnson
The Vanity of Human Wishes

In the *First Treatise* Locke observes that the real dilemma confronting political understanding is not whether there should be political power in the world, but who should have it: anyone claiming to be "a Reformer of Politicks," he insists, "should lay this sure, and be very clear in it. For if this remain disputable, all the rest will be to very little purpose."[1] As we have seen, in the *Treatises'* initial presentation of the state of nature the answer to this question is "everyone." Political power there makes its appearance as a natural characteristic of the species, and one that functions as the guarantor of moral order in that state insofar as it ensures the conformity of human action to the designed complementarity of law and right. In light of this, Locke's theoretical task in the *Second Treatise* is, on the one hand, to account for how the initial egalitarian distribution of this power could give way to legitimate inequalities of power and

1. John Locke, *Two Treatises of Government*, ed. Peter Laslett, rev. ed. (1960; reprint, with amendments, Cambridge: Cambridge University Press, 1963), by book and paragraph, 1.106.

jurisdiction in civil society. On the other hand, in view of the project of justifying resistance, that task entails as well the articulation of a mode of political understanding capable of ensuring that the particular persons into whose hands civil institutions condensed and channeled that power remained not only within the boundaries of law and right ordained by God's design, but terrestrially accountable for deviations from this rule.

In modern interpretations of the *Second Treatise* claims and counterclaims abound, justified both textually and contextually, as to just what is accomplished in Locke's description of the movement from the state of nature to civil society. Yet amidst the multitude of conflicting interpretations, none have paused long to ponder Locke's own most explicit statements of the rationale for that move: that the inconveniences eventually afflicting the state of nature spur the transition to civil society. Compared to Hobbes's account of the creation of political society in the pervasive violence and mutual predations of his state of nature, this notion of inconveniences would appear to minimize the issue—and if the term meant then what it does today, this would be an appropriate observation. A recent dictionary of current English usage, for example, defines "inconvenience" as a "want of adaptation to personal requirement or ease," and the prospect of ceaseless violence is certainly inconvenient in this sense.[2] But the subjectivity or, worse, triviality implied by this usage was but a minor part of the semantic field encompassed by the term among Locke's contemporaries. In the ordinary language of the period it possessed a far broader and morally significant range of meanings. In the most general sense, it could connote an "inconsistency with reason or rule" or "moral or ethical unsuitableness; unbecoming or unseemly behavior, impropriety."[3] The legal lexicon of the period, however, invested the term with considerable precision by formally distinguishing it from "mischief" or "injury." Where the latter were acts, in breach of law, attributed to or affecting specific persons, an "inconvenience" was an ill which lay upon the community as a whole—particularly in reference to situations in which the public law was disobeyed or an offense went unpunished.[4]

2. *The Concise Oxford Dictionary of English Usage*, 5th ed., s.v. "inconvenience."
3. *The Oxford English Dictionary*, 2d ed., s.v. "inconvenience," definitions 1 and 2.
4. Ibid., definitions 3b and 3c. A similar range is suggested by the adjectival form, s.v. "inconvenient."

Thus as "conveniency" evoked an image of harmony and order, so "inconveniency" suggested disharmony or disorder, and in Locke's usage both terms found their force importantly in an understanding of the necessary conformity of human action to the imperatives of morality and of the equally necessary operation of retributive justice. In the four passages of the *Second Treatise* where Locke asserts that it is the "inconveniences" of the natural state that prompt the creation of civil society, he quite explicitly identifies these with the uncertain or improper exercise of the executive right to judge and punish transgressions of the law of nature.[5] He thus associates the fundamental impetus for the transition to civil government with the desire of his natural agents "to avoid, and remedy those inconveniencies of the State of Nature, which necessarily follow from every Man's being Judge in his own Case."[6] The disorder, in other words, that besets Locke's natural state emerges neither from a Hobbesian perspective on the inevitability of violence in the absence of state power nor from a supposition about the pervasiveness of criminality. Rather, it is explicitly connected to a series of difficulties attending the just punishment of crime and injury in the natural condition, and hence is specifically evocative of the dilemma tapped by the broad juridical notion of "inconvenience."

With the emergence of these difficulties, Locke's state of nature is radically transformed. Once described as "a State of Peace, Good Will, Mutual Assistance, and Preservation," it degenerates into an "ill condition" rife with "Confusion and Disorder."[7] Locke repeatedly refers to the controversies afflicting this state as disputes over property taken in the broad sense of the term; thus the fundamental appeal of civil government lies precisely in its capacity to remedy or avoid the "Inconveniencies which disorder Mens Properties in the state of Nature."[8] He characterizes the disorder and the problem it represents in vivid terms:

> If Man in the State of Nature be so free, . . . If he be absolute Lord of his own Person and Possessions, equal to the greatest, and subject to no Body, why will he part with his Freedom? Why will he give up this

5. Locke, *Two Treatises*, 2.13, 90, 127, and 136.
6. Ibid., 2.90.
7. Ibid., 2.19, 127, 13.
8. Ibid., 2.136.

Empire, and subject himself to the Dominion and Controul of any other Power? To which 'tis obvious to Answer, that though in the state of Nature he hath such a right, yet the Enjoyment of it is very uncertain, and constantly exposed to the Invasion of others. For all being Kings as much as he, every Man his Equal, and the greater part no strict Observers of Equity and Justice, the enjoyment of the property he has in this state is very unsafe, very insecure. This makes him willing to quit a Condition, which, however free, is full of fears and continual dangers.[9]

But what is the specific source of this transformation? Why does the natural state, inhabited by reasonable beings and governed by a law "plain to a rational creature," the apparent epitome of tranquility and order, become one fraught with controversy and peopled by so few strict observers of the rule of reason? What, to put the question somewhat differently, is the relationship between "inconveniences," property, and the creation of civil society?

I Power, Property, and the Meaning of Inconveniencies

Locke explicitly describes the intimate connection between punishment, property, and the creation of civil government in chapter nine of the *Second Treatise*. There, in a brief summary of the larger argument, he explains why one rarely finds examples of humanity in their natural condition:

> The inconveniencies, that they are therein exposed to, by the irregular and uncertain exercise of the Power every Man has of punishing the transgressions of others, make them take Sanctuary under the establish'd Laws of Government, and therein seek *the preservation of their Property.* 'Tis this makes them so willingly give up every one his single power of punishing to be exercised by such alone as shall be appointed to it amongst them; and by such Rules as the Community, or those authorised by them to that purpose, shall agree on. And in this we have the original *right and rise* of both the *Legislative and Executive power,* as well as of the Governments and Societies themselves.[10]

Again the insecurity of property in the state of nature is identified as a result of improprieties in the exercise of the right to punish trans-

9. Ibid., 2.123.
10. Ibid., 2.127. See also 2.88–90, 131.

gressions of natural law "where every one is Judge, Interpreter, and Executioner of it too, and that in his own Case." In this version of the natural condition, "the Law of Nature being unwritten, and so no where to be found but in the minds of Men, . . . it serves not, as it ought, to determine the Rights, and fence the Properties of those that live under it." Locke's remedy for this dilemma, of course, is the establishment of a legislative authority, the duty of which is to "*dispense Justice, and decide the Rights of the Subject by promulgated standing Laws, and known Authoris'd Judges.*" He then reiterates the linkage between problems of judgment, property, and the rule of law: "To avoid these Inconveniencies which disorder Mens Properties in the state of Nature," he argues, "Men unite into Societies, that they may have the united strength of the whole Society to secure and defend their Properties, and may have *standing Rules* to bound it, by which every one may know what is his."[11]

Curiously, from this it would seem that at least one aspect of the problem confronting Locke's natural individuals in the original condition is the extent to which they are capable of understanding and applying the law of nature with sufficient certainty both to know what is theirs and to defend it effectively. By the same token, if it is the function of civil law and judges to decide the rights of the subject, this implies that knowledge of natural right and natural law has somehow become problematic. But as we have seen, it was also clear from the initial near-bucolic description of that state that this was not always the case. Far from being the subject of controversy or contention, property was so secure and the demands of the law of nature so clear with respect to it that there was "no doubt of Right, no room for quarrel."[12] In that earlier vision of the natural condition the convergence of right and conveniency was guaranteed by an epistemology of right that clearly defined what was proper to each and suggested measures of equitable punishment for such transgressions as might occur.

If, as I have argued, this harmonious vision of the natural state evoked broadly popular understandings of need and common notions of penal justice, so too does Locke's allusion to the source of its corruption reiterate widely held assumptions about the corruption

11. The four quotations are from ibid., 2.136.
12. Ibid., 2.39.

of moral character in the period. He was quite clear about what led to the beginning of the end of that system of natural justice: "This I dare boldly affirm, That the same *Rule of Propriety, (viz)* that every Man should have as much as he could make use of, would hold still in the World, without straitning any body, since there is Land enough in the World to suffice double the Inhabitants had not the *Invention of Money,* and the tacit Agreement of Men to put a value on it, introduced (by Consent) larger possessions, and a Right to them."[13] Locke's introduction of money is recognized by most modern interpreters as the crucial turning point in his characterization of the natural state. Usually, however, this is seen in the direct sense of engendering the whole panoply of human vices that (so the argument goes) ultimately render his version of that condition behaviorally indistinguishable from that of Hobbes. Typically, though in general agreement on this point, these perspectives then diverge widely in their interpretation of what is accomplished by the remedy of civil institutions, particularly as this involves a question about what class or group interests are (or are not) served by civil law. The stakes involved in Locke's account for the vast majority of these interpretations are predominantly worldly in nature. On this basis, he has been variously represented as a ventriloquist for such figures as rising capitalist entrepreneurs, agricultural improvers, gentry, artisans and Whiggish radicals, as well as for Calvinist social values or general male franchise and anticapitalist moralism.[14]

In contrast to interpretations that construe Locke's purpose as the justification or privileging of particular social classes or status groups, I have argued that the theistic framing of his political understanding centered on a moralistic rather than a sociological focus. The morally marked world of God's architecture provided a grid of meaningful order that both transcended particular historical social

13. Ibid., 2.36.
14. These are the interpretations, respectively, of Leo Strauss, *Natural Right and History* (Chicago: University of Chicago Press, 1953), and C. B. Macpherson, *The Political Theory of Possessive Individualism: Hobbes to Locke* (Oxford: Oxford University Press, 1962); Neal Wood, *John Locke and the Theory of Agrarian Capitalism* (Berkeley: University of California Press, 1984); Richard Ashcraft, *Revolutionary Politics and Locke's "Two Treatises of Government"* (Princeton: Princeton University Press, 1986); John Dunn, *The Political Thought of John Locke: An Historical Account of the Argument of the "Two Treatises of Government"* (Cambridge: Cambridge University Press, 1969); and James Tully, *A Discourse on Property: John Locke and His Adversaries* (Cambridge: Cambridge University Press, 1980).

orders and functioned as a broad measure of their conformity with
God's purposes. With respect to his own society, Locke's sociological
understanding, if such it may be called, was articulated in terms of
social statuses and callings, such as gentry, peer, merchant, artisan,
farmer, day laborer, servant, clergy, and the like. In moral terms,
however, his principal operative distinction was between the "industrious and rational" and the "quarrelsome and contentious," between
the innocence of those who kept peacefully and productively to their
calling, and to what was rightfully their own, and the corruption and
viciousness of those who vexed the peace of the world with conflict
and dissension.[15] In this division no social group was necessarily privileged. Moral innocence and corruption characterized individuals'
actions in relation to the law of virtue without regard to worldly
station. In both moral and political terms all were persons, equally
subject to law and equally accountable for the conformity of their
actions to its rule. The stakes in this ordering of things, however,
were not limited to one's interests in this world, for they touched as
well the question of one's fate in the next—an interest, on Locke's
account, with which no merely terrestrial consideration should compare.

It is, I would suggest, with this moral grid as a background that
Locke's treatment of money in the *Treatises* might productively be
read. Clearly, he understood the development of money to have
fundamentally transformed relationships between the human species and the natural world, as well as between individuals. As is generally recognized, it is money that overcomes the provisos limiting
the appropriation of property in the natural state. To interpret this
simply in terms of its economic or distributive implications, however,
not only brackets consideration of the centrality of retributive justice, it misses Locke's concern with how it is that people come to
know the just bounds of their property, maintain social peace, and
enact their created capacity for just and moral relations with their
fellows. Before money, the epistemology of right provided the criteria of need and use by which human agents limited their appropriation of nature to that which was justly theirs. Through that direct
and experiential way of knowing, Locke supposed that natural individuals could not only know the extent of their own property, but in

---

15. See also the discussion in Dunn, *Political Thought*, 254–55.

so knowing could avoid invading that of others as well as recognize and equitably punish any who might transgress the boundaries of moral order. Thus, to appreciate the nature and magnitude of the change wrought by money on the natural state, it is necessary to consider more than its subsequent effects on property relations in a narrowly economic or sociological sense. More important are its implications for the possibility of justice and moral order in human relationships in a world presumed to be morally marked by God's design. Before we turn to Locke's particular presentation of the moral meaning of money, however, it might be useful to consider some of the ways his contemporaries viewed the problem.

The equivocal moral status of money had, of course, long been an object of philosophical reflection. In the sixteenth and seventeenth centuries, though, the extensive monetarization of the English economy and the rapid development of national and international markets provided the impetus for a reexamination of the meaning of money and its role in the productive life of the community.[16] In the traditional moral economy of agricultural England, the localism of production and sustenance ensured the embeddedness of exchange in a social world that was structured by customary political, social, and religious duties. As Joyce Appleby has observed, economic relationships were represented in law as intimately connected "to a social context where duties and rights were closely tied to the needs of security and survival. As long as the principal elements in the economic structure remained visible and tangible, the understanding of the system was the possession of the whole society."[17] With the rapid expansion of trade and commerce, however, the forces that affected local markets and local experiences of dearth and abundance grew increasingly distant and anonymous. The moral meaning of production and consumption became increasingly obscure as goods became enmeshed in the web of commerce.

In the context of these developments, seventeenth-century perceptions of the meaning of money ranged from utilitarian appreciation to deep suspicion. In common understanding as well as law, it

16. The following discussion draws heavily upon Joyce Oldham Appleby, *Economic Thought and Ideology in Seventeenth-Century England* (Princeton: Princeton University Press, 1978), esp. chaps. 2 and 3. See also William Letwin, *The Origin of Scientific Economics: English Economic Thought, 1660–1776* (London: Methuen, 1963).

17. Appleby, *Economic Thought and Ideology*, 25.

was a peculiar substance. One aspect of its peculiarity, as well as its moral ambiguity, is evident in the curious character of Rochfield, a self-described "honest thief" in John Webster's *A Cure for a Cuckold.* As it happens, the woman he has chosen as his first victim in his new profession offers him her gold bracelets for lack of coin, but he finds this unacceptable:

> Ha, ready money is the prize I look for
> It walks without suspision anywhere
> When Chains and Jewels may be stayed and call'd
> Before the Constable[18]

Distinct from gems and other valuables which were recognizable by their quality or craftsmanship, money was anonymous and un-marked, lacking in identifiable particularity. A peculiar form of property in English law for which title passed simply with possession,[19] it was not only movable, but infinitely mutable. From the moral standpoint of a world concerned with personal character, money thus had the disturbing capacity to take on the moral personality of its possessor. In the hands of a good and charitable Christian it would relieve the necessities of the poor; in the possession of an engrosser of grain it was certain to add to the poor's distress in times of need. As the national wealth itself became an object of scrutiny and reflection, such commonly acknowledged differences in the moral meanings of various personal uses of money subtly developed into aggregate categories through the vehicle of social types. Thus in the hands of extravagant peers fond of foreign luxuries, money was as likely to dissipate the resources of the nation as it was likely to improve them in the possession of honest merchants and industrious artisans.

In still more abstract terms, money became seen as a vital element in the nourishment of trade and commerce, and the goal of policy was to ensure its supply in the hands that would best serve the end

18. John Webster, *A Cure for a Cuckold,* 2.2.86–89, in *The Complete Works of John Webster,* ed. F. L. Lucas (New York: Gordian Press, 1966), 3:46.

19. See Sir Frederick Pollock and Frederic William Maitland, *The History of English Law before the Time of Edward I,* 2nd ed., 2 vols. (1899–1923; reprint, with revisions, Cambridge: Cambridge University Press, 1968), vol. 2, chap. 4, sec. 7 (esp. 2:151–52, 178–79).

of national prosperity.[20] Seventeenth-century England was witness to a new form of intellectual activity, the aim of which was to name and understand the faceless forces affecting commercial life.[21] Variously termed "political anatomy" or "political arithmetick," later to develop into the discipline of political economy, contributions to this new genre of literature attempted to render intelligible the emerging economic processes that had insinuated themselves into the once personal and directly cognizable relationships of local production, consumption, and distribution. Although the direction of the causal relationship between the available stock of money and the quantity and quality of national trade remained a matter of debate, the increase of both was taken to be the measure of national wealth as well as the proper object of commercial policy in the period.[22]

But while William Petty, Josiah Child and their like grappled with the difficulties of imagining a national commerce in the context of an international flow of trade, others more committed to the older moral economy continued to seek an ethical understanding of the disruptions, social dislocations, and human costs of the emerging market system. Moralists continued to focus on the actions of those involved in the commercialization of the grain trade, the enclosure of common lands for private "improvement," and the practice of usury, particularly in terms of the manner in which these practices affected traditional rights or Christian duties.[23] Since both the securing of property and the relief of economic distress were taken as significant elements of the magisterial duty of protection, contributors to this literature no less than their more "scientific" brethren voiced their concerns in the form of political advice on state policy. From both perspectives, the freedom to pursue economic activities was understood as a matter bounded by law, and for both the central question to be addressed was what laws were necessary and desirable

20. Tax policy, in particular, was seen as a way of channeling money from the unproductive hands of luxury consumers into the public revenue, and hence back into circulation, in a manner more conducive to the public good. For a discussion of this, see William Kennedy, *English Taxation, 1640–1799: An Essay on Policy and Opinion* (1913; reprint, New York: Augustus M. Kelley, 1964), chaps. 1 through 5.

21. See Letwin, *Origin of Scientific Economics*; Appleby, *Economic Thought and Ideology;* and Michel Foucault, *The Order of Things: An Archeology of the Human Sciences* (New York: Vintage Books, 1973), chaps. 6 and 8.

22. Appleby, *Economic Thought and Ideology*, chaps. 2 and 4 through 7.

23. Ibid., chap. 3.

and why. The fundamental difference between the two, in other words, lay not in their understandings of the right, propriety, or desirability of political intervention in productive activities and commercial exchange, but rather in the manner in which the necessity of specific sorts of interventions might be recognized and defended in particular cases. Here, where the new writers on trade tended toward purely consequentialist arguments supporting the increase of national wealth and trade, the grounds of law from the perspective of moralists tended rather to rely on arguments from principles of justice and equity.

The commercialism of England's developing economy, however, was subject to more fundamental criticism than either traditional moralism or the emerging criteria of national productivity and efficiency could inspire. In the writings of Gerrard Winstanley at midcentury, this criticism erupted as an extreme variation on the Christian story of corruption, one spoken in the voice of revelation and invested as well with a radical egalitarian and activist vision. As money in the old adage was the root of all evil, so for Winstanley was monetarized commerce and the exchange of private properties for profit the source of all corruption. "When mankind began to buy and sell," he suggested, "then did he fall from his innocence; for then they began to oppress and cozen one another of their creation birthright."[24] In a world built around such commerce, "the cunning cheaters get great estates by other men's labours; and being rich thereby, become oppressing lords over their brethren; which occasions all our troubles."[25] Thus Winstanley's "free commonwealth" strictly prohibits the coinage of precious metals for domestic use: "For where money bears all the sway, there is no regard of that golden rule, *Do as you would be done by.* Justice is bought and sold: nay, injustice is sometimes bought and sold for money: and it is the cause of all wars and oppressions."[26] Whereas the political advice of

24. Gerrard Winstanley, "The Law of Freedom in a Platform," in *"The Law of Freedom" and Other Writings,* ed. Christopher Hill (Cambridge: Cambridge University Press, 1983), 286. For accounts of Winstanley and his relationship to seventeenth-century English political thought and practice see Hill's introduction, as well as Thomas Wilson Hayes, *Winstanley the Digger: A Literary Analysis of Radical Ideas in the English Revolution* (Cambridge: Harvard University Press, 1979); and George M. Shulman, *Radicalism and Reverence: The Political Thought of Gerrard Winstanley* (Berkeley: University of California Press, 1989).
25. Winstanley, "Law of Freedom," 371.
26. Ibid., 384.

the new economic perspectives as well as of the older moralistic ones urged that the welfare of the nation lay with the securing of money and property in the appropriate hands, Winstanley cut through the moral debate on commerce and money with a single stroke. For him, political tyranny and the corruption of commercial society were inextricably intertwined. Only the elimination of money, coupled with common access to the land, communal distribution of its product, and the appropriate reform of law to reflect these changes could promise peace and prosperity to the whole nation. Prophetically, from Winstanley's perspective, to alter England's "constitution" in any way short of this was "not to reform, but to baptize the law into a new name, from kingly law to state law."[27]

I mention these various perspectives on money and commerce not as a rehearsal of possible "influences" on Locke. Rather, I want to suggest more generally that the domain of discourse addressing the relationship between money, property, and political power was both diverse and extensive, its varied parameters loosely marked by traditional evocations of the moral economy and by radical Christian moral prophecy, as well as by emerging scientific or empirical perspectives.[28] What lent coherence to this range of interpretations, what made them accessible to contemporary understanding, was not their common status as economics, but their common dependence upon and deployment of current categories of moral and political meaning. Winstanley, no less than Locke, Petty, or even Filmer, inveighed against idleness, praising the virtues of productive labor and the industrious employment of the nation's resources. Despite their often substantial political differences, all saw the welfare and prosperity of the nation as a significant responsibility and charge of the political realm. Locke's relationship to these various ways of marking the connection between political power and commercial life, I would suggest, was in cognitive terms little different from our own intellectual relationship to the variety of perspectives that characterize the loose coherence of analogous contemporary discursive realms. Relative to the purposes we are pursuing or the issues we are addressing,

27. Ibid., 280.
28. In pointing to the loose parameters of a discursive field I am suggesting something very different from the idea of "ideological context" as this appears in the works of Skinner and Tully. Rather than attempting to capture the "fit" of Locke's "doctrines" or arguments into a structure of possible ideological positions, I mean to suggest his work's embeddedness in a fabric of ideas stretched across a highly unsettled discursive terrain.

what we don't beg from one perspective we may well borrow or steal from another as it seems to render the world more intelligible or to further our understanding of our chosen topic. To be sure, we may do this with a greater or lesser degree of self-consciousness, and with more or less awareness of the sources or implications of our borrowing. But that we do it, and often less than logically or reflectively, would be difficult to deny.

But Locke's project of justifying action against a corrupt administration by equating such action with the punishment of common criminality constrains his borrowing in certain ways. To so frame political power in a world for which politics, production, and morality were intimately bound together was to adopt a standpoint that appropriated such elements of existing discourses of morality and property as could render intelligible a politics centering on law and right, crime and punishment. For these purposes, the standpoint of supplicants to the proper exercise of political power, characteristic of assertions of the old moral economy, was wholly inadequate. That point of view might allow one to invoke the king's justice against the corruption of particular merchants or engrossers or even against lesser magistrates, but it offered no moral grounds for charges of political misrule against the government itself, writ large as it was upon the king's person. Inadequate, too, for such a project was the more narrowly economic concern of nascent political economy, which tended to take the legitimacy of constituted authority for granted and to concentrate rather on particular issues of policy and recommendations for the improvement of the nation's wealth or revenues.[29] The moral basis of Digger opposition to political corruption, of course, provided a more systematic critique, but its radical leveling of the social hierarchy was perceived by many as highly threatening. Even so, in practical terms Digger activism was limited, for its focus on voluntary conversion to a vision of utopian communalism eschewed any intention of assuming political power over an unregenerate nation.

As a point of critical leverage on the relationship between property and political power, however, Winstanley's strident moralism is far from unrelated to Locke's theistic articulation of God's purposes

29. Locke, of course, was himself a contributor to this genre, and an influential one at that. His own economic writings, however, are emphatic in their insistence not simply upon issues of national prosperity but upon a parallel concern for the maintenance of equity in the formulation of national policy.

and design for the natural community. It is true that the two men's relationship to the commercial society of their day was very different, but their points of difference are suggestive. Although Locke's work is markedly removed from Winstanley's radical social vision, neither is it sanguine about containing the corruption wrought by money and commercial life on the moral potentials of human character. But if the Digger's prophetic voice condensed antipathy to commerce into a resurrection of God's original design by regenerate believers in the simplicity of an agricultural community, Locke's perspective on money and commerce took a more equivocal, more worldly, more practical turn. Where Winstanley looked to a moral community of sufficiency, Locke's belief in the congruence of material abundance and the improvement of life's conveniences with God's purposes set him on a different path.[30] Specifically with respect to money, in place of the Digger's categorical rejection Locke accepted the benefits of commerce and of improved productivity and attempted, instead, to render money intelligible within his understanding of the moral categories of God's architecture and his perception of the character and function of political power in that design.

II   Money, Morality, and the Disruption of Judgment

While Locke's prowess as an economic theorist is certainly a matter of debate, his recurrent allusions to money suggest that his understanding of its meaning and function in human life was intimately connected to his concern for the moral basis of human action.[31] While the invention of money was an innocent thing, a matter of

30. For an interpretation of Locke's relationship to the "improvers," see Neal Wood, *The Politics of Locke's Philosophy: A Social Study of "An Essay concerning Human Understanding"* (Berkeley: University of California Press, 1983); and Wood, *Locke and Agrarian Capitalism.*

31. For specific discussions of Locke as an economic theorist see Letwin, *Origins of Scientific Economics;* Appleby, *Economic Thought and Ideology,* chap. 8; Karen Iverson Vaughn, *John Locke: Economist and Social Scientist* (Chicago: University of Chicago Press, 1980); Constantine George Caffentzis, *Clipped Coins, Abused Words, and Civil Government: John Locke's Philosophy of Money* (New York: Autonomedia, 1989); and, most recently, Patrick Hyde Kelly's excellent introduction to the collection of economic writings, John Locke, *Locke on Money,* ed. Patrick Hyde Kelly, 2 vols. (Cambridge: Cambridge University Press, 1991), 1:1–116.

fancy or delight in its appearance,[32] like any worldly property or possession, its moral meaning is not inherent in its substance but follows rather from the extent to which its use conforms to the imperatives of virtue and the prohibition of injury to others. As he suggests in a different context, "We cannot doubt there can be anything so good or innocent which the frail nature or improved corruption of man may not make use of to harm himself or his neighbor since the Apostle tells us we may abuse the *grace of God* into wantonness."[33] The moral meaning of money, in other words, can be no more or less ambiguous than the character and actions of its possessor and the purposes it is made to serve: what is a useful tool in the hands of one may well become a weapon in those of another.

Once again, we might recall that the understanding of order circulating through Locke's texts centered not simply on empirical regularities or patterns in the world, but on the necessary conformity of human action with God's rules of virtue. Whatever human agents might invent and however variously they might settle their inventions in social custom and practice, they still remained accountable for their actions toward their fellows. In this sense, as our previous discussion of the moral meaning of property suggested, it is not simply the possession of money that is at issue, but the meaning of its use in relation to the moral markings of God's architecture. Like other material goods, money was something that could be used for human purposes, and as such its meaning was both conditioned by and expressive of the moral character of those purposes. But unlike

32. Locke, *Two Treatises*, 2.46.

33. John Locke, *Two Tracts on Government*, ed. Philip Abrams (Cambridge: Cambridge University Press, 1967), by page, English Tract, 155. This allusion to the Apostle is particularly suggestive, for Paul's admonitions to the Galatians center on the relationship between God's law and human liberty: "Ye have been called unto liberty," he tells them, "only use not liberty for an occasion to the flesh, but by love serve one another" (Gal. 5.13 AV). Cautioning against envy, strife, malice, provocation, vainglory, and the like, he reminds them that "they which do such things shall not inherit the kingdom of God" (Gal. 5.21 AV). The task for Paul is one of keeping Christian liberty righteous within the bounds of law, while the law is summarized by the simple rule to love one's neighbor as one's self (Gal. 5.14). This book of the New Testament continued to fascinate Locke throughout his life, and provided the text of his last reflections. For his treatment of St. Paul's address to the Galatians in particular, see John Locke, *A Paraphrase and Notes on the Epistles of St. Paul to the Galatians, Corinthians, Romans, Ephesians. To Which is Prefixed an Essay for the Understanding of St. Paul's Epistles by Consulting St. Paul Himself*, in *The Works of John Locke in Ten Volumes* (1823, reprint, Scientia Verlag Aerlen: 1963), 8:27–72.

God's donation of property in the things and creatures of created nature, money was a peculiar sort of possession. For Locke, as for Winstanley, money was both the product of imagination and the vehicle of desire, and no part of God's original design. "Riches and Treasure," Locke observes, "are none of Natures Goods, they have but a Phantastical imaginary value."[34] The moral dilemma money presented to Locke had to do not with its role in commerce per se, as was the case for Winstanley, but with its potential for inciting or reinforcing a disproportionate desire for worldly goods and power, to the neglect of a concern for moral conduct and the care for one's soul.

This concern is articulated perhaps most pointedly in Locke's educational writings. There, for example, he advises parents never to reward their child's behavior with money or luxuries: "What do you by proposing these as *Rewards*, but allow them to be the good Things he should aim at, and thereby encourage his longing for them, and accustom him to place his Happiness in them?"[35] To the contrary, Locke insists, "a good, a wise, and a vertuous Man" should learn "to cross his Appetite, and deny his Inclination to *riches, finery, or pleasing his Palate*."[36] Genuine happiness lay not in such worldly goods, but in the right ordering of a life in conformity with the imperatives of virtue. Parents who do not understand this, he suggests, "sacrifice [their children's] Vertue, invert the Order of their Education, and teach them Luxury, Pride, or Covetousness, etc. For in this way, flattering those wrong Inclinations, which they should restrain and suppress, they lay the Foundations of those future Vices, which cannot be avoided, but by curbing our Desires, and accustoming them early to submit to Reason."[37] This curbing of desire, however, is not simply a matter of repression. Rather, it involves directing one's desires in a manner consonant with the imperatives of virtue and channeling them into an order that reflects the highest potential of the species. The desire for money and worldly riches, in this context, is a wrong inclination, a misplaced value, and one that by its relationship to the

34. Locke, *Two Treatises*, 2.184.
35. John Locke, *Some Thoughts concerning Education*, in *The Educational Writings of John Locke*, ed. James Axtell (Cambridge: Cambridge University Press, 1968), by paragraph and page, ¶52, 151. Hereafter cited as *Some Thoughts*.
36. Ibid.
37. Ibid.

vices of pride and luxury poses not only a temptation but the possibility of inverting the hierarchy of values embodied by the rule of virtue.

Discomfitted by the possibility of such inversion, Locke emphasizes the significance of moderation—an appreciation of the social virtue of liberality and an understanding of one's necessary relatedness to others. It is on these grounds that he urges parents to distinguish between the "Wants of Fancy" and those of "Nature." "Those are truly Natural Wants," he observes, "which Reason alone, without some other Help, is not able to fence against, nor keep from disturbing us. The Pains of Sickness and Hurts, Hunger, Thirst and Cold; want of Sleep, and Rest or relaxation of the Part wearied with Labour, are what all Men feel, and the best dispos'd Minds cannot but be sensible of their uneasiness."[38] Compared to these, Locke views a child's yearning for clothes of a particular fabric or color, or food of a certain kind, as an expression of fancy alone, a selfish and self-indulgent whim distant from genuine need. The objects of such desires are thus characterized as things of conceit, unrelated to the natural necessity that any number of other objects might answer. Restraining desire, in this context, is a question of avoiding the indulgence of fancy and excess, of discerning and understanding the difference between gratifying one's wants and fulfilling one's needs.

This self-restraint, however, is not simply self-involved. Locke also emphasizes the significance of social virtue in the conduct of one's life in general and one's relationship to worldly goods in particular. On these grounds, and in a language of moral character strikingly similar to that of the *Second Treatise,* he cautions parents to encourage in their children a proper attitude to both conduct and material possessions. "As to the having and possessing of Things," he suggests, "teach them to part with what they have easily and freely to their Friends," for this will engender both kindness and civility.[39]

---

38. Ibid., ¶107, 208–9. See also John Locke, *Essay concerning Human Understanding,* ed. Peter H. Nidditch (Oxford: Clarendon Press, 1975), by book, chapter, and paragraph, 2.21.45, where this appears as a distinction between the "ordinary necessities" such as "the *uneasiness* of *Hunger, Thirst, Heat, Cold, Weariness* with labour, and *Sleepiness* in their constant returns," and the "fantastical *uneasiness,* (as itch after *Honour, Power,* or *Riches,* etc.) which acquir'd habits by Fashion, Example, and Education have settled in us, and a thousand other irregular desires, which custom has made natural to us." Hereafter cited as *Essay.*

39. Locke, *Some Thoughts,* ¶110, 213.

"Covetousness, and the Desire of having in our Possession, and under our Dominion, more than we have need of, being the Root of all Evil, should be early and carefully weeded out."[40] No recognition should be accorded "to the *Complaints* of the *Querulous,*" but one should "curb the Insolence and Ill-nature of the Injurious."[41] In all this, "great Care is to be taken, that Children transgress not the Rules of *Justice;* and whenever they do, they should be set right, and if there be Occasion for it, severely rebuk'd."[42]

The conventionality of Locke's moral landscape is, of course, generally acknowledged, as is his concern for the inculcation of moral virtue and the avoidance of vice and corruption in the formation of personal character. Less commonly addressed, however, is the relationship between the moral character of money on this terrain and its role in Locke's account of the creation of civil society in the *Treatises.* There, in his presentation of the state of nature, against the naturalness of individual property right arising from material need, money is an expression of imagination, its value dependent upon human "Fancy or Agreement . . . more than real Use, and the necessary Support of Life."[43] The innocence of its invention, however, is accompanied not simply by moral ambiguity or uncertainty but by equivocality, for its use points in two directions simultaneously. On the one hand, the durability of money facilitates the production and exchange of the "truly useful, but perishable Supports of Life."[44] In this role it appears morally neutral; the convenience of its function in barter injures no one, since any particular individual's curious fascination with the glitter and sparkle of precious gems and metals cannot violate the right of others to nature's goods. On the other hand, the introduction of money into the natural community also generates the possibility of what Locke deems the most corrupt of human motives, the desire of having in one's possession more than one needs. It introduces, in other words, a vehicle for temptation and covetousness, and the potential for supplanting the natural order of need and sufficiency with the pursuit of private advantage and superfluity in the accumulation of worldly goods. In this, money

40. Ibid., ¶110, 213–14.
41. Ibid., ¶109, 213.
42. Ibid., ¶110, 214.
43. Locke, *Two Treatises,* 2.46.
44. Ibid., 2.47.

stands as a symbol of worldly purposes, and its utilitarian function in production and exchange is inseparable from its more disturbing capacity to engender temptation and encourage the inversion of the order of virtue.

Unlike his economic tracts, where he considers money's nature and the implications of its use and circulation at length, Locke's references to money in both the *Treatises* and the essay on education have the air of stating the obvious. This, of itself, is not particularly surprising, since its role in commodity exchange as a placeholder for the comparison of equivalent values between human necessities was generally acknowledged, as was its more morally problematic relationship to corruption and vice. To elucidate the political meaning of money in the *Treatises,* however, we need to go beyond a recognition of the apparent conventionality of Locke's attitudes toward it and consider as well its bearing on the rise of "inconveniences" attending the judgment and punishment of crime in the natural state. If, as I have argued, the epistemology of natural right lent experiential certainty to the just appropriation of property and the recognition and punishment of crime, how is the moral order of these natural politics affected by the introduction of money? To address this isssue, let us return to the *Treatises* and continue our speculative reconstruction of the cognitive processes of Locke's natural agents as they confront the introduction of money.

Locke's peaceful state of nature, as we have seen, evokes a harmonious vision of natural property relations and the administration of natural justice, a state in which a directly experiential knowledge of one's own, provided by the epistemology of right, guaranteed the convergence of right and conveniency. Taken together, Locke's notion of labor as the foundation of individuals' material property, his conception of need-based property rights, and his provisos limiting appropriation ensured the capacity of his natural agents to discern reliably the moral requirements of the law of nature. Where each could easily understand what was properly their own, their natural liberty to pursue their own individual judgments of private convenience could without difficulty be rendered consistent with the rule of virtue's prohibition of human injury. What was not experientially marked as their own clearly belonged to others, either because it remained in common or because it had been marked by the labor of another. In such a context the violation of right was easily seen, and such few controversies as might arise could be easily settled. We have seen how these criteria functioned in the premonetary state to order and define the conditions of judgment under which just and unjust acts could be distinguished and the latter equitably punished. But to grasp the specifically political meaning of money here, we need to consider its bearing upon these conditions of judgment as well as the exercise of the power which they ground, particularly as this is related to the inconveniences that eventually necessitate the creation of civil society. Clearly Locke presents the invention of money as opening the possibility for individuals in the natural state to appropriate more than they themselves could directly use. The issue that arises in this situation, though—given Locke's persistent concern for conduct and moral order—is how this might have affected their capacity to understand the moral requirements of natural law.

In the original state, reason provided three practical principles that allowed Locke's natural agents to conform their actions to the abstract demands of the law of nature that they preserve themselves and others. Of these—labor, "enough and as good," and spoilage— it is the last that is most directly affected by the introduction of money. While Locke viewed property inequalities and the scarcity of land as among the eventual consequences of its use,[45] the spoilage limitation on direct individual appropriation is most immediately transformed. Money is a "lasting thing that Men might keep without spoiling" that by tacit consent would be accepted for the "truly useful, but perishable Supports of Life."[46] Just as some might trade their fruit for a cache of nuts that would last longer, so might they provide for future necessities by trading their excess product for gold, silver, or gems that would last indefinitely. With this, the long shadow of commerce falls across Locke's presentation of the state of nature. Money affects the principle of spoilage, however, not so much by elimination as by attenuation. When the criterion of individual use is extended or expanded to include the exchange of products for money, that which an individual might appropriate for use is no longer contained within the boundaries of direct or natural need. The moral meaning of this, however, remains equivocal. On the one hand, though originating in fancy, the desire for money can

45. Ibid., 2.45, 50, 108.
46. Ibid., 2.47.

also be understood as an expression of the distinctly human characteristic of foresight, since its possession stands as a provision for future necessities. On the other hand, and more disturbingly, monetarized exchange also effectively removes the producer from a direct
relationship to, as well as responsibility for, the fate of the product.
At the same time, and again in more morally questionable terms, it
introduces imaginary wants and the accompanying possibility of unbounded desire into human agents' relationships both to nature and
to each other.[47] No longer driven simply and necessarily by natural
needs, their use of nature becomes potentially a matter not of sufficiency and need but of excess. Where spoilage limited the extent of
possession, the excesses of such few who might lean toward self-
indulgence could be easily recognized and, if necessary, equitably
punished. Where this boundary of natural appropriation is attenuated, however, the way is opened not only for the expanding
productivity of the industrious but for the ambitions of the covetous
in their immoderate pursuit of worldly wealth for its own sake as
well.

In addition to these cognitive and characterological implications,
money carries with it important practical consequences as well. Unlike values exchanged in barter transactions, the terms and measure
of which are set by the usefulness of the goods traded to the life of
man, the terms of monetary exchanges are influenced by the fanciful value attached to money itself. Gold, silver, and the like have no
more intrinsic value for human preservation and comfort than
rocks, but unlike the latter they are not only durable but scarce. On
Locke's rendering of the original state, the natural goods that individuals require for subsistence and comfort are all either already

47. For a striking example, see Locke's discussion in his economic tracts of the
different importance of "vent" in the analysis of commodities and the analysis of
money. The fluctuating vent of the former rests on variable consumption, an elasticity
of demand that nonetheless remains for Locke because nobody buys them "but according to the use he has of them, and that has its bounds." In the analysis of money,
on the other hand, vent is not a significant consideration, "everybody being ready to
receive Money without bounds and keep it by him, because it answers all things." John
Locke, *Some Considerations of the Consequences of the Lowering of Interest and Raising the
Value of Money*, 1691, 2d ed., corrected, in *Several Papers Relating to Money, Interest, and
Trade & c.* (London: A. & J. Churchill at the Black Swann, 1696; facsimile, New York:
Augustus M. Kelley Publishers, 1968), 71; reprinted in Locke, *Locke on Money*, 1:261.
Hereafter cited as *Some Considerations*. Pages cited will be from *Locke on Money*, with
original pagination following in parentheses for readers using the facsimile edition.

plentiful or become so with industry, and they are thus valued against each other by the primary criterion of usefulness. Precious metals and gems, to the contrary, are scarce, and the resultant value of things measured by monies thus has the potential of becoming highly unstable. As Locke put it in one of his economic tracts, that value is dependent upon the more abstract, indirect, and anonymous relationship between their "vent" which makes their price relative to the aggregate proportion of buyers to sellers, and the relative scarcity or abundance of such goods and money itself.[48] And, as Locke observed of the commercial society of his day, not only may the amount of available goods vary over time, but the amount of money may vary as well: "Thus it comes to pass that there is no manner of settled proportion between the value of an Ounce of Silver, and any other Commodity: For either varying its quantity in that Country, or the Commodity changing its quantity in proportion to its vent, their respective values changes, *i.e.* less of one will barter for more of the other."[49]

By considering the effect of money and its unsettling of the natural-use value of things upon human judgment of crime and punishment rather than upon property relations in the narrow sense, we can see that its invention has implications beyond the obvious fact that it allows individuals to appropriate for trade quantities that would spoil if personal use still bounded their efforts. Most immediately, in this juridical context it effectively eliminates any fixed or stable measure of value by which such direct personal injuries as theft might be equitably redressed. Under the criterion of use, as we saw previously, the debt due to the victim of theft would remain equivalent to that which had been stolen, regardless of how much time might have elapsed between the crime and the criminal's apprehension. But when money, to paraphrase Locke, alters the value of everything,[50] by what measure or rule might just reparation be deter-

---

48. Ibid., 1:252–57 (58–65).

49. Ibid., 1:255 (62).

50. Locke, *Two Treatises*, 2.37. See also Locke, *Some Considerations*, 1:258 (66), where Locke notes curiously that there both is and is not an "intrinsic" value of things in monetarized commerce: "1. That the Intrinsick Natural worth of any Thing, consists in its fitness to supply the Necessities or serve the Conveniencies of human Life; and the more necessary it is to our Being, or the more it contributes to our Well-being the greater is its worth: But yet, 2. That there is no such Intrinsick Natural settled value in any Thing, as to make any assign'd quantity of it, constantly worth any assigned quantity of another."

mined? By the market value of the stolen commodities at the time of
the theft? By their going price at the time of the thief's conviction?
By some other standard? Further, who is to determine which of
these rules most equitably answers the requirements of justice? Were
both the thief and the victim to be drawn more to the value of
money than to an equitable resolution of the debt, the former would
doubtless prefer the lower of the values, the latter the higher. Thus
money again has radically attenuated if not, indeed, eliminated the
previously direct linkage between crimes and their equitable punishment that had characterized the administration of natural justice in
the premonetary state.

    This, however, while perhaps the most direct, is not the only way
in which money compromises human access to the rule of virtue and
disrupts natural judgments of the requirements of justice in the
original condition. On Locke's account it is not only the introduction
of money, but its combination with increased population and stock
that lies at the root of the inconveniences that plague the natural
state. As the number of people in certain areas of the world grows,
so too does the need for increased production of nature's consum-
ables necessary for human preservation and comfort. When this supply ceases to be plentiful other sorts of practical problems begin to
emerge. In the *Considerations* Locke illustrates the principle in some
detail: "What more useful or necessary things are there to the Being
or Well-being of Men, than Air and Water, and yet these have generally no Price at all, nor yield any Money. . . . But, as soon as ever
Water (for Air still offers it self every where, without restraint or
inclosure, and is therefore no where of any Price) comes any where
to be reduced into any proportion to its consumption, it begins presently to have a Price, and is sometimes sold dearer than Wine."[51] In
the case of land, by transcending the spoilage limitation on direct
individual appropriation, money allows Locke's natural agents to enclose greater tracts than their personal use requires. This, as he observes in the *Treatises*, an individual could still do rightfully, just as
one might accumulate large sums of money, "*the exceeding of the*

    51. Locke, *Some Considerations*, 1:256 (63–64). Locke's faith in the sufficiency of
God's donations to answer the "natural" needs of the species comes through in the
remainder of the passage: "Hence it is, that the best, and most useful things are
commonly the cheapest; because, though their Consumption be great, yet the Bounty
of Providence has made their production large, and suitable to it."

bounds of his just *Property* not lying in the largeness of his Possession, but in the perishing of any thing uselessly in it."⁵² In Locke's view, though, the desire for money and the increasing private appropriation of land go hand in hand, for "where there is not something both lasting and scarce, and so valuable to be hoarded up, there Men will not be apt to enlarge their *Possessions of Land,* were it never so rich, never so free for them to take."⁵³ Were it not, then, for the fanciful attachment to money and the "hopes of Commerce," even vast quantities of land "would not be worth the enclosing." Indeed, for the individual without such prospect of worldly gain, "whatever was more than would supply the Conveniencies of Life . . . for him and his Family" would be returned "to the wild Common of Nature"⁵⁴

With the invention of money, however, and its rippled diffusion by the succession of private individuals' "tacit consent" to its use, the natural measure of sufficiency is dissolved. There is no longer a known limit on the size of private enclosures. Thus it was not simply the invention of money, but this in combination with the increase of population that "in some parts of the World . . . made Land scarce, and so of some Value."⁵⁵ By implication, until this occurs the criterion of "enough and as good" that ensured the justice of particular enclosures might remain unaffected by the use of money. But as this situation begins to develop, how might just and unjust appropriation be distinguished?⁵⁶ If two neighbors, for example, each wanted to enclose the last remaining parcel of waste adjacent to their properties, which could do so justly? The obvious answer, of course, is whichever did so first, for presuming the necessities of all others to be provided for, whatever the size of their holding, no one would be injured by the last enclosure. In this case, while property in excess of need can be rightfully appropriated, the law of nature provides no

52. Locke, *Two Treatises,* 2.46.
53. Locke, *Two Treatises,* 2.48. In terms of the implications of money for the question of political judgment, it is immaterial whether Lockean money is a capital to be loaned or invested, or a treasure to be hoarded.
54. Ibid.
55. Ibid., 2.45.
56. Robert Nozick, *Anarchy, State, and Utopia* (Oxford: Basil Blackwell, 1974), 174–82, considers a series of similar hypotheticals, but his emphasis upon the logical or analytical rather than the moral and theistic dimensions of the problem misses Locke's assumption that conformity to the moral imperatives of natural law has a significant bearing on one's prospects in the world to come.

principle for the particularization of that right, for on Locke's representation of God's design, what all as created equals may do by right
any one may do, and the individuation of property remains marked
by the human activity of labor alone, not by law. But what if all
others are not provided for? Here, even the first person deprived of
sufficient property for subsistence might justly claim that the right to
self-preservation had been compromised. And what then? Should
the last enclosure be reduced to accommodate the needy? Why not
the largest? The most productive? The least improved? Or perhaps,
as some modern interpreters would have it, anyone left landless at
this point would simply be excluded from property ownership in
land altogether, and compelled to labor upon the property of others
either as a rent-paying tenant or as a wage laborer. Still, even if this
were the case, what would be the appropriate relationship between
the use of another's property and rent, or between wages and labor?
How, by whom, and on what grounds might such ratios or propor-
tions be determined?[57]

There is, of course, no way of knowing whether Locke actually
considered anything resembling these imaginary scenarios, although
many of the issues they pose were common points of controversy in
both law and litigation in the period. Such hypothetical examples of
the moral dilemmas generated by the invention of money could be
multiplied at length, but the issue they point to is relatively straight-
forward. With money's elimination of the direct use or sufficiency
criterion, and with its consequent disruption of the practical principles that guided the conformity of human action with the demands
of the law of nature, the designed complementarity of law and right,
virtue and convenience, necessarily becomes problematic. Private
property and its appropriation remain rights of nature, but the attenuation of the relationship between the exercise of such individual
liberties and their social consequences severs their previous convergence with the conveniency or harmony of the whole. Right and
conveniency no longer go together. With this disordering of the cri-

---

57. Both Macpherson and Wood have argued that it is precisely in such contexts
that Locke's complicity with the rise of capitalism can be ascertained. From the perspective of moral responsibility, however, the issue here is not so clear, for the Tudor
and Stuart state was long held responsible for ensuring a living wage in many contexts, particularly through the regulation of the woolen industries and the periodic
revision of the Statute of Artificers.

teria and conditions of natural judgment, Locke's natural agents, once happily embedded in a community of sufficiency and contented with the fulfillment of their natural needs, now stand in danger of being lost in a sea of controversy. The rule prohibiting harm remains obligatory by the law of nature, but with the distancing of private appropriation from the boundary of direct use there are no longer any practical principles or commonly accessible measures to establish reliably the just limits of any particular property. As a result, the claims of those who profess injury, as well as the punishments of those who commit crimes, cannot be adjudicated with reference to any clear criterion of judgment.

Here, Locke's contention that "were it not for the corruption, and vitiousness of degenerate Men" all would remain in this "great and natural Community" is not at all inconsistent with his allegation that the general enjoyment of property is "unsafe" and "unsecure."[58] There are no longer direct, empirical, personally ascertainable criteria, as there were in the premonetary state, by which just and unjust acts of appropriation can be reliably distinguished. Lacking any such guide to determine the bounds of their possessions or the extent of their rights, all may well be "constantly exposed to the Invasion of others." The principle issue here, however, is not necessarily a matter of the inequality of possessions and the protection of the "haves" from the "have nots." Neither is it, strictly speaking, simply a question of defending the properties of the "industrious and rational" from the predations of the injurious or from the self-serving disturbances of the "quarrelsome and contentious." Before a property can be justly defended its title must be legitimately defined, but with the introduction of money and the eventual scarcity of land in some places there is no longer any sure way to determine whether the limits of any possession, however large or small, are justifiable. At that point the boundaries of all properties become potentially unsettled and subject to claims for revision, and the possessions and rights of both the "industrious" and the "contentious" are put in the same condition of jural uncertainty.

Substantial though they may be, however, the insecurity of property and the various forms of disorder and confusion that unsettle the practical affairs of the natural condition should not be conflated

---

58. Locke, *Two Treatises*, 2.128, 123.

with a state of war. From Locke's perspective, reasonable individuals may yet be able to settle their differences and agree upon boundaries between them, for the social virtues of promising and good faith belong "to Men, as Men, and not as Members of Society."[59] A state of war, on the other hand, refers to a relationship between individuals in which someone declares "by Word or Action, not a passionate and hasty, but a sedate settled Design, upon another Mans Life."[60] In particular it speaks to the intention to use "force without Right" against the person or property of another.[61] In this context, the conventionality of Locke's views on the moral meaning of money and its potential effect on human character becomes quite significant.

To begin with, in supplanting the natural or intrinsic value of things with an unstable measure of human artifice, money introduces into human judgments of convenience a worldly consideration that knows no bounds, an estimation of value that recognizes no natural limits. While it is not the cause of human perversity, money yet provides a vehicle for the contagion of corruption and encourages in human agents the wrong inclinations that Locke rails against in his educational writings. Despite its felicitous function in exchange, money's origin in imagination and fancy continues to render it suspect in moral terms, particularly as it facilitates a pride in worldly things, material indulgence, and the pursuit of excess in place of a proper concern for moral conduct and just relations with one's fellows. In cognitive terms, if access to the moral requirements of the law of virtue has been dissolved, the just determination of rights becomes a matter not of certainty, but of probability. In the *Essay* Locke suggests the dilemma this represents quite bluntly: "Let never so much Probability hang on one side of a covetous Man's Reasoning, and Money on the other; and it is easie to foresee which will out-weigh. Earthly Minds, like Mud-Walls, resist the strongest Batteries: and though, perhaps, sometimes the force of a clear Argument may make some Impression, yet they nevertheless stand firm, keep out the Enemy Truth, that would captivate, or disturb them."[62]

---

59. Locke, *Two Treatises*, 2.14.
60. Ibid., 2.16.
61. Ibid., 2.192, 207, 222, 226–28, 230, 232, 239, 242.
62. Locke, *Essay*, 4.20.12. The phrase "earthly minds," of course, suggests a mistaken and shortsighted emphasis on worldly concerns on the part of creatures created capable of salvation.

Although the general use of money may sufficiently distort human estimates of private convenience to render "the greater part no strict Observers of Equity and Justice,"[63] there nevertheless remains a significant difference between squabbling over property, however pervasive or vociferous, and the eruption of violence as a means of deciding controversies. It is in this context, however, that Locke's "strange doctrine" regarding the egalitarian distribution of the executive right of punishment combines with his curious introduction of money into the state of nature to set the stage for the transition to civil society. From a practical point of view, to the extent that Locke's natural agents have been beguiled by the imaginary value of money and have set upon the progressive enlargement of their properties, their estimates of private advantage will tend to take undue precedence over serious consideration of equity and justice. Such partiality to their own convenience and their stock of worldly goods might make them as quick to take offense at the slight misdeeds of others as they are unlikely to recognize their own excesses. But however unsettled property relations might become, however uncertain or doubtful the boundaries of what is justly one's own, Locke's natural agents should still be capable of recognizing that the use of force against another is only lawful as punishment for a crime.

With the dissolution of the epistemology of right, however, monetarized property relations have rendered the definition, recognition, and equitable punishment of crime quite problematic. To be sure, conventional forms of injury such as theft or robbery can still be known, but the just measures of their punishment have been rendered controversial. In more commercial contexts, however, as well as with respect to controversies over the size of possessions or provision for the needy, money has radically attenuated if not dissolved the previously clear relationship between the possession and use of property and the natural-law prohibition of human injury. As Locke notes in the *Essay*, "If one, who makes his complex *Idea* of *Justice*, to be such a treatment of the Person or Goods of another, as is according to Law, hath not a clear and distinct *Idea* what *Law* is, . . . 'tis plain his *Idea* of Justice it self, will be confused and imperfect."[64] Needless to say, in these circumstances both one's judgments and one's subsequent actions based on such mis-

63. Locke, *Two Treatises*, 2.123.
64. Locke, *Essay*, 3.11.9.

taken understandings will be equally confused. With the disordering of
natural judgment, this is precisely the dilemma wrought by money's
capacity to encourage or exacerbate the vices of selfish partiality in the
natural state. This, indeed, parallels Locke's own description of the
sources of the inconveniences attending his natural agents' exercise of
their right of punishment: "Self-love will Make men partial to themselves and their Friends," while "Ill Nature, Passion, and Revenge will
carry them too far in punishing others"; they will act "with too much
heat in their own cases" even as "negligence and unconcernedness will
make them too remiss in other Men's."[65]

Such excesses or neglect in the matter of punishment themselves
contribute to the further sundering of right and conveniency in the
natural state. The task of the rule of law for Locke is the protection of
property, taken broadly as life, liberty, and possessions; punishment is
necessarily the deprivation or forfeiture of these. Here, then, the exercise of executive right is no different from any other action in that its
justice consists in its conformity with certain rules.[66] Unjust or excess
punishment is itself an injury, for which its perpetrator becomes, in
turn, accountable. Although this situation surely holds the possibility of
escalating into a spiral of one injury upon another, each defended by
some notion of justice, even this is not necessarily the same as a state of
war. For it actually to become so, in Locke's terms, one party or another to any particular conflict would have to abandon the simple reac-
tiveness of haste or passion and embark upon a "sedate settled Design"
upon the life of another. However partial, self-concerned, or generally
remiss the bulk of Locke's natural agents might be, it is far more likely
that the possibility of a state of war rests primarily upon the shoulders
of the corrupt and vicious few whose covetousness and ambition mark
them as those whose understandings have been most distorted into a
"Mistake of true Power and Honour."[67]

Thus for Locke the general unsettling of property and the greater
or lesser probability of a state of war, each associated with the corruption of character wrought by money, are yet distinctly different problems besetting human agents in the final stage of the natural state.

65. Locke, *Two Treatises*, 2.13, 125.
66. For an extended discussion of punishment, see John Locke, *Second Letter concerning Toleration*, in vol. 6 of *The Works of John Locke in Ten Volumes* (1823; reprint,
Scientia Verlag Aalen, 1963).
67. Locke, *Two Treatises*, 2.16, 111.

Both, however, are emblematic of the disordering of the conditions and criteria of natural judgment that once guaranteed the complementarity of law and right and the associated convergence of right and conveniency. The lawful exercise of property right, the liberty of use with respect to one's own on the basis of one's private judgments of convenience, was dependent upon the capacity of human agents to discern the bounds of that liberty set by natural law. With the disruption of the epistemology of right this direct access to the rule of virtue is occluded. In a sense, the invention of money removes Locke's natural agents from the original order of God's design and deposits them in new circumstances, new social relations, plagued by a moral chaos of their own making. Individual judgments of private convenience in this context, potentially still within the bounds of right, no longer bear a necessary relationship to the convenience of the whole.

As many modern commentators have suggested, Locke's state of nature indeed comprises a strange amalgam of analytic abstraction and historical conjecture. And, as some contend, the monetary relations of commercial society are strategically placed there to evoke the problems that for Locke make civil society both necessary and desirable. On the interpretation developed here, however, they do this not by dividing society into a privileged class of rational and industrious property owners and a propertyless (and presumptively less rational) mass, but by negating the experiential criteria that ground moral judgments of particular actions and in terms of which the just bounds of individuals' properties, in the broad sense, can be both reliably discerned and effectively protected. When Locke's natural agents are freed from the bounds of natural need, the social consequences of individual acts of appropriation can no longer be located in or attributed to the particular acts of identifiable persons, but rather begin to assume the demeanor of anonymous forces affecting the community as a whole. In this context, principles of morality associated with the appropriation and use of property become beset by selfishness, partiality, and worldly ambition. The possibility diminishes that Locke's natural agents will order their actions in accordance with the moral imperatives of God's law that prohibit injury, just as the potential for fraud, corruption, and violence expands. Justice, which Locke characterizes as the treatment of the person and goods of others in conformity with the rule of virtue, if it is possible at all, becomes far more a matter of chance and good intentions than the application of clear rules and criteria of judgment to particular cases. For Locke, individuals' natural rights and duties to preserve themselves and others require practical principles differentiating just and unjust acts to link particular judgments of appropriation and criminality to the universal imperatives of natural law. In the original state labor and the provisos fulfilled such a function by providing experiential markers for moral judgment outside of subjective partiality. In combination with scarcity, money subverts these conditions of judgment and in so doing casts Locke's natural humanity adrift in a sea of moral uncertainty.

Locke's political meaning here, however, is quite emphatically focused upon the consequences of this state of affairs for the exercise of executive right. Access to the moral requirements of natural law eludes the confused as well as the corrupt, and the definition and just punishment of crime becomes impossible in a state devoid of common principles and practical criteria to guide judgments of right. As Locke describes it, "The Law of Nature being unwritten, and so no where to be found but in the minds of Men, they who through Passion or Interest shall mis-cite, or misapply it, cannot so easily be convinced of their mistake where there is no establish'd Judge: And so it serves not, as it ought, to determine the Rights, and fence the Properties of those that live under it, especially where every one is Judge, Interpreter, and Executioner of it too, and that in his own Case."[68] On Locke's account it is precisely the common recognition of this dilemma that leads all to cede their executive right to a common authority: "And thus all private judgement of every particular Member being excluded, the Community comes to be Umpire, by settled standing Rules, indifferent, and the same to all Parties; and by Men having Authority from the Community, for the execution of those Rules, decides all the differences that may happen between any Members of that Society, concerning any matter of right; and punishes those Offenses, which any Member hath committed against the Society, with such Penalties as the Law has established."[69] The establishment of civil government, then, with its characteristic features of declared law, known judges, and processes of adjudication and appeal, as well as established power to execute punishment, resolves the "disorder and confusion" of Locke's late state of nature.[70]

68. Ibid., 2.136.
69. Ibid., 2.87.
70. Ibid., chap. 9, entire.

Were Locke's theoretical project limited to suggesting only the practical necessity of civil power, his account of its origin and character might have stopped here. But in addition to this Locke was concerned as well to ensure the just and proper exercise of this power in the hands of those to whom it was entrusted and, more significantly still, to provide moral grounds for the justification of popular action against any who might be so corrupt as to violate that trust. If human access to the principles of morality has been rendered so problematic, the question arises how Locke's civil agents are to become so capable of recognizing the misdeeds of their governors as to equate resistance with the legitimate and morally justifiable punishment of common criminals. Since the deficiency of the natural state which civil society must remedy is not simply that of effective power but of moral knowledge as well, it behooves us to consider the moral dimensions of Lockean political power more closely. By taking up the question in the context of Locke's writings on toleration, and then returning briefly to the ground we have covered here, the next chapter will begin to consider Locke's positive construction of political power in civil society and the grounds of judgment upon which its exercise depends.

5

Morality Matters:
Civil Power and the
Reordering of Judgment

> Order is Heaven's first law.
> —*The Book of Common Prayer*

In elucidating Locke's hierarchically ordered cosmology I have
sought homologies and patterned resonances between his political works and his writings on religion, morality, education, and epistemology. By tracing some of these parallels I have suggested the
moral character of the connection between his theistic understanding of the human condition and the central terms of his political
vocabulary. I have also situated Locke's project of "justification" and
his treatment of money in the unsettled discursive terrain of seventeenth-century English political argument, urging that his defense of
political resistance was an attempt to reinscribe the core elements of
the traditional English political idiom in a framework of God's purposes. Throughout this account, I have suggested that Locke should
be read as intensely interested in the question of power. To the extent that he has been interpreted as a theorist of power, however, he
has most commonly been understood as concerned essentially with
its limitation and the prevention of its abuse. In general, such readings tend to reduce his notion of political power to governmental
power, and then go on to recount the manner in which such power
might be checked, restrained, or circumscribed in practice. Seen in
these terms, Locke's work may well seem not only single-minded, but
out-and-out repetitive, occasionally rising from pure monotony to
mere tedium, if at times enlivened by self-contradiction or confu-

sion. However many ways one might suggest that government should not be arbitrary or, to put it positively, that government should be limited, Locke seems to manage at one point or another to articulate at least as many as were perhaps conceivable to the mind of a seventeenth-century Englishman.

Recall his opening definition of political power in the *Second Treatise*—as "*a Right* of making Laws with Penalties of Death, and consequently all less Penalties, for the Regulating and Preserving of Property, and of employing the force of the Community, in the Execution of such Laws, and in the defence of the Common-wealth from Foreign Injury, and all this only for the Publick Good."[1] One might well see Locke's theoretical enterprise as giving historical and institutional specificity to these rights and purposes: the legislative power making laws, the executive enforcing them and through the federative power carrying on international relations. Indeed, many of Locke's interpreters have understood the *Treatises* as precisely this sort of project. With a nod to the polemical aim of refuting Filmer in the *First Treatise*, the *Second Treatise* has been commonly discussed as an argument about the legitimate exercise of political power in terms of the proper form, relations, or functions of political institutions. Julian H. Franklin, for instance, reads Locke for his contribution to theories of resistance right.[2] Here, Locke's doctrine of popular sovereignty and his account of the dissolution of government are seen as resolving a contradiction in earlier constitutionalist theories under conditions of mixed monarchy. These, for Franklin, failed to account for the tension in actual political practice between the alleged legislative supremacy of representative bodies and the equally acknowledged areas of substantial royal independence. Also locating the problem at the plane of institutional practice, John Gough addresses the question whether or not Locke presented a "false theory of sovereignty."[3] Phrased in these terms the issue becomes one of ascertaining the extent to which Locke offers, in Gough's terms, "an

1. John Locke, *Two Treatises of Government*, ed. Peter Laslett, rev. ed. (1960; reprint, with amendments, Cambridge: Cambridge University Press, 1963), by book and paragraph, 2.3. Hereafter cited as *Two Treatises*.

2. Julian H. Franklin, *John Locke and the Theory of Sovereignty: Mixed Monarchy and the Right of Resistance in the Political Thought of the English Revolution* (Cambridge: Cambridge University Press, 1978), esp. chaps. 1, 2, and 4.

3. John Gough, *John Locke's Political Philosophy, Eight Studies*, 2d ed. (Oxford: Clarendon Press, 1973), 23.

accurate description of the English Constitution in his own day."[4]
Characterizing Locke's derivation of political society from a state of
nature as "a mere product of the philosophical imagination" he
nonetheless observes that Locke's "resultant limitation of the power
of government was no figment, but a rationalization of accepted constitutional practice."[5] A similar perspective was offered by Sterling
Lamprecht in a much earlier work. In his analysis of Locke's treatment of legislative and executive power, Lamprecht observed "Just
as the English constitution was not a logical structure in which the
functions of the various departments were precisely defined, but an
historical compromise in which various unwritten precedents and
extra-legal conventions were followed as well as statute laws, so
Locke's theories present an inconsistent attitude on many points."[6]

It is, of course, not at all difficult to see Locke's *Treatises* as mirror-
ing the institutional mechanisms and controversies of his own day,
and I think it fairly clear from the text that at least a part of that
project does have to do, as James Tully suggests, with condemning
and condoning certain practices of that period. It is one thing, however, to say that the *Treatises* did this, but it is quite another to think
that this was all they did, or even that this was their primary or most
significant theoretical concern. Indeed, Locke himself cautioned
against too narrow an institutional reading. When he spoke of the
founding of a political commonwealth he explicitly asked to "be understood to mean, not . . . any Form of Government, but *any Independent Community*."[7] It is, in other words, within such a community
broadly conceived that Locke was concerned to pursue his principle
theoretical issue, "to understand Political Power right."[8] Without denying the significance he attached to political institutions, I think it
nonetheless clear that his theoretical emphasis fell more upon the
active exercise of their peculiar powers than on the particular historical forms in which these were manifested. "It is not," he insisted,
"Names, that Constitute Governments, but the use and exercise of
those Powers that were intended to accompany them."[9]

4. Ibid.
5. Ibid.
6. Sterling Lamprecht, *The Moral and Political Philosophy of John Locke* (New York:
Columbia University Press, 1918), 87.
7. Locke, *Two Treatises*, 2.133.
8. Ibid., 2.4.
9. Ibid., 2.215.

Hence from an epistemological perspective Locke's treatment of political power in the *Second Treatise* and elsewhere can be seen as analogous to his analysis of intellectual power in the *Essay*. There, his explorations of the boundedness of human capacities served to focus and condense the power of human intelligence upon the tasks for which he found it to be naturally suited. By respecting the limits of its constitution, so to speak, the mind could concentrate and intensify its power. And this power, on Locke's view, had been created capable of attaining the knowledge necessary to live a life of moral rectitude, social peace, and material comfort; God had endowed human agents with the capacities to discover what was necessary both to "the comfortable Provision for this Life and the Way that leads to a better."[10] That this possibility had remained unrealized throughout human history was not due to a defect in the created constitution of the species, but rather resulted from human agents' mistaken judgments of the ends or purposes to which their operative powers had been directed. Were we to focus attention narrowly upon what Locke considered to be the mind's inadequacies, we might well miss the audacity and substance of his positive claim: that in God's design human agents naturally possessed the intellectual power to provide not only for peace and plenty, but for salvation as well.

Similarly, the limitations or constraints that characterize Lockean government can be seen as constructed not so much to minimize or bound its power as to ensure what we might call its "properly political" exercise. To focus upon the mechanisms of containment or restraint, whether social or institutional, is to risk miscasting the intensity, scope, and character of his positive conception of political power—when it is directed to its proper ends. Here, as is the case for Locke's account of intellectual power, the fundamental question presented by political power lies, in the first instance, in distinguishing between the activities and endeavors for which he finds it suited and those which exceed the boundaries of its constitution. In both cases, Locke articulates the grounds for this distinction through an epistemological perspective on human agents' capacity to discern God's intentions for the species within the morally marked and hierarchically structured world of the architecture of order. As a conse-

10. John Locke, *Essay concerning Human Understanding*, ed. Peter H. Nidditch (Oxford: Clarendon Press, 1975), by book, chapter, and paragraph, 1.1.5. Hereafter cited as *Essay*.

quence, the positive tasks Locke assigns to the political realm are not only significantly charged with moral meaning but far more extensive than is often thought. My purpose in this chapter is to begin to develop this perspective—to characterize Locke's positive conception of political power and his construction of its character, scope, and proper aim in relation to the moral order required by God's design.

I   Politics and Morality in Locke's Early Work

The claim that Locke's positive conception of political power is explicitly concerned with moral order and is constituted as a carrier of moral meaning and purpose would seem liable to two significant objections. First, Locke's epistemological explorations were explicitly devoted to identifying the multiple sources of uncertainty and confusion attending moral judgment. This was obviously the case with respect to the question of saving knowledge and faith, but it was equally a matter of concern with regard to human access to natural law and the understanding of moral conduct more generally. Second, and largely on the basis of the epistemological difficulties described in the *Essay,* a significant portion of Locke's political writings were specifically directed to removing questions of faith and religious duty from the direct purview of political power. To respond to these objections adequately, it is necessary to speak of what remains conspicuously unremarked in the *Treatises,* the issue of the relationship between civil power, moral duty, and the possibility of salvation. To suggest how that work intimated this relationship, we shall return once more to the framing function of the architecture of order, for if Locke's account of the disordering of moral judgment by the imaginary value of money spoke to an issue of ongoing contemporary contestation, the conceptual tools he brought to its political resolution again resonate strongly with a decidedly theistic understanding of the human place in God's creation as well as with his epistemological explorations of the possibility of moral knowledge within that design.

Locke first addressed the question of the relationship between moral duty and political power in the context of the Restoration debate over the right of magistrates to impose ceremonies in religious worship. These early explorations, directed as they were to the specific issue of the connection between political power and the devotional duties required by God for salvation, tended to take the existence and accessibility of God's law for granted. In other words, rather than asking how one might know what God's law commands, the essays focus emphatically upon the question of the magistrate's power over "all things not comprehended in that law."[11] Here, although the categories structuring the essays suggest the general relationship between divine and human law, Locke's primary concern is with those precepts that define human duties to God and the particular status of these with respect to civil jurisdiction. Again resonant with the vertical imagery so common in Locke's work, the formal structure framing his argument in both essays consists in a hierarchical cascade of obligations:

> All the things that are indifferent so far as a higher law is concerned are the object and matter of a lower, and the authority of the individual prevails in all matters that are not wholly prescribed by superior law, and whatever is left, as it were, in the balance, inclining neither to this side nor to that, towards neither good nor evil, can be adopted and appropriated to either class by an adjoining and subordinate power. For where the divine law sets bounds to its action, there the authority of the magistrate begins, and whatever is classed as indeterminate and indifferent under that law is subordinate to the civil power.[12]

Within this hierarchy all laws of human artifice receive their obligatory force from divine precept, and no inferior law may void an obligation imposed by a superior.[13] Finally, with respect to the authority of human laws over things indifferent to God's rule, this obligation is but circumstantial or temporary, and is binding only so long as the inferior law continues in force.[14] Whatever civil law may require, in other words, the thing itself remains indifferent.

Locke's basic assumption in both tracts is that, with respect to di-

---

11. John Locke, *Two Tracts on Government*, ed. Philip Abrams (Cambridge: Cambridge University Press, 1967), English Tract, 124. Hereafter cited as *Tracts*. Abrams makes this point in his introduction (25–26); as does von Leyden in his introduction to John Locke, *Essays on the Law of Nature*, ed. Wolfgang von Leyden (Oxford: Clarendon Press, 1954), 28–29. Hereafter cited as *ELN*.

12. Locke, *Tracts*, Latin Tract (trans.), 227.

13. Ibid., 226.

14. Ibid.

vine or natural law, all possible human actions are either "necessary," that is, specifically required or prohibited by God's rule of
virtue, or "indifferent" to it. He emphatically asserts the rightful extension of civil power without exception over the latter category of
actions left free or undetermined by the law of God. Within the
morally marked world of the architecture of order, in other words,
all human actions that are not directly determined by God's law are
proper matters for political determination. Rejecting any ground for
distinguishing between civil and religious "indifferency," Locke contends that the particular rites and ceremonies of worship are no-
where stipulated by God's rule. As a result, he argues that such devotional practices are every bit as subject to political determination as
anything else left free by that law.[15] To oppose the civil imposition of
religious ceremonies, from this perspective, is tantamount to denying the civil magistrate power over anything at all. Locke's conclusion, after stating the argument in these terms, is that "the supreme
magistrate of every nation . . . must necessarily have an absolute and
arbitrary power over all the indifferent actions of his people."[16]

This, needless to say, is a striking conclusion for a thinker later
hailed as a champion of toleration and a defender of nonconformity
in matters of religion.[17] For my present purposes, however, the importance of these early essays lies, on the one hand, in their conception of a structured hierarchy of law and jurisdiction and, on the
other, in the categories of analysis within that structure that formally
distinguish the different tiers of law and the respective spheres of
activity in which they operate. Locke's formulation of the relationship between religious necessity and indifference parallels what I described earlier as his theistic understanding of God's dual purpose
for the human species within the architecture of order. In that design, as we have seen, the members of the species were to fulfill their
duty to their maker by honoring his glory and rendering him the
requisite worship, and they were to meet their duties to their fellows

15. Ibid., English Tract, 153; Latin Tract (trans.), 229.
16. Ibid., English Tract, 175.
17. For discussions of Locke and toleration more generally see Gough, *Locke's Polit-*
ical Philosophy; W. K. Jordan, *The Development of Religious Toleration in England*, 4 vols.
(London: G. Allen & Unwin, Ltd., 1932–40); and H. F. Russell Smith, *The Theory of*
Religious Liberty in the Reigns of Charles II and James II (Cambridge: Cambridge University Press, 1911). See also Abrams' introduction to Locke, *Tracts*; and von Leyden's
introduction to Locke, *ELN*.

by pursuing a peaceful life in society. Locke's argument in the *Tracts* distinguishes between these two purposes by positing a rigid and rather literal separation between human agents' created spiritual capacity for eternal life and the outward corporeal exigencies of their condition in society in earthly life. Divine necessity or religious virtue here becomes equated with the private or inward person, the subject of a kingdom "not of this world."[18] It commands "the actions of the inner virtues of all of which God is the object, as the love of God, reverence, fear, faith, etc.; this is that inner worship of the heart which God demands, in which the essence and soul of religion consists."[19] As terrestrial creatures, however, individuals' expression of such virtue requires bodily action as well: "Since God ordained that man should be composed of body as well as soul, he orders that he alone should be served by one of these, while by means of the other he has secured society and mutual association for mankind; for men cannot express the sentiments of their mind or benefit from mutual good will without the mediation and service of the body."[20] However privately true and constant one's inner voice might be to the commands of virtuous worship and true religion, the actions of the body for Locke are public and social, and hence particularized by a "host of circumstances . . . such as Time, Place, Appearance, Posture, etc."[21] These, he argues, are in their specific expression undetermined by Scripture and this indifferency leaves them to the jurisdiction of temporal authority. The civil magistrate may thus legitimately impose the form of external worship "as he should judge best in the light of the times and the customs of the people, and as the needs of the church should demand."[22] The broad criteria Locke suggests as appropriate to the magistrate's commands in this context are the same as those attending all his considerations of civil power, "the public peace and the welfare of the people,"[23] although here as elsewhere he gives the terms little content.

18. Locke, *Tracts,* English Tract, 133; see also Latin Tract (trans.), 233.

19. Ibid., Latin Tract (trans.), 214.

20. Ibid., Latin Tract (trans.), 214–15.

21. Ibid., Latin Tract (trans.), 215. A similar construction is used in Locke's general discussion of the nature of action, particularly in terms of its relationship to law; see Locke, *Essay,* 2.21.10.

22. Locke, *Tracts,* Latin Tract (trans.), 216.

23. Ibid., Latin Tract (trans.), 237. See also 219 and English Tract, 150. We will return to this point later.

In this formulation Locke construed religious virtue as inhering in the conformity of the mind to the general precept of divine law commanding the worship of God, but he left determination of the appropriate bodily expressions of this open to regulation by the authority of temporal powers. Locke thus defended imposition as a purely civil power, guided by civil necessity and exercised for the purposes of peace and social order as the exigencies of time and place require. Scripture may command, "Let all things be done decently and in order," but it is left entirely to the right and discretion of political authorities to judge the specific actions consistent with decency and order in their particular society.[24] The explicit charge of the political realm here becomes the peace, safety, and well-being of human agents as civil subjects in their bodily and temporal concerns. In this, Locke concluded his first attempt to work out the political implications of his understanding of the created condition of the species, whose members are beings designedly capable of eternal life, yet subject to the necessities and accidents of corporeal and social existence.

The sphere of religious belief and salvation was fundamentally associated with the relationship between the individual and God and had to do with the conformity of one's actions to his will. With respect to the worship he required, however, morally necessary actions consisted in the disposition of the mind, not the body. Further, and again consistent with the dual nature of the species, compliance with the divinely prescribed duty of worship fulfilled the first of the human functions in God's architecture, the glorification and reverence of the creator. But God had designed human agents with another function as well, to pursue a moral life in society with their fellows. Appropriate to this purpose they were also prescribed general rules of conduct consistent with God's will that their mutual relations be peaceful and orderly. Though, on Locke's view, the hierarchy of obligation morally forbade the magistrate to violate or void any element of the higher law, it was nonetheless well within the scope of political authority to include "what has already been enjoined by God" as part of civil law, particularly as this is required for social order.[25] The civil magistrate, in other words, may well legislate re-

24. Ibid., Latin Tract (trans.), 234. See also English Tract, 146.
25. Ibid., Latin Tract (trans.), 239; see also 223. Compare Locke, *Two Treatises,* 2.135, for a more mature and specific statement of this general point. A bare sugges-

garding murder or theft, not to mention usury or adultery, by adding civil encouragements to whatever God already requires. Thus, while religious belief necessary for salvation was a matter of individual conscience, moral actions could be stipulated and reinforced by civil command.

Here, the dual nature and purpose Locke ascribes to the created character of the species establish his initial grounds for distinguishing between the proper spheres of politics and religion. The latter becomes narrowly associated with the spiritual inward person, with one's individual relations with God as maker, and is substantially removed from the temporal concerns and worldly activities of ordinary life. With respect to the political realm, on the other hand, the *Tracts* empowered civil government to regulate virtually all external actions pertaining to the mutual relations of human agents in society. The repeated caveat that this jurisdiction was legitimate only insofar as required for the peace and welfare of earthly existence operated here not as a limitation of civil power, but as a highly elastic theoretical extension of its potential field over the entirety of social relations. While the criterion of the public good was asserted, it remained essentially vacuous, an empty conceptual space subject in terrestrial terms to whatever practical imperatives particular magistrates in particular times and places might deem appropriate. For this early Locke, rulers remained morally bound to observe the rules of virtue, but within the hierarchy of law and obligation God alone was their judge and civil subjects had no worldly recourse in the face of magisterial transgression.

It is certainly true that the point at which Locke demarcated the specific practices proper to the respective spheres of politics and religion changed substantially between the *Tracts* and his later essays on toleration.[26] This shift, however, represents neither a blurring of his notion of the species' dual nature nor a reversal of his judgment of the proper place and moral function of the political realm in the larger design of God's architecture. Rather, it rests upon three as-

tion in the *Tracts*, this theme is treated at some length in Locke's first defense of toleration, the unpublished "An Essay concerning Toleration" (1667), in H. R. Fox-Bourne, *The Life of John Locke* (London: H. S. King, 1876), esp. 181–83.

26. Three letters on the subject were printed in Locke's later debate with Jonas Proast in 1689, 1690, and 1692. A fourth remained unfinished at Locke's death in 1704. All are printed in Vol. 6 of *The Works of John Locke in Ten Volumes* (1823); reprint, Scientia Verlag Aalen, 1963.

pects of Locke's intellectual development within this framework: his growing interest in epistemology, his formulation of a more nuanced understanding of the role of conscience in religious belief, and following from these, his consequent refinement of the criteria for specifying the content of the public good as a ground for judging the bounds of properly political power. To understand Locke's positive conception of political power and its relationship to moral duty, it is important to recognize that this shift in Locke's judgment of policy was significantly driven by his adoption of a sensationalist philosophy of knowledge. This in turn, as we shall see, provided him with a plausible ground for distinguishing between the just and unjust exercise of civil power, as well as a moral basis for resistance to the latter. Let us turn, then, to consider this shift in some detail.

II Civil Power and the Privatization of Religion

Confronted with the problematic relationship between moral duty, salvation, and political power, Locke's first forays onto the terrain of political discourse were directed to the narrow question of religious virtue. In the face of diverse interpretations of those elements of God's law stipulating human duties to their maker, Locke defended the civil imposition of religious ceremony and extended the scope of political power to all outward acts, all physical and material aspects of life in society. As early as the "Essay on Toleration" of 1667, however, his writings begin to indicate a shift away from this broadly inclusive grant of civil power and toward a more finely focused exploration of the possibility of distinguishing between civil and religious indifferency. Culminating in his extensive letters in support of toleration, Locke's mature treatment of indifferency attempted a clear epistemological separation of one's duties to God in worship and one's duties to others in temporal life. In particular, these later works are devoted to defining the relationship between such outward acts as these very different sorts of rules might require or prohibit and the proper scope and purpose of political power in the hands of the civil magistrate.

In effect, Locke's later defense of toleration abandons his initial separation of mental duty and bodily performance in favor of a construction that differentiates between worldly acts of public and private concernment on the basis of experiential and epistemological rather than abstract or formal grounds. As a result, his broad theoretical distinction between the public purposes of civil power, pertaining to earthly peace and the preservation of social order, and the ends of religion, concerned with things necessary to salvation and the ordering of private souls, remains unchanged. What does change, however, is Locke's development of the epistemological grounds for this distinction and his consequent refinement of each category in terms of the manner in which and certainty with which each might be known. In his later writings on toleration it is these shifts that enable the relegation of religion to a private concern and allow a more perspicuously framed notion of civil power. Locke announces this project as well as its temporal significance succinctly in his *Letter concerning Toleration*: "I esteem it above all things necessary to distinguish exactly the Business of Civil Government from that of Religion, and to settle the just Bounds that lie between one and the other. If this be not done, there can be no end put to the Controversies that will be always arising, between those that have, or at least pretend to have, on the one side, a Concernment for the Interest of Men's Souls, and on the other side, a Care for the Commonwealth."[27] It is, of course, hardly new to cast Locke's politics as intended to ensure the peace, safety, and security of human agents in worldly terms, nor is there anything the least surprising in the claim that his theoretical energies were devoted to distinguishing politics from religion. Indeed, Locke's decidedly worldly focus was shared not only with such now canonical political writers as Machiavelli and Hobbes, but with multitudes of his less illustrious English contemporaries as well.[28] But where the secular emphases of others excluded both salvation and suprapolitical moral categories as central political con-

27. John Locke, *A Letter concerning Toleration*, ed. James Tully (Indianapolis: Hackett Publishing Co., 1983), 26.

28. See, for examples, Quentin Skinner, "The Ideological Context of Hobbes's Political Thought," *Historical Journal* 9, no. 3 (1966): 286–317; and Quentin Skinner, *Foundations of Modern Political Thought*, 2 vols. (Cambridge: Cambridge University Press, 1978). See also the treatment of seventeenth-century England in J. G. A. Pocock, *The Ancient Constitution and the Feudal Law: A Study of English Historical Thought in the Seventeenth Century*, 2d ed. (Cambridge: Cambridge University Press, 1967); and J. G. A. Pocock, *The Machiavellian Moment: Florentine Political Thought and the Atlantic Republican Tradition* (Princeton: Princeton University Press, 1975). The secularism of the period, however, is not articulated simply from the standpoint of authority, as one can see from the individualist perspectives typical of the Leveller tracts of the Civil War years. A good source for the latter is Don M. Wolfe, ed., *Leveller Manifestoes of the Puritan Revolution* (New York: Humanities Press, 1967).

cerns, both Locke's theism and his theoretical intent to justify the
morality of resistance entailed the necessary retention of moral categories as a characteristic element of political understanding. Indeed,
as we shall see in a moment, Locke's privatization of religion was
accompanied by an affirmation of civil determinations of moral order.

Locke's formulation of a distinction in temporal terms between
actions expressing one's duties to God and those concerning one's
duties to others is theoretically significant, for it grounds his attempt
to retain the latter as a criterion establishing the legitimate scope and
purpose of political power, while banishing the former to the purely
private realm of individual conscience. By virtue of their shared concern for mutual obligations in ordinary life, Locke's arguments for
toleration and his discussion of the "Original, Extent, and End of
Civil Government" in the *Second Treatise* can thus be read as complementary expressions of a common theoretical purpose. This purpose, broadly characterized, consists in advancing a mode of political
understanding capable of distinguishing properly political power
from its despotic corruption and, at the same time, of offering a
moral justification for resistance to the latter as consistent with a care
for the fate of one's soul. The complementarity of the two projects
inheres in their differential articulation of the epistemological
morass in which, on Locke's account, the question of the grounds of
moral judgment had become mired. Both, to put the point differently, emerge from his explorations of the difficulty of attaining
moral knowledge, and both are significantly concerned with the relationship between a care for one's soul and the moral meaning, purpose, and implications of political judgment and action in civil society.

In theoretical terms, Locke constructs the conceptual bridge between the two projects in the notion of political power. This concept,
however, is held in place within each project differently, as it re-
ceives its theoretical content through its juxtaposition with contrast-
ing categories drawn from two very different levels of God's architecture of order. In the works on toleration this power and the civil
interests that constitute its proper end are defined and delimited as
finite, public, and temporal concerns for the things of this life, in
contrast to the private and individual, but ontologically higher, concern with God's promise of salvation for the faithful. In the *Second*

Treatise, by contrast, political power is juxtaposed not against the infinite and eternal, but against the bestial and brutal. There it appears as a power both proper to human agents by virtue of their unique subjection to God's moral law and expressive of their natural right and capacity to enforce that law as it pertains to their mutual obligations amidst the finitude of temporal existence.

In the opening pages of the first letter on toleration, Locke denominates as civil interests such things as "life, liberty, health and indolency of body," as well as the possession of worldly goods.[29] With respect to these he characterizes the proper tasks of political power as well as its distinctive means, in relatively short compass:

> It is the Duty of the Civil Magistrate, by the impartial Execution of equal Laws, to secure unto all the People in general, and to every one of his Subjects in particular, the just Possession of things belonging to this Life. If any one presume to violate the Laws of Publick Justice and Equity, established for the Preservation of those things, his Presumption is to be check'd by the fear of Punishment, consisting of the Deprivation or Diminution of those Civil Interests, or Goods, which otherwise he might and ought to enjoy. But seeing no Man does willingly suffer himself to be punished by the Deprivation of any part of his Goods, and much less of his Liberty or Life, therefore is the Magistrate armed with the Force and Strength of all his Subjects, in order to the punishment of those that violate any other Man's Rights.[30]

Here, Locke describes the proper business of the political realm in the conventional terms of the English political idiom: the rule of law, the security of property, and the rightful use of force in punishment. "All civil power, right, and dominion," he continues, "is bounded and confined to the only care of promoting these things: . . . it neither can nor ought in any manner to be extended to the Salvation of Souls."[31]

For the purpose of understanding Locke's positive construction of political power, two of his arguments for this prohibition are particularly germane, each of which centers on defining the proper place and function of political power with reference to the species' created

29. Locke, *Letter concerning Toleration*, ed. Tully, 26.
30. Ibid. Again, this theme is extensively developed in the second of Locke's letters on toleration.
31. Locke, *A Letter concerning Toleration*, ed. Tully, 26.

potential for eternal life. On the one hand, he insists, the performance of one's duties to God must carry the inward persuasion of
one's conscience, and this can only be gained through admonition
and argument. The distinctive and rightful activities of political
power to "give laws, receive obedience, and compel with the sword"
are neither suitable nor fitting to the task of engendering faith:
"Penalties in this case are absolutely impertinent, because they are
not proper to convince the mind. . . . It is only Light and Evidence
that can work a change in Mens Opinions; which Light can in no
manner proceed from corporal Sufferings or any other outward
Penalties."[32] On the other hand, Locke continues, even if it were possible to compel belief, there is only one way to heaven and many
worldly princes of many different and conflicting religious persuasions. If the salvation of souls were the concern of magistrates, one's
ultimate fate would necessarily be bound up with whatever religion
"either Ignorance, Ambition, or Superstition had chanced to establish" in one's country of birth. This, for Locke, is simply absurd, for
it "ill suits the Notion of a Deity" that people "would owe their eternal Happiness or Misery to the places of their Nativity."[33] In addition
to this reductio, however, Locke offers an epistemological argument
for opposing the political determination of religious belief and practice. Although, he suggests, differences in religion have generally to
do with "frivolous things" of little importance to God's positive command of worship, there remain both animosity and doubt even
among Christians as to which way leads to salvation. Thus "Neither
the care of the Commonwealth, nor the right enacting of Laws does
discover this way that leads to Heaven more certainly to the Magistrate, than every private mans Search and Study discovers it unto
himself. . . . Princes indeed are born Superior unto other men in
Power, but in Nature equal. Neither the Right, nor the Art of Ruling, does necessarily carry with it the certain Knowledge of other
things, and least of all of the true Religion."[34]

Locke's defense of toleration thus condenses theoretical attention
on two fundamental deficiencies of the political realm with respect
to religion. First, the distinctive means of political power—that
is, the right of command and the rightful use of force in punishment

32. Ibid., 27.
33. Ibid., 28.
34. Ibid., 36.

—are neither useful or effective in engendering religious conviction. Secondly, with respect to one's duties to God, which are the distinct purpose of religion, earthly magistrates remain mere mortals and are not invested with any special access to saving knowledge by virtue of their political function and position. Following from these limitations, political society must disclaim both effective power and privileged knowledge with respect to the other-worldly ends of individuals' duties to God in worship. Thus bounded, the proper task and positive charge of political power is to guarantee the civil rights and worldly goods of human agents in their earthly sojourn. On the necessary separation of these two realms Locke is clear and emphatic: "The Boundaries on both sides are fixed and immovable. He jumbles Heaven and Earth together, the things most remote and opposite, who mixes these two Societies; which are in their Original, End, Business, and in every thing, perfectly distinct, and infinitely different from each other."[35]

From the vantage point of subsequent history this defense of religious toleration and its apparent separation of public and private concerns might be seen as the entering wedge for later claims of individual rights against the state. However accurate this characterization at the level of the historical practice of opposition and the political rhetoric of later liberal individualism advanced to justify it, in epistemological terms Locke's perspective is hardly so clear or simple as this more modern dichotomy between state and individual may suggest. To be sure, the political realm Locke evokes in the letters on toleration is epistemologically deficient with regard to the speculative truths of religion and its civil subjects' private concerns for their duties to God. It does not, however, follow from this that Locke denies civil power access to all aspects of God's rule of virtue that pertain to moral conduct. While the direct concern for salvation expressed in ceremonies and in matters of belief are certainly a part of God's law, there remain as well imperatives regarding duties to one's fellows in worldly life. In this context, no less than his earlier defense of imposition, Locke's defense of toleration invests civil power with moral purpose. "A Good Life," he suggests, "in which consists not the least part of Religion and true Piety, concerns also the Civil Government: and in it lies the safety both of Mens Souls

35. Ibid., 33.

and of the Commonwealth. Moral Actions belong therefore to the Jurisdiction both of the outward and the inward court; both of the Civil and Domestic Governor; I mean both of the Magistrate and Conscience."[36]

Locke does not, however, treat all moral duties as subject to political determination. "Covetousness, Uncharitableness, Idleness, and many other things are sins," he notes, "by the consent of all men, which yet no man ever said were to be punished by the Magistrate." In distinguishing between such sins as these and moral wrongs properly subject to civil penalty, Locke articulates his concerns not in the language of salvation, but in the traditional English idiom of law and right. Such private vices, whatever they may bode for the future state of one's soul in the eye of God, "are not prejudicial to other men's Rights, nor do they break the publick Peace of Societies."[37] Indeed, "even the sins of Lying and Perjury" cannot be punished by laws except, he notes, with a significant qualification, "in certain cases in which the real Turpitude of the thing and the offense against God are not considered, but only the Injury done unto men's Neighbors and to the Commonwealth."[38] Throughout these discussions, Locke reproduces his distinction between political and religious purposes in the world at the level of understanding itself. The criterion, in other words, that he suggests as appropriate for judging the proper scope of political power is not to be drawn from religious discourse and its necessary concern for otherworldly ends, but rather must be drawn from a civil concern for injury and a moral concern for the earthly purposes of peace and preservation. These

36. Ibid., 46. Compare Locke, *Tracts*, Latin Tract (trans.), 223, 239. An example will clarify the point. Civil power might both reinforce moral obligations mandated by natural law (or Scripture) and impose new obligations pertaining to civil society alone, and within Locke's notion of a hierarchy of obligations, practical morality looms far larger than doctrinal adherence as a marker of Christian belief. In the civil prohibition of theft or murder, for example, the political order may give greater specificity to the natural duties to abstain from stealing and killing. These things are not indifferent to natural law, and in Scriptural terms are already prohibited by God's command. The magistrate in this case adds nothing new to the previous obligation, except of course its more effective worldly enforcement. The civil order may also require that taxes or tolls be paid to support public highways. Concerned with a matter of public convenience, something not of direct concern to God's law, this is in itself not only religiously but morally indifferent.

37. Locke, *A Letter concerning Toleration*, ed. Tully, 44.

38. Ibid., 42.

two considerations may indeed overlap, operating in Christian societies as alternate descriptions of the act in question. But the political meaning of the act itself, Locke insists, must be understood and framed in terms of a civil discourse of unlawful harm and the violation of right, not in terms of sinfulness and the language of salvation.

Although Locke's successive treatments of toleration consistently exclude salvation from a proper understanding of political power, they offer little in the way of guidance for distinguishing between the legitimate and illegitimate exercise of such power in the field of worldly concerns. Focused as they are upon the deficiencies and incapacities of magistracy with respect to the questions of salvation and religious belief, they remain largely though not wholly silent about its positive character, scope, and boundaries with regard to those worldly matters that comprise its rightful domain. This, I would suggest, is precisely the project Locke undertakes in the *Second Treatise,* where his discussion of the "Original, Extent, and End of Civil Government" is cast in relation to a subordinate level of God's architecture of order. There, in other words, his construction of political power is concerned not with the Christian promise of salvation per se but with the moral problem of defining the right order of relations between individuals with respect to their worldly interests and their concern for social peace in earthly life. In descriptive terms, to be sure, Locke characterizes political power in both contexts as the guarantor of worldly order through law and the rightful use of force in punishment. But while the defense of toleration presents such power as ineffective and epistemologically deficient with respect to the highest of human concerns—that is, with regard to the fulfillment of one's duties to God in worship—in the *Second Treatise* that power is constituted as a distinct and properly human capacity to ensure moral order and enforce social virtue in stark contrast to the violence and brutality of beasts of prey.

The meaning and function Locke ascribes to natural law in the structured hierarchy of God's architecture is significant here, as is his theistic attribution of facticity to that design as a whole, for it is the conformity of their actions to that moral rule that distinguishes and elevates human agents from the temporal finitude of the lower orders of nature. At the same time, though, despite the insistent presence of natural law as the regulative principle of order in

Locke's representations of the created world, it is but a pale reflection of the richness and complexity of earlier natural law theories. Similarly, in comparison to the detailed and diverse duties to others represented within Christian theology, the moral order it embodies is narrowly defined. Mention is made, of course, of parental and filial duty, of charity and forgiveness, and of obligations to keep promises, but in general Locke effectively reduces the specifically political meaning of natural law to the prohibition of harm. Consistent with this emphasis, he constitutes political power in terms that center attention on the definition, prohibition, and punishment of injury.

In so doing, Locke advances a political sensibility, a mode of political understanding, that takes its measure from worldly and experiential considerations, and thereby sidesteps the dilemma of making the moral meaning of political power dependent on a demonstration of the true ground of virtue in all its complexity and contestedness. Different Christian sects as well as different ages and cultures may differ over what constitutes injury or over the reasons adduced for avoiding it, but that harm is to be prohibited and punished is for Locke a transhistorical given of God's creation. As he notes in the *Essay*, "Christians," "*Hobbists*," and "old *Heathen* Philosophers" may well agree on many rules of morality, but differ widely in their accounts of why those rules should be obeyed.[39] Such differences notwithstanding, for Locke the natural-law prohibition of harm remains a necessary structural element of God's design, independent of whether human agents ever discern what he considers to be the "true ground" of obligation, the "Will and Law of a God."[40] Other moral duties may be contestable or obscure, religion itself may have become corrupt, and "unassisted reason" may have fallen short of its divinely appointed task of discerning the necessary connections between all of God's moral laws.[41] On Locke's account, however, the fact of God's prohibition of injury remains the one moral rule inextricably linked to the exercise of political power, and it is this fact that underwrites Locke's conviction that such power is necessarily everywhere the same.

39. Locke, *Essay*, 1.3.5–6.
40. Ibid.
41. John Locke, *The Reasonableness of Christianity*, in *The Works of John Locke in Ten Volumes* (1823; reprint, Scientia Verlag Aalen, 1963), 7:139–40.

To return to the figuration of political power in the *Treatises*, by condensing the political meaning of natural law into the prohibition of harm and articulating the natural condition of the human species in the language of law, right, liberty, equality, and property, Locke both reinscribes his native political idiom in a context of God's purposes and, at the same time, renders it independent of Scripture and safe from theological controversy. In this sense, his contribution to the welter of casuistic and constitutionalist political debate of the period lay in his insistence upon the connection between the central terms of the English political vocabulary and the moral obligation to observe the essential social virtue of God's framework of order. In so doing he proffers an alternative foundation for that language, a foundation that not only sustains the familiar experiential character of ordinary political practice, but explicitly invests that practice with a moral rather than historical grounding. This in turn establishes an indirect relation between Locke's political realm and the question of salvation that so preoccupied many of his contemporaries. Whatever else God may require, the obligation to abstain from injuring one's created equals remained a fundamental characteristic of a moral life. Different religions or cultures, indeed even different Christian understandings of duty and morality, may add to this moral baseline. But for Locke they are incapable of altering its structural status as the given of God's architecture that marks the dividing line between human and animal existence.

It is, in other words, a fact of creation that human actions must conform to this rule to be properly human and that in the absence of such conformity no human group can cohere. Locke's observation regarding gangs of thieves is again pertinent: "Justice and Truth are the common ties of Society; and therefore, even Outlaws and Robbers, who break with all the World besides, must keep Faith and Rules of Equity amongst themselves, or else they cannot hold together."[42] By the standard of Christian duty and conscience, as we have seen, these practices would hardly be considered virtuous. Observing justice and equity among themselves only as "Rules of convenience," such outlaws fail to recognize their necessary moral ground in the will of God or natural law. For Locke, however, the facticity of the architecture of creation enfolded believer and non-

42. Locke, *Essay*, 1.3.2.

believer alike in a framework of God's purposes, and all instantiations of human community must by definition adhere to this rule. God, he asserts, has "by an inseparable connexion, joined *Virtue* and publick Happiness together; and made the Practice thereof, necessary to the preservation of Society, and visibly *beneficial* to all."[43] Whatever else God might require, the prohibition of mutual injury remains the necessary precondition of a moral life for creatures designedly capable of salvation, but it is also the bottom line of social cohesion for any human group.

It is with respect to this necessity that the *Treatises'* presentation of political power as a natural endowment of the species in the created condition takes on moral weight and significance. As we have seen, Locke's parable of the natural state marshaled the traditional English political vocabulary onto a terrain of God's design in a manner that not only articulated a certain means of access to the requirements of natural law but thereby ensured the moral autonomy and individual accountability of his free and equal possessors as responsible moral agents. Within this construction, however, Locke presents two distinct aspects of political power. Its operation and active expression lie, on the one hand, in an individual's right to employ "such means for the preserving of his own Property, as he thinks good, and Nature allows him." On the other hand, it inheres also in the rightful exercise of executive power to "punish the Breach of the Law of Nature in others so, as (according to the best of his Reason) may most conduce to the preservation of himself, and the rest of Mankind."[44] Both forms of this power, though differing in their objects, are to be exercised by Locke's natural political agents within the bounds of natural law, and both are represented as integral to the moral order of the natural community. Both, in other words, are constituted as consistent with the moral potential of human agents as creatures fit for salvation and created capable of knowing the moral boundaries of their liberty.

The right of punishment, however, is exceptional, for it is the single site in Locke's state of nature in which "*one Man comes by a Power over another*," the single instance in which the use of force, characterized as lawful harm, is permitted against another human creature.

43. Ibid., 1.3.6.
44. Locke, *Two Treatises*, 2.171.

It is only in the exercise of this power for doing "Justice on an Offender" that one of Locke's natural agents may "take away, or impair the life, or what tends to the Preservation of the Life, Liberty, Health, Limbs, or Goods of another." To be sure, Locke cautions that the exercise of this power is to be guided by the "calm reason and conscience" of its executor, and not the "passionate heats, or boundless extravagancy of his own Will."[45] And certainly, from the standpoint of God's design, it is a morally precarious power, for its distinctive means, the use of force, must conform to the rule of virtue to sustain the ordained separation between properly human agents and beasts of prey. To exceed this boundary, to punish wrongly or in excess, is itself an injury that renders its perpetrator beastlike and subject to punishment in turn. But to recognize this requirement is only to acknowledge that in Locke's view the exercise of this right, like all other forms of properly human liberty in the architecture of order, must conform to the imperatives of law and virtue. Far from an exception to the prohibition of harm granted solely to magistrates answerable to God alone, it is a democratically distributed and properly human right to enforce the law of nature where "all the Power and Jurisdiction is reciprocal" and each is accountable to all for its lawful exercise.[46] Thus despite its moral precariousness, the presence of such a power and the specification of its proper bounds in the created condition of the species invest its exercise with moral purpose and render the use of force it entails consistent with a regard for moral duty and the fate of one's soul.

III Civil Power and Moral Purpose

With these observations on the relationship between political power, moral virtue, and the promise of salvation in mind, we are prepared to discern the moral stakes of Locke's disordering of judgment in the *Second Treatise* and, following from this, to consider the specifically moral freighting of his positive conception of political power in civil society. Having banished the expression of individual duties to God in worship from a properly political understanding, Locke presents natural political power as coextensive with moral

45. Ibid., 2.8.
46. Ibid., 2.4.

judgment of duties to others with respect to the things of this world. Here, his reduction of natural law to the prohibition of injury condenses the exercise of political judgment and power into the active preservation of the boundary between law and right, virtue and convenience—and this in two quite specific contexts. Locke's natural agents, his free and equal possessors, are political creatures insofar as they conform their private judgments of "convenience" to the imperatives of virtue in the two distinct spheres of action specified by the two aspects of "natural" political power. On the one hand, in the use and preservation of their property—taken broadly as life, liberty, and worldly possessions—they are each empowered to do as they "think good" and "Nature allows" them. On the other hand, as executors of the law of nature they are empowered to retribute to transgressors of that law such punishment as is "proportionate" to their crime.[47]

In Locke's original presentation of the created condition of the species, the epistemology of right guaranteed the proper exercise of political power in each of these spheres of action. Secured within the finitude of an economy of needs, each agent was guaranteed experiential certainty of the just limits of what was rightfully their own, and thus established the moral bounds of their private judgments of convenience. It established, in similarly direct and experiential terms, equitable measures of punishment for such few transgressions as might occur. The rights of each were easily known and the complementarity of law and liberty was assured by the fact of common access to the lawful limits of private convenience. "Right and conveniency went together," the species expressed its moral potential in action, and the harmonious operation of the whole was ensured and enforced by the common possession of the executive right of punishment. All of this, as we have seen, is precisely what is undone by Locke's introduction of money in the natural condition of the species. Its moral meaning and significance in this context, however, far exceeds both its conventional characterization as an incentive to greed and its role in generating the practical confusions and instabilities that we noted in the previous chapter. In its disruption of the epistemology of right, the invention of money effectively dis-

---

47. For Locke's own quite explicit separation of these powers in parallel terms, see *Two Treatises*, 2.128–30.

solves human access to the ordained complementarity of law and right by eliminating the minimal experiential grounding for human agents to know what is justly their own, and in so doing it compromises the minimal condition of moral order required by the natural-law prohibition of injury. To be sure, "Truth and the keeping of faith" as well as promises and "bargains for truck" still belong "to Men as Men,"[48] but with the invention of money such controversies as do arise can no longer be settled by reference to any commonly accessible criterion of injury or any sure measure of just and equitable punishment. Just as the exercise of moral judgment is confounded by the difficulty of determining what is properly one's own or one's due, so too is the exercise of executive right beset by a parallel uncertainty.

With respect to Locke's representation of political power, this disruption of judgment is portentous. Where money has dissolved certain knowledge of the lawful bounds of one's property, the political power of each to judge what is suitable for preservation and convenience is similarly disordered. Without the epistemological grounding of labor and personal need, and with the consequent elimination of the provisos limiting the extent of private acquisition, there is no longer any common criterion for determining the lawful bounds of appropriation. The right to property indeed remains, but what has disappeared is any moral ground for its properly human possession, any criterion for its individuation in private title consistent with the preservation of all. Individual judgments of private convenience no longer bear any necessary relationship to natural law or to the convenience and harmony of the whole that the observation of that law entails. Under such conditions the divinely designed harmony of individual property rights with the good of the whole is threatened with dissolution.

It is in this context that the second aspect of Locke's characterization of political power assumes a central theoretical importance. As a distinctly human power to sustain the minimal conditions of virtue through the use of lawful force, the designed function of executive right as a vehicle of moral order has become fundamentally problematic. Like the moral claim to individual property, the natural right remains, but once again the criteria of judgment governing its

48. Ibid., 2.14.

proper exercise have become obscure. In particular, controversies over things valued in money are bereft of any common criterion that might resolve the issue and render one party or another subject to lawful retribution. Since punishment, for Locke, is equated with the lawful and, if necessary, forceful deprivation of liberty or property for the commission of crime, where the definition of criminality is uncertain such force cannot be exercised rightfully. What was once morally precarious for individuals becomes in practice pernicious for all, as monetarized property relations dissolve any semblance of a boundary between rightful force and force without right, between properly political power and the predatory ways of beasts.

In light of this, Locke's observation that "God hath certainly appointed Government to restrain the partiality and violence of Men"[49] takes on new meaning, for the creation of civil society in a context of moral confusion implies that its task is far greater than the centralization of the power of coercion. It is not, in other words, simply the practical efficacy of the natural rights to property and political power that has been dissolved by the invention of money, but the knowledge and moral grounding essential to their properly human exercise in the morally marked world of God's design. Locke's separate and autonomous moral agents, to put the point differently, have in their creation of the imaginary value of money generated new matters of moral judgment that elude the previously direct linkages between knowledge of one's own and the identification and just punishment of crime and injury in the possession and use of worldly things. Severed from the original criterion of natural need, both private judgments of convenience and individual understandings of injury have been rendered, in many situations, matters of subjective perception devoid of any necessary relationship to the moral imperatives of natural law. With this development the fundamental charge of political power in civil society becomes the reordering of moral judgment and the reconstitution of the right order of relations between individuals with respect to the just determination and peaceful use of that which is properly their own. Locke's civil constitution of political power, to put the matter directly, is thoroughly saturated with moral purpose. By settling property relations in public law, determining common definitions of crime with known punishments,

49. Ibid., 2.13.

and providing indifferent judges and certain enforcement, Lockean civil power is responsible for resurrecting the necessary preconditions for moral order and the observation of human duties to their fellows with respect to the things of this world. Its task, in short, is to reconstitute through civil law the possibility of moral order once guaranteed by the epistemology of right, and in so doing, to reconstruct through human artifice the structural distinction between human action and bestiality required by God's design.

Considered in the context of the architecture of order, this broad construction of the political realm inserts civil power as an intermediate level of authority in the hierarchy of God's creation. As articulated in the letters on toleration and the *Two Treatises*, Locke's late political theory thus replicates in significant respects the imagery of a structured hierarchy of obligation advanced decades previously in the *Tracts*. It differs substantially from the *Tracts*, however, in its refinement of the purposes and proper objects of political power to a care for the things of this world and the determination of such duties to others as are necessary to give worldly content to the natural-law prohibition of injury. In its settling and preserving of individual title to what is rightfully one's own, the political realm is thus charged with ensuring, through the making and execution of civil law, the essential precondition of moral order in temporal life—and this in the broadest sense, for even such conventional virtues as charity and liberality require a settled self-propriety for their proper expression.

In this new situation, however, the divinely ordained complementarity between virtue and convenience, between the obligations of natural law and properly human liberty, still stands as the measure of the moral potential of the species in God's architecture of order. Here, by linking political power with the rightful possession of property, Locke has done more than simply exclude a direct consideration of salvation from a proper understanding of political right. For if institutionalized political power is necessary to guarantee to each the just possession and use of what is legitimately their own, its scope and function is itself morally framed by this purpose. Though the law of nature requires the use of force for its worldly efficacy, it also requires that such force conform to the imperatives of moral order if it is to count as a legitimately human and properly political power. If, in other words, Locke's natural agents create civil institutions to reconstitute propriety and reaffirm the distinction between human agency and the violence of beasts, they can hardly be expected to tolerate a deviation from this purpose in civil power itself. As Locke suggests early in the *Second Treatise,* "wherever violence is used, and injury done, though by hands appointed to administer Justice, it is still violence and injury, however colour'd with the Name, Pretenses, or Forms of Law."[50]

With these remarks Locke intimates the moral legitimacy of resistance against those who exceed their rightful power. What remains to be seen, however, given money's disruption of moral judgment in the natural state, is precisely how the rightful scope of such power is to be known in the context of particular political orders and how, consequently, its excess or violation is to be recognized in practice. Here, as we shall see, Locke's sensationalist philosophy and its theoretical emphasis upon the experience of injury may well have endowed civil government with a power far less limited and far more problematic than is generally taken to be the case. Let us shift, then, from the moral underpinnings of Locke's positive conception of political power to its temporal exercise in worldly practice and action.

50. Ibid., 2.20.

6

A Politics of Judgment:
Political Understanding,
Resistance Right, and the
Rule of Law

> There are two sorts of Contests amongst Men, the one
> managed by Law, the other by Force: and these are of that
> nature, that where the one ends the other always begins.
> —John Locke
> *A Letter concerning Toleration*

The concern with reason and judgment in the face of uncertainty is a recurrent theme across all of Locke's writings. Typically, he examines the potential development and control of individual judgment as essential to the proper direction of human
appetites, desires, and inclinations in a manner consistent with God's
design. This is especially the case with respect to moral conduct,[1] but
his political writings, too, are rooted in a consideration of the possibility and scope of human reason as a primary determinant of political knowledge and action. For example, the argument for toleration
can, as we have noted, be understood in part as the consequence of
an epistemology that emphasizes the inherent boundedness or limitations of reason in matters of faith.[2] But in temporal concerns as

---

1. See, for instance, John Locke, *Some Thoughts concerning Education*, in *The Educational Writings of John Locke*, ed. James Axtell (Cambridge: Cambridge University
Press, 1967), by paragraph, esp. 29, 38.

2. John Locke, *A Letter concerning Toleration*, ed. James Tully (Indianapolis: Hackett Publishing Co., 1983), 36: "Neither the care of the Commonwealth nor the right
enacting of Laws, does discover the way that leads to Heaven more certainly to the
Magistrate, than every private Mans Search and Study discovers it unto himself. . . .

well, Locke stressed differential levels of cognitive access to the world, ranging from knowledge of demonstrative certainty at the highest level through judgments of probable truths distinguished by degrees. Where the former requires recognition of the "necessary and undubitable connexion" between all the ideas that comprise its object, the latter involves a perception of the "probable connexion" between such ideas. The uncertainty or tentativeness of such probable truths, however, is a practical and ethical as well as an epistemological problem. Indeed, as Locke notes, "most of the Propositions we think, reason, discourse, nay act upon, are such, as we cannot have undoubted Knowledge of their Truth."[3] Containing as it does not only many practical propositions but moral notions as well, this realm of probable knowledge poses the possibility of moral chaos, for where this probable connection is not perceived "there Men's Opinions are not the product of Judgment, or the Consequence of Reason; but the effects of Chance and Hazard, of a Mind floating at all Adventures, without choice, and without direction."[4]

This chaotic disordering of human judgment can well be taken as an appropriate description of the moral dilemma faced by Locke's natural agents in the corrupt state of nature in the *Second Treatise*. With respect to his account of the formation of political society, though, we have seen in his narrative of that original condition two distinctly different visions of the human capacity to reason with certainty to the moral requirements of natural law. In the beginning, concerned only with the usefulness of things to life itself, Locke's equal and autonomous moral agents could be relied upon to discover common principles by which the moral character of particular actions could be both guided and judged. The postmonetary state, to the contrary, with no such criterion of right immediately accessible to reason, generates a condition of moral uncertainty in which individuals' biases, partiality, and self-interest engender inconveniences in any controversy touched by money. In such a condition, all being

---

Those things that every man ought sincerely to inquire into himself, and by Meditation, Study, Search, and his own Endeavors, attain the Knowledge of, cannot be looked upon as the Peculiar Possession of any one sort of men." See also John Locke, *Essay concerning Human Understanding*, ed. Peter H. Nidditch (Oxford: Oxford University Press, 1975), by book, chapter, and paragraph, 4.16.4. Hereafter cited as *Essay*.

3. Locke, *Essay*, 4.15.2.
4. Ibid., 4.17.2.

equal, no one interpretation of right or equity in any particular case is necessarily superior to any other. Locke's civil society is generated to mitigate this confusion and disorder through the authoritative determination of right in the form of legal rules and through the certain enforcement of these rules by a centralized executive.

Locke's creation of political society thus reintroduces the possibility of moral order in worldly concerns by establishing a public authority to create and enforce common rules for human action. By the promulgating and executing of known laws with fixed punishments, the potential scope and intensity of arbitrary judgments of right that characterized the postmonetary state of nature is overcome. In establishing political society, however, Locke's natural agents generate not only new institutions, but new relations with their fellows as well. The equality of power and jurisdiction that defined the natural state gives way to a condition of inequality between those who are empowered to make and execute laws and the members of the community who empower them. This authority relation, in effect, substitutes the judgment of civil authority for the potentially confusing multitude of individual judgments that characterized the late state of nature. In this new condition the fundamental imperatives of the law of nature proscribing injury and mandating the preservation of all are still binding, but the task of determining the specific actions that conduce or fail to conduce to these ends is taken out of the hands of private individuals and entrusted to public institutions and officers. Locke refers repeatedly in the *Second Treatise* to the civil power thus constituted as a "trust."[5] In relinquishing their "power to punish Offenses . . . in prosecution of [their] own private Judgment," individuals agree to conform their actions to the judgments of public authorities. These authoritative judgments, however, which Locke considers equivalent to the individual's "own Judgements," are confined to such activities and purposes as conduce to the "*Peace, Safety,* and *publick good* of the People."[6] Where this trust is violated, where power is exercised contrary to the ends for which it was established, it is no longer properly political power at all and is stripped of its authority. At that point, on Locke's account,

5. For example, see John Locke, *Two Treatises of Government*, ed. Peter Laslett, rev. ed. (1960; reprint, with amendments, Cambridge: Cambridge University Press, 1963), by book and paragraph, 2.136, 139, 142, 171. Hereafter cited as *Two Treatises*.

6. Ibid., 2.88, 131.

civil subjects are relieved of the obligation of obedience: "All former Ties are cancelled, all other Rights cease."[7] The state of war which then results *"levels the parties,"*[8] the equality of jurisdiction that characterized the state of nature is resumed, and the members of Locke's civil society recover their natural power to punish any who would invade their properties by unlawful force.

That Locke's civil agents may recognize and take action against the excesses of their governors underlines the capacity for political judgment that they retain, as a matter of right, in civil society. Although, while civil government exists, they give up their right actively to execute their private judgments of the rules and actions required by the law of nature, they do not and cannot cede either their ability or their right to consider and judge the extent to which their own lives and the affairs of their community conform to the principles and ends of that law. For Locke this capacity for judgment, like the rational faculty upon which it rests, can only be a matter of individual conviction, as it is ultimately a matter of individual responsibility for creatures subject to a moral law and potentially capable of salvation. This Lockean defense of resistance right, of course, was hardly unique, nor was his particular formulation of that right as an analogue to the punishment of common criminality original. In this, as in many other aspects of his political thought, his participation in the intellectual tenor and tendencies of his day was fairly conventional. To say, however, that his political concerns were perhaps less striking than is often considered to be the case is not by any means to suggest that the way in which he articulated and defended them was unimportant, or that they were merely commonsensical. Quite to the contrary, it is precisely the manner in which he draws upon, condenses, recombines, and reshapes various common configurations and controversies of the political thought of his time that constitutes his distinctive political and theoretical contribution.

As I suggested earlier, the broader theoretical enterprise of the *Treatises* might fruitfully be seen as a form of political education, but it might be useful to think more precisely about what such a characterization might mean. It cannot, for instance, refer exclusively to what a particular thinker says about the political realm in explicit

7. Ibid., 2.232.
8. Ibid., 2.235.

terms, for what is said is both said in a particular way and said to someone. This in turn suggests that to read a theoretical text as a form of political education one must consider not simply what is written, but who it is written for as well as how it might speak to their prior understanding of the issues and themes that it addresses. Because political discourse is itself set within larger historical, cultural, and linguistic frameworks, it suggests as well that in such texts allusions, asides, metaphors, and rhetorical constructions are as much vehicles of political meaning as are the more obvious and explicit conceptual formulations. On this view, it was perhaps less the logic or coherence of Locke's argument that carried his political meaning than it was his evocation, condensation, and restructuring of a variety of perspectives framing political controversy and moral concern into a justification of resistance. Most significant in theoretical terms, I have argued, was his attempt to affirm, without reliance upon the contested terrain of Scripture, a moral grounding for the English political idiom of law, right, liberty, equality, and property in the context of God's purposes.[9] His political meaning, however, is not simply a matter of an abstract argument about the relationship of political power to natural law, natural right, or the preservation of property. Certainly it is this, but it is also more than this. For Locke's politics are located as well in the discursive linkage he articulates between the worldly purpose of political power and the ongoing controversies over law and right spawned by increasingly monetarized property relations. In this context, as we have seen, the relationship Locke suggests between political power and property is framed primarily by moral rather than narrowly economic considerations, particularly in terms of the epistemological privilege it lends to the use and preservation of one's own as a fundamental experiential grounding for political and moral knowledge.

In this, Locke both affirms and replicates the characteristic law-mindedness of his contemporaries' understanding of political power. He sustains without question the conventional primacy of retributive

9. This is not, of course, to say that Locke made no recourse to Scripture. His refutation of Filmerian patriarchy in the *First Treatise* made extensive use of biblical materials. The *Second Treatise*, too, abounds in Old Testament references, but at no point does it explicitly depend on Scriptural counterweights to the Pauline injunction to obey the powers that be. For a related discussion see Deborah Baumgold, "Pacifying Politics: Resistance, Violence, and Accountability in Seventeenth-Century Contract Theory," *Political Theory* 21, no. 1 (1993): 6–27.

justice, as well as a traditional emphasis upon property as the epitome of right and that which the political order must by all means
preserve. He does this, however, in two rather distinctive ways. First,
instead of significantly shifting the internal meanings attached to the
traditional juridical idiom by the culture of law, he moralizes that
vocabulary by aligning it with the realization of God's purposes. Secondly, he instantiates these concerns by portraying in the *Treatises* a
mode of political understanding that invokes experiential grounds
for distinguishing the boundaries of properly political power and,
simultaneously, that lends credence to the moral legitimacy of resistance to the exercise of such power as exceeds these purposes in
practice. In this regard, the political sensibility articulated in the
Treatises functions not only as a theoretical umbrella capable of comprehending extant forms of anti-absolutist argument, but as an exemplar of political understanding and judgment capable of informing political action.

All this we have seen before in a variety of contexts and registers
of meaning. My purpose in this chapter, however, is to consider this
mode of political understanding as it stands in relation to Locke's
positive conception of political power. I shall be particularly concerned to elucidate the grounds and criteria of judgment that condition the exercise of this power in civil practice and to characterize
the politics of Locke's civil polity in light of the conception of political understanding, knowledge, and action on which it rests. With this
characterization in hand, we will be prepared to examine, in the final
chapter, the problematic of judgment at the heart of Locke's political
theory and to open the question of its implications for the subsequent
historical development of liberal political discourse and practice.

I   Civil Facticity and the Culture of Law

Locke's summary position on the character of political understanding generally appears as an aside or an offhand remark in the
context of reflections on other topics. Often articulated but rarely
analyzed, the conventionality of this position within the historical
practice and intellectual traditions of Anglo-American liberalism has
tended to insulate it from critical attention. In a section of his *Conduct of the Understanding* entitled simply "Observation," for example,

Locke states his position succinctly: "Particular matters of fact are the undoubted foundations on which our civil and natural knowledge is built; the benefit the understanding makes of them is to draw from them conclusions which may be as standing rules of knowledge, and consequently of practice."[10] But what, in this formulation, is a particular matter of fact? What kind of conclusions might such facts entail? And what, with respect to specifically civil facts, is the relationship here implied between political knowledge and political practice?

The answers to these questions, I would suggest, are among the theoretical issues that Locke works through in his letters on toleration and, more positively and concisely, in the *Second Treatise*. In the former, as we have seen, matters of faith are characterized as speculative truths, and are facts only insofar as they are actual opinions held by actual persons. On Locke's account, however, they are not properly to be considered of political concern, for their facticity, as it were, is of a wholly private character. Such facts, Locke argues, are matters of personal belief that cannot be demonstrated to be true or false, and therefore are restricted in their meaning to individuals' private and particular care for the future state of their souls. Lacking this-worldly consequences, in other words, they are as good as politically nonexistent. For Locke, however, the uncertainty and political irrelevance of such speculative religious opinions is most emphatically not the case for other kinds of facts, particularly those known directly from experience and sensation. "I think," he notes in the *Essay*, "no body can, in earnest, be so sceptical, as to be uncertain of the Existence of those Things which he sees and feels."[11] The certainty of those facts "when we have *the testimony of our Senses* . . . is not only *as great* as our frame can attain to, but *as our Condition needs*."[12] Our cognitive faculties, he continues, in an implicit evocation of God's design, are not fit to "the full Extent of Being, nor to a perfect, clear, comprehensive Knowledge of things free from all doubt and scruple; but to the preservation of us, in whom they are; and accommodated to the use of Life."[13]

10. John Locke, *Of the Conduct of the Understanding*, ed. Thomas Fowler, 2d ed. (1882; New York: Lenox Hill, 1971), sec. 13, p. 36.

11. Locke, *Essay*, 4.11.3.

12. Ibid., 4.11.8.

13. Ibid.

The example Locke offers of such certain knowledge is suggestive, for it speaks of the kinds of facts that, on his account, human understanding was designed to know best: "He that sees a Candle burning, and hath experimented the force of its Flame, by putting his Finger in it, will little doubt, that this is something existing without him, which does him harm, and puts him to great pain: which is assurance enough, when no Man requires greater certainty to govern his Actions by, than what is as certain as his Actions themselves."[14] In quite similar terms he evokes an equivalent and parallel certainty for political understanding in the *Second Treatise*. "Are the People," he asks, "to be blamed, if they have the sence of rational Creatures, and can think of things no otherwise than as they find and feel them?"[15] Even so, as he notes there with specific reference to the exercise of political power by civil governors, much will be *"born by the People, without mutiny or murmur."*[16] At some point, however, such quietude will give way to cognition, and Locke articulates the character of this understanding in the emphatically sensory language of his epistemological explorations: "If a long train of Abuses, Prevarications, and Artifices, all tending the same way, make the design visible to the People, and they cannot but feel, what they lie under, and see, whither they are going; 'tis not to be wonder'd, that they should then rouze themselves, and endeavor to put the rule into such hands, which may secure to them the ends for which Government was at first erected."[17]

At a distance of three hundred years such formulations may appear simply rhetorical. But substance and rhetoric are not necessarily so easily distinguished, and serious consideration of the privileged status that Locke's epistemology accords to sensation and experience suggests a rather different reading, particularly in light of his insistent condensation of natural law into the prohibition of injury. Locke's theistic individuation of the species into autonomous moral agents in God's architecture of order allows him to cast the English political idiom of law, right, liberty, equality, and property as a hierarchically organized conceptual field focused upon the moral integrity of individuals' self-propriety. This, as I have suggested, is

14. Ibid.
15. Locke, *Two Treatises*, 2.230.
16. Ibid., 2.225.
17. Ibid.

not limited to property in the narrow sense of material possessions, but extends further to each human agent's moral personality, so to speak, as this expresses itself in their accountability for the use of that which is proper to them, that which is their own. Knowledge of this self-propriety is for Locke the necessary precondition of moral relations between individuals capable of salvation; the certainty with which one knows one's own serves to ground one's observance of the parallel distinctions between law and right, virtue and convenience, obligation and liberty that structurally frame the meaning of properly human action in God's design.

If, in these terms, Lockean political power finds its expression in securing and preserving property, it does so by defining and defending that which is properly one's own. From the standpoint of individual judgment and cognition, the property that Locke insulates from injury in the original condition of the species in the *Second Treatise* is equivalent to the "civil interests" he affirms as the proper matter of political consideration in the *Letter concerning Toleration*. The "Life, Liberty, Health, Limb or Goods" secured as rights by natural political power and natural law in the former, in other words, run parallel to the civil concern in the latter for "life, liberty, health, and indolency of the body" as well as "the possession of outward things."[18] In both cases, that which is established as one's own is to be both morally and practically protected from injury. But it is not simply this, for on Locke's account it is also that which is most personally, most immediately, and most viscerally known by both natural and civil subjects through direct experience—and, by the same token, it is precisely that with respect to which injury is most clearly, most substantially, and most directly felt.

There is, in short, no difference between Locke's natural and civil conditions at the level of individuals' cognitive relationship to, and accountability for the use of, that which is properly their own, as this is determined by the relevant structure of law. Whether that law be natural or civil, in either context one's self-propriety is broadly understood as one's person, actions, life, limb, labor, health, and goods. Liberty, too, is at this level identical, for in both the natural and the civil condition it is embodied in the discretionary power individuals have over their self-propriety. In each case, property right is syn-

18. Ibid., 2.6; Locke, *Letter concerning Toleration*, ed. Tully, 26.

onymous with the liberty of action each has in the free use of these things as they each judge convenient within the bounds of law. Locke thus attributes to both his natural and his civil agents a direct cognizance, an extended sensation, if you will, of that which is properly their own as this is circumscribed by law. In both conditions, one's self-propriety is invested with an experiential certainty. One knows it, Locke implies, as directly and assuredly as one knows one's body. In effect—and central to the mode of political judgment proffered by the *Second Treatise*—one experiences a violation of one's self-propriety in terms analogous to the experience of physical or bodily harm. In this sense, I would suggest, individual cognizance and experience of injury to one's propriety are precisely the particular matters of fact that on Locke's account constitute the foundation of political knowledge.

What differs between Locke's natural and civil states—and differs significantly—is the manner in which this self-propriety is established and bounded in the first place. In this context Locke's narrative construction of the movement from the original peaceful state of nature, through its corruption by money, to the creation of civil society tells a rather different story from the one that is generally assumed. It evokes at its beginning God's intentions for the peace, goodwill, and mutual assistance of the species and presents their created condition as one in which the boundaries of one's self-propriety were easily known and the designed complementarity between natural law and natural right easily observed. One knew, grounded, and limited that self-propriety through personal action, through the labor of one's body and the work of one's hands, and the epistemology of right endowed those actions with a moral certainty that was, in Locke's ever recurrent phrase, easily seen. Title was certain, controversies were few, and violations of rightful propriety were both easily recognized and justly punished. Political power, as a natural endowment of the species as a whole, was the mechanism through which self-propriety was both established and ensured, and its rightful use of force guaranteed the conformity of worldly practice to the designed complementarity of law and right.

By introducing monetarized property relations as the instrument by which this peaceful condition is corrupted, Locke evokes a matter of controversy hardly to be missed by his contemporary readers. If this may have struck a biblical resonance for some, money being the root of all evil, it doubtless struck others as both a moral and political problematic, as the increasing role of money in English society had generated fundamental controversies in social, legal, and economic relations. Here, I would suggest, Locke places the invention of money in his state of nature not to justify the commercial society of his day, but rather to insist upon the moral necessity of civil law to establish the boundaries of self-propriety, the limits of private right and convenience, the definition of crime, and the determination of just measures of punishment where money has divested the expression of right from its necessary connection with the law of nature.[19] Where money has severed the convergence of right and conveniency, the task of civil society and the function of civil law is to restore personality to property, to resurrect, to name and make known the boundaries of what is properly one's own in a manner consistent with God's design. Far from being an unqualified approval of the monetarized market economy, in other words, Locke's work affirms the moral necessity of civil determination of both the limits of right and the definition of injury within a realm of human artifice in which the law of nature lacks the necessary specificity to guide human action.

The natural law prohibition of injury remains a fundamental imperative here, just as the complementarity between virtue and convenience, between moral obligation and human liberty, remains the measure of properly human action. In the structured hierarchy of God's creation this boundary remains firmly and universally in place. With the dissolution of the natural epistemology of right, however, its worldly markings for existential human agents are reconstituted by the specific "private" or "particular Political Society" in which they are historically located.[20] This is significant both in terms of the general relationship Locke establishes between property and political power and with respect to the mode of political understanding and judgment he offers for distinguishing between properly political power and its excess. While natural law, for example, demands that property in the broad sense be guaranteed, with re-

19. Patrick Hyde Kelly's observation that ethics and civil prudence (rather than science) provided the method for Locke's economic writings is germane. See his introduction to John Locke, *Locke on Money*, ed. Patrick Hyde Kelly, 2 vols. (Cambridge: Cambridge University Press, 1991), 1:91–96.
20. Locke, *Two Treatises*, 2.128.

gard to the narrower sense of material possession that law does not specify how, or in what measure, or to whom it is to be distributed.[21] As we have seen in Locke's presentation of the natural state, even before the invention of money, natural law may have given and bounded the right to material property, but its individuation in fact and practice was a product of human judgment and action.[22] Thus in Lockean civil society, although liberty and property remain identified in theoretical terms with the free use of one's own on the basis of private convenience, the title to this self-propriety as well as the bounds of individual liberty and the definition of criminality are determined by civil authority in particular polities rather than by direct and individual reflection upon one's experience and needs. Similarly, the executive use of lawful force to punish violations of right remains the worldly guarantor of moral order, but the laws that it enforces are now those of particular historically constituted commonwealths.

We have, of course, already noted the moral character and status of civil power so construed. What is important for understanding its operation in both theoretical and practical terms, however, is the manner in which its determining function in the definition of property simultaneously reconstitutes the capacity of Locke's civil agents for moral and political judgment in the context of their own specific political society. As Locke himself suggests at the close of the chapter on property in the *Second Treatise*, "in Governments the Laws regulate the right of property, and the possession of land is determined by positive constitutions."[23] Thus wherever property has been, in Locke's terms, settled by the development or creation of civil communities, knowledge of one's own is reestablished by civil law. This settling, or civil reconstitution of the boundaries of private rights, necessarily recreates an experiential basis for the recognition of injury as a civil fact, but its frame of reference is given content and

21. " 'Tis true, [*who would have his conscience imposed upon?*]," Locke observes in the *Two Tracts*, "and 'tis as true, who would pay taxes? who would be poor? who almost would not be a prince? And yet these (as some think them) burdens, this inequality, is owing all to human laws and those just enough, the law of God or nature neither distinguishing their degrees nor bounding their possessions." John Locke, *Two Tracts on Government*, ed. Philip Abrams (Cambridge: Cambridge University Press, 1967), English Tract, 138.

22. Locke, *Two Treatises*, 2.31.

23. Ibid., 2.50.

specificity by each particular political community's definition of self-propriety in civil law.

We shall have occasion to look more closely at this issue presently, but let us pause here a moment to consider what this construction might have suggested to Locke's contemporary readers. To begin with, his constant reference to the settling of property by particular political societies was spoken to a public whose understanding of their own civil constitution was preeminently framed by the culture of common law as the practical expression and summary of centuries of political experience. English law, in short, was the animating force of political consciousness and practice. However obscure or contestable the historical origins of particular legal principles, their multiple and combined expression in the myriad operations of the common law was taken to constitute a whole fabric—a fabric which, however complex, remained for the English public a distinctive element of "the Frame" they had "been accustom'd to."[24] The insistent legalism of English political culture, in other words, was for Locke's reading public sufficiently entrenched that merely to speak the language of law, right, liberty, equality, and property was to evoke the complex web of that constitution as the peculiar expression of the English polity.

To locate Locke's work within this cultural context is to offer an account of what has generally been taken to be a significant theoretical ellipsis on his part. It is to suggest that his particular articulation of contract theory can itself be seen as an instance of his participation in the culture of law.[25] His concern to establish the worldly sov-

24. Ibid., 2.223.

25. For accounts of the pervasiveness of legal metaphors and imagery in the political discourse of the period see Howard Nenner, *By Colour of Law: Legal Culture and Constitutional Politics in England, 1660–1689* (Chicago: University of Chicago Press, 1977); as well as J. G. A. Pocock's classic discussion of "the Common-law mind" in his *The Ancient Constitution and the Feudal Law: A Study of English Historical Thought in the Seventeenth Century*, 2d ed. (Cambridge: Cambridge University Press, 1987), chaps. 2 and 3, and its critical revisitation in the second edition (pt. 2, chap. 1). Mark Goldie, "The Revolution of 1689 and the Structure of Political Argument," *Bulletin of Research in the Humanities* 83, no. 4 (Winter 1980): 473–564, suggests linkages between natural law and constitutionalist arguments. The best work specifically addressing intersections between the *Treatises* and constitutionalist theory includes Lois Schwoerer, "Locke, Lockean Ideas, and the Glorious Revolution," *Journal of the History of Ideas* 51, no. 4 (1990): 531–48; Martyn P. Thompson, "Significant Silences in Locke's *Two Treatises of Government*: Constitutional History, Contract, and Law," *Historical Journal* 31, no. 2 (1988): 275–94; and James Tully, "Placing the *Two Treatises*," in *Political Discourse*

ereignty of civil law and the moral integrity of one's self-propriety in this sense highlights what, in the contemporary political understanding, English laws were presumed ideally to do: "*To dispense Justice, and decide the Rights of the Subject by promulgated standing Laws, and known Authoris'd Judges.*"[26] Rather than divorcing himself from the cultural frame of English law, Locke presumes the historical legitimacy of the English constitution in terms of the proper purposes of political power broadly understood. It is, in turn, the very givenness of this legitimacy that allows him to focus his theoretical concern on providing both a moral framework for such power and an exemplar of political judgment capable of discerning the violation of its proper purposes in practice. Thus over the course of the *Second Treatise* what appears initially as an abstract discussion of the moral character and worldly purposes of political power is gradually and pointedly infused with an increasingly particular and obviously English frame of reference. Through this narrative, I would suggest, Locke affirms an essential connection between, on the one hand, the experiential grounds of moral and political judgment offered in his presentation of the natural state and, on the other, the historical situation and political traditions of his contemporary public.

To put the point somewhat differently, the general theoretical purpose of Locke's civil power is to reconstitute the minimal conditions of social morality in worldly terms. By securing to each their own, it rearticulates the right order of relations between individuals in a manner consistent with the natural law prohibition of injury. The political meaning of this in its contemporary context, however, no less than the language of the Ancient Constitution, included in the definition of one's own the inheritance of common law and traditional notions of the English constitution as the framing structures of political judgment and practice. Locke's project, in other words, is not to abandon, much less to undermine, the traditional legalism of his culture, but to articulate more closely the moral grounds upon

---

in Early Modern Britain, ed. Nicholas Phillipson and Quentin Skinner (Cambridge: Cambridge University Press, 1993), esp. 256–62. The strength of the relationship between the *Treatises* and common law was noted much earlier this century by Sir Frederick Pollock, "Locke's Theory of the State," *Proceedings of the British Academy, 1903–1904*: 237–49.

26. Locke, *Two Treatises*, 2.136.

which it rests and the purposes, terrestrial and otherwise, to which it is answerable. Governments may be "every where antecedent to Records," but the recognition of the legitimate scope and purpose of political power is properly a determination of those subject to its exercise in the present.[27] This, for Locke, is a matter of practical judgment, an expression of what he refers to in another place as "the other part of politics," a concern for "the art of government."[28] In this small phrase the culture of law enters Locke's theory, as it were, through the back door, for on his account this kind of political knowledge is "best to be learned by experience and history, especially that of a man's own country."[29]

In this context, however, the facticity attributed to the self-propriety of Locke's English readers might be understood in two senses, one of which is quite familiar while the other opens out onto a more curious terrain. First, and most obviously, it refers to the property they each have in their persons, liberties, and possessions. Of this more than enough has been said already. Second, however, and of no small moment to Locke's contemporary audience, because these properties are themselves defined and secured by civil law, self-propriety includes the historical practice of common law and right itself, as well as the image of that great and immemorial English constitution as the loom upon which this complex fabric of law and right was woven in time. In moralizing the political vocabulary of this constitutional idiom, Locke thus extends both the cognizance of civil facts and the perception of injury to one's "self-propriety" to include the political inheritance of the constitutional tradition itself.[30] It is this that subtends his characterization of rebellion as "an Opposition, not to Persons, but Authority, which is founded only in the Constitutions and Laws of the Government," and it is this that allows him to paint

27. Ibid., 2.101.
28. John Locke, "Some Thoughts concerning Reading and Study for a Gentleman" (1703), in *The Educational Writings of John Locke*, ed. James Axtell (Cambridge: Cambridge University Press, 1968), 400.
29. Ibid.
30. The constitution, in this respect, appears as something akin to the "incorporeal things" that Pollock and Maitland characterize as among the most medieval categories of medieval law. See Sir Frederick Pollock and Frederic William Maitland, *The History of English Law before the Time of Edward I*, 2d ed., 1899–1923; reprint with revisions, (Cambridge: Cambridge University Press, 1968), vol. 2, chap. 4, sec. 6.

the character of any who might "by force break through, and by
force justifie their violation" of the constitution and established law
as "truly and properly *Rebels.*"[31]

Locke's political theory might be read in this respect as conservative or, perhaps more accurately, conservationist in its aim, since it
seeks to preserve the established frame of political sensibility and
juridical practice against the threat of such change or innovation as
fails to conform to its underlying principles.[32] This, of course, is the
strangely equivocal core of Locke's justification of resistance right.
Modeled on the image of retribution against criminals, a corrective
rather than creative act, it is more clearly a restoration than a revolution in the modern sense. Locke's language here, however, is not
simply quaint or archaic, and to recognize its distance from more
recent representations of revolution as the birth of a new social order is to do more than note a linguistic curiosity. It is to point to a
pattern of thought, a mode of political cognition, if you will, that is
essentially reactive or responsive in nature, one that equates political
agency with the defense of a settled self-propriety against criminal
violation. The cognizance, in other words, of civil facts that for
Locke provides an experiential grounding for the moral justification
of resistance is modeled primarily as a retrospective judgment of
injury to one's own, where this has already been determined and
secured by law.

The theoretical significance of this formulation, however, lies not
simply in the evidence it provides for the orthodoxy of Locke's polit-

31. Locke, *Two Treatises,* 2.226. See 2.227 for the extension of this reasoning to
legislators, and 2.228 for Locke's analogizing of the remedy to self-defense against
common criminals. The full force of this position appears at 2.230: "This I am sure,
whoever, either Ruler or Subject, by force goes about to invade the Rights of either
Prince, or People, and lays the foundation for *overturning* the Constitution and Frame
of *any Just Government,* is guilty of the greatest Crime, I think, a Man is capable of,
being to answer for all those mischiefs of Blood, Rapine, and Desolation, which the
breaking to pieces of Governments bring on a Countrey. And he who does it, is justly
to be esteemed the common Enemy and Pest of Mankind; and is to be treated accordingly."

32. John Dunn, *The Political Thought of John Locke: An Historical Account of the Argument of the "Two Treatises of Government"* (Cambridge: Cambridge University Press,
1969), 182, offers a similar reading: "It is thus partly the intellectual resources, as well
as the conventional pieties, of English constitutionalism which enable Locke to com-
bine his theological individualism with an articulated and differentiated theory of the
right to resistance, and to make this a theory of the restoration of an existing degree
of legality."

ical principles or for his apparent complacency toward the way the English constitution had settled the property relations of his day, in either the broad or the narrow sense of the term. For if Locke's theoretical project is conventional in this sense, its very conventionality offers a glimpse of a moment in the history of the language of rights—in the history, more specifically, of what was to become liberal political discourse—a moment in which the relationship between its valorization of experience and its positive conception of the purposes of political power is laid bare. As we shall see, the Lockean construction of the political both embodies and reveals a significant tension between the worldly purposes attributed to political power and the experiential mode of political understanding it affirms as appropriate to judge the proper exercise of this power in practice. To begin to delineate the contours and implications of this tension, let us look more closely at the relationship between Locke's theoretical project to justify resistance, the experiential grounds it adduces as proper to political judgment, and its positive conception of political power.

II   Resistance Right and the Rule of Law

Locke's preface to the reader of the *Treatises* both invokes the image of reclaimed order and characterizes his own project retrospectively as one of justification. William appears as the "Great Restorer," his "Title" to the throne secured by the actions of a people whose "love of their Just and Natural Rights" and "Resolution to preserve them, saved the Nation when it was on the very brink of Slavery and Ruine."[33] Here, though Locke situates his discourse in the context of the events of 1688, this revolution is distinctly coded as a restoration, as the preservation or recovery of rights previously secured to the "Nation." To characterize Locke's positive conception of political power, however, it is necessary to distinguish between the particular political edge of his presentation in its immediate context, on the one hand, and its broader political, theoretical, and historical implications on the other. In effect, the *Treatises'* announced purpose to render resistance consistent with morality focuses attention upon particular aspects of Locke's notion of properly political power,

33. Locke, *Two Treatises*, introd., 171.

while allowing other elements of his larger theoretical construct to recede into the background. As we shall see, this selective foregrounding is itself both significant and problematic, but before moving to a more critical perspective let us follow the *Treatises*' elaboration of this project a bit further.

Having characterized the proper business of political power as the preservation of property, in the broad sense of the term, and framed political understanding as the cognizance of one's self-propriety, Locke closes the *Second Treatise* with discussions of tyranny and the dissolution of government. Whether viewed in the context of the Exclusion Crisis or in the context of the Glorious Revolution, both of these chapters offer their contemporary readers an indictment of power directed beyond its proper bounds as well as an evocation of the specific senses in which Stuart rule had violated the self-propriety of English subjects. They offer, in other words, characterizations of the particular "Abuses, Prevarications, and Artifices" that on Locke's account evidenced a design upon the lives, liberties, and properties of the English people and condemned their perpetrators as the greatest of criminals. If legitimate resistance is predicated upon seeing and feeling the abusive design of arbitrary power, these chapters are devoted to stimulating the perception and recognition of that design.

Locke's distinction between tyranny and the dissolution of government follows from the two senses of self-propriety suggested above as characteristic of the culture of law. The civil facts that for Locke constitute the stuff of political understanding, as we have seen, operate at two levels of experience, each of which is defined by a different object of political cognition. First, at the primary level of direct individual experience they refer to the property or propriety one has in one's person, liberties, and possessions as this is established by civil law, and this is the sense that Locke invokes throughout the chapter on tyranny. One's experience of injury in this context is personal and visceral, for a violation of what the law has determined to be properly one's own is directly and immediately felt. Cognitively analogous to the individual's experience of criminal violation in the state of nature, it is to this form of self-propriety that tyranny stands as a transgression. *"Tyranny,"* Locke suggests, *"is the exercise of Power beyond Right,"* the exercise of "unjust and unlawful *Force*."[34] The in-

---

34. Ibid., 2.199 and 2.204 respectively.

jury entailed by such tyranny, however, is particularized to the personal self-propriety of specific individuals: *"Where-ever Law ends Tyranny begins,* if the Law be transgressed to another's harm. And whosoever in Authority exceeds the Power given him by the Law, and makes use of the Force he has under his Command, to compass that upon the Subject, which the Law allows not, ceases in that to be a Magistrate, and acting without Authority, may be opposed, as any other Man, who by Force invades the Right of another."[35] Locke's analogy here between tyranny and criminality, on the one hand, and resistance right and justifiable self-defense on the other, turns importantly upon the absence of recourse to law and civil authority for its political meaning. He continues, "Where the injured Party may be relieved, and his damages repaired by Appeal to the Law, there can be no pretence for Force, which is only to be used, where a Man is intercepted from appealing to the Law."[36] Where no such recourse is possible, obligation ceases. And where obligation ceases resistance through force is morally permitted—though Locke hastens to add that it may well be prudentially ill advised. If such "manifest Acts of Tyranny," he suggests, "reach no farther than some private Mens Cases, though they have a right to defend themselves, and to recover by force, what by unlawful force is taken from them; yet the Right to do so, will not easily ingage them in a Contest, wherein they are sure to perish."[37]

Toward the end of the discussion of tyranny, however, Locke's description of the character of such injury undergoes a subtle but significant change. In the closing paragraphs of the chapter his referents shift from the direct experience of particular individuals to an evocation of the extended meaning of self-propriety, the sense in which one's law and constitution itself is a matter of political cognition. "But if either these illegal Acts have extended to the Majority of the People; or if the Mischief and Oppression has light only on some few, but in such Cases, as the Precedent, and Consequences seem to threaten all, and they are perswaded in their Consciences, that their Laws, and with them their Estates, Liberties, and Lives are in danger, and perhaps their Religion too, how they will be hindered

35. Ibid., 2.202. See also ibid., 2.203–8 and 2.232–5 regarding Princes or Kings as chief magistrates.
36. Ibid., 2.207.
37. Ibid., 2.208. The possession of such a right, in other words, does not make the worldly consequences of its assertion 'convenient'.

from resisting illegal force, used against them, I cannot tell."[38] But
this dangerous state of things, Locke contends, is "easie to be
avoided."[39] Again invoking the sensory and experiential character of
political judgment, he insists that it is "impossible for a Governor, if
he really means the good of his People, and the preservation of them
and their Laws together, not to make them see and feel it."[40] If,
however, "all the World shall observe Pretenses of one kind, and
Actions of another," if they see the law artfully eluded and power
"employed contrary to the end, for which it was given," if "the People shall find" subordinate magistrates chosen for their willingness
to pursue these corrupt purposes, "if they see several Experiments
made of Arbitrary Power," and if "*a long Train of Actings shew the
Councils* all tending that way,"[41] the public, on Locke's account, can
hardly help but see and feel it. What is "seen and felt," in such situations, however, is not simply an attack upon the personal property of
specific individuals, but an assault upon the laws and constitution of
the commonwealth itself, upon their self-propriety in its broadest
sense. It is this extended sense of self-propriety that provides Locke
with a conceptual bridge into his examination of the dissolution of
government and his most explicit justification of resistance.

This closing chapter of the *Second Treatise* both focuses Locke's
theoretical criticism of arbitrary power and sharpens his indictment
of Stuart rule by invoking an unmistakably English frame of reference.[42] Having demonstrated the dependence of personal self-propriety upon the rule of civil law, he turns from the individuated and
personally specific injury of tyranny to the question of misrule as an
attack upon the constitution of the commonwealth and the principle
of law itself. It is not, for our present purposes, necessary to linger
over the details of Locke's exposition here, for in all cases his emphasis falls upon the disruption of civil law and established constitutional arrangements by the actions of those "who misuse the Power
they have."[43] In all instances, in other words, what dissolves the gov-

38. Ibid., 2.209.
39. Ibid. Locke ascribes a similar dynamic to the proper exercise of prerogative
power at ibid., 2.161–66.
40. Ibid.
41. Ibid., 2.210.
42. Ibid., "Of the Dissolution of Government," esp. 2.213.
43. Ibid., 2.213. Again, this discussion is foreshadowed in Locke's treatment of
prerogative. See esp. ibid., 2.167–68.

ernment is some manner of studied assault on the security or due execution of legislative power, the civil power singularly responsible for remedying the epistemological deficiency of Locke's state of nature by determining the self-propriety of each and all by law. On the sanctity of such a duly constituted legislative power, Locke is quite insistent: "The Reason why Men enter into Society, is the preservation of their Property; and the end why they chuse and authorize a Legislative, is, that there may be Laws made, and Rules set as Guards and Fences to the Properties of all the Members of the Society, to limit the Power, and moderate the Dominion of every Part and Member of the Society."[44]

Of signal importance here is the primacy accorded civil law as the source of terrestrial order. Whether the attack on law comes from the executive or from corrupt members of a particular legislative body itself, what is at stake in the assault is the possibility of worldly peace itself. Since on Locke's rendering only known law can settle propriety in a manner conducive to moral order, any alternation of the established constitution of the legislative power signifies the death of the polity, for "this is the Soul that gives Form, Life, and Unity to the Commonwealth: From hence the several Members have their mutual Influence, Sympathy, and Connexion."[45] The only other source for the dissolution of government lies in the executive's neglect or abandonment of the duty of enforcing such laws as already exist:

This is demonstratively to reduce all to Anarchy. . . . For Laws not being made for themselves, but to be by their execution the Bonds of the Society, to keep every part of the Body Politick in its due place and function, when that totally ceases, the *Government* visibly *ceases*, and the People become a confused Multitude, without Order or Connexion. . . . Where the Laws cannot be executed, it is all one as if there were no Laws, and a Government without Laws is, I suppose, a Mystery in Politicks, unconceivable to humane Capacity, and inconsistent with humane Society.[46]

44. Ibid., 2.222.
45. Ibid., 2.212.
46. Ibid., 2.219. Locke's recourse here to organic or corporate imagery is striking, but it elaborates the view of law introduced in the opening description of the state of nature. See ibid., 2.7.

Here, as in Locke's state of nature, the purpose of law is to "preserve the innocent and restrain offenders,"[47] and in both conditions the power to execute the law justly is essential to effectively guarantee the right order of relations between individuals' proprieties. From the perspective of civil agents, however, what distinguishes the natural from the civil condition is not the character of law as a guide to human action, but the condensation of its promulgation and rightful enforcement into the hands of superior authority.[48] As the law of nature and the epistemology of right in the created condition establish the boundaries of right between Locke's equal and autonomous moral agents, so does civil law set boundaries to the propriety and limit the power of each member of the commonwealth. Thus, in practical terms, for Locke's contemporary public the theoretical weight and centrality he accorded to law both presumed the solidity of English political practice and reinforced the sanctity accorded to the rule of law within their constitutional frame. The purpose of Locke's civil law, in short, remains in significant respects highly traditional, keeping "every part of the Body Politick, in its due place and function."[49] In this way Locke invests civil power with the task of ordering social relationships and sustaining the existing constitutional coherence of the community as a whole.

The subversion of the constitution which Locke equates with an assault on law is represented as a "design" of those in power evidenced by "*a long Train of Actings.*"[50] While much has been made of Locke's theoretical emphasis on trust and consent, in the final analysis it is the consistency of rulers' particular actions with the rule of law—taken broadly as the prohibiton of injury—that enacts their political character. By the same token, it is the capacity of civil agents to see and feel this consistency or its absence in present practice that provokes their political understanding. One consents that political power be established, authorized and exercised to certain ends, and trusts that the particular persons in whose hands it rests will conform their actions to these purposes. The political understanding of Locke's civil agents is thus directed to judging the actions of their

47. Ibid., 2.7.
48. Ibid., 2.19 and 21.
49. Ibid., 2.219. As Laslett observes, this is not to be confused with the notion of a general will. See his introduction to the *Two Treatises*, ibid., 128–31.
50. Ibid., 2.210.

governors in very much the same way and on very similar grounds
as his natural agents judge one another in the original condition. In
both cases one's political judgment derives from one's moral personality as this is identified with a settled self-propriety. And in both
cases, violators of that self-propriety forfeit their human status, for
their actions relegate them to the rank of "noxious beasts" justly subject to punishment by those whom they have injured. It is here that
the significance of Locke's "strange doctrine" of executive right
comes assertively to the fore, for when rulers violate civil subjects'
self-propriety, this right reverts to the members of the commonwealth in their severalty. Drawing on Barclay's discussion of kings
"unkinging" themselves, Locke insists that both civil power and lawful force inhere not in the persons of governors but in lawful authority. Where that power and force is exercised contrary to its
proper purpose in the preservation of self-propriety, it ceases for
Locke to be properly political power at all and has no authority. The
magistrate in such cases disappears, and the obligation to obey the
particular person once entrusted with civil power evaporates as well.
Titles and names notwithstanding, in exceeding the scope of lawful
authority he "becomes like other Men who have no Authority."[51] In
this move Locke asserts precisely the claims that advocates of passive
obedience had been concerned to deny: that rulers were not only
morally bound by God's rule of virtue, but subject to terrestrial sanctions for the misuse of their power.

On Locke's account, however, this business of canceled obligations
to a king who unkings himself, this business of resistance to those
who refuse to take the laws as their guide whatever their station,
would appear to be more than an alchemy of naming. Here, though
Locke urges a formal democratization of resistance right, he nonetheless attempts to contain its legitimate expression within the realm
of experience—albeit a notion of experience that is both framed by
and, more important, extended to include the extant system of legality. Justifiable opposition to those who have abused their power is
thus not to be confused with the disquiet engendered by a "raving
mad Man, or heady Male-content."[52] Rather, Locke represents the

---

51. Ibid., 2.239.
52. Locke, *Two Treatises,* 2.208. Locke's uneasiness over such fevered imaginings is
interestingly explored by Uday Singh Mehta, *The Anxiety of Freedom: Imagination and
Individuality in Locke's Political Thought* (Ithaca: Cornell University Press, 1992).

experience of injury and the recognition of constitutional subversion as matters of civil fact, and characterizes the political judgment that recognizes this unkinging of kings as a matter of public acknowledgment that rulers' actions have exceeded the bounds of properly political power. This, of course, is precisely the theoretical function of his account of property.

Two aspects of Locke's formulation of legitimate resistance stand out as particularly important here. First, because the experiential judgment that grounds its expression is a cognizance of civil injury, its necessary frame of reference for existential civil agents must be a preexisting constitutional order, for as we have seen, after the invention of money it is only such a regime that can establish an identifiable self-propriety. Second, and following from this, what is resisted in this context is particular individuals whose successive actions over time evidence a design against this self-propriety, broadly understood as including the accustomed frame of the legal order itself. Taken together, these elements suggest, once again, that Lockean resistance is fundamentally different from more modern understandings of revolution as the installation of a new social order. Dependent upon the prior operation of a system of law to define one's self-propriety, the political agency of Lockean resistance is not directed against an oppressive political *system* as an object of human cognition. Rather, and consistent with Locke's thoroughgoing moral and cognitive individualism, it speaks, on the one hand, to the moral culpability of specific persons in power whose misdeeds have divested them of authority and, on the other, to the moral liberty of civil subjects, acting in their own persons or through their representatives to restore order.[53]

---

53. As Locke put it, for example, with regard to an alteration of the legislative: "When any one, or more, shall take upon them to make Laws, whom the People have not appointed to do so, they make Laws without Authority, which the People are not bound to obey; by which means they come again to be out of subjection, and may constitute to themselves a *new Legislative*, as they think best, being in full liberty to resist the force of those, who without Authority would impose any thing on them. Every one is at the disposure of his own Will, when those who had by the delegation of the Society, the declaring of the publick Will, are excluded from it, and others usurp the place who have no such Authority or Delegation." Locke, *Two Treatises*, 2.212. Amidst the continuing instabilities of the period immediately following the Revolution of 1688, Locke's missive to Edward Clarke held James alone responsible for the miscarriages of the previous government and recommended a general act of oblivion for all others to "restore us to as much innocency as the law can doe." See

Locke's conception of politics in the *Second Treatise* is thus every bit as concerned with the necessity of sustaining lawful order as his earlier "conservative" vision of political order in the *Tracts*. What distinguishes the *Treatises* is both their secular narrowing of the purposes of political power to the prohibition of worldly harm and their attendant presupposition of a legally constituted self-propriety as the experiential basis on which civil subjects might distinguish between the lawful and unlawful exercise of such power in practice. Whether considered in the context of its composition or in that of its publication, Locke's indictment of Stuart misrule may appear loose or imprecise. Given the comprehensiveness of the culture of law, however, this looseness is overshadowed by the conventionality of its constitutionalism and the orthodoxy of its defense of lawful self-propriety as the moral basis of political judgment and action. To the extent that it accounts for the dissolution of obligations to obey those who by obstinacy or design had meddled with the constitution, it was arguably adequate to its purposes in either context.

In this respect, the *Second Treatise* is very much a document of its times. The political and theoretical implications of its conventionality, however, exceed the simple recognition that it offered a rather complex account of what a more or less numerous proportion of its contemporary readers may have already believed. For here, amidst the conceptual apparatus of consent and trust, Locke's articulation of the English political idiom of law, right, liberty, equality, and property asserted an individualistic construct of political understanding and civil agency that was long to outlive the theistic conception of moral order that provided its original inspiration and grounding. Considered in light of this broader trajectory of historical development, Locke's selective foregrounding of a lawfully settled propriety as an experiential basis for individual judgment is not simply a curious artifact of his largely silent assumptions regarding the legitimacy of the English constitution. Rather, it both articulates and affirms the connection in common understanding as well as political practice between the traditional language of law and right and a pattern of political cognition that centered on the security and protection of one's own as this was defined by law. Conceived and mor-

---

James Farr and Clayton Roberts, "John Locke on the Glorious Revolution: A Rediscovered Document," *Historical Journal* 28, no. 2 (1985): 385–98.

alized as a lawful defense against the abuse of power, Locke's justification of resistance thus embodies a model of political judgment that both centers on individuals' cognizance of their lawfully established propriety and sanctions an understanding of political agency that is personal, retrospective, reactive, and remedial in character.

Significantly though, amidst the insistent legalism of Locke's theoretical construct, the general character of law itself remains unquestioned. His theological and epistemological individualism combines with the characteristic law-mindedness of English political culture to focus attention upon both the moral necessity of civil law as a guide to the limits of individuals' rightful liberty and the moral function of executive right in defending self-propriety through the due operation of retributive justice. The content of particular laws, however, and the issue of precisely how and on what basis such individual proprieties are ordered, are not subject to critical scrutiny in the *Treatises*. This exclusion, as we shall see, is politically and theoretically important, especially in light of Locke's presentation of money as the mechanism for the disordering of natural property relations and the spur to the creation of civil society. The *Treatises'* focus on the right of resistance eschews such specificities, however, in favor of an attempt to delineate in general terms the moral boundaries and purposes of properly political power. This, as we have seen, directs theoretical concern to its active exercise in practice rather than to a discussion of the particular institutional forms in which this might take place, the particular substance of law, or the specific measures of punishment in any given context.

Locke's civil society can thus be seen less as a definitive solution to the moral confusion of his state of nature than as a way of organizing or conceptualizing possible solutions. As such, it poses its own peculiar set of difficulties with respect to the problems of reasoned judgment, moral knowledge, and political action, for the obscurity attending the determination of right in monetarized property relations does not end in civil society. Civil laws may provide a hedge against chaos and confusion, but their authoritative, public, and common character neither invests them with moral certainty nor endows them with any necessary connection to the requirements of natural law. The political issue that arises here, given the centrality of individual injury to Locke's justification of resistance, is the theoretical relationship between the political understanding of his civil subjects and his positive construction of political power as a *"Right* of making Laws" and fixing penalties "for the Regulating and Preserving of Property."[54]

III The Problematic of Law

Lockean civil society, I have argued, answers to the disruption of moral knowledge and the transformation of the conditions of political judgment developed in his presentation of the state of nature. In the face of the moral uncertainty engendered by the invention of money, Locke's natural agents relinquish specific elements of their original power to be exercised by the institutions of political governance.[55] Recall, however, that on Locke's account there are two distinct aspects of the political power proper to individuals in the original condition. They are empowered, on the one hand, to provide for themselves and to act as they see fit and convenient for their own preservation and that of their fellows, within the bounds of the law of nature. On the other hand, they are endowed with the right to punish breaches of that law by others.[56] Confronted with the inconveniences that arise in the exercise of these two powers in the context of monetarized property relations, they give up a portion of the former to be regulated and determined by civil law for the public good. The latter is ceded entirely to public authority "in all cases that exclude [them] not from appealing for Protection to the Law established by it."[57] The civil society created by this transfer of powers thus compensates for the deficiencies of the postmonetary state of

54. Locke, *Two Treatises,* 2.3.

55. Again, as suggested earlier, for Locke the form of the institutions exercising these powers is morally irrelevant: "By *Common-wealth,*" he notes, he should "be understood all along to mean, not a Democracy, or any Form of Government, but *any Independent Community* which the *Latines* signified by the word *Civitas,* to which the word which best answers in our Language, is *Commonwealth.*" Locke, *Two Treatises,* 2.133. This is not to suggest that Locke saw no difference between different constitutional forms. Since political power was everywhere the same, however, the choice between them was not a moral issue but a matter of convenience and prudential judgment of the tendency or probability of each form to generate inconveniences. See, for instance, Locke, *Two Treatises,* 2.107, 110–11.

56. Ibid., 2.128.

57. Ibid., 2.87. See also 2.128–30.

nature by providing common rules, impartial authorities, and reliable enforcement.[58]

In Locke's positive articulation of civil authority, both of these aspects of political power are important, particularly with respect to the capacities of his civil agents to distinguish between the exercise of properly political power and its excess. At the same time, though, their importance inheres in two very different matters and modes of political understanding and judgment. The civil expression of both powers, in other words, derives from the disordering of moral judgment in the state of nature, but each is derived in a distinctly different way and with markedly different implications. To put the issue more concretely, although the political power to make civil laws and the right to punish their violation are theoretically and practically interdependent in Locke's civil society, they yet differ substantially in their respective relationships to the epistemological problem of moral knowledge that plagues his late state of nature. On the one hand, and most importantly as we shall see, the purpose of civil power is to remedy directly the disorder, insecurity, and moral confusion introduced by money's dissolution of the epistemology of right. Here, where direct access to the natural boundary of law and right has been disrupted, the task of legislative power is to reconstitute the bounds of particular proprieties as well as private right through "*standing Rules* . . . by which every one may know what is his."[59] In this, as I have suggested, Locke shifts the epistemological problem of reconstructing the moral markings of God's architecture—and thus the dilemma of reconstituting the boundaries of individual rights and the lawful limits of private judgments of convenience—into the domain of law and legislation. On the other hand, the power of punishment and the employment of the force of the community is rendered dependent upon and subordinate to this civil determination of the boundary between law and right in political society.[60]

Locke's justification of resistance right, as we have seen, drew at-

58. Ibid., *Second Treatise*, chap. 9, entire.
59. Ibid., 2.136.
60. The signal exception to this is the prerogative power, a ruler's "Power to act according to discretion, for the publick good, without the prescription of the Law, and sometimes even against it." Ibid., 2.160. For all of Locke's emphatic legalism, this is a more than curious power, as we shall see with regard to instances of regulation in the next chapter.

tention to the latter of these, and more particularly to the misuse of executive power, as the primary source of political disorder in civil society.[61] By casting such resistance as a defense of property against the exercise of force without right and characterizing the political changes it accomplished as a restoration, Locke's account derived its political edge from the presumption that the English constitution and its laws were generally legitimate civil articulations of the just and natural rights of the English people. The experience of injury to one's self-propriety at the hands of corrupt and designing rulers stood for Locke as a sufficient indication of the abuse of power to render opposition legitimate. This foregrounding of resistance right and executive abuse, however, constitutes an identity in both theoretical and practical terms between civil law and individuals' understanding of their own self-propriety. Locke's construction of civil agency as a defense of lawfully established property thus necessarily elided theoretical consideration of civil subjects' relationship to the law itself as a properly political power to regulate and preserve property for the public good.

In light of the insistent law-mindedness of English political culture and the specific purposes of the *Treatises,* this theoretical lacuna is perhaps unremarkable, but in historical perspective it is far from unproblematic. During Locke's lifetime both English law and English understandings of the law were undergoing significant changes in focus and emphasis.[62] In the most general terms, to be sure, the law continued to symbolize justice, order, and moral rectitude. This was the case in the realm of religious discourse, of course. It was equally typical, however, of the language of the Ancient Constitution, where the association of English law with the longevity of immemorial custom lent credence to the presumption of its consistency with God's intentions. As a framework for adjudicating controversies, however, the law was subject to an increasingly diverse range of social, economic, political and demographic pressures. In a period of great change, the traditional legal mechanism of precedent neces-

---

61. "No other part of the Legislative, or the People is capable by themselves to attempt any alteration of the Legislative, without open and visible Rebellion, apt enough to be taken notice of." Ibid., 2.218.

62. This account is based largely upon Nenner, *By Colour of Law*; and Sir Charles Ogilvie, *The King's Government and the Common Law, 1471–1641* (Oxford: Basil Blackwell, 1958).

sarily called forth the application of law to new matters of dispute, new arenas of conflict and contention. Under the weight of these pressures, new understandings of law were beginning to emerge. In particular, these processes of change and adaptation began to generate a shift of emphasis in legal understanding from the moral status of law to its worldly function, from the image of law as the near-sacred embodiment of moral order to a more instrumental notion of law as a "secular tool to be addressed to the needs of the community at large."[63] Law in the first of these understandings was immutable, suggesting an eternal order of right by which the social world was to be regulated. To refer a controversy to law so understood was to frame its adjudication in terms of finding or discovering the appropriate general rule to cover, whether by analogy, extension, or inference, the particular present case at issue. In the second of these understandings, however, the law itself was potentially mutable or fluid, a tool that was subject to adaptation according to the character and substance of the circumstances it addressed or the dispute it was to resolve. As in the earlier moralistic sense, its purpose could be to remedy a wrong, but it could answer other purposes as well. In either case, on this latter view law was less an unchanging source of moral order than an instrument of human artifice, contingently directing human action and susceptible to change as the social world generated new needs and new matters of dispute.

These two images of the law, however, are not mutually contradictory, nor are they necessarily even mutually exclusive. Like most retrospective characterizations of the past, the neatness of such a dis-

---

63. Nenner, *By Colour of Law*, 15–16. This distinction could be handled in Christian understandings of law by reference to a difference between duties that were matters of eternal obligation imposed by God's law itself and duties that were temporary or circumstantial and dependent upon contingent states of the world. The obligation not to murder is of the first sort, the duty of charity of the second (those who have nothing are not bound to it). Locke, following Hooker and rather standard Anglican interpretations of the issue, uses this sort of formulation extensively in his early tracts on the civil magistrate. Though exploring the connection here would take us too far afield, a similar conundrum over a rift between the status and function of law in the early modern period is noted by Michel Foucault, "Governmentality," in *The Foucault Effect: Studies in Governmentality with Two Lectures by and an Interview with Michel Foucault*, ed. Graham Burchell, Colin Gordon, and Peter Miller (Chicago: University of Chicago Press, 1991), 87–104. For a recent attempt to bring Foucauldian insights to bear on Lockean texts, see James Tully, "Governing Conduct: Locke on the Reform of Thought and Behavior," in *An Approach to Political Philosophy*, 179–241.

tinction sacrifices historical specificity to purchase analytical breadth. In English practice from the sixteenth century onward, the shift in emphasis from status to function was manifested more clearly in some areas of the law than others. Matters of criminal jurisdiction like murder and theft, for instance, remained preeminently framed in the language of moral order and continued to evoke images of God's design for worldly peace and individual security. This continuity of emphasis on the moral status of law, however, was not the case in other areas of legal jurisdiction and statutory regulation. In particular, the highly formalized and precedent-bound writ system of the common law proved increasingly inadequate to resolve new matters of controversy and litigation generated by emerging forces of social and economic change. Significantly, the creation of new law and new rights was distinctively centered on the law of property, particularly with respect to mortgages and contracts, torts, uses, debt, and inheritance.[64] Over the course of the sixteenth and seventeenth centuries, the task of compensating for the inadequacies of the common law devolved principally upon emerging and increasingly powerful state institutions. The centralized authority of parliamentary statutes, Courts of Chancery and other equitable jurisdictions, as well as executive power over foreign trade and coinage, increasingly eclipsed the older, more local emphasis and practice of the common law, not only as appellate jurisdictions but also as primary sites of legal adjudication and redress. To be sure, the law continued to enjoy mythic status both as a source of moral order and as a framing device for rights and remedies in the social world. But the areas of law in which its social function and mutability became most pronounced were precisely those upon which the forces of social change pressed most insistently. It was in these areas of the law that the articulation of new obligations and liberties, as well as new forms of property, by the action of state authority took precedence over older understandings of remedying injuries done to a settled self-propriety.[65]

64. These observations are based on the discussion of the common law in G. W. Keeton, *An Introduction to Equity*, 5th ed. (London: Pitman & Sons, 1961), pt. 1, esp. chap. 2.

65. Hence Nenner's reinterpretation, contra Hexter, of the century's political conflict between the Crown and Parliament not as a contest between lawful government and despotism, but as a struggle between Parliament and the Crown for the control of

Again, however, the clarity of this distinction between the moral status and functional character of the law remains largely a product of historical distance. For contemporaries of the period the issue was not sorted out through such neat conceptual categories. To the extent that it was possible, their perception of change in the meaning of law was far more likely to be phrased in prudential terms of the wisdom or risk involved in adapting existing law to new circumstances or, more pointedly, in terms of a distinction between the presumption of justice in old law and the uncertain validity and suspicious character of newer formulations. In either event, the law was the law was the law: an authoritative set of rules to guide human action, and a set of rules that remained undergirded by God's injunction to social peace and moral duty. In light of this, neither Locke's complacency with regard to the moral character of law nor his neglect of the relationship between civil agents' experiential political understanding of their propriety and the character of civil law itself should be particularly surprising. But viewed in a broader historical and critical perspective this inattention is far from insignificant, for as we have seen, his theoretical justification of resistance and his understanding of political power are both deeply embedded in the older understanding of the status of law as a stable guarantor of moral order. This is not to claim that the functional perspective is absent from his work, but rather to suggest that it is consistently subordinated to the more moralistic framework. That emphasis, however, has important implications, for it renders the moral credibility and theoretical solidity of the Lockean civil subject dependent upon an image of stable moral order and an understanding of law that was gradually being eroded by the forces of social change. This dependence, in turn, establishes a decisive tension between the experiential political understanding of Locke's civil subject and the potential mutability of civil rules that stands at the center of more modern functional understandings of law. Far from peripheral to Locke's concerns, this tension is built into the core of his political

---

the law. This in itself is interesting, but its focus on the high politics of central institutions takes the increasing centralization of state power as a given, with the consequence that it misses much of the political and cultural meaning of the phenomena it traces for the practice and practical judgment of rights by ordinary citizens. See Howard Nenner, *By Colour of Law: Legal Culture and Constitutional Politics in England, 1660–1689* (Chicago: University of Chicago Press, 1977).

theory, for the functional character and moral status of law converge in his account of the necessity of civil law to overcome money's disordering of judgment and propriety in the state of nature. As we shall see, at the same time that he constitutes a civil subject capable of recognizing and justified in resisting the abuse of political power, Locke creates a central political authority with extensive powers to regulate the possession and use of material goods as well as the exercise of individual liberties for what it determines to be the public good.

It has become fairly commonplace to note that Locke invests civil authority with considerable latitude over property relations in civil society. Typically, this is granted as a matter of course, but little consideration has been given either to how this might be the case or, more importantly, how it relates to his justification of resistance as just retribution against the abuse of power. If property right, as I have suggested, is for Locke a liberty of use in that which is legally established as one's own, and if the purpose of civil law is to determine, settle, and regulate property for the public good, the question of the relationship between the political understanding of his civil subjects and laws affecting property is a significant one. This is particularly the case since, on Locke's account, individuals' experiential judgments of injury to their self-propriety on the part of civil authority constitute a sufficient moral ground for legitimate resistance. In this context, there are two aspects of the political regulation of property that bear critical examination: the theoretical grounds upon which Locke invests civil authority with the rightful power to determine what is properly one's own, and the extent to which and grounds upon which the Lockean state is empowered rightfully to limit or condition the liberty of use one has in a property so defined. In both cases, as we shall see, the reactivity and self-protectiveness of Locke's civil subjects with respect to civil interferences with their propriety, broadly understood, generate a situation much like his late state of nature, particularly as the law begins to assume a more mutable and functional character with respect to the regulation of property in civil society.

7

Legal Trouble: The Public Good and the Limits of Consent

For forms of government let fools contest, Whate'er is best administered is best.

—John Locke
An Essay on Man

B y casting knowledge of one's self-propriety as the fundament of political understanding, Locke avoids many of the epistemological difficulties attending moral judgment that he explored at length in the *Essay*, where bias, partiality, and an uncritical acceptance of the authority of others are isolated as the chief sources of wrong judgment. In contrast to the dilemmas posed by these obstacles to reliable knowledge, such civil facts as injury to one's life, limb, or health, restriction of one's liberty, deprivation of one's property, and, of course, the experience of force without right, stand in Locke's account on far more solid cognitive ground. In this respect the consideration of civil interests that Lockean political authority embodies in public law and political action appears to speak the same experiential and present-minded language that characterizes the political understanding of his civil subjects. The Lockean political realm is thus one in which individual experience and reasoned judgment are not only central concerns but defining features. Unlike the law that governs the natural community, however, the laws of particular political societies are themselves of human making. Embodying an authority relation not between the species as a whole and its infallible maker, but between finite beings prone to partiality and error, civil power itself may be called to the court of reason. Indeed, as we have noted before, to those duly informed by both morality

248

and common law Locke explicitly recommends such sustained inquiry
into civil statutes to "shew the true ground upon which they came to be
made, and what weight they ought to have."[1] In this context, just as
Locke's natural individuals were accountable for injurious actions
based on error or willful disregard of the rule of reason, so too are his
civil agents culpable for unreasonable judgments. All are accountable,
governors and subjects alike, for the use they make of their liberty, and
the authoritative character of civil power so constituted is contingent
upon a condition of agreement that the political judgments and actions
of the former are reasonable and necessary.

In the broadest sense, the issue this poses is one of consent. As
John Dunn has noted, however, Locke's notion of consent is not simply a matter of positive affect or psychological assent, for what his
political agents "can rationally assent to is limited by their own
rights."[2] The political power transferred by Locke's natural agents to
civil authority can only be such as they had by nature over themselves in the original condition, and they cannot cede such powers as
they do not themselves naturally possess. Dunn suggests, noting the
suicide taboo as an example, that this limitation establishes a significant moral boundary for political power, since it provides one of the
grounds for Locke's derivation of resistance right. As we have seen
from a different perspective, that taboo is a pivotal element in his
critique of tyranny: because his natural agents lack arbitrary power
over their own lives and propriety, no attempt to exercise such
power in a civil condition can, on his account, be properly political.
The matter, however, is not nearly so clear with respect to the
boundaries of political power relative to such rights and powers as
Locke's natural agents can and do transfer to civil authority. Most
crucially, it is unclear with regard to the power of the individual to
do "*whatever he thought fit for the Preservation of himself, and the rest of
Mankind.*"[3] This, Locke asserts, is given up "to be regulated by Laws

1. John Locke, *Some Thoughts concerning Education*, in *The Educational Writings of
John Locke*, ed. James Axtell (Cambridge: Cambridge University Press, 1968), by paragraph, 187.

2. John Dunn, "Consent in the Political Theory of John Locke," in *Life, Liberty,
and Property: Essays on Locke's Political Ideas*, ed. Gordon Schochet (Belmont, Calif.:
Wadsworth Press, 1971), 134.

3. John Locke, *Two Treatises of Government*, ed. Peter Laslett, rev. ed. (1960; reprint, with amendments, Cambridge: Cambridge University Press, 1963), by book and
paragraph, 2.129. Hereafter cited as *Two Treatises*.

made by the Society, so far forth as the preservation of himself and the rest of that Society shall require," and such laws "in many things confine the liberty he had by the Law of Nature."[4] To be sure, these civil laws as well as the penalties they impose can only be such as are necessary for the public good. And again, with particular reference to laws setting taxes and regulating property, Locke insists that they require consent. The precise character of this consent as a limitation of civil power, however, is far less obvious than it may appear, for the supremacy of the Lockean legislative power to define the boundaries of propriety in law renders the consent of representatives identical with the making of law itself.

If, as I have argued, the political understanding of Locke's civil subjects is framed by the civil fact of their own propriety as this is settled by law, the question of their relationship to the civil regulation of this propriety would appear to be a significant one. Here, then, as we near the end of our exploration of the problematic of judgment in Locke's political theory, we confront an issue that was relegated to the background of his thought by the conventional moralism of his notion of law and by the *Treatises'* emphasis on the right to resist executive abuse. As we have seen, however, early modern legal understandings were caught up in a subtle shift of emphasis from the moral status of law to its social function, particularly with respect to laws affecting property—and this transformation suggests that Locke's legal moralism was embedded in an understanding of the relationship between law and right that was slowly being supplemented by a rather different sensibility. And yet, by marshaling that moralism to demonstrate the consistency of resistance with a care for one's soul, Locke may have limned, however unwittingly, an unsettling tension attending the historical elaboration of the secular civil subject of later liberalism. Though perhaps not so stridently acquisitive as some have suggested, Locke's civil agents are nonetheless cognitively individualistic, protective of their propriety, and morally justified in opposing the exercise of such power as is not, on Locke's account, properly political. In light of this, the question of the relationship of the Lockean civil subject to law itself can be seen as a matter of both theoretical and historical import.

To the extent that the individual "subject of rights" becomes a sta-

4. Ibid.

ple of liberal thought, and to the extent that its "proprieties" become matters of concern for a more functional view of civil law, its relationship to civil order grows increasingly problematic. As the laws governing its propriety come to be seen neither as matters of immemorial prescription nor as immutable rules of right consistent with God's design, but as secular tools susceptible to intentional change in the face of new circumstances and new social needs, what then becomes of its defensive relationship to civil power? In this regard, Locke's political writings offer an unusual opportunity to examine the rights-bearing subject in light of this shifting emphasis in legal understanding, for although the *Treatises'* justification of resistance gives pride of place to the moral status of civil law, his treatments elsewhere of the political power to regulate propriety are infused with a far more functionalist perspective. In the latter context, as we shall see, the moral individualism and experiential political understanding of the *Treatises'* civil subjects confront the regulatory powers of the nascent state with a rather significant difficulty. To develop this claim, we will begin by exploring the theoretical bases for Locke's civil power to regulate propriety as this appears in his writings on money and toleration, particularly as these suggest the criteria of judgment appropriate to such regulation. Following this, we will consider examples, in turn, of both the moralistic and the functional understandings of the lawful regulation of propriety, with an eye to their implications for Locke's construction of legitimate authority. In closing, I will attempt to characterize more broadly the relationship between Lockean property and political power in terms of the politics of judgment this suggests, as well gesture toward what may be some of its thornier implications for the subsequent historical development of the politics of rights.

I Civil Law and the Settling of Propriety

If, as the root of inconveniences in Locke's state of nature, money is the mechanism establishing the moral necessity of civil power, it generates on the worldly terrain of property relations the same sort of essential contestedness that differing religious beliefs produce with regard to the question of salvation. Its free-floating imaginary values, like the speculative truths of religion, are subject to controversies that cannot be resolved by reference to any clear experiential criterion of justice, either with regard to questions of just possession and use or with regard to issues of injury and punishment. But quite unlike religious opinions, to which Locke ascribes a private character, money is an emphatically worldly substance: what one may properly or improperly value as necessary to salvation has no effect upon others' prospects for redemption, but the price one puts on grain or other essential commodities can have considerable impact on their daily lives. The function of money as a measure of value and a vehicle of desire in the exchange of worldly goods thus endows it with a kind of public consequence, civil facticity, and moral weight that Locke's epistemology denies to the speculative truths of religion.

For Locke no less than Winstanley, money symbolized the new commercial order and the faceless character of monetarized market relations, in contrast to the more personal and directly perceived moral economy of an older imagery of property. But while Locke rejected neither commercial society nor the coinage that drove its trade, the *Treatises* nonetheless represent money as disruptive of the epistemology of right that had, prior to its invention, ensured a settled order of property relations by guaranteeing to natural agents hands-on knowledge of their own in an economy of needs. The moral meaning of money, however, remained equivocal. On the one hand, as a magnet for greed and partiality it stimulated the most corrupt of human motives. Similarly, although the inequalities of property that it enabled were not inherently immoral, wealth and poverty were each attended by their own peculiar forms of vice. On the other hand, money facilitated exchange and encouraged productivity, thereby increasing the stock of necessities and conveniences available for human use. In light of this equivocality Locke asserts the rightful power of the political order to control the controversies that money generates and to assure, where necessary, the conformity of commercial relations to the moral prohibition of injury. In effect, his perspective seeks to mitigate the more pernicious of money's worldly consequences by extending the moral framework of God's architecture into a reaffirmation of political jurisdiction over the unsettled terrain of monetarized property relations. To put the point somewhat differently, for Locke the problematic relationship between property and political power is not a question of whether civil authority may or may not legitimately intervene in property relations. This is evidenced by the explicit responsibility he assigns the legislative power to "decide the Rights of the Subject" and make "*standing Rules*" to bound the properties of civil subjects so that "every one may know what is his," for in the absence of such "*declared Laws*" property would "still be at the same uncertainty, as it was in the state of Nature."[5] The issue, in other words, is not whether the state may rightfully concern itself with the self-propriety of its citizens, for this jurisdiction over both their liberties and their possessions is precisely what is created by the institution of political society and civil government. Rather, given the *Treatises'* representation of the moral necessity and legitimacy of the jurisdiction, the question becomes how, for what purposes, and on what grounds particular state actions within this domain are to be determined and defended.

In theoretical terms, as we have seen, the moral character of this jurisdiction invests civil law with the task of giving renewed specificity to the parallel distinctions between law and right, virtue and convenience, as the measure of properly human liberty. In deciding the rights of the subject, civil authorities thus set the legal limits of private liberty through their "Power to set down what punishment shall belong to the several transgressions which they think worthy of it."[6] On Locke's account, this is precisely the way in which the obligations of natural law are "drawn closer, and have by Humane Laws known Penalties annexed to them, to inforce their observation."[7] Most significantly, then, with money's denaturalization of the extent of private possession and the criterion of harm, it is the peculiar charge of the political realm to determine what is to count as lawful possession and what as criminality, as well as to establish measures of punishment proportionate to the severity of the crime. Thus in any particular political society, the function of Lockean civil power is to reestablish the boundary between the lawful and unlawful pursuit of private convenience in a manner consistent with the good of each and the welfare of all. While Locke's clear approval of industriousness and property may appear to accede to acquisitive individualism, this acquiescence is implicitly mediated by the assumed presence of

5. Ibid., 2.136.
6. Ibid., 2.88.
7. Ibid., 2.135.

civil law to differentiate between such things as honest industry and fraud or just possession and criminal injury. The criteria appropriate to such civil line-drawing, however, remain to be seen. In this context Locke's theoretical deployment of money as the mechanism disrupting both property relations and the administration of natural justice is far more fundamental to his positive conception of political power than has heretofore been recognized. In Locke's theoretical narrative the invention of money generates a transformation of human society from an economy of sufficiency, in which the fundamental moral imperative is the preservation of life itself, to one of potential superfluity, in which perceptions of injury are caught up by inherently controversial reckonings of imaginary values. With the monetarization of natural property relations, the presumptively direct connection between individual property rights and the needs of life has been radically attenuated. Where one may rightfully possess more than one needs, private determinations of convenience in the use and appropriation of property no longer bear any necessary relationship to the preservation of each and all in accordance with God's intentions. In this altered condition Locke places the burden of resolving the moral and epistemological dilemmas that attend monetarized property relations squarely on the shoulders of civil authorities.

In so doing, Locke reaffirms the moralistic understanding of lawful order and its commitment to the needs of life itself as the baseline criterion of legitimate civil jurisdiction over personal propriety. His primary concern, however, is not with the extent of possession, whether of material goods or of liberty itself, since both are by definition matters enabled by civil determination in any case. As he noted in the *Tracts*, worldly differences between individuals in such things as fiscal responsibilities, as well as economic and political inequalities, are "owing all to human laws and those just enough, the law of God or nature neither distinguishing their degrees nor bounding their possessions."[8] Instead, his emphasis falls upon the moral necessity of civil laws to give specific content to the natural-law prohibition of injury in particular contexts where the boundary between law and right is in question. The justice of such laws, in other

8. John Locke, *Two Tracts on Government*, ed. Philip Abrams (Cambridge: Cambridge University Press, 1967), English Tract, 138. Hereafter cited as *Tracts*.

words, follows not from any elaborate criterion of distributive justice, for on this the law of nature is silent. Rather, it derives from the natural-law prohibition of injury and the imperative of worldly preservation per se. Thus even the liberty of use that one has in a lawfully established propriety is subject to moral and political limitation should circumstances require.

One of Locke's most pointed articulations of this position appears in his discussion of just price in the "Venditio." He suggests that, though in conditions of dearth a merchant does no injustice by selling his grain at the highest price he can get,

> yet if he carry it away unless they will give him more than they are able, or extorts so much from their present necessity as not to leave them the means of subsistence afterwards he offends against the common rule of charity as a man and if they perish any of them by reason of extortion is no doubt guilty of murder. For though all the selling merchants gain arises only from the advantage he makes of the Buyer's want whether it be a want of necessity or fancy . . . yet he must not make use of his necessity to his destruction, and enrich himself so as to make another perish. He is so far from being permitted to gain to that degree, that he is bound to be at some loss and impart of his own to save an other from perishing.[9]

That some are enriched by their vocations in trade is thus neither a moral dilemma nor a political question for Locke—unless in so doing they violate the prohibition of harm and thereby become criminally accountable. The moral clarity with which Locke here represents the connection between murder and profiteering in the grain trade, however, does not really capture the character or potential scope of Lockean civil jurisdiction. As the gravity of the term "murder" might suggest, however, what it does indicate is his continuing embeddedness in the traditional assumption of a directly cognizable moral economy of needs and its corollary understanding of the moral imperatives of natural law as establishing the right order of relations between individuals as such.

At the same time, though, this example suggests some of the difficulties encountered by that traditional view in the face of extended market relations and the expansion of trade well beyond the person-

9. John Locke, "Venditio," in John Dunn, "Justice and the Interpretation of Locke's Political Theory," *Political Studies* 16, no. 1 (1968): 86.

ally known and need-centered dynamics of the local community. In the "Venditio," for instance, Locke's insistence upon individual accountability and the prohibition of personal injury as the controlling moral criteria of human actions can be seen as an attempt to draw those categories of political and moral judgment forward into the considerably broader domain of extended commerce.[10] The actions of his extortionary grain trader, in this sense, manifest the personally perceived consequences that informed common judgments regarding the questionable moral character of the local engrosser or monopolist in the older view. But with Locke's stretching of his individualist vocabulary to cover an expanded market situation comes the silent assumption that direct personal accountability can be ascertained. In practice, however, the situation was likely to be far more complex than Locke, in that brief reflection, managed to acknowledge. In all likelihood it would not entail a single grain seller to whose pricing practices one could impute personal responsibility for the starvation of particular individuals. More realistically, the market would include several merchants, none of whose direct responsibility for such deaths as might occur could be clearly determined. Given the facelessness of market forces and the attenuation of personal responsibility for either the fate of products or the social consequences of their movement through the market, such clarity is precisely what monetarized commerce operated to subvert.

Locke's neglect of this complexity in the "Venditio," however, should not be taken as lack of concern for, let alone ignorance of, the problem; for such controversies fall by definition under the jurisdiction of his civil authority. And in this context Locke was prepared to go further than an abstract discussion of moral responsibility, and further in ways that have important implications for understanding the character and scope of Lockean civil power over personal propriety in both the broad and the narrow senses of the word. While the "Venditio" example owes its force to the moral enormity of murder in universalistic terms, the rightful power of Locke's civil authority to determine the measure of injury in such worldly controversies more often relied upon a narrower—and in

10. As Kelly observes, "Venditio" contains an odd amalgam of scholastic notions, Aristotelian reasoning, and individualist morality. See his introduction to John Locke, *Locke on Money*, 2 vols., ed. Patrick Hyde Kelly (Cambridge: Cambridge University Press, 1991), 1:150–51.

fundamental respects more problematic—frame of reference. Here, as was the case in his justification of resistance, a general focus on the formal universalism of Locke's moral language can obscure his practical presumption that existential civil agents live out their lives not on the abstract plane of moral philosophy or casuistic debate, but in particular political societies. Thus, such rights over their own property as they transfer in theoretical terms to civil society are in practice yielded in a continuous fashion to specific historically consti-tuted polities. As Locke himself observes in the *Treatises,* with the initial creation of a civil order each natural agent "is to part with . . . as much of his natural liberty in providing for himself, as the good, prosperity, and safety of the Society shall require," and in this sense the Lockean civil power to regulate and preserve property must be understood in terms of contingent judgments of circumstances in particular civil states.[11] Locke's theoretical transfer of natural rights to civil determination, in other words, invests particular govern-ments with such jurisdiction over propriety as the necessity·of the case shall require for the good, prosperity, and safety of the com-monwealth as a whole.

Thus while the self-propriety of Locke's civil subject, once estab-lished, is perhaps not to be meddled with lightly, it is by no means insulated from the continuing if circumstantially contingent purview of political power. In one of his economic tracts, for example, Locke notes, "Private mens interests ought not . . . to be neglected, nor sacri-ficed to any thing but the manifest advantage of the Publick"[12]—a con-struction that circumscribes rather than prohibits such jurisdiction. As Dunn has suggested, one issue this presents is how the "right of the political society to regulate and articulate the property rights of individuals" can credibly be squared with "their right to do with it whatever they wish."[13] Locke's answer to this, fragile though it may seem, is that such regulation must conform to the public good as the

---

11. Locke, *Two Treatises,* 2.130.
12. John Locke, *Some Considerations of the Consequences of the Lowering of Interest and Raising the Value of Money,* 1691, 2d ed., corrected, in *Several Papers Relating to Money, Interest, and Trade & c.* (London: A. & J. Churchill at the Black Swann, 1696; facsimile, New York: Augustus M. Kelley Publishers, 1968), 13; reprinted in Locke, *Locke on Money,* 1:220. Hereafter cited as *Some Considerations.* Pages cited will be from the first volume of *Locke on Money,* with the page of the facsimile edition following in paren-theses.
13. Dunn, "Consent in Locke," 147.

only proper and legitimate end of all actions undertaken by civil authority. The apparent vacuousness of this criterion notwithstanding, its liturgical recitation as the Lockean measure of properly political power exhausts neither its theoretical nor its political significance. For in his legitimation of resistance to the exercise of such power as exceeds its proper bounds, Locke has constituted his civil subjects as creatures both wary of incursions upon that which the law has established as their own and justified in opposing such political tampering with this propriety as they do not see and feel to be consistent with the public good. This suggests that the problem cannot be conceptually contained in the difficulties attending Locke's notions of consent or representation, but extends as well into a consideration of the grounds upon which political regulation can be demonstrated as necessary or desirable for the good of the whole. If the legitimacy of Lockean political authority is a matter of agreement between rulers and ruled that civil actions are necessary, the problem of civil order becomes one of establishing the grounds or terms upon which such agreement depends. This in turn suggests the question of how Lockean civil agents are to distinguish between arbitrary interferences with their propriety and reasonable regulation for the public good. What, in other words, are the criteria of judgment upon which political intervention in citizens' proprieties can be credibly justified as contributing to the good, prosperity, and safety of the community itself?

II Regulating Propriety: Public Visibility and the Criterion of Injury

When we explored the moral status of Locke's civil power we looked briefly at his early essays on the civil magistrate. In charging the political realm with the maintenance of decency and order, Locke there extended civil jurisdiction broadly over whatever aspects of social life the magistrate deemed necessary for the public good. With his later defense of toleration, as we have seen, Locke refined this criterion of political purpose to a care for "civil interests": "The safeguard of men's lives, and of the things that belong unto this life, is the business of the Commonwealth; and the preserving of those things unto their Owners is the Duty of the Magistrate."[14] In the same work, and paralleling his construction of political power in the *Treatises,* Locke characterizes force as the distinct means of civil authority and "the Possession of all outward Goods" as its proper matter of concern.[15] Articulated in the context of the question of toleration, Locke's concern here is to secure the religious use or nonuse of such property as wine, bread, surplices, articles of clothing, and the like from magisterial imposition, and the criterion he offers for this exclusion is a purely civil one: so far as the use of such property is permitted in ordinary life, so must it be allowed in the ceremonies of religious associations. Its insulation from political determination, in other words, is not a matter of its being symbolically marked as devotional, but rather is derived from the fact that its religious and ceremonial employment is consistent with the moral and civil prohibition of injury.

The ground, in other words, for Locke's toleration of diverse religious practices is their conformity to the experiential standard of civil facticity that was, for him, the sine qua non of properly political understanding. Thus infant sacrifice and other such "heinous enormities" could be legitimately prohibited to religious congregations: such things "are not lawful in the ordinary course of life, nor in any private house; and therefore neither are they so in the Worship of God, or in any religious Meeting."[16] Once again, it is not the strangeness or sinfulness of such practices that make them subject to political control, but their violation of the moral and civil prohibition of personal harm. The ceremonial sacrifice of beasts, to note Locke's counterexample, though doubtless repugnant to his contemporary readers, is another thing entirely. By Locke's civil criterion, this must be permitted, "for no Injury is thereby done to any one, no prejudice to another mans Goods."[17] Whether such practices please God or not are topics of speculation, not matters of civil fact, and the function of the magistrate with respect to them "is only to take care that the Commonwealth receive no prejudice, and that there be no

14. John Locke, *A Letter concerning Toleration,* ed. James Tully (Indianapolis: Hackett Publishing Co., 1983), 48.
15. Ibid., 30.
16. Ibid., 42.
17. Ibid.

injury done to any man, whether in life or estate."[18] Here, the experience and use of one's own, in the sense of both liberty and material possessions, remains a matter regulated by law on the basis of the prohibition of injury. Only the lawfully established indifferency of such usages in ordinary life renders them equally indifferent in religious practice.

This assertion of a civil criterion for the religious use of worldly goods offers a point of entry for considering the relationship between Locke's positive conception of political power and the civil interests it is established to regulate and preserve. As we noted in our initial exploration of the architecture of order, on Locke's account God's moral imperatives for the human species were all of a piece: "The duties of life are not at variance with one another."[19] In terms of the scope and purposes of political power, though, the centrality accorded to the natural-law prohibition of injury to others is both the precondition and the controlling minimal criterion of virtue for all worldly acts. With respect to religious observances, then, God could never require for his worship any use of worldly things that would violate this fundamental imperative. While in most cases this effectively insulates religious practices from civil purview, Locke's follow-up qualification on the question of animal sacrifice affirms the contingent and worldly character of the criterion of injury and begins as well to suggest something of the scope and character of his civil power over the things of this world. The limiting condition attached to the political toleration of such sacrifice, in particular, is an unequivocal assertion of the public good—this time not in the *Tracts'* vague language of "decency and order" but in emphatically worldly and material terms. In developing this argument Locke offers an example of legitimate civil interference with religious practice that is tremendously suggestive. If a nation's stock of cattle had been decimated by disease, "the Interest of the Commonwealth" in restoring that stock might require that "all slaughter of Beasts should be foreborn for some while." In that situation even the sacrifice of animals for religious purposes could be prohibited, regardless of how this might bear upon the religious beliefs of those whose ceremonial

18. Ibid.
19. John Locke, *Essays on the Law of Nature,* ed. Wolfgang von Leyden (Oxford: Clarendon Press, 1954), Eighth Essay, 213.

practice includes it.[20] However central they may believe such sacrifice to their prospects for salvation, the injury to the public entailed by the continuation of such a ritual in those circumstances renders it inconsistent with the moral duty to abstain from harm. "Who sees not," Locke asks, "that the Magistrate, in such a case, may forbid all his Subjects to kill any Calves for any use whatsoever? Only 'tis to be observed that, in this case, the Law is not made about a Religious, but a Political matter: nor is the Sacrifice, but the Slaughter of Calves, thereby prohibited."[21]

Here, as we saw earlier with respect to such sins as lying and perjury, Locke's reference to political matters asserts a civil language centering upon the recognition of injury and a concern for earthly preservation as appropriate to a properly political understanding, and explicitly denies the applicability of religious discourse to these purposes. In such a situation a slaughter for the purpose of religious observance remains a slaughter—and if, in the judgment of the magistrate, the necessity of the commonwealth requires its forbearance, calling it a "sacrifice" cannot exempt it from civil jurisdiction. The magistrate's determination of the interest of the commonwealth takes clear precedence over the private right of believers to dispose of their property as they see fit. We shall return momentarily to this question of the interest of the commonwealth, but before we do let us pause to consider its civil character more closely, for in addition to particular examples of such political matters Locke offers a more broadly theoretical construction as well. Political society, he reiterates, is established "only to secure every mans Possession of the things of this life"; the care for one's soul can neither "belong" to the commonwealth nor "be subjected to it" and is thereby "left entirely to every mans self."[22] In this context, Locke goes on to suggest the insolence of civil penalties for religious belief and the wrong done by magistrates who use their jurisdiction over property to reward or punish civil subjects for their religious persuasions. The magistrate, he contends, "cannot take away these worldly things from this man, or party, and give them to that; nor change Propriety amongst Fellow-Subjects, (no, not even by a Law), for a cause that has no relation

20. Locke, *Letter concerning Toleration*, ed. Tully, 42.
21. Ibid.
22. Ibid., 48.

to the end of Civil Government, I mean for their Religion, which whether true or false does no prejudice to the worldly concerns of their Fellow-Subjects."[23]

By implication, though, such political intervention in property relations or propriety is perfectly conceivable for a cause that does pertain to the proper ends of civil government. Indeed, given the extended sense of personal "propriety" in the period, Locke's clear presumption that such intervention could be legitimate operates not only with regard to material possessions but with respect to personal liberty as well—provided, of course, that its necessity be both demonstrated and justified in purely civil terms. This is most obviously the case in another example he uses to distinguish between civil and religious ends. "Let it be granted," he argues, "that the washing of an infant with water is an indifferent thing. Let it be granted also, that if the Magistrate understand such washing to be profitable to the curing or preventing of any Disease that the Children are subject unto, and esteem the matter weighty enough to be taken care of by a Law, in that case he may order it to be done."[24] The "extreame difference," he suggests, between a command so framed and a law ordering the baptism of children with sacred water to purify their souls "is visible to every one at first sight."[25] In all such instances Locke affirms the legitimacy of civil regulation of propriety, but insists upon a specifically civil discourse, focused on the prevention of harm or injury, to demonstrate its consistency with "the public good."

At the same time, throughout such examples Locke constantly attributes an obviousness to the public character of the good provided and clearly associates this with its easy "visibility." Here we encounter the other side, so to speak, of Locke's experiential coin. As his civil subjects are accounted viscerally aware of intrusions upon their propriety, so in Locke's civil discourse is the legitimacy and contingent necessity of political regulation for the public good presumed to be easily seen, visible to all at first sight. Whatever the law has determined to be properly one's own, in other words, it remains subject to political jurisdiction insofar as circumstances render its disposal on the grounds of private convenience potentially injurious or prejudi-

23. Ibid., 48–9.
24. Ibid., 39–40.
25. Ibid., 40.

cial, either to particular others or to the public more generally. Here, as in his state of nature, Locke aims at a complementarity of law and right as a guarantee against harm, a balance wheel, so to speak, for maintaining the right order of relations between individuals amidst the flux and contingency of temporal life.

At first glance Locke's examples of killing calves and washing babies appear simply commonsensical. Similarly, it seems hardly arguable that someone's house might be razed to forestall the spread of an urban fire, or that one might be prohibited from hoarding or destroying necessities in time of famine.[26] But consider the modes and matters of cognition upon which the obviousness of these various examples rest. Here, I would suggest, no less than in his presentation of the state of nature, Locke's civil knowledge is cast as a matter of direct perception and experience, a civil analogue to his construction of firsthand knowledge in the original condition, and a social analogue to his example of an individual's physical sensation of pain. "Sense," on his account, has specifically to do with external objects, with material things.[27] Ideas stemming from the sensation of such things, he contends, are quite distinctly knowable; they are "real, and not fictions at Pleasure."[28] What makes such sense "common" for Locke is not, in the first instance, the likelihood of general assent it might command, but the degree of certainty that attends the kind of knowledge it is. In other words, its viscerally known character assures its commonality, rather than common agreement establishing its certainty.

A goodly proportion of Locke's examples, however, are invested with an obviousness and directness at the level of individual cognition that is more problematic than he manages to recognize. Recall, for instance, his ascription of legitimacy to a civil command requiring the washing of children to cure or prevent disease. The health of individuals, to be sure, is one of the civil interests with which his political authority is specifically concerned. Yet the relationship between one's experience of a particular disease (or even one's perception of another's experience) and one's knowledge of what causes or

26. The first of the latter two examples appears in Locke, *Two Treatises*, 2.159. The second was conventional political practice.

27. John Locke, *Essay concerning Human Understanding*, ed. Peter H. Nidditch (Oxford: Clarendon Press, 1975), by book, chapter, and paragraph, 2.1.3–4.

28. Ibid., 2.30.2.

cures it is not at all as analogous to the relationship between one's experience of an urban fire and the knowledge of the actions necessary to prevent its spread as Locke seems to assume. In Locke's own terms, of course, neither case is simply a matter of sensation, for sensation itself is a "Perception," an "Idea formed by our Judgment."[29] In most aspects of ordinary life, he suggests, this is so quick and habitual a process that it is barely noticeable, if it is noticeable at all. The judgmental connection between the sight of a fire and one's knowledge of what to do about it, however, may be rather different from the connection between the perception of illness and the knowledge of how to cure it. Here, in effect, Locke's characteristic focus upon the knowing subject, upon the cognitive processes of the individual, links things that—when bumped upward to the level of state policy—arguably differ in their political implications. True, a physician's observation of disease and experimentation with remedies may follow the same cognitive pattern as one who observes a fire and "experiments" with ways to put it out. But the latter was a phenomenon of general experience, whereas the same cannot be said about the former.

In the seventeenth century, as Locke well knew, specialized medical knowledge as a matter of scientific expertise was beginning to supplant folk remedies and traditional understandings of prevention and cure. As a matter of practice, to be sure, this shift was taking place primarily in urban contexts and among the more privileged classes, but this in itself begins to indicate a certain slippage between the emphatically experiential knowledge of Locke's civil subjects and the grounds of judgment he attributed to his civil authorities. Locke's phrasing—"let it be granted that the magistrate understand" a particular practice "to be profitable to the curing or preventing of any disease"—is thus charged with significant implications for the operation of his civil power in practice, for what magistrates might understand as beneficial in such a case was by no means necessarily coincident with what those subject to their authority might understand as appropriate or necessary. Moreover, a command to perform certain actions in such a context sits uneasily with Locke's construction of legitimate civil power as a condition of agreement between governors and subjects that political interference with one's

29. Ibid., 2.9.9.

propriety, in this case the private right to care for one's children as one sees fit, is demonstrably necessary for the public good. To the extent, for instance, that political care for and jurisdiction over the health of subjects are informed by such uncommon knowledge as medical expertise, the command in the matter of washing babies runs the risk of being perceived as an excessive intrusion on conventional views of parental liberty. But this example only suggests the leading edge of the difficulty. In the practice of the period, political regulation of behavior during epidemics was commonly accepted as legitimate. Further, in such a case the success of the commanded practice in curing or preventing disease might well be a matter of direct experience readily apparent to all. The obviousness of the public good achieved in this case and its intimate connection with the preservation of life itself could perhaps conform comfortably to the standard of civil facticity that informs the political understanding of Locke's civil agents. Although the form of knowledge that justified the exercise of such power might not be widely shared, its positive consequences might nonetheless still be "visible to everyone" in more or less immediate terms. Although the discrepancy or asymmetry of knowledge between rulers and ruled in the example of disease suggests a potential for disagreement, the direct personal cognizance of benefits and their close relationship to the primary virtue of protecting human life may well render the intervention if defended relatively safe from opposition.

In all these instances, as with civil prohibitions of hoarding or destroying necessities in times of dearth, Locke's construction of civil facticity remains deeply indebted to the immediate and visible criteria of danger and benefit typical of traditional views of the moral economy of needs and traditional understandings of the moral status of law. In this, again, Locke's theoretical project can be read as an extension or, perhaps more accurately, a transposition of the more direct ways of knowing typical of local communities—that is, of town or village or parish life—into the necessities of a far larger public. As we briefly noted with respect to the extortionary grain merchant of the "Venditio," however, this transposition was not without its difficulties in the context of expanded trade and commercial practice. In the domain of commerce in particular, as we shall see in a moment, political interferences with subjects' propriety may present Locke's understanding of political authority with an intractible dilemma, for in this context his own construction of the regulation of "propriety" for the public good was neither so clearly tied to the preservation of life itself nor so closely linked with such a common, direct, and experiential recognition of benefits.

III   The Public Convenience and the Politics of Judgment

Locke's earliest formulation of civil power affirmed the duty "cheerfully to obey the commands of the magistrate in all things that God hath left us free," that is, in all indifferent things[30]—and among the things left free by the law of God and nature was the private possession of outward goods. After the duty to support public necessities, "both ownership and the rights of property [are] in general entirely free," and it is "open to every one individually either to harvest his wealth or to give away his riches to anyone else."[31] "Whether they are ours or another's," he observed, is "a matter of complete indifference" to the law of nature.[32] It is precisely this "indifferency," as we have seen in Locke's later writings as well, that renders such goods subject to political jurisdiction should the necessity of the case require. Thus in Locke's civil society, just as in his state of nature, the boundary of property right remains firmly drawn at the injury of others. Though in political society this is determined by civil legislation, obedience to this law remains a matter of moral obligation.

We have briefly explored the potential for disagreement over political incursions upon subjects' propriety and noted that in practice, at least with respect to questions relating to life itself, Locke's criterion of civil facticity was probably adequate to secure agreement as to the necessity of political intervention for the public good. There is, however, another side to Locke's positive conception of political power and the proper care of his civil authority. As we have seen, his theoretical construction of civil power presumes the historical creation and individuation of societies into independent communities, each of which is concerned not only with the good that inheres in the preservation of its members' lives, but with the good that per-

30. Locke, *Two Tracts*, English Tract, 159.
31. Ibid., Latin Tract (trans.), 229.
32. Ibid.

tains to the prosperity and safety of the commonwealth itself. In effect, just as Locke's individual agents have a legitimate care not only for their moral duty but for their comfort and convenience as well, so too does the civil government of each independent community have a concern not only for defining the just bounds of private liberties but for ensuring the material welfare and prosperity of the society as a whole. Here, though, the "interest of the Commonwealth" poses an issue rather different from the preservation of life itself and implies a rather different power over subjects' "proprieties" from that of preventing injury in the extreme situation of contingent emergencies. It presents, I would suggest, both an odd category in Locke's architecture of order and a new criterion of judgment as appropriate to the exercise of political power. Given the distinction between virtue and convenience, if the establishment of laws defining injurious acts can be seen as mandating a minimal standard of public "virtue," the public charge to care for the welfare and prosperity of the community can be seen as a matter of pursuing the public "convenience." Law, in the first of these contexts, is securely attached to morality, its moral status and social function converging in its articulation of connections between various worldly actions and the natural law prohibition of harm. As a means of ensuring the public convenience, however, law assumes a far more instrumental character. Although theoretically still bounded by the natural-law prohibition of injury, its social function is channeled into a consequentialist consideration of the public good in material terms.

It is difficult to characterize the conundrum introduced into Locke's account of civil power by this notion of the public good or public interest. To begin with, it is not an altogether novel category within his theistic rendering of the architecture of order, nor is it foreign to his account of the hierarchy of laws that govern human actions within it. With respect to the law-boundedness of all proper judgments of convenience, Locke's earliest articulations of that hierarchy in the *Tracts* quite clearly designated a conceptual space for such a category. Noting that God's law and civil law were vertically ordered, he suggested an equally hierarchical dimension to consequential judgments of convenience as well. Thus "the magistrate is to consider the consequences of those things which God hath left free before he determine them by his public decrees, and the subject to consider the consequences of those things which the magistrate hath left free before he determine them by his private resolution."[33] In that early formulation, to be sure, the magistrate was to judge consequences by the broad criteria of decency and order, but Locke's later construction of civil facticity channeled civil power into a closer consideration of material effects. This increasing emphasis on a worldly, material, and ostensibly experiential conception of the public good operated to prohibit political interference with matters of religious belief, but with the inclusion of the community's prosperity as a proper civil concern this centering of attention on material consequences adds a new dimension to Locke's positive conception of political power.

There is, to put the point directly, a significant disjuncture between a civil care to define, prohibit, and remedy personal injuries to the members of a community and a concern to produce material benefits for that community as a whole. The former, consistent with Locke's construction of civil knowledge, takes primary cognizance of civil subjects' personal and individual experience of harm. Attending to worldly actions by the criterion of virtue, it attempts to frame the right order of relations between civil subjects consistent with the natural-law prohibition of injury. The latter, on the other hand, projects an image of the public as a whole, and its consequential judgments derive not from considerations of virtue, but of convenience—particularly as this is expressed in maintaining or improving the quality of the nation's material life. In the civil care for prosperity, in other words, we find Lockean political concern primarily centered not on the moral task of preventing or remedying injurious acts between individuals, but rather on sustaining or increasing in the aggregate the various comforts and conveniences of the commonwealth itself. Retrospectively, through the historical filter of later liberal concerns, the dilemma this presents might appear as a tension between the "interests" of particular civil subjects and those of the public at large, a tension easily phrased as an opposition between the individual and society, or between individualism and collectivism. If we take full account of Locke's indebtedness to a theistic frame for his defense of resistance, however, we shall see that the dilemma goes far deeper.

The difficulty is not simply a matter of whether or to what extent

33. Ibid., English Tract, 156.

individuals' rights may be limited, constrained, or sacrificed for the welfare of the whole. This, as we have seen, is precisely the business of Locke's civil jurisdiction. Rather, the question is how such regulation is to be defended, how its necessity or desirability is to be demonstrated, to civil subjects whose civil knowledge is cognitively framed in personal and experiential terms and whose political sensibility is focused on the security of their own proprieties. Locke's civil agents, to put the point somewhat differently, are individually constituted to know what affects their own propriety in direct and immediate terms. But they have little or no basis for a conception of the public beyond their own experience or observation, and hence their cognitive access to the interest of the commonwealth can only be articulated in these terms. Locke's civil subjects are, in this respect, rather prickly creatures, closely attuned to what affects their own as their primary cognitive connection with what affects the public at large. By making the prosperity of the nation a properly political concern, Locke generates a significant problem of political legitimation, a problem rendered yet more acute by his moral justification of resistance to such political interferences with propriety as are not seen and felt by his civil subjects to be beneficial.

This is not, of course, to suggest that Locke would have recognized the dilemma in these terms. As was the case with respect to public health, the rightful power of civil authority to regulate trade and production, establish standards of quality in manufacture, set wages, and broadly encourage domestic industry through public policy had long been assumed. The very stuff of early modern mercantilism, such policies had been vigorously pursued by the English state since the sixteenth century. In this respect the significance Locke attributes to money in the origin of political society as well as the resulting right of his civil power to regulate propriety are advanced to defend what had become decidedly conventional political practices. Indeed, among his contemporaries even those who opposed particular forms of such regulation did so not by denying the right of central authority to intervene in such matters, but by offering consequential arguments as to the efficacy of such regulation and the probability with which it might produce the desired effects.[34] For

---

34. Joyce Oldham Appleby, *Economic Thought and Ideology in Seventeenth-Century England* (Princeton: Princeton University Press, 1978), chap. 5, esp. 99.

them, as for Locke himself, neither precedent or tradition was adequate in itself as a reason for doing anything, and the acknowledged fact that the state had a right to regulate propriety was no guide to how, or even whether, it should do so in particular cases.

Locke's focus on observable consequences thus offers an alternative to tradition or customary practice as a way of accounting for the reasonableness or necessity of political policy and action. As we have seen, though, his assumption of the public visibility of the benefits of regulation, like his more general emphasis on what I have called civil facticity, remained centered upon the prevention of injury and highly indebted to notions of direct and personal knowledge embedded in older, more localistic understandings of a moral economy of needs. In this, however, Locke's acceptance of the moral legitimacy of possession beyond need may be less indicative of a "confusion in his mind between the remnant of traditional values and the new bourgeois values,"[35] than it is symptomatic of a tension involved in translating elements of that older view into the new conditions of extended commerce. If so, the political significance of Locke's acceptance of such excess possession may be substantially more pointed than its broad conformity with bourgeois attitudes toward property. Rather, it is concentrated in his insistence upon a factual or empirical standard of benefit or harm as the measure of public policy, as well as in his affirmation of the power of the state not only to maintain its traditional purview over the moral limits of private right but to embrace the task of ensuring the material welfare of the nation in positive terms.

Here we can begin to discern the dilemma of judgment that attends Locke's positive conception of political power. On the one hand, his elaborate reweaving of the personal and experiential knowledge of one's self-propriety typical of the moral economy into the warp of natural law and the woof of ancient constitutionalism gave moral texture and worldly detail to his justification of political resistance. In the context of the predominantly casuistic political debate of the period this extension and moralization of the English political idiom through the framework of God's purposes permitted the characterization of such resistance as consistent with a conscien-

---

35. C. B. Macpherson, *The Political Theory of Possessive Individualism: Hobbes to Locke* (Oxford: Oxford University Press, 1962), 220.

tious care for one's soul. Yet on the other hand, in charging political authority with ensuring national prosperity Locke confronts his civil subjects with the welfare of a public that transcends the limits of their political cognition. Encouraged to be wary of political interferences with their propriety save those conventionally accepted as necessary for the public good, they are epistemologically bereft of any cognitive grounds for recognizing such necessity outside of their own experience. Although in the political practice of the period this dilemma was perhaps eased by the legitimacy traditionally accorded state regulation, it nonetheless points to a difficulty attending Locke's theoretical transposition of the language of that older, localistic cognitive frame onto new conditions and a more general national frame of reference. In particular, given his devaluation of tradition as a mode of justification and the potential touchiness of his civil subjects toward political initiatives affecting their propriety, it imposes upon even traditional forms of regulation the task of demonstrating the connection between specific forms of intervention and the public good. It generates, to put the point in rather different terms, the need for a language of political justification capable of bridging the cognitive gap between civil subjects' personal experience and the interest or welfare of the public as a whole.

In theoretical terms for Locke, as well as in historical practice for later liberalism, the resolution of this dilemma centered upon the notion of consent, particularly consent secured through representative or participatory institutions. In view of the epistemological or cognitive dimension of Locke's articulation of rights, however, this resolution can be seen as veiling a more fundamental problematic. Such institutions may provide an effective mechanism for marking civil subjects' willingness to abide by particular contingent definitions of the public interest, but the consent they secure rests upon a deeper level of political meaning. To the extent that consent signifies agreement or persuasion regarding the necessity or desirability of civil intervention in propriety, it directs us to an examination of the cognitive ground of that agreement itself. More specifically, it calls attention to the political character of such knowledges as would claim to forge a connection between individual experience and the welfare of the public as such. In political practice, to be sure, consent and representative institutions have historically operated both as permissions for and as limitations upon the regulation of propriety by civil authority. But these, in turn, are framed by the parameters and limitations of, as well as controversies within, the broader forms of political discourse that both generate and mediate the cognitive relationship between particularly located civil subjects and the condition of the public as a whole.

Another, more politically fraught way of putting this dilemma is to say that Locke's justification of resistance confronts the positive task of his state to ensure prosperity with the problem of accounting for the connection between individuals' personal experience and the welfare or prosperity of the political community as such. In this sense the public right of Lockean civil authority to regulate its subjects' proprieties for the public good requires a way of representing that public to itself or, more precisely, a way of imaging their place in that public to the particular civil subjects that constitute it. Given the cognitive individualism of Locke's construction of civil facticity, in other words, such regulation requires a mode of conceptualizing material connections between citizens' perceptions of their particular condition and the welfare or prosperity of the commonwealth itself. To point to this cognitive gap, of course, is not to suggest that Locke had no way to span it. His various contributions to policy debates in the period concerning recoinage as well as the regulation of interest can be seen as attempts to provide precisely such a bridge. Rather, it is to suggest that the political and theoretical significance of his attempts to vindicate state economic policy goes beyond what we might now describe as the ideological content of their recommendations. More broadly, in light of the cognitive individualism of the Lockean civil subject, their significance lies in their articulation of a mediating language to defend state policy, a political language devoted to framing the relationship between individuals' experience and the convenience of the territorial public to which they belong.

To grasp the political difficulties this produces, recall our earlier example of public health, and how Locke's individualistic construction of civil knowledge presented a potential difficulty for his notion of political authority. The production of public benefits in that example was a matter contingently defined by the discretionary judgment of civil authorities, but to the extent that their judgment was framed by such uncommon knowledge as medical expertise, it generated a cognitive gap between what the magistrate might understand to be necessary to cure or prevent disease and what those subject to such commands might believe. That difficulty, as we noted, might be mitigated not only by the traditional acceptance of such regulation but by the immediacy, generality, and moral status of the benefits produced. Bodily health as a public good could be regarded as a commonly observable benefit and also as a matter of general concern, experience, and identification. As a component of the public good, however, the civil care for prosperity is only partially analogous to the concern for public health; its difference from the latter suggests a far more fundamental dilemma for Locke's conception of public authority as a condition of agreement between rulers and ruled that the civil regulation of propriety is necessary or desirable. As in the example of public health, of course, the legitimacy of such actions turns upon a judgment of consequences, but these consequences are not so much identified with the moral status of preserving life and preventing personal injury as they are embroiled in the far more subjective and unstable realm of evaluations of convenience. In terms of Locke's construction of political understanding as individual cognizance of one's propriety, this opens up a rather large area of potential dispute. As we saw in the example of disease, one might readily assent to a restriction on one's liberty to save a life or to ward off an immediate danger. Limiting personal freedom or restraining the use of one's possessions to enhance the national prosperity, however, presents a significantly different problem of political cognition and understanding. Here, I would suggest, we confront the most trenchant difficulty engendered by Locke's displacement of the problem of moral knowledge onto central political authority in the context of an extensive and monetarized national commerce.

The dilemma might be best illustrated by imagining a typical instance of early modern regulatory policy. Although the particular case is amenable to description in the more common modern political language of a conflict of interests, for the purposes of exposition let us consider it rather in terms of Locke's language of convenience. England's national prosperity in the period was widely acknowledged to be in part due to the productivity of its woolens industry. To maintain domestic employment levels in that industry as well as to ensure domestic markets for its products, civil authority might restrict or levy a tax on the importation of competing goods such as silk or cotton cloth. Confronted with the legal obligation to restrict their commerce or to pay such a tax, however, the domestic merchants of such imported commodities might well see such policies as sacrificing their convenience to that of the woolens industry. Phrased in Locke's visceral language of political cognition, what they would "see" and "feel" would be the restriction of their liberty and propriety for the benefit of others. Such a comparison of direct personal conveniences entails evaluations beset by precisely the problems of bias and partiality that plagued Locke's late state of nature and rendered it so unstable. Conversely, those whose prosperity depended upon a thriving woolens industry might well see the absence of such regulation as encouraging the willingness of such merchants to pursue their own private convenience to the detriment of others' welfare. Indeed, perhaps from the perspective of unemployed woolens workers, it could be seen as a deprivation of necessities. In either case the controversial character of such disparate evaluations of convenience stems from the notion of a public good abstracted from the local and particularized experience of individuals and displaced onto the generality of the nation itself.

In effect, from the perspective of Locke's civil subjects, the pursuit of national prosperity as a proper goal of political power lacks what we might call a standpoint of identification. To draw again upon the example of an epidemic, the early modern experience of health and disease could be cast as viscerally known and common to all, and there could be no public health distinct from the particular health of the individual members of the society. As an object of both emergent medical science and traditional policies protecting the health of the population, it fell comfortably within Locke's standard of civil facticity, for what cured or prevented disease in one was not only observable but sufficiently generalizable to be broadly identified with the health of any and all members of the public. This ease of identification and presumptively obvious generality of benefit is precisely what the civil end of prosperity lacks. While individuals, to be sure, may experience their own material well-being as certainly and directly as they experience their own health, there is yet no necessary connection between their particular condition and the condition of the community as a whole. In Locke's example of disease, what cures an illness in one is unlikely to infect another, but in matters of trade and finance what enhances the prosperity of some may well be understood to diminish substantially the welfare of others. Any individual experience of plenty or deprivation is thus only contingently related to the welfare or need of the larger public of which they are a part, and in this respect the standpoint of identification that Locke's account assumes in the domain of public health is conspicuously absent in the pursuit of public prosperity.

As in the case of disease, Locke's civil magistrates come to understand the prosperity of the nation through the intellectual frameworks provided by emerging scientific expertise. The specialized economic knowledge that takes the prosperity of the nation as its end, however, differs substantially from the medical expertise of the earlier example, and the cognitive gap it entails is of a far more problematic character. Most important, the object of such investigation is constructed as significantly different. Where Locke's specialized medical knowledge was modeled on the health of individuals as a generalizable civil fact, the national prosperity that is the object of economic knowledge is, within Locke's categories of cognition, itself a complex idea, an entity of human artifice quite removed from the naturalistic level of individual sensation and perception he deployed to ground the political understanding of his civil agents. To the extent that Lockean civil authority bases its regulation of propriety in a vision of national welfare provided by such expertise, it assimilates a cognitive category and standpoint quite foreign to the individualistic standard of civil facticity that frames the political sensibilities of those subject to its commands.

Here we confront the dilemma of judgment intrinsic to Locke's positive conception of political power. In charging public authority with the regulation of propriety and defining the limits of private convenience, he channels the myriad controversies of monetarized commerce into the domain of civil jurisdiction. Where this power sustains its association with the moral status of law, where it centers on the prevention of personal injury—as for example with respect to the criminality of theft or fraud—it remains consistent with his individualistic construction of civil knowledge. But as the object of such power shifts to a more functional understanding of regulation, as it pursues the public interest or convenience of prosperity, the scope of its charge escapes the personal and individualistic cognitive standpoint of Locke's civil subjects. In effect, by taking on the task of producing positive material benefits and ensuring the economic welfare of the nation as a whole, Lockean civil authority must move beyond his construction of civil facticity and seek more general frameworks to delineate the material connections between particular individual activities and the good of the whole. Civil power in this context necessarily becomes dependent upon forms of knowledge significantly removed from that characteristic of the civil subjects whose proprieties it regulates.

To view this from the ground up, however, Locke's civil subjects lack any standpoint of identification with such constructs as the national prosperity. They have presumptively immediate access to knowledges of the productive and distributive dynamics within a more limited local community, but Lockean individuals have no direct cognitive access to their position or function within the economy of the nation. Whereas they may personally know and witness the vicissitudes of commerce in a context of known needs, persons, and practices, they are cognitively unequipped to envision their place within the economic exigencies and processes of that larger civil community as a whole. As a result, because the form of knowledge they do have provides a moral ground for resistance, despite the right of Lockean civil power to regulate propriety for the public good, his civil subjects are theoretically constituted to find virtually any civil interference with their propriety suspicious. In important respects, by charging civil authority with the pursuit of national prosperity Locke has substantially replicated the conditions of judgment that rendered the determination of right so problematic in his postmonetary state of nature. Again, albeit now in a civil context, there are no directly accessible practical principles or experiential criteria which might provide grounds for common agreement upon the necessity of specific forms of regulation. Again there is no obvious relationship between individuals' experiential perceptions and claims of rights and the convenience of the whole.

The essential difference, however, between this and Locke's natural state is the existence of centralized political institutions, institutions vested with the power to make and enforce judgments that are binding upon all members of the community. In effect, by carrying into the broader context of a national state both the traditional right of civil magistrates to regulate propriety for the public good and the model of personal and local knowledge typical of the moral economy, Locke endows that central political authority with a scope of concern inaccessible to the understanding of his civil subjects. However mitigated in historical practice by the appropriateness generally accorded such regulation by custom, in theoretical terms the dilemma of legitimation this suggests is severe. Notwithstanding its ostensible or formal grounding in consent, we might see in Locke's positive conception of the political realm not the limited government of later liberal commentary, but the articulation of a central power that is in significant respects at once overpowered and underauthorized—a state, that is, for which what we now might refer to as "legitimation crisis" is discernible as both constituent feature and constitutive dilemma.

Once again, though, to note this theoretical dilemma from the vantage of historical retrospect is not to suggest that Locke and his contemporaries lacked intellectual resources to address it. As I briefly noted earlier, amidst the legitimacy traditionally accorded the power of magistrates to legislate for the convenience of the whole, Locke's and others' various contributions to the policy debates over recoinage and the statutory regulation of interest rates can be seen as providing variations on the sort of legitimation required in particular cases. The political function of such economic analyses may, however, have been indebted far less to their scientific character than to their rhetorical capacity to represent the public interest to its constituent members—to their capacity to phrase the contingent relationship between individual experience and the economic condition of the nation as a whole. If so, the political significance of these analyses lay less in their validity as what later moderns would call economics than in their articulation of a mediating language through which individuals might not only identify themselves with the prosperity of an entity beyond their personal experience, but, in effect, "see" conceptually their place and function in the economy of the nation itself.

The dilemma of legitimation evident within Locke's theoretical project can thus be understood as emblematic of a parallel dilemma confronting the political practice of the period and the economic imperatives of the emerging national state. If the capacity of civil authority to pursue public prosperity depends upon the knowledges generated by emergent frameworks of economic analysis, so then does the legitimacy accorded its policies become linked to the diffusion of these new perspectives among the public whose propriety it is empowered to regulate for the common good. Civil subjects can consent to regulations affecting their propriety only to the extent that they come to identify with and accept the relationship between the effects of such regulation on their own propriety and the welfare of the nation as a whole. If it is not to be a matter simply of habitual obedience, consent itself becomes an artifact of civil agents' willingness or capacity to mediate or interpret their immediate personal experience of benefit or harm through the conceptual representations of emergent economic discourses—in effect, to see themselves in the categories such discourses provide. And in this sense, the order or stability of the Lockean state is fundamentally dependent upon civil subjects' assimilation of the broad conceptualizations of the nation's prosperity and welfare that guide the judgments of public authorities.

This, in any case, is the difficulty in theoretical terms. In practice, that assimilation had been proceeding apace. In addition to the massive outpouring of political and religious pamphlets and the equally vast literatures on agricultural improvement and moral conduct, over the course of the seventeenth century economic writings too had become a standard offering of the popular press. Beginning with the economic crisis of the 1620s, this new genre of materials focused on such issues as trade, credit, agricultural productivity, and employment. For better and for worse, city and county alike had become enmeshed in the web of commerce and, as Joyce Appleby suggests, the genre provides a glimpse of "the way Englishmen used their imagination to explain the new market forces in their lives."[36] Addressed to an increasingly literate public, these pieces of economic advice attempted to visualize the world of trade that had begun to knit together England's scattered localities into a single national market. The form these imaginings took, however, as well as the language in which they were articulated was a far cry from what later became recognizable as scientific economics.[37] What they represented had little to do with such now-standard abstractions as gross national product and unemployment statistics, much less supply and demand curves, estimates of elasticity, preference orderings, or calculations of diminishing marginal utility. Rather, their images were directed to tracing the ebb and flow of goods as well as the circula-

36. Appleby, *Economic Thought and Ideology*, 5.
37. Kelly also stresses the difference between these writings and the analyses of later economic science. See his introduction to Locke, *Locke on Money*, 1:67–71.

tion of money through the "hands" of the nation. Their tracts were peopled, one is tempted to say literally, with the characters, callings, and activities of the familiar social landscape. Landlords, freeholders, tenants, day laborers, merchants, shopkeepers, grain traders, bankers, clothiers, weavers, paupers, widows and orphans on fixed incomes—like characters in a drama each and all were called upon to perform their part in the new narratives mapping the economy of the nation. In significant respects, the nation brought to life by these writings could be understood in terms generally cognizable as the local community writ large, and in this sense such images were in large part readily assimilable to the immediacy of perception presumed characteristic of local knowledge.

Locke's own contributions to the balance-of-trade theory in the period offer a number of particularly vivid examples of this and are sufficiently rich in their evocations of cognitive immediacy to be reproduced here in some detail. Attempting at one point to draw out the implications of a scarcity of money for the domestic economy, he introduces the stock characters of common homily and casts them as actors on the national stage. In such a situation, he observes, "People not perceiving the Money to be gone, are apt to be jealous one of another; and each suspecting anothers inequality of Gain to rob him of his share, every one will be imploying his skill, and power, the best he can, to retrieve it again, and to bring Money into his Pocket in the same plenty as formerly."[38] Locke's images, however, become yet more intimate and familiar than this, for the connecting metaphors he employs move from local personages to the family itself. Recast as a bedtime squabble between siblings, for example, the domestic jealousy and suspicion alluded to above is "but scrambling amongst our selves" that "helps no more against our want, than the pulling of a short Coverlet will, amongst Children, that lye together, preserve them all from the Cold. Some will starve, unless the Father of the Family provide better, and enlarge the scanty Covering."[39] The father of the family, of course, metaphorically evokes the government itself, and in this example the danger Locke points to is the promulgation of inappropriate laws. This "pulling and contest" for the economic "coverlet," he suggests, "is usually between the

38. Locke, *Some Considerations*, 290 (115).
39. Ibid.

Landed-man and the Merchant,"[40] but he goes on to add the "Mon-ied Man" to the social landscape of the national economy and to describe the contest in some detail:

> The *Landed Man* finds himself agrieved, by the falling of his Rents, and the streightning of his Fortune; whilst the Monied Man keeps up his Gain, and the Merchant thrives and grows rich by Trade. These he thinks steal his Income into their Pockets, build their Fortunes upon his Ruin, and Ingross more of the Riches of the Nation than comes to their share. He therefore endeavors, by Laws, to keep up the value of *Lands,* which he suspects lessened by the others excess of Profit: But all in vain. The cause is mistaken and the remedy too. 'Tis not the *Merchants* nor *Monied Man's* Gains that makes Land fall: But the want of Money and lessening of our Treasure wasted by extravagent Expences, and a mis-manag'd Trade, which the Land always first feels.[41]

Particular policy debates were not alone, however, in receiving this sort of figurative treatment, for such analogies were equally charac-teristic of attempts to represent the economy as a whole in temporal terms. Again, Locke's own contribution to the genre relies upon the most intimately familiar images of the predominantly agrarian order of seventeenth-century England. "A Kingdom," he notes, "grows Rich, or Poor, just as a Farmer doth, and no otherwise."[42] He then compares two such farmers of equal productivity, one of whom spends nine-tenths of the income on "Salt, Wine, Oyl, Spice, Linen, and Silks," while the other, "contenting himself with his Native Com-modities, buys less Wine, Spice, and Silk at Market" and spends only half.[43] The latter, Locke observes, at the close of a decade will be five times the richer, but to suggest a temporal process of corruption threatening to such thrift and industry he goes on to evoke the equally familiar imagery of familial inheritance. The wealthy farmer dies,

> and his Son succeeds, a fashionable young Gentleman, that cannot Dine without *Champagne* and *Burgundy,* not sleep but in a Damask Bed; whose Wife must spread a long Train of Brocard, and his Children be always in the newest French cut and Stuff. He being come to the Estate, keeps

40. Ibid., 290–91 (115).
41. Ibid., 291 (116).
42. Ibid., 230 (26).
43. Ibid., 230 (27).

on a very busie Family; the Markets are weekly frequented, and the Commodities of his Farm carried out, and Sold, as formerly, but the Returns are made something different; the fashionable way of Eating, Drinking, Furniture and Clothing for himself and Family, requires more Sugar and Spice, Wine and Fruit, Silk and Ribons, than in his Fathers time. . . . What comes of this? He lives in Splendor, 'tis true, but this unavoidably carries away the Money his Father got, and he is every year . . . Poorer.[44]

To the arithmetic of this image of decay Locke adds a moralistic flair as well, again replicating the homilies of the contemporary pulpit to draw the cognitive connections between the experiential knowledge of individuals and the welfare of the nation:[45] "To his Expences, beyond his Income, add Debauchery, Idleness, and Quarrels amongst his Servants, whereby his Manufactures are disturbed, and his Business neglected, and a general Disorder and Confusion through his whole Family and Farm: This will tumble him down the Hill the faster, and the Stock, which the Industry, Frugality, and good Order of his Father had laid up, will be quickly brought to an end, and he fast in Prison." All these familiar images laid end-to-end, Locke hammers home the cognitive correspondence he is attempting to establish by analogizing his parable of the farm to the nation itself. The two, he observes, again slipping rapidly between local cognizance and national identification, "differ no more than as greater and less." And like the fictive son, "we may Trade, and be busie, and grow Poor by it, unless we regulate our Expences; If to this we are Idle, Negligent, Dishonest, Malitious, and disturb the Sober and Industrious in their Business, let it be upon what pretence it will, we shall Ruine the faster."[46]

As Locke's own imagery might suggest, to a considerable degree this literature followed precisely the sort of reasoning he once characterized as appropriate to the "well management of publique or private affairs."[47] The latter, he suggests, are questions of "politie and prudence . . . not capeable of demonstration," depending as

44. Ibid., 230–31 (27–28).
45. Ibid., 231 (28).
46. Ibid.
47. Journal entry for 26 June 1681; reproduced in John Locke, *An Early Draft of Locke's "Essay," Together with Excerpts from His Journals*, ed. Richard I. Aaron and Jocelyn Gibb (Oxford: Clarendon Press, 1936), 116.

they do upon the "various unknowne humours, interests and capacitys of men" rather than "any setled Ideas of things physique."[48] Instead, he continues, "a man is principally helped in them by the history of matter of fact, and a sagacity of enquireing into probable causes and findeing out an analogie in their operations and effects."[49] By representing the productive and commercial processes of the nation in terms analogous to the more intimately known cast of characters and callings that populated the local scene, the economic writings of the period provided intellectual frameworks capable of mapping the cognitive terrain between the experience of individuals and the public that they severally embodied. So framed, the emerging conceptualizations of the national economy began to forge a new political language, initially augmenting but eventually supplanting the individuated moral imagery of local knowledge, for understanding and legitimating political interventions in propriety for the public good.

IV   A Legacy of Lockean Judgment: The Disjuncture of Knowledge and the Politics of Legitimation

In these last considerations of the relationship of Locke's civil agents to the law that preserved and regulated their proprieties, I have adopted a perspective foreign not only to Locke's definition of his project, but to what was in all likelihood even conceivable to a seventeenth-century political consciousness. My approach here has strayed considerably from the political questions and the categories of analysis that engaged Locke and his contemporaries. Where they may have contested the wisdom of particular laws or speculated as to their consequences, I have focused on the cognitive frames, associations, and assumptions that circulated through the language of such controversies and that structured judgments within them. I have used the interpretation of Locke developed in previous chapters to provide a window, so to speak, onto a scene in the pre-history of liberal political theory and practice. In effect, by pointing to some of the difficulties of Locke's construction of civil knowledge and political understanding, given the tasks he attributed to political author-

48. Ibid.
49. Ibid.

ity, I have made him to respond to a question he could not have asked. The problems I have brought to light, however, are indications neither of incoherence nor of disingenuousness on his part. Rather, they expose the limits or boundaries of his political, theoretical, and cognitive frames and suggest, albeit in retrospect, the fragilities of his construction of civil knowledge under the pressure of the regulatory activities not only acknowledged by him as legitimate in principle, but actively pursued in practice by civil authority in the period. Most important, though, these difficulties point to an emergent disjuncture in the language of rights and to an emergent contradiction between its political purchase within the moralistic framework of natural law and the economic responsibilities of the nascent state.

This interpretation points, at least retrospectively, to a certain irony at the heart of Locke's political theory. In his attempt to understand political power right, he draws upon the resources of natural law to inscribe the English political idiom of law, right, liberty, equality, and property within a framework of God's purposes. Acutely conscious of the disruptions and controversies that beset individual property relations as well as judgments of right in the context of monetarized property relations, Locke invokes these dilemmas as a mechanism to establish the moral necessity of civil power. In combination with his mingling of natural law and constitutionalist idioms, this not only allows him to argue for moral boundaries to the exercise of such power but provides him with a moral basis for the justification of resistance. In the casuistic debate of the period, and more particularly with regard to the dilemmas of conscience spurred by debates over obligation and allegiance, this enables him to render magistrates subject to worldly sanctions for the misuse of their power and suggests the consistency of such resistance with a conscientious care for the fate of one's soul. Driven by its theological and cognitive individualism, however, Locke's construction of the scope and purpose of properly political power remains focused primarily on civil law as a vehicle for maintaining moral relations between individuals in conformity with the natural law prohibition of injury, for this is what provides both the moral purpose of civil power and the measure of its proper exercise. Similarly, the resistance right of his civil subjects is operationalized, so to speak, through a form of civil knowledge centered upon the experi-

ence of injury to their lawfully established propriety. But in accepting national prosperity as a proper concern of political authority,
Locke's perspective allows the disruptive potentials of monetarized
commerce to resurface at the level of national policy. In following a
more functionalist understanding of law in this context, Lockean political power is invested with a task that cannot be accommodated to
the individualistic standard of civil facticity that he privileges
throughout as the proper mode of political understanding. The responsibility of ensuring the convenience and pursuing the prosperity
of the nation thus leaves the legitimacy of the Lockean state on
rather unstable ground, to say the least. Indeed, in terms of Locke's
construct of civil knowledge, it has little in the way of factual
grounding at all, for its acts in this realm are no longer addressed to
the moral and civil prohibition of individual injury. Informed and
directed rather by the images, analogies, and metaphors of the nation proffered by nascent economic discourse, its legitimacy becomes
dependent upon civil subjects' habituation to interpreting their individual experience of dearth and plenty within such allegorical representations of the community as a whole.

This irony, however, is accompanied by a second one, all the more
curious because Locke's effort to understand political power right is
often taken to advance a conception of limited government. From
one perspective this is doubtless the case, for his justification of resistance and defense of propriety from arbitrary action indeed established boundaries for civil interferences with both individual liberty
and property rights. Yet as Locke himself noted in a different context, "Even *absolute Power,* where it is necessary, is *not Arbitrary* by
being absolute, but is still limited by that reason, and confined to
those ends, which required it in some cases to be absolute."[50] In this
sense, the capacity of Lockean political power to determine the
rights of subjects and regulate propriety for the public good is no
exception. In the pursuit of national prosperity and convenience,
however, this limitation and confinement is no longer limited or confined with reference to the presumptively direct experience of injury, but instead has become mediated by mimetic constructs of the
economy of the nation as a whole. Paradoxically, Locke can be seen
here as simultaneously a proponent of limited government and a

50. Locke, *Two Treatises,* 2.139.

strong state theorist, for what confines state action in this context is not individual rights per se, but the capacity of emerging economic discourses to legitimate the lawful inconveniencing of various categories of its constituent members for the convenience of the nation itself.

Commenting on the emergence of systematic economic thought in the period, Appleby has suggested that the significance of economic changes for reshaping society rendered attempts to conceptualize them "necessarily ideological."[51] "Observations, recommendations, and assertions about reality," she argues, "were necessarily intertwined, making facts the most powerful carriers of values."[52] This, on the one hand, can be seen as an appropriate description of the various formulations of the national economy that were advanced thoughout the seventeenth century. On the other hand, taken by itself, such a description offers no account of why, or how, or to what extent such formulations were politically credible or, indeed, of their relationship to the myriad sources of conflict and dissension that made all such questions of policy potentially volatile.[53] To the extent that Locke's political writings suggest something of the cognitive individualism attending the language and practice of rights in the period, the various articulations of economic thought at the time can be seen not simply as value-laced expressions of fact, but as the invention of a new understanding, one might even say a new order, of facticity itself. With the integration of local communities into a national market and the gradual erosion of religion and tradition as legitimating frames for political interventions in propriety, such new representations of the relationship between individual experience and the welfare of the community as a whole were inextricably linked to the historical and practical articulation of the economic,

51. Appleby, *Economic Thought and Ideology*, 5.

52. Ibid.

53. This difficulty, admittedly, extends well beyond the scope of Appleby's study. The conception of ideology she uses is drawn from anthropological and sociological perspectives that emphasize its function as a "bridge between the individual and society" and "the constructive role of shared beliefs" (ibid., 6). That economic theory became such a bridge, however, does not account for its relationship to the older bridges which it displaced or for the character of the political conflicts and controversies through which that displacement occurred. For a glimpse of some of the intense social and political dissensions that undergirded this formative period of economic theory see Margaret James, *Social Problems and Policy during the Puritan Revolution, 1640–1660* (New York: Barnes and Noble, 1966).

administrative, and regulatory capacities of the emerging national state.

Viewed with the privilege of hindsight, one of Locke's first considerations of the political dilemma posed by private estimations of convenience acquires a new significance. It is impossible, he suggested, for human prudence to frame any law "which whilst it minds the good of the whole will not be inconvenient to several of the members, and wherein many will not think themselves hardly and unequally dealt with."[54] The original point of this formulation had to do with the problem of conscience and religious imposition, but the conclusions Locke draws from it may be equally appropriate to the question of regulating propriety more generally:

> The magistrate in his constitutions regards the public concernment and not private opinions which, biased by their own interest, or misled by their ignorance and indiscretion, are like to make them but ill judges of reasons of state or the equity of laws; and when we find the greatest part of men usually complaining, we may easily conclude, that they think that precept of "do as thou wouldst be done unto" but ill observed by their superiors. Were magistrates to gratify the desires of men in all things to which by a partial interpretation they would extend this rule, they would quickly stand in need of a power not to make laws but worlds.[55]

For the self-protective and retrospective Lockean civil subject to consent to the civil ordering of propriety for the prosperity of the nation, the representations of the public good proffered by nascent economic theory were indeed such world-creating projects. In these projects the seventeenth century witnessed the beginning of a process that was long to out last it: the fusion of the language of law, right, liberty, equality, and property with emerging scientific constructions of social processes. Gradually dissassociated from their complementary relationship to the moral status of law in a theistic understanding of God's design, gradually assimilated to a more securely secular, functionalist, and instrumental understanding of civil regulation, individual rights became less of a moral claim against the exercise of power than a civil definition of lawful liberty to be administered for the good of the whole.

54. Locke, *Tracts*, English Tract, 137.
55. Ibid.

Epilogue

The John Locke presented over the course of this book is an equivocal figure. My focus on the problematic of judgment rather than the more obviously "political" aspects of his work has suggested a somewhat less confused, if perhaps rather more complicated, thinker than a good deal of twentieth-century commentary might allow. Concurring, albeit from a different interpretive angle, with contextualists' insistence on the salience of ethical thematics in his work, I have suggested that Locke's political writings were structured by a theistic concern for moral order. He appears here neither as a champion of nor an apologist for the historical development of social or economic systems that he had little in the way of conceptual resources for imagining as possible, and as for his constitutionalism—well, it bears little resemblance to that of the apostle of liberal democracy and representative government many of us first encountered as students in the heat of the Cold War. Devolving not from "the rights of man" but from the resolutely hierarchical imagery of early modern political culture, Locke's constitutionalism drew on the lessons of history and experience to recommend the rule of law and the differentiation of powers as civil remedies for monarchical excess.[1] Less a matter of democratic principle than a sign of political

1. In such circumstances, as Locke suggests in the *Treatises*, "the People finding their properties not secure . . . could never be safe or at rest until the Legislative was placed in collective Bodies of Men" (2.94). A note to Hooker here, interestingly repeated at 2.111, elaborates: Communities that initially entrusted power to the rule of one often found his successors far less virtuous. Thus "by experience they found this for all parts very inconvenient, so as the thing they had devised for a Remedy did indeed but increase the Sore, which it should have cured. They saw that to live by one Man's Will became the cause of all Mens misery. This constrained them to come unto Laws wherein all Men might know their duty beforehand and know the penalties for transgressing them."

prudence, within the theistic image of God's architecture Locke's endorsement of representative institutions was a judgment of "convenience." In theoretical terms his political subjects are free to devise such regimes—and they would be both wise and prudent to institute them—but they are not morally obliged to do so by the rule of virtue, for such institutions have no necessary relationship to the moral order of God's design. Locke's God may have given his creatures political power, but he had little interest in the institutional forms in which they organized it on the historical plane of temporal existence.

At the same time, though, while a theistic world view may be fundamental to the Lockean political sensibility, the meanings of that sensibility cannot be secured within the confines of a religious impulse neatly relegated to the past, nor should they be insulated from later historical developments. Locke's theism, in effect, was rife with secular permissions—and as a theorist concerned with the boundaries of properly political power, he elaborated those permissions through a vocabulary that continues to frame political thought and action. In this regard the historical horizon of his political thought is at once more restricted than that implied by more conventionally "political" and present-minded interpretations and more extended than that suggested by more assertively contextualist perspectives. In drawing this account to a close, I would like to make these claims a bit more concrete by offering a more general characterization of Lockean politics than the narrative structure and topical sequence of the book has thus far permitted. In particular, I would like to say something further of Locke's political and theoretical contribution to the controversies of his period as well as speculate about some of the implications of his work for reconsidering the problem of judging rights in the theory and practice of later liberalisms.

The tensions and turmoils of Stuart England, of course, are matters of historical fact. In religious, political, social, cultural, and economic terms it was a century fraught with change. The alleviation of subsistence crises, the growth of trade and finance, as well as marked shifts in traditional patterns of social status and political power went hand in hand with changes in traditional property relations and massive social dislocation. The century was marked by recurrent foreign wars, fiscal crises, regicide, revolution, and the rise of a recognizably modern state. These phenomena, however, are "facts" for us in a quite specific way, for the period provides us with an unprecedented volume of surviving documents in the form of treatises, essays, pamphlets, broadsides, private correspondence, and state papers. The Reformation emphasis upon individual access to Scripture and the publication of the Bible in the vernacular spurred extraordinarily high rates of literacy. Combined with the refinement of print technology, the relaxation of censorship at mid-century, and improvements in transportation and distribution networks, these developments generated a broad popular audience for an astonishing outpouring of literary production on religion, politics, economics, natural science, husbandry, mechanical inventions, and the arts. More than any earlier historical epoch, the multiple conflicts and cleavages of the period had and continue to have a public face. In this regard it is a century laid bare to its successors as none before it.

From the promontory of the present we can abstract and generalize from this wealth of material, reconstructing such things as the rise and decline of classes or social groups, the bases of their power, and the systems of conflict within which they operated. Today we speak of the dynamic processes of historical change at work in the period—more often than not invoking the operation of social, political, economic, or cultural processes—to trace the lineages, the cul-de-sacs and continuities, of a world that both has and has not become our own. Such reconstructions, however, do not simply mirror the past to us in its "original" form, much less in a manner that would necessarily be recognizable to its denizens. Rather, and I take it quite inescapably, they reflect various organizations of knowledge in our own time, themselves both historical accretions and systems of power. Contemporary disciplinary canons, methods of interpretation, rules of inference, and criteria of validity not only define, organize, and codify but legitimate and valorize representations of the past just as they do understandings of the present. In both cases methodological considerations are neither objective nor benign but rather are necessarily political in character, however indirect or arcane their political bearing might appear.

Thus controversies in historical scholarship, as is so often the case in studies of contemporary phenomena, tend frequently to cleave along lines that are as much political as they are methodological, with opposing positions not infrequently defined less in terms of disagreements over "facts" than in terms of the interpretive approaches within which such facts are rendered significant, coherent, or meaningful. The political issue in this context is not whether contemporary theoretical or conceptual categories are deployed, but which ones are given currency or credence. That this pertains to the analytic and evidentiary commitments of Whiggish or liberal or Marxist historiography is sufficiently familiar, but it is no less the case with regard to less conventionally "ideological" perspectives. To take an example from the history of political thought—even the admonition to "think for ourselves," when articulated as a historiographical commitment to the pastness of the past as an object of present knowing, necessarily implies a position on the question of modern knowledges—a position, ironically, that by endorsing the autonomy of the present construes its own political stance in the image of a guard against temporal seepage.

In speaking of the relationship of Locke's theoretical project to the strife and tensions of his time, I have attempted to bracket a wide range of modern knowledges in order to characterize some of the cognitive categories, conventions, and presuppositions that broadly framed political knowledges in the period and to situate Locke's various intellectual efforts within them. Relative to what counts as social knowledge in the late twentieth century, of course, one can attribute specific and assuredly differential class effects to the various issues of law and policy that appear in Locke's works. Indeed, particularly given the wealth of surviving documents, such attributions can be highly compelling. It is one thing, however, to note such social consequences from the perspective of historical distance and quite another to conflate them with Locke's intentions, or even more diffusely to suggest that they capture his meaning. Although Locke addressed the social world whose traces appear in surviving records, the theistic ground and moral freighting of his theoretical categories impose on that world a grid of meaning fundamentally different from those retrospectively applied by more modern constructions of social knowledge. In light of this, I have characterized the Lockean political sensibility as predominantly moralistic in character, concerned with maintaining the right order of relations between individual moral agents and centered on the due operation of retributive justice. This account of Locke's "moralism," however, should not be taken to imply that he excluded consideration of such aspects of his social world as were later to provide the raw materials for more scientific understandings of social processes and dynamics. I do not mean, in other words, to rest content with the affirmation of Locke's moralism and claim simply that he could not have intended its social effects because he had no way of knowing them.

Rather, I have attempted to elucidate some of the ways in which the theistic elements of Locke's theoretical project cast the moral and political meanings of that social world in terms irreducible to the post-theistic sensibilities of modern social theory. The claim here is not that he did not know the world later times would call "the social" but that he knew it differently, and that the difference is important for glimpsing not only the political edge of his thought in its own time, but its internal tensions and lingering implications for later political theory and practice as well. For if the intricate dynamics of worldly processes in the creation of social groups and classes had yet to be theorized in a manner credible to later moderns, there nonetheless remained rich and complex conceptual fields surrounding such things as money, property, and political power, not to mention morality and law, through which various accounts of the social world might be articulated. As a consequence, there is something lost in reducing Locke's political meaning to his moral or theological commitments, despite their centrality to his work. To be sure, he was concerned with individuals' obligations to labor productively in their respective callings, and the political realm he envisioned was importantly centered on securing sufficient order in the world for them to do so peacefully. Yet he was no less emphatic that such power was essential not simply to ensure peace through the power of punishment, but to guarantee through law what was properly one's own to labor upon. In effect, Locke's moralistic regard for duty and his appreciation for worldly comfort and convenience are less mutually exclusive than they might appear. Both, I have suggested, found their roots in his inflection of the theistic imagery of God's design for the human species—both are theoretically dependent on the right that imagery allocated to civil power to settle, preserve, and regulate property for the public good, and both are implicated in a more general cultural configuration for which the right of punishment was the central signifier of political power.

Construed in these terms, Locke's *Two Treatises* can be seen as advancing a distinctly political resolution to the problem of moral knowledge that both drove his epistemological investigations and haunted his thinking on religion and toleration. Concurrent with the

Essay in its composition, the narrative of the *Treatises* proffers the disordering of natural judgment and the dissolution of moral certainty as the worldly consequences of monetarized commerce. If the *Essay* implied doubt as to the possibility of knowing the imperatives of natural law, the *Treatises* cast a world ruled by money as the source of the most significant obstacles to such knowledge and stipulated political power, civil law, and state authority as a remedy for the dilemma. In effect, Lockean politics repair the disruption of moral judgment by making civil law the guarantor of moral order in a world corrupted by the partiality of imaginary values. As the moral duty of Lockean civil agents was to keep peacefully to their own, so was the duty of properly political power to define what was lawfully to be theirs by giving substance and specificity, in particular times and places, to the natural law prohibition of injury. Attempting simultaneously to secure the political order from the speculative uncertainties of religious disputes and to deprive particular creeds of the force of politically mandated conformity, Lockean politics were thus fashioned to attend to the worldly concerns and welfare of civil subjects as these were epitomized in God's moral prohibition of harm. Whether this freed the political order from religion or religion from the political order is itself a judgment call, but it liberated no one from the demands of moral duty in everyday life.

In this context, the complementarity of law and right and the moral meanings of liberty, equality, and property that characterized Locke's theistic cosmology persist as the conceptual scaffolding of his political sensibility. With the dissolution of cognitive access to natural law making the boundaries of properly human liberty uncertain, the moral task of civil law is to reconstruct these boundaries in conformity with God's intentions. Once such boundaries have been settled by particular constitutions, it is the moral duty of magistrates to abide by them, and the moral right of civil subjects to hold their rulers accountable—in the extreme case by recourse to the retributive power of resistance right. To put the point differently, in Locke's articulation of the language of rights both his moral commitments and his social assumptions were mediated by his construction of political power as the necessary condition for moral relations between individuals in terrestrial life. If that construction, in formal terms, was widely shared amidst the conflict, disorder, and uncertainty that characterized the religious and political discourse of the period, the *Treatises* gave its conventional truth an uncommonly radical edge. Convinced of the enormity of royal misdeeds, confronted with the inconclusiveness and ambiguities of casuistic debate, and yet resolute about the moral stakes of obligation for creatures capable of salvation, Locke marshalled the cognitive and conceptual resources of his culture into a defense of resistance in the name of order. Drawing in particular on the insistent legalism of that culture, as well as on the personal and localistic ways of knowing typical of the practice of rights and the administration of justice at common law, his account of the political sought refuge in the cognizance of one's lawful "propriety" as a reliable experiential ground for civil knowledge and, by extension, as a moral baseline for recognizing the limits of consent on the worldly terrain of the English polity. As the "settling" of such propriety was the moral charge of properly political power, so was its unsettling through "force without right" a crime of the highest order, and it was this in turn that justified the revocation of consent necessary to political resistance.

In this regard, both the juridical cast of Lockean politics and his emphasis on individual judgment and experience might best be understood not as the declaration of something new in the way of civil knowledge but as a theoretical elaboration of the practice of rights within the localistic perceptual frame of the moral economy. Committed to an understanding of law that emphasized its moral status, however, Locke's extension of this construct of civil knowledge to the politics of a national state contains the seeds of its own undoing. In privileging injury to one's lawfully established propriety as a moral ground for resistance, he affirms an understanding of individual rights that renders the contingent civil regulation of such propriety highly problematic, for the functional view of law this entails and the knowledges it requires in significant respects exceed the model of political cognition that sustains the moral status and practical limits of his notion of consent. Thus as Locke's positive construction of political power shifts from the moralistic and juridical tasks of "settling" and preserving propriety to the instrumental project of ensuring national prosperity, it not only invites but demands supplementation by conceptual frameworks capable of reconfiguring the experiential limits of its civil subjects' political understanding in relation to the dynamics of a national commerce. As the state turns to more functionalist understandings of law in pursuit of public con-

venience, the consensual basis of Lockean political authority finds its
limits in a second register of meaning, for that authority becomes
dependent on the mediation of new forms of social knowledge as a
precondition for public acquiescence in civil regulation.

From the vantage of retrospect, then, the theistic and cognitive
individualism of Locke's justification of resistance can be seen to represent both a radical extension of the moral resources of the language of rights in the period and their conceptual fragility in the
face of the practical tasks taken on by state institutions amid the
social dynamics and dislocations of an expanding commerce. The
reverberations of this disjuncture through the subsequent development of liberal politics are both subtle and complex, though here I
shall only gesture to what seem to me to be some of the more significant among them. Most obviously perhaps, and in terms now conventional, the necessity of new social knowledges to mediate between
the experiential understanding of the Lockean civil subject and the
contingent needs of the nation points to a tendency to translate political issues of benefit and injury into questions of expertise. To conceive the dilemma in these terms, however, is already to inhabit a
more modern frame of reference than that available to Locke. It is
to imagine a political world divided not simply by substantive issues
or material interests, but between those who know and those who
don't—between those fluent in the requisite modern knowledges
and those uninformed by such competencies—with the implication
that the uglier faces of political conflict might be at least ameliorated
by education. But this is not the sense in which the prospect of legitimation crisis is written into Lockean politics from the outset, for my
point here is not that Locke's seventeenth-century analogues to modern experts knew more about the world than his civil subjects nor is
it simply that they knew that world differently or more deeply. I'm
suggesting, rather, that they knew a different world, a world epis-
temically at odds with the standards of self-propriety and civil facticity that framed ordinary understandings of political judgment—
and, by virtue of that, a world politically at odds with the form of
civil knowledge and political judgment that both supported Locke's
notion of consent and justified its revocation.

What I've characterized as the constitutive dilemma of Lockean
politics, however, is more than an artifact of the emergent historical
differentiation between the moral status of law and its social func-

tion, for it touches matters of political and theoretical significance as well. Heir to the epistemic difference Locke inscribes between the knowledges informing each view of law, Locke's state is overpowered and underauthorized because that difference generates a tension at the core of his positive conception of political power—a tension that manifests itself in two modalities of political judgment splayed across the differential tasks he accorded to state activities with respect to property. Juridically devoted, on the one hand, to guaranteeing to each their own and securing that possession against violation, Lockean politics are infused with a retributive moralism that identifies political power with the preservation of one's own against injury and the due exercise of the executive right of punishment in conformity to the law of virtue. Charged, on the other hand, with the task of managing the welfare and prosperity of the nation as a whole, Lockean politics are caught up in judgments not of virtue but of public convenience. Inflected by a more instrumental view of law, such judgments are prospective rather than retrospective in character, aimed less at preserving to each their own than ensuring to each their due—and Locke's functionalist commitments in this context are shadowed by the myriad dilemmas of distributive justice that silently follow in their wake.

It is at the level of political practice, however, that this tension takes on worldly weight and significance. In effect, though his state is empowered to regulate proprieties for the public good, the priority of the retributive frame in Locke's justification of resistance makes such regulation particularly problematic, for the distributive dilemmas Locke leaves unaddressed are indistinguishable from injury. From the standpoint of his civil subjects—and, indeed, in the political practice of eighteenth-century England—Locke's writings suggest little if any basis for regarding the regulatory activities of the state as anything other than violations of individuals' rights to a settled self-propriety, designs on their liberties, or manifestations of the corruption of power by those who benefit from regulation. From the perspective of the state, however—that is, from the perspective of what magistrates might understand to be necessary in the way of regulating proprieties—those writings suggest equally little reason to regard such protestations of violation as arising from anything other than ignorance, self-interest, or ambition.

In the gap between these two perceptual possibilities, Locke's notion of trust bears a heavy burden. Speaking to a world of contingency, unloosed from the legitimating bonds of precedent, the power to regulate propriety begins strongly to resemble the power of prerogative—and, like the latter, its authority rests, finally, on civil subjects' capacity to "see" and "feel" the consistency of its exercise with the public good. Despite the inferential props provided by the familial and localistic imagery of seventeenth-century policy debates, the capacity of trust to span that gap in practice would seem to rest more on deference and credulity than on the sorts of individual judgment and civil facticity that the *Treatises'* justification of resistance reserved to civil agents as a matter of right. Assimilated, however, to the orders of facticity and scenarios of national identification proffered by new social knowledges, the political prospects of trust brighten considerably. One might note, though, that trust so conceived has migrated to the other horn of the Lockean dilemma, collecting its allegiances around the functionalist view of law. Relieved of its proximity to retributive justice, what is trusted is neither the preservation of a settled self-propriety nor the conformity of governors' actions to the standards of a pre-existing legality. Linked rather to the pursuit of public benefits and to the promulgation of such policies as particular exigencies might require, what is trusted is the knowledges such policies rely on and the efficacy with which they achieve their desired results. Uncoupled from the epistemic support of a settled self-propriety, the question confronting political judgment in this context is less whether one's own has been preserved from injury—Locke's litmus for distinguishing properly political power from its excess—than whether the government's management of the public convenience has delivered one's due. As such judgments are assimilated to the circulation of new social knowledges, as they are divested, like trust, of their connection to retribution, so too are their political concerns freed to migrate into the domain of public convenience and the dilemmas of distribution entailed by a national frame of reference.

Worldly instances of the political dilemmas these migrations posed for the language of rights awaited a more modern moment of modernity, a moment in which the notion of order undergirding that language was unmoored from the theistic understanding of divine command, ultimate judgment, and final retribution that provided Locke's formulations with their moral anchor. Over the course of the eighteenth century and continuing through the nineteenth, perspectives were forged that displaced the seventeenth-century conceit of a divinely designed architecture. Substituting mechanistic or organic metaphors of temporal processes for static hierarchies, such perspectives blurred the Lockean distinction between moral laws definitive of properly human action and the physical necessities governing animal existence. Absent the theistic ontology of a morally marked world, in these later perspectives human actions shed their individual and performative character, their status as discrete events to be judged in relation to God's prohibition of injury, to be conceived rather as elements of social and behavioral processes operating independent of the will or intentions of human agents. With this shift the social world was no longer regarded, as it was in Locke's inflection of God's architecture, as a domain of flux and contingency. Instead, subtended by naturalistic understandings of dynamic social processes and providentialist understandings of divine intentions, that world became seen as one of patterned regularities unfolding in time, of laws of relation immanent within social life to which civil laws, if they were wisely framed, must accommodate themselves if they were not to defeat their own purposes.[2]

In one sense, and seemingly contrary to the intuition that first incited this exploration of Lockean political judgment, the effective history of this shift suggests at its outset not an augmentation but a diminution of the breadth of state power characteristic of Lockean politics. Against the more ascetic tendencies of Locke's mercantilism, for example, Mandeville's account of the processes through which private vices generated public benefits pressed forcefully.[3] Though ethical flaws in the estimation of a long-lingering Calvinism, such things as acquisitiveness, consumption, and display were in his view nonetheless positive in their aggregate effects and thus functional to

2. Elements of the older linkage of individual judgment and action with responsibility and retributive justice continued to inform the domain of criminal law, but even this, over time, became caught up in the supposition of underlying social dynamics. For the most challenging contemporary theorization of these developments, see Michel Foucault, *Discipline and Punish: The Birth of the Prison* (New York: Pantheon Books, 1977). A more historically nuanced account of English developments can be found in Michael Ignatieff, *A Just Measure of Pain: The Penitentiary in the Industrial Revolution,* 1750–1850 (New York: Columbia University Press, 1980).

3. Bernard Mandeville, *The Fable of the Bees; or, Private vices, Public benefits* (London, 1714).

the convenience of the nation as a whole. Similarly, as an extension
of this notion of unanticipated consequences, Adam Smith's theorization of an unseen hand ordering economic processes toward equilibrium discredited many of the substantive prerogatives of economic regulation that Lockean theory allocated to civil government
as a matter of course. We might be wary, however, of the impulse to
imagine such containments of state power simply as blows struck for
individual liberty, as if that were some transhistorical essence. It
would seem worth noting, for instance, that such restrictions on the
state's regulatory powers were defended not by recourse to retrospective judgments of individual rights to a juridically settled self-
propriety but by reference to prospective expectations of benefits,
both public and private, to be achieved by unfettering the natural
operation of social processes. It is one thing, in other words, to say
that such regulation violates individual rights in the sense specific to
the retributive face of Lockean politics—with the cognitive individualism and prospect of resistance this implies—but this was not the
claim made by the new social knowledges. It is another thing to say
that specific sorts of regulation restrict individual rights for no good
reason or that good reasons exist for avoiding their adoption, and it
was these sorts of claims that such knowledges advanced.

Though disengaged from the retributive moralism that justified
resistance, the latter criticisms were nonetheless quite in keeping
with the regulatory logic of the Lockean political sensibility, and the
new arguments against state interference were no less dependent on
the supplementation of emergent social knowledges than Locke's
were in its defense. In this regard, the idea that political regulation
impeded the production of benefits that would arise naturally in its
absence indeed provided late-eighteenth-century political economists
with a counter to the mercantilist strictures of the preceding century.
It did so, however, not by giving up but by reconceiving the notion
that the state had a pivotal role to play in the production and maintenance of worldly order. Recast as the caretaker of processes it was
incompetent to command, the state of Enlightenment political economy was charged with the elimination of obstacles to the natural
operation of underlying social processes—a charge that naturalized
distributive dilemmas even as it linked state activities all the more
firmly to the ongoing articulation of new social knowledges. In effect, though confining state power to interfering with interferences,

that limitation pertains not to the limits of its rightful jurisdiction in the regulation of proprieties but to the limits of its capacity to do so productively. And these limits, finally, were to be established by the knowledges that, by discerning the effects of institutional artifices on the operation of natural processes, both defined that capacity in general terms and legitimated its deployment in particular instances.

Such views, however, did not so much transcend as transform the Lockean problematic of legitimacy, rearticulating its terms into alternative and for the most part extra-juridical frameworks of political meaning. To elaborate the point in credible detail would doubtless call for another book, but a few further speculations might not be out of order.[4] Malthus's *Essay on the Principle of Population* may suffice as a token of the ways in which various facets of the Lockean political sensibility could be orchestrated into new configurations of meaning under the pressure of providential and naturalistic notions of underlying social dynamics. As a scientific counter to Enlightenment notions of human perfectibility, for example, Malthus pointed to the "principle of population" as a limit imposed by natural processes on all schemes for the alleviation of social distress. Relating the quantum of human misery to the operation of a natural ratio between the arithmetic increase of subsistence and the geometric increase of population, he took specific issue with the English poor laws and the institution of parish relief. Such things as overseers and restrictions on geographic mobility, he observed, subjected the poor "to a set of grating, inconvenient, and tyrannical laws, totally inconsistent with the spirit of the constitution."[5] Though the adjective "inconvenient" in this formulation still describes an ill that lays upon the public as a whole, neither "tyranny" nor "the constitution" here carries the assertively moral and juridical meanings that each had for Locke. "Tyranny" in this context is both dejuridicalized and depersonalized, relieved of its primary Lockean construal as arbitrary injuries perpetrated by particular rulers against a settled self-propriety. Recast rather as a characteristic of witless or incompetent legislation, this tyranny is to be

4. My initial explorations of this transformation are elaborated in "Taking Liberties in Foucault's Triangle: Sovereignty, Discipline, Governmentality, and the Subject of Rights," in *Politics, Identities, and Rights,* ed. Austin Sarat and Thomas Kearns (Ann Arbor: University of Michigan Press, 1995).

5. Thomas Malthus, *An Essay on the Principles of Population,* ed. Antony Flew (New York: Viking/Penguin, 1985), p. 100.

remedied not by resistance, retribution, and the restoration of an order of legality but by knowledge and the adequation of policy to the natural laws of population. Similarly, "the constitution" that Malthus refers to is unhinged from the institutional referent of "King, Lords, and Commons" that Locke shared with the common law sensibility and attached, in Montesquieu's fashion via the idea of its "spirit," to the notion of an appropriate relation between political institutions, the stage of civilization attained by a particular polity, and the environmental constraints of natural processes that such elements of human artifice must respect to survive and prosper.[6]

The poor laws, on this account, are a political problem not because they are morally wrong but because they are socially dysfunctional. Residues of an age ignorant of the laws of population, they are prudentially wrong-headed—inappropriate, that is, on the functionalist view of civil law—for in their promise to alleviate misery they inescapably increase it by encouraging the growth of population without stimulating the increase of subsistence necessary to support it. Again, however, what is at issue here is not the right of the state, in the Lockean sense, to regulate proprieties. Indeed, for Malthus, the right to property was itself a creation of positive law, contingently modifiable in the interest of the public welfare.[7] The problem, rather, is the extent to which the state's beneficent intentions in the poor laws are, in the nature of things, incapable of realization. Malthus put it bluntly: "We tell the common people that if they will submit to a code of tyrannical regulation they should never be in want. They perform their part of the contract. But we do not, nay cannot, and thus the poor sacrifice the blessings of liberty and receive nothing that can be called an equivalent in return."[8]

On Malthus's view, however, the poor were not simply to be abandoned to the operation of nature. Although Malthus argued for the elimination of the poor laws, he also urged the provision of "premiums" for opening up new arable lands and of encouragements to agriculture over manufactures and cultivation over pasturage. Similarly, he advocated policies that would "weaken and destroy" such institutions as corporations and apprenticeships that elevated the re-

---

6. See, in particular, the last two chapters of Malthus's *Essay*.

7. Thomas Malthus, *A Summary View of the Principle of Population* (1830), in the Flew edition of the *Essay* noted above, p. 269.

8. Ibid., p. 103.

ward of labor in trade and manufacture over that of agricultural employment. Finally, he recommended the establishment of workhouses at the county level, to be supported not by parish rates on local landholders but at national charge.[9] In all such recommendations the relief of hardship has nothing to do with the customary claims of the poor to public support, but it persists (as do the poor) as an object of policy nonetheless. In this context, however, the requisite policies are to be governed not by moral or juridical considerations of rights, but by considerations specific to political economy, in particular by accounts of the ways in which various natural tendencies of the population could be foreseen and managed to best effect by the appropriate design of public policy and institutions.

Malthus, of course, was but one of many for whom scientific accounts of underlying natural processes provided a basis for the criticism of "positive institutions." Despite their many differences, Adam Smith, William Godwin, Jeremy Bentham, Robert Owen, David Ricardo, and a host of others marshalled such accounts in ways that sought to minimize—indeed, in Godwin's and Owen's cases to eliminate—the retributive or penal dimension of state power that the Lockean political sensibility figured as its essential characteristic. Variously presuming the systematicity of the social to be manifested in such regularities as laws of population, laws of the market, or laws of psychology, such writers imagined political power less on the juridical model of crime and punishment than as an art of governance or science of legislation. Charged with the task of ensuring the welfare of "society" as a whole, legislators addressed themselves to the desires and aversions that motivated human behavior. Whether directly in the form of commands and prohibitions, or indirectly by the provision of incentives and disincentives, legislation and policy were the instruments through which the natural dynamics of society might be encouraged to sustain public benefits or to minimize public harms.

Between the arrival of the nineteenth century and its meridian, the dispersion of political economy as a mediating vocabulary for political understanding was accompanied by its diversification into multiple schools and tendencies as well as its appropriation to the service of a disparate range of political purposes. The marketplace

9. Ibid., pp. 101–2.

of ideas, however, was bullish on knowledges of all sorts, and political economy was but one of the commodities in demand. As "the condition of England question" assumed the center of national attention, other forms of social knowledge, in various degrees of relation to political economy, vied for public credence as well. Incited by the investigations of individual researchers and polemicists, philanthropic and benevolent associations, Parliamentary commissions and private statistical societies, reform policies found justification in the orders of facticity adumbrated by an array of new social knowledges. Public health, hygiene, and allied sanitary sciences figured prominently, as did the nascent scientific disciplines of psychology, criminology, and sociology. For many such perspectives, a concern not with the juridically framed property or rights of individuals but with the health and welfare of the population was the order of the day. Indeed, over the decades following the end of the Napoleonic wars, even as the gradual and piecemeal adoption of free trade evidenced the increasingly powerful sway of both laissez-faire economics and the "philosophical radicalism" that promoted it, the same school of reform allied with a variety of other tendencies to advocate a wide array of regulatory initiatives and social interventions. The principle of individual rights, of course, was central to the defense of Catholic emancipation, as well as to campaigns for the expansion of the franchise and the elimination of laws forbidding workers' combinations. In other areas of social concern, however—most notably in arguments for the restriction of child labor, the limitation of adult working hours, the regulation of hazardous employments, and the institution of mandatory public education—progressive reformers required the subordination of individual rights to the welfare of the public as a whole.

In the crucible of political contestations that such reforms both accommodated and engendered, British liberalism achieved ideological specificity as a signifier of political identity and partisan investment. It was this liberalism that nominated Locke among its principal progenitors—a nomination repeated by heirs and critics alike as the nineteenth century gave way to the twentieth and as the decades of the twentieth retreated in turn. To note this is to suggest that the creature long bruited about as Lockean liberalism has its initial historiographical site not in the constitutional crises of Stuart England but in the social conflicts and regulatory problematics of late Georgian and Victorian Britain. Simultaneously committed to the critique of positive institutions in the name of individual liberties and to the elaboration of state policies to secure such public conveniences as health, welfare, and prosperity, this liberalism took shape not as a systematic philosophy or unitary theory but as a site of multiple and often conflicting variations. Within such variations, the ostensibly Lockean political vocabulary of law, right, liberty, equality, and property persisted, even as it was assimilated to a governing notion of order quite distant from the retributive moralism of Locke's theistic frame. "Liberal" concerns, in this context, centered not on the relation between institutions of human artifice and a moral order of God's design, but on the relation between such institutions and the natural dynamics or patterned regularities of underlying social processes. Home to Herbert Spencer not less than to John Stuart Mill, this liberalism harbored divergent perspectives on what "nature" might entail or require as well as how such requirements were to be known. Arguably however, the commonality that permitted such disputes was the privilege their participants accorded both to the functionalist understanding of law and to the social knowledges that understanding relied upon to justify its political expression in social policy.

For this liberalism—or, perhaps more accurately, for the mode of governance and understanding of the political within which this liberalism developed—the problematic of distribution displaced Locke's retributive moralism as the central signifier of political power. Like Locke, nineteenth-century liberals looked to a strong state, a state still charged, if now more subtly, with maintaining the worldly order, prosperity, and welfare of the society it governed. But despite the continuity of Locke's political vocabulary, the state nineteenth-century liberals imagined was not a Lockean state; the society they imagined was not a Lockean society; and the politics they pursued were not Lockean politics—at least not on the account of such things presented here. Expected to operate indirectly, through the provision of incentives and disincentives to behaviors affecting the welfare of the nation as a whole, this state was construed not as the worldly source of moral order but as a modulator of social processes, a steering mechanism for the pursuit and maintenence of the public good over time. Concerned with ascertaining the appropriate role of political institutions in the distribution of social

goods broadly conceived, this liberalism was thus never simply
laissez-faire. The latter perspective, indeed, achieved prominence
for its commitment to individual enterprise and ingenuity as a principle for distributing economic energies and expectations in the interest of national prosperity. The range of social goods open to
questions of distribution, however, extended well beyond economics,
and the public conveniences to be pursued by national policy could
be variously imagined to include the health, education, talents, and
virtues of both the present and future generations of the population.
As the nineteenth century wore on, it was in this context that the
narrowing of state power, once promoted by scientific critiques of
legislative incompetence, gave way to its expansion and refinement.

   That transformation developed amid a variety of pressures and
contestations. Reform agitation, economic crises, and popular mobil-
izations pushed it along, as did the practical imperatives of imperial
administration and, finally, world war. Such pressures, however,
both accumulated and converged in the modernization of the British
state, a process that whatever else it might be taken to entail resulted
in the infusion of social scientific competences not only into the legislative processes and administrative apparatuses of political governance, but into the languages of public discussion and debate as well.
And it was over the course of these developments that the tendency
to translate issues of public benefit and harm into questions of expertise—a dilemma set aside some pages ago as too recent to capture
the Lockean problematic of legitimacy—began to take on considerable political weight. True, echoes of the Lockean form of that dilemma resonated well into the nineteenth century. As Robert Owen
and others, for instance, hoped to educate an unruly population to
understand their various places and functions in a complex social
whole, so Carlyle and Dickens mocked political economy and statistics as absurd departures from ordinary competences to judge questions of benefit and harm. By the end of the century, however, with
the dissemination and popularization of social scientific perspectives—not to mention the curricular installation of those perspectives in the newly institutionalized public education—such traces of
earlier sensibilities could be read as romantic nostalgia or literary
imagination, but in any event distant from the forms of civil knowledge requisite to modern governance.

   Historically, of course, in the political practice of modern polities more generally both the extent of state regulatory power and the political intensity of the dilemma of expertise have varied widely, as have their relationships to liberal politics. Liberal or not, in other words, the assimilation of modern social knowledges to political understanding has been both gradual and uneven, and in constitutional orders the assertion of rights as claims against state power has continued to play a significant role in political controversy. With the collapse of natural law and theistic understandings of God's design, however, such claims have typically been phrased as civil rather than natural rights—and, as the history of labor organizing and struggles for racial and sexual equality over the last century might suggest, the evidentiary basis of the injuries they contest has been increasingly drawn from the domain of social scientific expertise. At the same time, and in large part again linked to the elaboration of knowledges of social processes, the political expression of such movements has tended to look to state power for the regulation or administration of social dynamics in time. In historical practice, in other words, such claims have been cast as appeals to state management and adjudication, a context in which their resolution has not infrequently rested less on widely public processes of deliberation or broadly participatory processes of change than on the marshalling of social scientific evidence before the appropriate state institutions. Under the restricted franchise of nineteenth-century Britain, for example, the findings of the public commissions and private statistical societies that spoke to the "condition of England question" undergirded both industrial and social legislation throughout the century. Similarly, under the expanded suffrage of the United States, the sociological innovation of the Brandeis briefs, the psychological and sociological studies that lent justification to the Brown decision desegregating public education, and, more recently, the Meese report on pornography—all point to an increasingly powerful state as an administrator of social practices, however favorably or unfavorably one might regard the particular appeals for regulation that such analyses have supported. In the U.S. context, however, the success of such claims in securing legislative redress has been met of late by a reassertion of rights claims by those whose "liberties" have been most directly limited or constrained by political regulation. And, given the pervasive contemporary assimilation of such questions into the realm of social scientific discourse, these contestations have generated their own

growth industry of expert counterassessments of the costs and benefits of such reform.

This, in turn, points to a further and perhaps more fundamental
contemporary political dilemma. With the emergence of national, let
alone international, politics and markets, the "obviousness" and experiential immediacy with which Locke's early modern articulation
of the language of rights endowed individual judgments of the public good appears an epistemological impossibility. In this context the
various social knowledges through which we moderns have come to
imagine the political world carry an equivocal, indeed, contradictory
message. On the one hand, not unlike the things Locke's magistrate
came to "understand" from such early modern sciences as political
arithmetic or medicine, they reflect a devaluation or depoliticization
of individual judgment and experience. However seventeenth-century civil subjects may have "seen" themselves in the familiar moral
typologies and casts of characters that early economic writings
shared with Christian homiletics, the same is hardly true of the modern citizen's relation to the theoretical categories and mathematical
functions of contemporary economic and social sciences. Nonetheless, such frameworks have become integral to the operations of the
modern governance—so much so, perhaps, that by analogy to the
extraconstitutional status of political parties, it would not be too extreme to refer to social science as an institution of the modern state.

Yet the cognitive gap between perceptions of individual experience and the condition of the nation still remains, and where that
experience can be articulated as one of injury or deprivation, the
language of rights still provides a significant resource for political
claims. Markedly distant from Locke's retributive imagery, most contemporary versions of such claims themselves bear witness to the the
historical migration of that language into the prospective problematics of distributive justice. Here, as was the case for the competing
public visions of free trade and balance of trade theories in the seventeenth century, that cognitive gap continues to offer a discursive
space for the articulation of diverse representations of the political
community as a whole and the distribution of rights within it. One
might, of course, easily recognize the political character of this space
in the conflicting realities and differential distributive commitments
characteristic of, say, Keynesian, supply-side, and neo-Marxist economic analyses. But as non-economic or indirectly economic do-

mains of social experience and controversy have become sites of both scrutiny and contestation for other social scientific disciplines, the political character of these too has become evident. Studies of deviance and criminality might come most immediately to mind or studies of educational achievement, but related analyses of the social dynamics of race, ethnicity, gender, and sexuality are no less subject to the political conundrum I'm suggesting—particularly as such analyses are regarded as pertinent to the condition of the nation as a whole and the distribution of social goods and opportunities within it. With respect to the practice of rights, in any case, as the problem of judgment attending such distributive dilemmas becomes increasingly administrative and scientized, so too do competing frames for analyzing them, as well as representing their public character and import, become increasingly politicized.

In light of this, recent historical and philosophical perspectives critical of the "neutrality" or "objectivity" of science are significant, for the politics of science that they point to transcend issues of bias or partiality as distortions of an otherwise pure enterprise. Focusing rather on the discursive or constructed character of scientific categories, the intersubjective nature of scientific understanding, and the circulation of power within and between various communities of scientific practitioners, such perspectives may offer possibilities for reconceptualizing the political relation between expertise and more conventionally understood political institutions and practices. The emergence of such critical perspectives, however, may bode more unsettling possibilities as well, for they may themselves be symptomatic of the incapacity of the social sciences to fulfill the function of political legitimation that they inherited from the disordering of tradition and religion in the early modern period. The closing page of a study of John Locke is hardly the place to explore such issues further. But if, as I've suggested, the temporal trajectory of the language of rights is marked by a disjuncture between the moral valence of individual rights as experiential claims and the historical assimilation of scientific discourse to popular political understanding, the question of what this might entail for the politics of judgment, the practice of rights, and the limits of consent will be both challenging as a site of theoretical reflection and unavoidable as a site of political engagement.

Selected Bibliography

Aaron, Richard. *John Locke* 3d ed. Oxford: Clarendon Press, 1971.

Aarsleff, Hans. "The State of Nature and the Nature of Man in Locke." In *John Locke: Problems and Perspectives*, ed. John W. Yolton, 99–136. Cambridge: Cambridge University Press, 1969.

Appleby, Joyce Oldham. *Economic Thought and Ideology in Seventeenth-Century England*. Princeton: Princeton University Press, 1978.

Ashcraft, Richard. "Locke's State of Nature: Historical Fact or Moral Fiction." *American Political Science Review* 68, no. 3 (1968): 898–914.

——. *Revolutionary Politics and Locke's "Two Treatises of Government."* Princeton: Princeton University Press, 1986.

Axtell, James. Introduction to *Locke's Educational Writings*. Cambridge: Cambridge University Press, 1968.

Ayers, Michael R. "Locke versus Aristotle on Natural Kinds." *Journal of Philosophy* 78, no. 5 (1981): 247–72.

——. "Mechanism, Superaddition, and the Proof of God's Existence in Locke's *Essay*." *Philosophical Review* 90, no. 2 (1981): 210–51.

Baker, H. H. "Criminal Courts and Procedure at Common Law, 1550–1800." In *Crime in England, 1550–1800*, ed. J. S. Cockburn. Princeton: Princeton University Press, 1977.

Barbeyrac, Jean. "A Historical and Critical Account of the Science of Morality." In Samuel Pufendorf, *Of the Law of Nature and Nations*, ed. Jean Barbeyrac. Trans. Basil Kennett. London: 1729.

Baumgold, Deborah. "Pacifying Politics: Resistance, Violence, and Accountability in Seventeenth-Century Contract Theory." *Political Theory* 21, no. 1 (1993): 6–27.

Black, Max. *Models and Metaphors: Studies in Language and Philosophy*. Ithaca: Cornell University Press, 1962.

Brewer, John, and John Styles, eds. *An Ungovernable People: The English and Their Law in the Seventeenth and Eighteenth Centuries*. London: Hutchison and Co., 1980.

Burtt, E. A. *The Metaphysical Foundations of Modern Science: A Historical and Critical Essay.* New York: Doubleday, 1954.

Caffentzis, Constantine George. *Clipped Coins, Abused Words, and Civil Government: John Locke's Philosophy of Money.* New York: Autonomedia, 1989.

Chappell, Vere, ed. *John Locke: Theory of Knowledge.* New York: Garland Publishers 1992.

Cherno, Melvin. "Locke on Property: A Reappraisal." *Ethics* 68, no. 1 (1957): 51–55.

Cockburn, J. S., ed. *Crime in England 1550–1800.* Princeton: Princeton University Press, 1977.

Coles, Elisha. *An English Dictionary.* 1676. Reprint, Menston: Scolar Press, 1971.

Colman, John. *John Locke's Moral Philosophy.* Edinburgh: Edinburgh University Press, 1983.

Cox, Richard Howard. *Locke on War and Peace.* Oxford: Clarendon Press, 1960.

Crimmins, James E., ed. *Religion, Secularization, and Political Thought: Thomas Hobbes to J. S. Mill.* London: Routledge, 1989.

Curtis, T. C. "Quarter Sessions Appearances and Their Background: A Seventeenth-Century Regional Study." In *Crime in England, 1550–1800,* ed. J. S. Cockburn. Princeton: Princeton University Press, 1977.

Day, J. P. "Locke on Property." *Philosophical Quarterly* 16, no. 64 (1966): 207–20.

Dickson, P. G. M. *The Financial Revolution in England: A Study in the Development of Public Credit, 1688–1756.* London: Macmillan, 1967.

Dollimore, Jonathan. *Radical Tragedy: Religion, Ideology, and Power in the Drama of Shakespeare and His Contemporaries.* Chicago: University of Chicago Press, 1984.

Dumont, Louis. *Homo Hierarchicus: The Caste System and Its Implications.* Rev. ed. Chicago: University of Chicago Press, 1980.

———. "Religion, Politics, and Society in the Individualistic Universe." *Proceedings of the Royal Anthropological Institute for 1970:* 33–41.

Dunn, John. "Consent in the Political Theory of John Locke." In *Life, Liberty, and Property: Essays on Locke's Political Ideas,* ed. Gordon J. Schochet. Belmont, Calif.: Wadsworth Publishing Co. 1971. First published in *The Historical Journal* 10, no. 2 (1968): 153–82.

———. "The Identity of the History of Ideas." *Philosophy* 43, no. 164 (April 1968): 85–104.

———. "Justice and the Interpretation of Locke's Political Theory." *Political Studies* 16, no. 1 (1968): 68–87.

———. *The Political Thought of John Locke: An Historical Account of the Argument of the "Two Treatises of Government."* Cambridge: Cambridge University Press, 1969.

——. "The Politics of Locke in England and America." In *John Locke: Problems and Perspectives*, ed. John W. Yolton. Cambridge: Cambridge University Press, 1969.

Eisenach, Eldon J. *The Two Worlds of Liberalism: Religion and Politics in Hobbes, Locke, and Mill*. Chicago: University of Chicago Press, 1981.

Farr, James, and Clayton Roberts. "John Locke on the Glorious Revolution: A Rediscovered Document." *Historical Journal* 28, no. 2 (1985): 385–98.

Foucault, Michel. *Discipline and Punish: The Birth of the Prison*. New York: Pantheon Books, 1977.

——. "Governmentality." In *The Foucault Effect: Studies in Governmentality with Two Lectures by and an Interview with Michel Foucault*, ed. Graham Burchell, Colin Gordon, and Peter Miller, 87–104. Chicago: University of Chicago Press, 1991.

——. *The Order of Things: An Archeology of the Human Sciences*. New York: Vintage Books, 1973.

Franklin, Julian H. *John Locke and the Theory of Sovereignty: Mixed Monarchy and the Right of Resistance in the Political Thought of the English Revolution*. Cambridge: Cambridge University Press, 1978.

Gatrell, V. A. C., Bruce Lenman, and Geoffrey Parker, eds. *Crime and the Law: The Social History of Crime in Western Europe since 1500*. London: Europa Publications, 1980.

Goldie, Mark. "The Revolution of 1689 and the Structure of Political Argument." *Bulletin of Research in the Humanities* 83, no. 4 (Winter 1980): 473–564.

Gough, John. *John Locke's Political Philosophy, Eight Studies*. 2d ed. Oxford: Clarendon Press, 1973.

Haraway, Donna. *Crystals, Fabrics, and Fields: Metaphors of Organicism in Twentieth-Century Developmental Biology*. New Haven: Yale University Press, 1976.

Harrington, James. *Aphorisms Political*. In *The Political Works of James Harrington*, ed. J. G. A. Pocock. Cambridge: Cambridge University Press, 1977.

Harrison, John, and Peter Laslett, eds. *The Library of John Locke*. Oxford Bibliographical Society Publications, n. s., 13. Oxford: Oxford University Press, 1965.

Hay, Douglas, Peter Linebaugh, John G. Rule, E. P. Thompson, and Cal Winslow, eds. *Albion's Fatal Tree: Crime and Society in Eighteenth-Century England*. New York: Pantheon, 1975.

Hayes, Thomas Wilson. *Winstanley the Digger: A Literary Analysis of Radical Ideas in the English Revolution*. Cambridge: Harvard University Press, 1979.

Hefelbower, Samuel Gring. *The Relation of John Locke to English Deism*. Chicago: University of Chicago Press, 1918.

Hesse, Mary. *Models and Analogies in Science*. South Bend, Ind.: Notre Dame Press, 1966.

Hexter, J. H. *Reappraisals in History: New Visions of History and Society in Early Modern Europe*. 2d ed. Chicago: University of Chicago Press, 1979.

Hill, Christopher. *Change and Continuity in Seventeenth-Century England*. Cambridge: Harvard University Press, 1975.

———. *Puritanism and Revolution: Studies in Interpretation of the English Revolution of the Seventeenth Century*. London: Secker and Warburg, 1958.

———. *Society and Puritanism in Pre-Revolutionary England*. New York: Schocken Books, 1964.

———, ed. *"The Law of Freedom" and Other Writings*, by Gerrard Winstanley. Cambridge: Cambridge University Press, 1983.

Hooker, Richard. *The Laws of Ecclesiastical Polity*. In *The Works of That Learned Divine Mr. Richard Hooker*. Ed. John Keble. 2d ed. 3 vols. Oxford: Oxford University Press, 1841.

Horwitz, Henry. *Parliament, Policy, and Politics in the Reign of William III*. Manchester: Manchester University Press, 1977.

Horwitz, Henry, and James Oldham. "John Locke, Lord Mansfield, and Arbitration in the Eighteenth Century." *Historical Journal* 36, no. 1 (1993): 137–59.

Huizinga, Johann. *The Waning of the Middle Ages: A Study of the Forms of Life, Thought, and Art in France and the Netherlands in the XIVth and XVth Centuries*. London: E. Arnold & Co., 1937.

Hundert, Edward J. "The Making of *homo faber*: John Locke between Ideology and History." *Journal of the History of Ideas* 32, no. 1 (1972): 3–22.

———. "Market Society and Meaning in Locke's Political Philosophy." *Journal of the History of Philosophy* 15, no. 1 (1977): 33–44.

Ignatieff, Michael. *A Just Measure of Pain: The Penitentiary in the Industrial Revolution, 1750–1850*. New York: Columbia University Press, 1980.

Ingram, M. J. "Communities and Courts: Law and Disorder in Early-Seventeenth-Century Wiltshire." In *Crime in England, 1550–1800*, ed. J. S. Cockburn, 110–34. Princeton: Princeton University Press, 1977.

James, Margaret. *Social Problems and Policy during the Puritan Revolution, 1640–1660*. New York: Barnes and Noble, 1966.

Jones, W. J. *Politics and the Bench: The Judges and the Origins of the English Civil War*. London: Allen and Unwin, 1971.

Jordan, W. K. *The Development of Religious Toleration in England*. 4 vols. London: G. Allen & Unwin, Ltd., 1932–40.

Keeton, G. W. *An Introduction to Equity*. 5th ed. London: Sir Isaac Pitman & Sons, 1961.

Kendall, Willmoore. *John Locke and the Doctrine of Majority Rule*. Urbana: University of Illinois Press, 1941.

Kennedy, William. *English Taxation, 1640–1799: An Essay on Policy and Opinion*. 1913. Reprint, New York: Augustus M. Kelley, 1964.

Kenyon, J. P. *Revolution Principles: The Politics of Party, 1689–1720.* Cambridge: Cambridge University Press, 1977.

——. *The Stuart Constitution, 1603–1688: Documents and Commentary.* Cambridge: Cambridge University Press, 1966.

Kersey, John. *Dictionarium anglo-britannicum.* London: J. Wilde, 1708.

King, Lord Peter. *The Life of John Locke, with Extracts from His Correspondence, Journals, and Common-Place Books.* 2 vols. London: H. Colburn and R. Bentley, 1830.

Koyré, Alexandre. *From the Closed World to the Infinite Universe.* Baltimore: Johns Hopkins University Press, 1957–68.

Lamont, William M. *Godly Rule: Politics and Religion, 1603–60.* London: Macmillan, 1969.

Lamprecht, Sterling. *The Moral and Political Philosophy of John Locke.* New York: Columbia University Press, 1918.

Larkin, Paschal. *Property in the Eighteenth Century, with Special Reference to England and Locke.* Dublin: Cork University Press, 1930.

Laslett, Peter. "Market Society and Political Theory." *Historical Journal* 7, no. 11 (1964): 150–54.

Letwin, William. *The Origin of Scientific Economics: English Economic Thought, 1660–1776.* London: Methuen, 1963.

Locke, John. *The Correspondence of John Locke.* Ed. E. S. De Beer. Cambridge: Cambridge University Press, 1978.

——. *An Early Draft of Locke's "Essay," together with Excerpts from his Journals.* Ed. Richard I. Aaron and Jocelyn Gibb. Oxford: Clarendon Press, 1936.

——. *Essay concerning Human Understanding.* Ed. Peter H. Nidditch. Oxford: Clarendon Press, 1975.

——. "An Essay on Toleration" (1667). In *The Life of John Locke,* ed. H. R. Fox-Bourne. London: H. S. King, 1876.

——. *Essays on the Law of Nature.* Ed. Wolfgang von Leyden. Oxford: Clarendon Press, 1954.

——. *A Letter concerning Toleration.* Ed. James Tully. Indianapolis: Hackett Publishing Co., 1983.

——. *Locke on Money.* Ed. Patrick Hyde Kelly. 2 vols. Cambridge: Cambridge University Press, 1991.

——. *Of the Conduct of the Understanding* Ed. Thomas Fowler. 2d ed. 1882. Reprint, New York: Lenox Hill, 1971.

——. "Of Study." In *The Educational Writings of John Locke.* Ed. James Axtell, 406–22. Cambridge: Cambridge University Press, 1968.

——. *A Paraphrase and Notes on the Epistles of St. Paul to the Galatians, Corinthians, Romans, Ephesians. To Which is Prefixed an Essay for the Understanding of St. Paul's Epistles by Consulting St. Paul Himself.* Ed. Arthur Wainwright. Oxford: Oxford University Press, 1987.

——. *The Reasonableness of Christianity.* In vol. 7 of *The Works of John Locke in Ten Volumes.* 1823. Reprint, Scientia Verlag Aalen, 1963.

——. *Second Letter concerning Toleration.* In vol. 6 of *The Works of John Locke in Ten Volumes.* 1823. Reprint, Scientia Verlag Aalen, 1963.

——. *Some Considerations of the Consequences of the Lowering of Interest and Raising the Value of Money* (1691). 2d ed., corrected. In *Several Papers Relating to Money, Interest, and Trade & c.* London: A. & J. Churchill at the Black Swann, 1696. Facsimile, New York: Augustus M. Kelley Publishers, 1968. Reprinted in *Locke on Money,* ed. Patrick Hyde Kelly, 1:1–116. Cambridge: Cambridge University Press, 1991.

——. *Some Thoughts concerning Education.* In *The Educational Writings of John Locke,* ed. James Axtell. Cambridge: Cambridge University Press, 1968.

——. "Some Thoughts concerning Reading and Study for a Gentleman" (1703). In *The Educational Writings of John Locke,* ed. James Axtell. Cambridge: Cambridge University Press, 1968.

——. *Third Letter on Toleration.* In vol. 6 of *The Works of John Locke in Ten Volumes.* 1823. Reprint, Scientia Verlag Aalen, 1963.

——. *Two Tracts on Government.* Ed. Philip Abrams. Cambridge: Cambridge University Press, 1967.

——. *Two Treatises of Government.* Ed. Peter Laslett. Rev. ed. 1960. Reprint, with amendments, Cambridge: Cambridge University Press, 1963.

——. "Venditio." In John Dunn, "Justice and the Interpretation of Locke's Political Theory." *Political Studies* 16, no. 1 (1968): 68–87.

——. *The Works of John Locke in Ten Volumes.* 1823. Reprint, Scientia Verlag Aalen, 1963.

Lovejoy, Arthur O. *The Great Chain of Being: A Study in the History of an Idea.* Cambridge: Harvard University Press, 1965.

Mabbott, J. D. *The State and the Citizen.* London: Hutchinson's University Library, 1947.

Macfarlane, Alan, and Sarah Harrison. *The Justice and the Mare's Ale: Law and Disorder in Seventeenth-Century England.* New York: Cambridge University Press, 1981.

Macpherson, C. B. "Locke on Capitalist Appropriation." *Western Political Quarterly* 4, no. 4 (1951): 550–66.

——. *The Political Theory of Possessive Individualism: Hobbes to Locke.* Oxford: Oxford University Press, 1962.

——. "Scholars and Spectres: A Rejoinder to Viner." *Canadian Journal of Economics and Political Science* 29, no. 4 (1963): 559–62.

Mahoney, Edward P. "Metaphysical Foundations of the Hierarchy of Being according to Some Late-Medieval and Renaissance Philosophers." In *Philosophies of Existence: Ancient and Medieval,* ed. Parviz Morewedge, 165–257. New York: Fordham University Press, 1982.

Malthus, Thomas. *An Essay on the Principles of Population.* Ed. Antony Flew. New York: Viking/Penguin, 1985.

Mandeville, Bernard. *The Fable of the Bees; or, Private vices, Public benefits.* London, 1714.

Marshall, John. *John Locke: Resistance, Religion, and Responsibility.* Cambridge: Cambridge University Press, 1994.

———. "John Locke's Religious, Educational, and Moral Thought." *The Historical Journal* 33, no. 4 (1990): 993–1001.

McClure, Kirstie M. "Difference, Diversity, and the Limits of Toleration." *Political Theory* 18, no. 3 (1990): 361–91.

———. "Taking Liberties in Foucault's Triangle: Sovereignty, Discipline, Governmentality, and the Subject of Rights." In *Politics, Identities, and Rights,* ed. Austin Sarat and Thomas Kearns. Ann Arbor: University of Michigan Press, 1995.

McLachlan, Herbert. *The Religious Opinions of Milton, Locke, and Newton.* Manchester: Manchester University Press, 1941.

Mehta, Uday Singh. *The Anxiety of Freedom: Imagination and Individuality in Locke's Political Thought.* Ithaca: Cornell University Press, 1992.

Monson, C. H. "Locke and His Interpreters." *Political Studies* 6, no. 2 (1958): 120–33.

Morewedge, Parviz, ed. *Philosophies of Existence: Ancient and Medieval.* New York: Fordham University Press, 1982.

Nenner, Howard. *By Colour of Law: Legal Culture and Constitutional Politics in England, 1660–1689.* Chicago: University of Chicago Press, 1977.

Nozick, Robert. *Anarchy, State, and Utopia.* Oxford: Basil Blackwell, 1974.

Oakley, Francis. *Omnipotence, Covenant, and Order: An Excursion in the History of Ideas from Abelard to Leibniz.* Ithaca: Cornell University Press, 1984.

Ogilvie, Sir Charles. *The King's Government and the Common Law, 1471–1641.* Oxford: Basil Blackwell, 1958.

Olivecrona, Karl. "Appropriation in the State of Nature: Locke on the Origin of Property." *Journal of the History of Ideas* 35, no. 2 (1974): 211–30.

———. "Locke's Theory of Appropriation." *Philosophical Quarterly* 24, no. 96 (1974): 220–34.

Pearson, John. *Exposition of the Creed* (1659). Ed. Robert Sinker. Cambridge: Cambridge University Press, 1899.

Phillipson, Nicholas, and Quentin Skinner, eds. *Political Discourse in Early Modern Britain.* Cambridge: Cambridge University Press, 1993.

Pitkin, Hannah. "Obligation and Consent." Pts. 1 and 2. *American Political Science Review* 59, no. 4 (1965): 990–99 and 60, no. 1 (1966): 39–52.

Plumb, J. H. *The Growth of Political Stability in England, 1660–1730.* London: Macmillan, 1967.

Pocock, J. G. A. *The Ancient Constitution and the Feudal Law: A Study of English Historical Thought in the Seventeenth Century.* 2d ed. Cambridge: Cambridge University Press, 1987.

———. *The Machiavellian Moment: Florentine Political Thought and the Atlantic Republican Tradition.* Princeton: Princeton University Press, 1975.

Polin, Raymond. "Locke's Conception of Freedom." In *John Locke: Problems and Perspectives,* ed. John W. Yolton, 1–18. Cambridge: Cambridge University Press, 1969.

———. *La politique morale de John Locke.* Paris: Presses universitaires de France, 1960.

Pollock, Sir Frederick. "Locke's Theory of State." *Proceedings of the British Academy, 1903–1904:* 237–49.

Pollock, Sir Frederick, and Frederic William Maitland. *The History of English Law before the Time of Edward I.* 2d ed. 2 vols. 1899–1923. Reprint, with revisions, Cambridge: Cambridge University Press, 1968.

Rabb, Theodore K. *The Struggle for Stability in Early Modern Europe.* Oxford: Oxford University Press, 1975.

Reay, Barry, ed. *Popular Culture in Seventeenth-Century England.* New York: St. Martin's Press, 1985.

Reddy, William M. *Money and Liberty in Modern Europe: A Critique of Historical Understanding.* Cambridge: Cambridge University Press, 1987.

Rogers, G. A. J. "Locke, Law, and the Laws of Nature." In *John Locke: Theory of Knowledge,* ed. Vere Chappell, 502–18. New York: Garland Publishers, 1992.

Russell Smith, H. F. *The Theory of Religious Liberty in the Reigns of Charles II and James II.* Cambridge: Cambridge University Press, 1911.

Ryan, Alan. "Locke and the Dictatorship of the Bourgeoisie." *Political Studies* 13, no. 2 (1965): 219–30.

———. *Property.* Minneapolis: University of Minnesota Press, 1987.

Scanlon, Thomas. "Nozick on Rights, Liberty, and Property." *Philosophy and Public Affairs* 6, no. 1 (1976): 3–25.

Schochet, Gordon. *Patriarchalism in Political Thought: The Authoritarian Family and Political Speculation and Attitudes, Especially in Seventeenth-Century England.* Oxford: Basil Blackwell, 1975.

———. "Radical Politics and Ashcraft's Treatise on Locke." *The Journal of the History of Ideas* 50, no. 3 (1989): 491–510.

———. "Toleration, Revolution, and Judgment in the Development of Locke's Political Thought." *Political Science* 40, no. 1 (1988): 84–96.

Schochet, Gordon J., ed. *Life, Liberty and Property: Essays on Locke's Political Ideas.* Belmont, Calif.: Wadsworth Publishing Co., 1971.

Schwoerer, Lois. *The Declaration of Rights, 1689.* Baltimore: Johns Hopkins University Press, 1981.

———. "Locke, Lockean Ideas, and the Glorious Revolution." *Journal of the History of Ideas* 51, no. 4 (1990): 531–48.

Seliger, Martin. *The Liberal Politics of John Locke.* New York: Frederick Praeger, 1969.

Shapiro, Barbara. *Probability and Certainty in Seventeenth-Century England: A Study of the Relationships between Natural Science, Religion, History, Law, and Literature.* Princeton: Princeton University Press, 1983.

Sharp, Buchanan. "Popular Protest in Seventeenth-Century England." In

Popular Culture in Seventeenth-Century England, ed. Barry Reay, 271–308. New York: St. Martin's Press, 1985.

Sharpe, James A. "Enforcing the Law in the Seventeenth-Century English Village." In *Crime and the Law: The Social History of Crime in Western Europe since 1500,* eds. V. A. C. Gatrell, Bruce Lenman, and Geoffrey Parker, 97–119. London: Europa Publications, 1980.

———. "The People and the Law." In *Popular Culture in Seventeenth-Century England,* ed. Barry Reay, 244–70. New York: St. Martin's Press, 1985.

Shirley, F. J. *Richard Hooker and Contemporary Political Ideas.* London: Society for Promoting Christian Knowledge, 1949.

Shulman, George M. *Radicalism and Reverence: The Political Thought of Gerrard Winstanley.* Berkeley: University of California Press, 1989.

Singh, Raghuveer. "John Locke and the Theory of Natural Law." *Political Studies* 9, no. 2 (1961): 105–18.

Skerpan, Elizabeth. *The Rhetoric of Politics in the English Revolution, 1642–1660.* Columbia: University of Missouri Press, 1992.

Skinner, Quentin. *Foundations of Modern Political Thought.* Cambridge: Cambridge University Press, 1978.

———. "History and Ideology in the English Revolution." *Historical Journal* 8, no. 2 (1965): 151–78.

———. "The Ideological Context of Hobbes's Political Thought." *Historical Journal* 9, no. 3 (1966): 286–317.

———. "Meaning and Understanding in the History of Ideas." *History and Theory* 8, no. 1 (1969): 3–53.

Soles, David E. "Locke's Empiricism and the Postulation of Unobservables." *Journal of the History of Philosphy* 23, no. 3 (1985): 339–69.

Spellman, W. M. *John Locke and the Problem of Depravity.* Oxford: Clarendon Press, 1988.

———. "Locke and the Latitudinarian Perspective on Original Sin." In *John Locke: Theory of Knowledge,* ed. Vere Chappell. New York: Garland Publishers, 1992.

Spencer, John. *A Discourse concerning Prodigies: Wherein the Vanity of Presages by Them Is Reprehended and Their True and Proper Ends Asserted and Vindicated.* 2d ed., corrected and enlarged. London: J. Field for Will Groves, 1665.

Steiner, Hillel. "The Natural Right to the Means of Production." *Philosophical Quarterly* 27, no. 1 (1977): 41–49.

Strauss, Leo. "Locke's Doctrine of Natural Law." *American Political Science Review* 52, no. 2 (1958): 490–501.

———. *Natural Right and History.* Chicago: University of Chicago Press, 1953.

Tarlton, Charles D. "'The Rulers Now on Earth': Locke's *Two Treatises* and the Revolution of 1688." *Historical Journal* 28, no. 2 (1985): 279–98.

Thompson, E. P. "The Moral Economy of the English Crowd in the Eighteenth Century." *Past and Present* 50 (1971): 76–136.

Thompson, Martyn P. "The Reception of Locke's *Two Treatises of Government*, 1690–1705." *Political Studies* 24, no. 2 (1976): 184–91.

———. "Significant Silences in Locke's *Two Treatises of Government:* Constitutional History, Contract, and Law." *Historical Journal* 31, no. 2 (1988): 275–94.

Tillyard, E. M. W. *The Elizabethan World Picture.* New York: Macmillan, 1944.

Tuck, Richard. *Natural Rights Theories: Their Origin and Development.* Cambridge: Cambridge University Press, 1979.

Tully, James. *An Approach to Political Philosophy: Locke in Contexts.* Cambridge: Cambridge University Press, 1993.

———. *A Discourse on Property: John Locke and His Adversaries.* Cambridge: Cambridge University Press, 1980.

———. "Placing the *Two Treatises.*" In *Political Discourse in Early Modern Britain,* ed. Nicholas Phillipson and Quentin Skinner. Cambridge: Cambridge University Press, 1993.

Ullmann, Walter. *History of Political Thought in the Middle Ages.* Hammondsworth: Penguin, 1965.

———. *Principles of Government and Politics in the Middle Ages.* London: Metheun, 1961.

Urdang, Elliot W., and Francis Oakley. "Locke, Natural Law, and God." *Natural Law Forum* 11 (1966): 92–109.

Van Leeuwen, Henry G. *The Problem of Certainty in English Thought, 1630–1690.* The Hague: Martinus Nijhoff, 1963.

Vaughn, Karen Iverson. *John Locke: Economist and Social Scientist.* Chicago: University of Chicago Press, 1980.

Viner, Jacob. "'Possessive Individualism' as Original Sin." *Canadian Journal of Economics and Political Science* 29, no. 4 (1963): 548–59.

von Gierke, Otto. *Natural Law and the Theory of Society, 1500–1800.* Trans. Ernest Barker. Boston: Beacon Press, 1960.

von Leyden, Wolfgang. "John Locke and Natural Law." In *Life, Liberty and Property: Essays on Locke's Political Ideas,* ed. Gordon Schochet. Belmont, Calif.: Wadsworth Publishing Co., 1971.

Waldron, Jeremy. *The Right to Private Property.* Oxford: Clarendon Press, 1988.

Walter, John. "Grain Riots and Popular Attitudes to the Law: Malden and the Crisis of 1629." In *An Ungovernable People: The English and Their Law in the Seventeenth and Eighteenth Centuries,* eds. John Brewer and John Styles, 47–84. London: Hutchison and Co., 1980.

Walzer, Michael. *Revolution of the Saints: A Study in the Origins of Radical Politics.* Cambridge: Harvard University Press, 1965.

Webster, John. *A Cure for a Cuckold.* In vol. 3 of *The Complete Works of John Webster.* Ed. F. L. Lucas. New York: Gordian Press, Inc., 1966.

Weston, J. R. *Monarchy and Revolution: The English State in the 1680s.* London: Blanford Press, 1972.

Willey, Basil. *The Seventeenth-Century Background: Studies in the Thought of the Age in Relation to Poetry and Religion.* Garden City, N. Y.: Doubleday, 1953.

Winstanley, Gerrard. "The Law of Freedom in a Platform." In *"The Law of Freedom" and Other Writings,* ed. Christopher Hill. Cambridge: Cambridge University Press, 1983.

Wolfe, Don M., ed. *Leveller Manifestoes of the Puritan Revolution.* New York: Humanities Press, 1967.

Wolin, Sheldon S. *Politics and Vision: Continuity and Innovation in Western Political Thought.* Boston: Little, Brown and Company, 1960.

Wood, Neal. "The Baconian Character of Locke's *Essay.*" *Studies in the History and Philosophy of Science* 6, no. 1 (1975): 43–84.

———. *John Locke and the Theory of Agrarian Capitalism.* Berkeley: University of California Press, 1984.

———. *The Politics of Locke's Philosophy: A Social Study of "An Essay concerning Human Understanding."* Berkeley: University of California Press, 1983.

Wooton, David. "John Locke: Socinian or Natural Law Theorist?" In *Religion, Secularization, and Political Thought: Thomas Hobbes to J. S. Mill,* ed. James E. Crimmins, 39–67. London: Routledge, 1989.

Wrightson, Keith. "Two Concepts of Order: Justices, Constables, and Jurymen in Seventeenth Century England." In *An Ungovernable People: The English and Their Law in the Seventeenth and Eighteenth Centuries,* eds. John Brewer and John Styles, 21–46. London: Hutchison and Co., 1980.

Yolton, John W. *Locke and the Compass of Human Understanding: A Selective Commentary on the "Essay."* Cambridge: Cambridge University Press, 1970.

———. "The Science of Nature." In *John Locke: Problems and Perspectives,* ed. John W. Yolton, 183–93. Cambridge: Cambridge University Press, 1969.

Yolton, John W., ed. *John Locke: Problems and Perspectives.* Cambridge: Cambridge University Press, 1969.

Index